Soul-Centered Astrology

SOUL-CENTERED

ASTROLOGY

A Key to Your Expanding Self

ALAN OKEN

THE CROSSING PRESS
FREEDOM, CA

Quote from *The Hidden Glory of the Inner Man* by Torkom Saraydarian,
(Aquarian Educational Foundation, Agoura, CA, 1985) is reprinted
by permission of author.

Illustrations from Rider-Waite Tarot deck reproduced by permission of
U.S. Games Systems, Inc., Stamford, CT 06902 U.S.A. Copyright © 1971 by
U.S. Games Systems, Inc. Further reproduction prohibited.
Illustration of Diagram 13 by Luis Ribeiro

Library of Congress Cataloging-in-Publication Data
Oken, Alan.
    Soul-centered astrology: a key to your expanding self/ Alan Oken.
      p. cm.
    Originally published: New York: Bantam Books, 1990.
    Includes bibliography references and index.
    ISBN 0-89594-811-7
    1. Astrology 2.Soul-Miscellanea. 3. Self-actualization (Psychology)--Miscellanea.
    4. Seven rays (Occultism) I.Title. [BF1711.038 1996]
    133.5--dc20   96-3683
                                                                   CIP

This book is gratefully dedicated to:

The Tibetan Master, Djwhal Khul

Mrs. Frances Adams Moore

The Family of Brothers and Sisters
who work on and through Meditation Mount,
Ojai, California

The New Group of World Servers

Acknowledgments

I am decidedly blessed. Wherever I have traveled, I have had a constant opportunity to learn, teach, and share with others. Throughout my life, I have been guided and protected by hands both visible and invisible. In the late 1960s, when I first came upon the Tibetan's books, especially *Esoteric Astrology,* I realized that there was a need to contribute to the distribution of this incredible, loving wisdom. It has taken me over twenty years to assimilate enough of this information so that I could synthesize it into my own experiences as a practicing astrologer and metaphysician. In addition, I have had the great privilege of participating in hundreds of conversations and seminars with men and women far wiser than myself, who have made their observations and research concerning the relationship between the Soul and the personality available to me.

The Work and Energy of the Tibetan Master has been at the conscious center of my life and heart since October 24, 1967. The group focus that my small part in this One Work entails has helped me move from a totally egocentric individual to one who, at this point in his life, is aware of the great joy available in the service to others. So it is to the Tibetan, His group, and my coworkers in astrology and world service that I offer my deepest thanks and my continued love and energy.

In this respect, I would like to acknowledge some of the many teachers and friends who have helped me along my way. With many blessings, thank you: Isadore Friedman; Ellen Resch; dearest Isabel Hickey; Pak Suyono of Surakarta, Java; Madeline Haddon, who brought me to Meditation Mount; Georgia Cooper, whose grace, beauty, and wisdom have been a source of inspiration to so many; Frances Adams Moore, who has acted as my mentor and spiritual mother for nearly fifteen years; Michael Robbins, Ph.D., whose brotherhood, profound understanding, and total dedication to the Work we share have inspired me to increase my efforts; Sir John Sinclair, who agreed, his own abundantly filled schedule notwithstanding, to write the foreword to this book; Tobi Sanders, my editor at Bantam Books from my beginnings there in 1969 to her untimely passing in 1987, who encouraged me to undertake this project; and to my other Family at the Church of Religious Science in Santa Fe, New Mexico, who consistently offered me their love and collective strength while I was preparing this manuscript. Thank you, everyone!

My list could fill many more pages, as so many people have contributed to the experiences which are distilled in *Soul-Centered Astrology*, but I shall limit myself to three last mentions of my sincere appreciation. The first is to the members of the Meditation Group for the New Age, who have been so generous in their support of the writing of chapter 4, "The Laws and Principles of the New Age." The second is to the readers of my other books, the participants in my various public talks and seminars, and the many other friends who have encouraged me to produce a work that would speak to the consciously evolving humanity of our times. I hope that *Soul-Centered Astrology* meets with their approval and is a proper response to their request.

And last, to Rose Ewald, who has assisted me in the preparation of this manuscript, offered consistently sage advice, kept me focused when the circumstances of life made going off on tangents easier than sitting at the word processor, and who generally has been a great friend and dedicated co-worker.

Love and blessings to you all.

ALAN OKEN
Santa Fe, New Mexico
April 1988

If, in the presentation of this vast subject (of astrology), and in the process of indicating the attitude of the Ageless Wisdom to this new and coming (yet very ancient) "science of effective energies," as it has been called, I may present a new approach . . . I am hoping that some astrologers may be found who will be sensitive to that which is new. I am believing that there are investigators along astrological lines who will be open-minded enough to recognize possible hypotheses and then to make fair experiment with them . . . I am looking for these fair-minded astrologers to make experiment with the factors and suggestions which I may indicate.

—the Tibetan, quoted in
Alice A. Bailey's *Esoteric Astrology*

Contents

Index of Diagrams

Index of Tabulations

Index of Horoscope Charts

Mantra and Invocations

Foreword

Popular magazines and journals are filled with articles discussing energy in its myriad types of manifestation—in terms of exercise and health, food and diet, the care required for environmental resources, the multitude of scientific skills employed in computerization, medical practice, educational equipment, electrical household appliances—the list could go on and on. Energy, in different modes, flows through all these channels.

Then, if we wish, we can shift the emphasis and consider how often we talk about the impact of someone's emotional energy, the quality of his thought radiation, or the general energy of his being.

And if we are inclined to consider the modern researches of physicists, astronomers, biologists, mathematicians, and others probing the nature of the universe in which we find ourselves, we discover that their reports are often couched in terms of the energies they are discussing.

Beatrix Potter, the famous writer of the Peter Rabbit children's books, who was herself a great naturalist, once announced that she did not often consider the stars—she reportedly found it sufficient that there were forty-two thousand known species of fungus. But whether the subject is fungi or supernovas, we consider energy in the motions of manifestation, according to type and kind. There is around us a veritable welter of impacting energies, conditioning, melding, rebuffing, and relating one with another in an extraordinarily creative rough-and-tumble that we blanket with the term *life*.

It is one of the glories of humankind that, over the course of evolution, we have been able to employ our native intelligence to register such energies and, whether by mechanical, intellectual, or intuitive means, come to at least a partial understanding of their meaning and purpose. Astrology is one of the time-honored systems devised to this end.

However, any growth process has to be prepared to admit that as additional light comes onto a subject and new discoveries are made, our knowledge, along with the disciplines which brought it through, is seen to have registered as "through a glass, darkly." Consequently, it needs to be overhauled, reconsidered, subjected to spring cleaning, expanded, and constantly brought up-to-date. The ancient and almost mythic art of astrology is no exception.

It is toward this expansion of awareness that Alan Oken focuses his considerable knowledge. And, in this valuable effort to shift gears and give us all some workable perspective on Soul-centered astrology, he incorporates many other types of subtle energy quality besides the well-known planetary and zodiacal influences.

If we inhabit and are, indeed, ourselves constructed of a great soup of differentiated energies, then we need to know as much as possible about the ingredients, or rather the particular energies that represent the human soul. Also, just as it is interesting to know about the qualities which particular planetary influences may invest in our particular orbit of operations, it is also valuable to consider the inspirational radiation that particular principles of altruistic or spiritual life may also impart when associated with them. This our author does by considering the various subtle Laws and Principles of the Aquarian Age which his researches have brought to his notice, and which are available to us all for study.

It must be clear to everyone who is prepared to entertain at least the hypothesis of subtle radiatory influences energizing the field of human life that, just as modern living brings most of us into contact with a multitude of mechanical appliances driven by energy, so our subtle and invisible nature is also in contact with probably countless energy influences, which can be of increasing practical usefulness as we gain greater understanding of them.

In this respect, Alan Oken goes quite deeply into the infant study of the Seven Ray energies, or psychological types of quality, which interweave with astrological radiation. At first, this may seem a picture of great complexity; however, his skill in blending the whole range of his researches illustrates the miraculous ingenuity of the unique energy pattern, tapestry, or blueprint which represents our individuality. And this comes about even while we all share in the same universal energies.

Of course, it may require some small effort to follow our author into those particular areas of research. It will no doubt be pioneering territory for many of us. But the reward will be that we are lifted from any overly simplistic and relatively superficial astrological view of human nature.

Carl Jung, the great psychologist, once pictured consciousness in terms of a mountain range. Individual consciousness was like separate little peaks peering through cloud cover. Supporting and joining these were the various hill groupings of family, and still more embracing national and racial consciousness, with the whole range seen to be grounded on the bedrock of total human consciousness itself, making us all part of one entity, without loss of individuality. In a similar, though more subtle type of picture, the many different kinds of invisible energy quality that Alan Oken brings to our notice reveal that Soul-centered astrology does not just concern the spiritual or essential nature of human beings. Planets and other great radiatory influences in life also have their spiritual nature, as well as their outward and forceful forms of phenomenal appearance. And all—be they constellation, planet, human being, or one of Beatrix Potter's many fungi—interweave our vital energies within one magnificent, albeit mysterious, flow of life.

The prospect may almost seem too daunting, or alternatively, so fascinating in its multitudinous detail, as to be hypnotic. Fortunately, Alan Oken has brought forward a central, and indeed pivotal thesis of the Tibetan teacher who has inspired him. This he features early in his work as the Rainbow Bridge, or Path, which we construct within our own subtle nature out of the many energies which come within our orbit, and which can beneficially enhance life, consciousness, and creativity.

The Tibetan meditation master calls this ongoing development, or growth unfoldment, *Antahkarana,* a Sanskrit term which is said to mean "inner instrument." As each of us, through our own best endeavors in consciousness, lets this inner instrument come into working existence, our reception center for the apprehension, appreciation, and broadcast of increasingly finely tuned, subtle, yet nonetheless practically effective energy, is set up. And then, the grand design and almost infinite perspective of Soul-centered astrology makes increasing good sense. To this adventure Alan Oken beckons us and, generous guide that he is, puts the treasure map into our hands.

SIR JOHN ROLLO SINCLAIR, BT.
London, 1988

PART ONE

SOUL-CENTERED ASTROLOGY: A KEY TO YOUR EXPANDING SELF

1

Why a Soul-Centered

Astrology?

Matter is the vehicle for the manifestation of soul on this plane of existence, and soul is the vehicle on a higher plane for the manifestation of spirit, and these three are a trinity synthesized by Life, which pervades them all.

—H. P. Blavatsky, *The Secret Doctrine*

There is a new awakening which is expanding and transforming the minds and hearts of a great multitude of humanity. Those of you reading these words are part of this evolutionary current of our collective experience. You are finding that your needs, perspectives, and approach to life are taking a radical turn in their orientation. This is bringing about certain new crises and tensions, joys and victories, in your life. Yet, just a short time ago, these transformational circumstances were not part of your frame of reference, or at best, were mere mental abstractions.

You may be finding, as individual students of astrology or as professional practitioners, that you are being confronted with certain dynamics of human psychology and relationships that current trends in astrological interpretation and counseling no longer satisfy. The nature of your aspirations, as well as those of your friends or clients, has changed and continues to change remarkably. In recent years, the speed and pervasive quality of this reorientation of life values and perspective have been increasing systematically. Furthermore, you are also discovering that neither you nor your associates are being supported in your individual spiritual quests by a personality-centered,

"Mommy and Daddy did it to me" approach to the horoscope and your lives. In other words, you are discovering that your urges for self-fulfillment, and the blockages and tests that occur as a part of this process, can no longer be attributed to your early behavioral conditioning and family background.

Where at one time it was enough to know that you were a Libra and could define yourself by Libran characteristics, you are now asking yourself an entirely different quality of question. You are now seeking to apply your Libra attunement of balance and harmony as an energy within the larger framework of social contribution. You are seeking an essential experience of yourself which goes beyond personality characteristics and enters into the realm of the purpose for being. In this respect, you are also finding that your experience of planetary and other astrological influences is no longer easily substantiated by traditional—even "modern" traditional—methods of horoscope delineation and interpretation. And yet, you know and trust the validity of astrological symbolism and its scientific and practical expressions. You recognize the ability of astrology to serve as a mirror of the continual expression of cosmic reality. And you are right to hold such trust and belief in this beautiful and ancient art.

Those of you drawn to this book because of its title are finding that you are turning more and more to the reality of yourself as a Soul. This means that you are part of that increasing number of people who are developing the vision and the experience of the physical world and the physical body as vehicles for the expression of a transcendental existence. This existence is one in which the orientation and the exigencies of the inner life of the Soul—the "vertical" life, rather than the "horizontal" life of the personality—are becoming a predominating theme in your daily experience of the world around and within you. (See chapter 3 for a detailed discussion of this most important point.)

What has been the major focus of life for the few initiates and mystics down through the ages will shortly become—is, indeed, becoming—an integrated facet of life for many. The Waters of the Man with the Urn are indeed being distributed, and Aquarius is most certainly the ruler—not just of the coming age, but of astrology and its practitioners.[1]

The aspiration to Soul alignment—the endeavor to merge the personality life of external, material existence with the increasing inner experience of Soul perceptions and the Life Force—creates a very different life perspective. In this respect, we are exploring and con-

---

[1]The Christ, Jesus, gave a vision of this coming New Age when, in Luke 22:10 he told his Disciples: "When ye are entered into the city, there shall a man meet you, bearing a pitcher of water; follow him into the house where he entereth in."

fronting those changes, transformations, and crises which are part of this natural path of union. There is a structure, rhythm, and series of Laws which are universal and intrinsic to the joining of the lower and Higher selves. These struggles and victories are different to each one of us in their outer forms, but absolutely united in their inner, essential energies and cyclic unfoldment. This is the nature of the relationship between the inner and the outer, the essence and the form, the esoteric and the exoteric. We are One Essential Whole, expressing Itself through a limitless number of forms and varieties. Astrology—especially esoteric astrology, and the Soul Force Itself— seeks to give a structure and focus to this process of Self-realization.

Astrology is a system of thought and a vehicle of interpreting daily life through the unfolding of meaning contained within its symbolism. Such symbology is representative of the very fabric of human experience. As symbology is transcendental by its very nature, astrology is quite a flexible system. This highly developed system has evolved over the course of thousands of years, and its methods, techniques, and applications are constantly in the process of being expanded, developed, and synthesized. The symbols of astrology give a structure to the rational mind so that a relationship between external events and their more subtle factors of causality may be perceived, predicted and appreciated. It can thus be a successful interpreter of human evolution and events, even as the quality of human consciousness, and the forms of those events, change. Astrology is, after all, a system that seeks to interpret the nature of the Universal Life Force as It moves, shapes, and creates human life and all events. The planets, signs, and houses, in any case, are *not* the causal elements of manifestation. They are, rather, the reflections of a transcendental synchronicity manifesting through the rhythms and timing of a cosmic clock.

In this respect, astrology permits several things to occur, and it is in the following that we may appreciate the gifts of this wonderful invention:

1. Astrology allows the astrologer to attune himself to the essential *qualities* of the energies embodied in the planets, signs, houses, and other astrological factors.

2. Because of its flexibility, astrology engenders many levels of perception of the rhythms of the "celestial and terrestrial dancing partners" as they interface within the Being of the Life Force. It is important to note, however, and this will be a very important theme throughout the book, that such perceptions of the essential Life Force on the part of the student are totally relative to the level of his consciousness. This level of *perceptive* awareness expands or contracts according to his evolutionary path.

3. The relationship between cause and effect is at the very core of metaphysics and is the reason why, of all the occult sciences and

methods of investigation, astrology is the most refined revealer of occult laws and principles.

4. Astrology allows, on a social level, a growing group of men and women to speak a common language of perception, no matter what their differences may be in personal life-style. Astrology is thus not only a tool for the viewing of an increasingly unifying humanity, but a vehicle for the gathering of those people who seek to know and share what they have discovered. This approach, in terms of group endeavor and unanimity (not to be confused with *uniformity*)—is a major principle of contemporary life and is explored in much greater detail in chapter 3.

5. Astrology adds to the appreciation of the basic unifying principle of life. This we continue to discover both within the study of astrology itself, and without, in our daily life experiences. Astrology teaches that everything moves in cycles and circles:

> Everything the power of the world does is done in a circle. The sky is round, and I have heard that the earth is round like a ball, and so are all the stars. The wind, in its greatest power, whirls. Birds make their nests in circles, for theirs is the same religion as ours. The sun comes forth and goes down again in a circle. The moon does the same, and both are round. Even the seasons form a great circle in their changing, and always come back again to where they were. The life of a man is a circle from childhood to childhood, and so it is in everything where power moves.

—Black Elk, Oglala Sioux[2]

This unifying rhythm is called the Law of Attraction—the Law of Love in Action. If astrology brings the astrologer into attunement with these two Laws (actually, one and the same), it has then accomplished for the individual its greatest gift of all.

The present cycling and circling of events, the current ticking of the cosmic clock, is revealing a quantum transmutation of human consciousness. This is resulting in a rapidly shifting (although essentially predictable) direction in both our inner life experience and our outer life-styles and events. Individually and collectively, we are at the threshold of an incredible reorientation of our life directions. This is indicated by the movement from one World Age (Pisces) of some 2,160 years, to another (Aquarius), within a unit of time known as a "Great Year" (equaling 25,920 Earth years). This transitional point in the universal rhythm for our planet creates vastly increased tensions for each of us. It also offers great opportunities to consciously

[2]Neihardt, J. *Black Elk Speaks.* New York: Washington Square Press, 1972.

co-create the dynamics of both our inner and outer lives through the right use of will. If astrology is to remain a useful tool for healing and service in the present era, as well as in the future, certain techniques of horoscope delineation must be developed to answer the special needs of these times. Such a system has to possess a framework for delineation and counseling which can meet the challenging problems (as well as the special joys and victories) inherent in our evolving individual and collective destinies. There also has to be a group of astrologers equal to the task of creating, developing, and applying such a system.

The astrologer for the New Age must be thoroughly trained and intellectually centered in the science of astrology in order to be able to measure and interpret celestial movements. But he or she must be equally heart-centered and intuitively focused in order to apply such data to the level of consciousness through which others are functioning. This will require of the astrologer, as well as give the opportunity for, great personal, mental, and spiritual growth. Fortunately, both the seeds for this kind of astrology, and the presence of this initial seed group of astrologers, already exists. (See Bibliography for further information on esoteric astrology and its related field of esoteric psychology.)

Soul-centered astrology is part of a larger exteriorization of esoteric astrology, the many principles of which are currently being unfolded and synthesized into the collective body of astrological studies. My present effort lies within the body of a much larger work now being created by an international group of esoteric astrologers. It is hoped that this entire collection of work will be utilized to perceive the structure, quality, and meaning of these evolving crises of transformation and the energies which they embody. In this respect, a service may be rendered both to astrology and to humanity.

Our struggles and victories as we progress—and regress—along the Path are very special. What makes them so extraordinary is that we are consciously aware that these transformations are currently taking place. We are witnesses to a very incredible kind of growth process! The magic of our Self is alive and well and living in Pittsburgh (or Atlanta, or even Los Angeles!). What's more, these changes are occurring to millions of people simultaneously. The expressions "soul brother/soul sister," "soul mate," "group soul," "New Age brothers and sisters," "companions along the Way," etc., have begun to take on new and profoundly loving meanings among a huge number of people, and with good reason! There is an affinity of experience that seems to be uniting people from every social stratum and human experience. But that is indeed the very essence of the Soul of Humanity at work. The Soul is a unifying, collectivizing energy whose power of attraction and magnetism is Love. Our task both individually and collectively is to create those necessary channels for the Soul's expression in our daily lives. This is our great challenge, and it is to this process of unfoldment that *Soul-Centered Astrology* will address itself. As we create the avenues for the outer expression of the inner life, we, in effect, consciously co-create our own destiny. This type of creative spiritual responsibility is at the center of the current course of human evolution.

In the process of reorienting yourself to these collective changes, you may experience the following:

1. You are consistently seeking those methods of self-improvement which give you a feeling of greater wholeness.

2. You are interested in methods and processes which serve to heal other people from addictive and negative behavior patterns.

3. You are becoming increasingly aware of others outside of your immediate family and social circle.

4. You are finding it often easier to relate with people connected to you through similar ideological or belief systems than through simple biological or other social ties.

5. You are exhausted and undernourished (either emotionally or mentally) by those civic, social, or spiritual activities which at one time used to be enjoyable, or at least tolerable. Now, such activities represent a distinct drain on your vitality.

6. You are finding yourself increasingly more attracted to love, and less attracted by desire. At the very least, you are finding a distinct conflict between the two and are trying somehow to unite them. This is resulting in a reorientation of your sexual attitudes (it's not just a symptom of growing older—wiser, maybe, but not necessarily older!).

7. You are finding that you are growing increasingly dispassionate, detached, and discriminating. Sometimes this makes you feel guilty; sometimes, fearful of loss.

8. You are definitely searching (and even finding!) a greater purpose for the use of your life energies. Service is becoming a very important factor in your life, and the need to create a field of service through which you may express yourself is becoming a very dominant theme to your life.

9. You are seeing through and are clearly dissatisfied with the "game structures" of nonregenerative, egocentric habit patterns! You would like to have a clearer understanding of how to become more detached from these magnetic traps which block the proper use of your energy. (Understanding the Ray qualities of the planets and the signs will do much to help you sort this one out.)

10. You are sensing, perceiving, and experiencing another aspect of Love in your life—one which has a more impersonal and detached quality to it. It is very different from the more personal kind of love. It is unconditionally supportive, demands nothing in return, and

may be experienced by you as a "nurturing presence." You find your-self radiating it, and being drawn to others who also express this non-demanding quality of the heart. This attraction goes beyond all differences in gender, and in ethnic, religious, and social orientations.

11. You feel a growing need to be part of a group of people who are working toward these same inward and outward goals.

12. Perhaps most important, you are finding that you are becoming increasingly impersonal to all things that are personal, and increas-ingly personal to all that is impersonal. As the Tibetan Master, D. K., would advise at this point: "Ponder on this."

If you have had a majority of these experiences, then you and I, and all the others reading these words, are kindred spirits. We are, in essence, a seed group working to externalize the new archetypes of human consciousness and relationships for the New Age.

In the course of your own growth and development, you have come across the ancient science and beautiful art of astrology. If this is your first astrology book, you have opened yourself to a great spiritual and intellectual journey. A warm welcome to you.[3]

The majority of you have probably already absorbed and synthe-sized many of the cosmic principles outlined in current astrological teachings. At this time, you may be seeking new ways to express your evolving perceptions of both your inner and outer lives. This perspec-tive of the relationship of the Life within the Form, the conflict between the Higher and the lower selves (also called the Path of Union), and the true purpose for your life and present struggles, are revealed through an esoteric and Soul-centered astrology.

The quality of human consciousness as expressed through astrol-ogy, in general, is conditioned by three primary factors. On a collec-tive level, it is the historical age and the generation into which you are born and raised (as indicated in part by the signs and interrelationships of the three outer planets—Uranus, Neptune, and Pluto). Individually, a number of factors determine the levels of energy/consciousness through which the planetary forces express themselves. These include your racial and national origins, and other factors of biological karma, as well as your general degree of personal evolution. The latter can only be determined through the lens of the intuitively focused astrolo-ger (true intuition being one of the faculties of Soul awareness). This will be discussed further in chapter 2.

There is no doubt, however, that the evolution of human con-sciousness and culture has its parallel in the types of astrology prac-ticed during each social era. The astrology of the European Middle

---

[3]For insight into more traditional astrological teachings with a spiritual perspective, read *Alan Oken's Complete Astrology.*

Ages, for example, was replete with dire predictions of gloom, pestilence, death, and assorted other astral negativities. It focused on a fated, sin-filled, and guilt-ridden reality. It represented a life of little hope, except through the redemption of a (preferably) martyred physical death, and revealed very little, if any, degree of free will.

The astrology of Classical Greece was "cleaner"—more orderly and logical in its presentation. The planetary gods lived with humanity and played a very active role in the unfolding of life's archetypical dramas.

The astrology of the Chaldeans and ancient Hebrews was steeped in metaphysics and the interpretation of Cosmic Laws. This is a most fitting view of the use of astrology, as the Judaic legacy to humanity includes much in the way of understanding the "geometry of God" and the outworking of Universal Principles.

Like the minute subdivisions of its caste system, and the abundantly populated heavens of its incredible pantheon of devas, devis, and other emanations of the One, Hindu astrology is a vastly complex, labyrinthine system of rulers, sub-rulers, and sub-sub-rulers. All of these powers express themselves and interrelate by means of a rather fated Capricornian structure, through an unmovable zodiac of fixed constellations.

Victorian Age astrology books have made their influence felt well into the present era. These works are filled with moral repressions. They interpret natal and transiting planetary aspects in terms of severe moral judgments, and warnings of fiery repercussions should one stray from the appropriate behavior of the times. This type of astrology (and its reflection on the human life-style it sought to counsel and advise) was much more concerned with transitional morality and the outer-form life than on an understanding and support of Cosmic Law. Mars was depicted as the penultimate rogue, with Saturn as the even more malignant Keeper of the Gates, who doled out the hellish retribution of a dominant, patriarchal, polarized theology and society. Yet the "other side" of the veils of Neptune shone through this last segment of the Age of Pisces, and several illuminati appeared. Alan Leo, Helena Blavatsky, the young Krishnamurti, Rudolph Steiner, and Alice Bailey, as well as their various groups of students and co-workers, emerged to plant the seeds of an astrological and spiritual future.

American and European astrology in the twentieth century has had several major trends. Since the 1930s, there has been a great increase in various psychological approaches to the delineation of the natal chart. These approaches have also extended themselves into the integration of certain methods of healing and therapy in counseling situations. Jung's work with archetypes (and with astrology and metaphysical symbology, as well) has perfectly lent itself to a most helpful and beautifully developed humanistic movement in astrological interpretation. The work of Liz Greene, Jeff Jawer, and the late Richard Ideman stands out as prime examples of this humanistic tendency in modern astrology. Roberto Assagioli's work in psychosynthesis has also contributed much to the knowledge of several contemporary astrologers (including the author). In both traditional and esoteric astrology, Jungian psychology and psychosynthesis deal with the Law of Correspondences (also known as the Hermetic Law—As Above, So Below). Astrology, as well as these two psychological approaches, attempts to relate the macrocosmic and the microcosmic in terms of the human experience.

The 1960s through the 1980s brought in a great many experimental methods of horoscope delineation. The advent of personal computers expanded and revolutionized the codification of data and hence astrological research. This period also saw the birthing of a heightened interest in the more spiritual and esoteric aspects of astrology. In this respect, Eastern religions and philosophies found their way into an astrology that was already taking a decidedly metaphysical, and particularly occidental, humanistic turn.

A new astrology is emerging today which neither supersedes any existing system nor asserts its superiority. Esoteric, Soul-centered astrology, by its very nature, is inclusive. It adds a dimension to the scope of astrological analysis and delineation that has heretofore not been fully synthesized into the collective body of astrological work and literature. This new development in astrological research and counseling has emerged today because humanity is evolving rapidly enough to recognize the need for it. People are inquiring with heightened excitement and awareness into the nature of their subjective reality and its relationship with the external world of form. *This is happening not only on an individual level, but is a state of contemporary, collective planetary evolution!*

The preponderant characteristic of the majority of twentieth-century astrology has been to focus upon the need to clarify one's individual identity, which is the usual focus of popularist newspaper and "supermarket" astrology. This has been coupled with those counseling techniques involved in the resolution of such personal problems that may arise in this preliminary phase of the individualization process. This phase is intimately connected to those characteristics of the ego/lower self, and from those situations which arise from egocentric confrontations with life. In effect, this is an astrology based around the exoteric significances of the Ascendant, the M.C., and their planetary rulers. It is an astrology which is also primarily focused on the inner planets (Sun, Moon, Mercury, Venus, Mars, Jupiter, and

Saturn), and their effects on the world of personality. At best—and there has been some very fine and useful information published in this genre—this orientation leads to the synthesis of the personality, and is a major step toward individual growth. At worst, it promotes the continued glorification and glamorization of the characteristics of the personality, and it sells enormously well!

One of the most important contributions that psychological, personality-centered astrology has made is to allow people to take an objective look at themselves through the universal archetypes contained in astrological symbology. Natal charts reveal a person's fundamental energy patterns—his blockages, as well as his more fluidly expressed creative potentials. Professionally executed, humanistic and psychological astrology definitely helps clarify the nature and relationships existing within a person's component parts. Thus personality-centered, exoteric astrology, when practiced by highly trained individuals, facilitates the understanding and integration of our many pieces and personae.

Modern, humanistic, psychologically oriented astrology allows us to see our individual, lower self as an expression of a conglomeration of energies and forces which give rise to certain modes of action and response. It also shows us how to look a bit more objectively at ourselves—to see ourselves as energies, in fact—and perhaps even to grasp a certain universality to our being. We are certainly asked, if we wish to have any happiness at all, to envision a bigger picture of life than the one blindly seen through our navels—and if we insist on staying at the navel point, to garner a glimpse of the fact that our umbilicus is connected to the World Mother and to the greater Human Family.

A strongly integrated ego structure is essential to a healthy life, and is of primary importance to our spiritual growth. The lower self is the anchor upon which the rest of our being is based. The outer life of the physical body and its associated feelings and thoughts (the fundamental trinity of the structure of the lower self), is the vehicle of expression of the human Soul. The Soul is that essential, inclusive, and intelligent Love Principle which, when joined and fused with the lower self, creates a whole person who is most definitely greater than the sum of his or her parts. And the nature of the relationship, purpose, and structure of Soul unfoldment to the outer life of the personality is at the core of Soul-centered astrology.

The crises, tensions, and opportunities inherent in the present shifting of the World Ages are of great significance insofar as the vastness of their inclusivity is concerned. Both as the human race and as planet Earth, we are taking a huge step in our collective, as well as individual, evolution. The effects of planetary and constellational energies on our lives are also mutating accordingly. (Please refer to parts 2 and 3 for greater detail about the astrological significances and applications of these energies in horoscope delineation.)

One of the characteristics of the multitude of men and women of goodwill who aspire to greater personal growth and mutual understanding is that they are neither exclusively personality-oriented nor entirely egocentric. Such individuals—and here I am speaking to and about many of my readers—have indeed achieved varying degrees of Soul awareness, and are heartily at work serving others (or, at the very least, aspiring to serve others) in a variety of ways.

This gigantic human network is constantly growing, as people of like minds recognize their unity within a larger path of unfoldment. Such individuals are working not only to discover their place and function in their lover's life, or in their professional life, or in their family life, but, more important, in the *planetary life*! Many of us are sincerely aspiring toward those pathways which will reveal ways to share and serve one another. Thus, we may better learn how to contribute effectively to the well-being of the collective life, and by so doing, continue to discover the meaning of the Soul's purpose and function.

The nature of the transitions that result from the crossing of the World Ages will continue to increase personal as well as world tensions. The juxtaposition of the forces and forms of expression inherent in the past Age of Pisces and the coming Age of Aquarius directs our attention to the tremendous polarizations which are manifesting in our lives. In addition to the omnipresent and lengthy change in the World Ages, Pluto is in Scorpio until late 1995, intensifying the processes of personal and collective transformation and reorienting desires. No easy task in (or at) any Age!

There is the very real threat of total planetary annihilation, as well as the seemingly never-ending stream of moral and physical pollution rising to the surface for cleansing. At the very same time, we are living in a period in which global spiritual awareness and the positive, creative opportunities it brings to humanity have never been greater. Never have separatist egos, thoughts, feelings, and actions been so threatening to world peace. And never has humanity demonstrated more convincingly the power of group endeavor, collective goodwill, and the urge for spiritual unity. (See chapter 4, "The Laws and Principles of the New Age.")

There is a way to resolve the current crises and tensions our polarized nations and their conflicting political systems are experiencing. It is known by various names: the Path of Synthesis, the Third Way, the Way of the Disciple, or simply, the Way of the Soul.

In terms of the study and practice of astrology, there is a need to create a system which serves the needs of those individuals who are seeking (and finding!) their place in a more planetary and collective orientation to life. For such individuals, the question: "How may I more effectively serve my community, nation, and world through the fulfillment of my true and inner purpose in life?" has become much more important than asking: "I am a Capricorn and my boyfriend is a Libra. How can we better get along?" There is nothing wrong with such a question—it is one of the most natural, and in its way, most beautiful questions one could ask. We hope that the two of them will get along, unite, and resolve any polarities they may have into the creative synthesis of an uplifting relationship. Once this takes place, then perhaps they may ask: "How may we better serve humanity and the Plan?" It is for those emerging Souls who are aware that they are more than just their thoughts, desires, and physical body that another focus and system of astrology is required. Soul-centered astrology is an initial facet of such a system—one which is being developed by an international group of esoteric astrologers. This collective body of work will certainly be an important contribution to the astrology of the New Age.

As the current Age begins to unfold, certain aspects of the Ancient Wisdom Teachings are being externalized and adapted for our benefit and use. The Tibetan Master, Djwhal Khul, has provided a significant foundation for a more Soul-oriented approach to astrology and to the Life it seeks to symbolize and interpret. As one of the Tibetan's many students, I owe a great debt to Him for His Love and Wisdom.

2

The Soul,

the Personality,

and the Rainbow Bridge

The real world consists of a balanced adjustment of opposing tendencies. Behind the strife between opposites there lies a hidden harmony of attunement which is the world.

—Heraclitus

There are a number of fundamental metaphysical laws and structures which must be examined before we can begin to integrate the principles of Soul-centered astrology into the practical outworking of the natal chart. In addition, several of the major steps and stages in the evolution of personal consciousness have to be recognized in order to apply these astrological indications correctly. This requires three vital factors:

1. An understanding of the meaning and applications of the planets, signs, houses, and their geometric aspect patterns when considered from the perspective of the personality or lower self. This is exoteric astrology.

2. The same scope of understanding, but studied from the level of the Soul or the Higher Self. This is esoteric astrology.

3. The intuitive ability to recognize the level on which these energies are expressing themselves, and the nature of their interrelationship. This is the Path.

The comprehension and integration of these first two factors require a strong mind, plus an ability and an eagerness to learn. The third factor is somewhat more challenging and complex, in that it necessitates a quality of personal development on the Soul level itself. This is another example of how astrology serves the astrologer: in striving for such a degree of Soul awareness, personal fulfillment and individual growth are achieved.

There is an ancient, esoteric tradition which has accompanied such Soul-focused aspirations down through the Ages: It is an Inner Teaching coming from what are called the "Mystery Schools," and offered through Love to those who have earned the right to this understanding. (See the Bibliography for further information about these Teachings.)

In this and in the several chapters which follow, we shall be examining certain facets of the Ageless Science (Ancient Wisdom), of which astrology has ever been a primary branch. We will be doing this so that our understanding of Soul-centered astrology is grounded through an attunement to patterns of cosmic structure. Meditations, visualizations, and contemplative exercises are also provided, both here and elsewhere in the present work. These will serve to deepen our essential awareness of the Energies and Principles we are seeking to contact and know. These experiences will enable us to practice an astrology based in Law and applied with Love and Wisdom. Such a process will produce a balanced and wholistic framework of support both for our efforts at service to others and for our own focus of personal development.

One of the most fundamental and important structural relationships in our lives is that between the personality and the Soul, and the linking force field that joins them. The latter is known either by its Sanskrit name, the Antahkarana, or lately, by a more popular term, the Rainbow Bridge. There are many definitions and interpretations of the functions of this major triad. My own understandings are rooted in a tradition called the Ancient Wisdom Teachings, which I have been studying, meditating, testing (and been tested by!), practicing, and living since 1967. The words and diagrams that follow are intellectual devices designed to aid the reader (and the writer) in the pursuit of a greater intuitive understanding of and contact with the Life Force. In the final analysis, the truth of any study is only relative to the voice of one's own inner truth; finding that voice coincides with walking the Path.

To reveal our own personal truth, we must prepare our personality to receive the Presence of the Soul. Only then may we say: "What I seek to present through my life I identify, experience, and take responsibility for as the truth for me." Without this Presence as the central focus and synthesizing essence of our life, our existence tends toward an intellectual morass of conjectures and opinions. This is often accompanied by a series of partially fulfilled or frustrated desires, as well as an alternating current of elation or depression, depending on our physical appearance or the state of our material possessions. It is only through attunement and alignment with the Soul that a consistent approach to a life of endless inconsistencies is made possible.

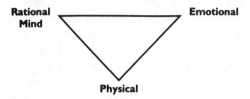

Diagram 1: The Symbolic Structure of the Personality (Lower Self or Lesser Ego)

As we can see in diagram 1, the personality consists of the physical body, the emotional (also known as the "astral" or "desire") body, and the lower mental body (the rational mind). In a fully developed personality, these three vehicles are synthesized into a harmoniously working unit. This means that there is an alignment of the mind and the feelings so that our outer actions are expressed in a balanced manner. (The positions of the planets in the natal horoscope will, of course, indicate the ease or difficulty in bringing about this integration of the personality. The transcending force—the use of the will to "weave" the pattern of the horoscope into a cohesive whole—is a primary factor leading to the free use of that will and the co-creation of our character and destiny.)

This type of personality is usually quite creative or, at the very least, quite able to function under all social pressures and circumstances. It is the goal of every spiritually active and aspiring person to create such an integrated lower self, for it is only with the correct alignment of forces that consistent Soul contact can occur. The individualization of the lesser ego is a major step in personal evolution—a step which millions are currently taking. Millions more are making the actual link between the lower and the Higher selves as the awakening to the Rainbow Bridge and the Soul's Presence become ever-increasing realities.

Until a fairly advanced state of personal evolution is reached, in which there is a fusion between the lower and the Higher selves, everything about the personality is either inherited (biological karma), or created and assumed temporarily (factors of response to social conditioning). The exception to this is the eternal and immortal Life Principle, which animates and vivifies all existence. The *forms* of the personality—whether these are the actual forms of the physical body, the thought-forms of the mind, or the forms for the expression of personal desire—are mortal and temporary in nature. The Life Force remains ever *essentially* formless, yet it is constantly creating these temporary "containers" for Itself through the work and function of the Soul-Personality relationship.

When viewed and interpreted both from a traditional, personality-centered perspective, as well as from a Soul-centered one, the natal horoscope reveals an illuminating understanding of this fundamental form-essence relationship. Such a juxtaposition will clearly demonstrate the relationship between an individual's inner Soul purpose ("Why am I here?") and the nature of those outer circumstances, that is, the "world" of the personality, through which this Purpose is to be externalized. As the goal inherent in the struggle between these two natures is their eventual harmonious union, such an astrologically revealed perspective is of great service. The path that the astrologer must take to obtain this knowledge, quality of attunement, and insight is an incredible and often difficult journey, as well as a great gift.

When we speak of the personality, or lower self, we are referring to an entity composed of three vehicles of consciousness: the physical body, the emotional or astral body, and the lower mental body (the rational, logical mind). *Vehicle* also implies the structure of matter which conveys the more subtle life energy or consciousness. Thus, we could compare a vehicle to a thought, and consciousness to the energy which that thought contains. A vehicle is composed of the matter of its corresponding plane (see diagram 2). The important thing for us to remember is that these vehicles, and their planes of consciousness, are actual centers of force. These centers, as we shall soon discover, are affected by, and correspond to, the planets, signs, and Rays which constitute other centers of force. The interconnections between these energies are at the core of Soul-centered astrology.

Traditional astrology teaches that all the planets have effects on the personality and its three vehicles. We know that the actual shape and temperament of the physical body is often characterized by the sign of the Ascendant and any planets found within or in aspect to the first house. (See *Alan Oken's Complete Astrology*, as well as the Bibliography, for further details about astrophysiology.)

Jupiter in the first house, for example, indicates a large and gregarious person, while with Saturn in this position, one is generally slender, with a prominent, bony body structure, and tends to be rather introverted or serious by nature. But the Earth and the Moon, regardless of their placement in the natal chart, exert the most essential qualities on the nature of the physical body.

The Earth is easily found in the natal chart. It is always exactly opposite the position of the Sun. Thus, if the Sun is located at 14

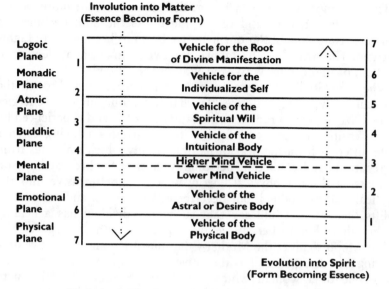

Diagram 2: The Seven Planes of Matter and Their Corresponding Vehicles of Consciousness

degrees of Taurus, the Earth will be found at 14 degrees of Scorpio. The physical matter of the Earth *is* our physical body. This is the primary reason we are affected by the gravitational and other force fields exerted by the Sun, Moon, and other celestial bodies on our planet. From the purely physical standpoint: "We are dust, and to dust we return." What animates our physical organism and all the other heavenly spheres is not dust, but Light, and it is to Light that we also return. *It is this relationship of dust to Light that constitutes the core of the Ancient Science and all metaphysical inquiry.*

Thus the more we are attached to the personality, the more we are materially oriented, in and of the Earth. As the Soul becomes an ever-increasing Presence in our lives, we begin to become more Light-oriented. The struggle to harmonize the two is an essential element of the Path of the Middle Way—the Way of the Disciple.

When the Soul's Presence enters and is experienced through the physical body, a very noticeable change in our physical energies occurs. We appear to radiate. This radiance is felt and experienced by those sensitive enough to perceive it as warmth—a loving essence quite different from the heat of natural vitality which emanates from a gregarious and exuberant personality. Such a Soul-realized person emanates a distinct physical energy which is not intrusive into the physical space of others, but nevertheless penetrates and most often uplifts them. One could say that such an individual has a healing quality about him or her, as well as a quiet strength of purpose.

The Moon signifies the Mother—that nurturing and formative urge existing within us, as well as the universe. It is the Moon in the natal horoscope of a woman which reveals much about her ability to conceive, support in her womb, birth, and nurture a child. On a more collective level, the Moon indicates much about our biological and inherited karma. She is the significator of our racial memory, and indicates how our genes finally express themselves as the various facets of our personality.

The Moon is our tribal history and roots. She signifies, in her most specific indications, the nature of our own family. And, in the more collective sense, she reveals our relationship to the entire human family. Thus, the Moon is the storehouse of our genetic pool, and from this ancient conglomerate, an individual, synthesized unit is born. As our consciousness evolves to the level of the Soul, we begin to see, with ever-increasing understanding, those biological and karmic links which unite us to others, and which eventually unite the entire Human Family as One. The experiential quality of this unity of focus is a key factor of personal evolution and interpersonal relationships in the New Age. (See chapter 3.)

A subconscious or unconscious attachment to the Moon from the personality level is indicative of a person who has not severed the psychic umbilical cord which links us to our physical mother, and thus to our tribal roots and family karma. Such a state denotes a frame of reference that is basically subjective and separative. The individual is a "blind unit," fearful of its own individual expression and unaware of the nurturing quality of that Life Who sustains us all. Here is where we suffer most and where the prejudices and fears of tribal and racial conflicts have their origins. As the Soul's Presence becomes a greater reality, we become increasingly more inclusive in our attitude both to ourselves and to life. From a blind unit only aware of its navel point (and only dimly, at that!), evolving people become increasingly and inclusively aware of the rest of the world. This vision expands until, with loving detachment, we perceive the Womb that holds us all.

The Moon is also highly influential in terms of the emotional or astral body. The Moon acts like a magnet, forming and focusing our needs and desires, based upon our subjective links to our personal and tribal past. It is the prime factor which deals with our feelings of emotional and material security—factors which are conditioned, to a very large extent, by our past experiences. A person may discover, for example, that her fear of not having any money is not so much her own, but an attitude she has inherited from her father and unconsciously adopted from her racial antecedents. By making this attitude her own, she has given her own form and focus to this fear. As the Soul's Presence becomes more prevalent in her life, her ego structure will individualize, and she can begin to objectify this inherited attitude. She can lovingly (but forcefully) detach herself from it, and then *create her own attitude* toward material abundance, regardless of the Moon's position! Thus, attunement to the Soul allows for the reorientation of personality attachments and an ability to co-create our destiny from the Soul's perspective.

Mars is another important planetary influence on the nature of the emotional vehicle. While the Moon gives focus and form to needs and desires, Mars is the energy of their activated expression into the environment. While the Moon represents the inner urge for possession of what is perceived to be our own, Mars creates that into a territorial imperative, and in this respect, acts out its role as the archetype of the god of war. It is the interrelationship between the forces of Mars and the Moon on the personality level that produces the blind devotion to ideals and demagogues which so often leads to interpersonal and international conflicts. Yet, as the Soul's Presence unfolds—either individually, or in terms of the Soul of a nation— Mars and the Moon combine to give direction and power to the inclusive, loving, and transcendental creative urge. Thus are born new forms to the Soul's expression, and evolution proceeds.

Mercury, as the traditional ruler of the sign Gemini, is known as the "Messenger of the Gods," and acts as the communicator. Mercury and the force of the rational mind weave the patterns of cohesiveness that endow focus, logic, and reason.

Mercury expresses itself through several levels, in terms of the lower mental vehicle of the ego. In its most basic form, the mind is used to gratify instincts and primary desires: "I am hungry. How do I go about getting food?" The mind is not particularly rational—it is not used for any level of abstract reasoning. Here it is used for, and subject to, the physical and emotional vehicles.

When functioning at a higher level, the mind formulates and communicates ideas and opinions. Yet, when based in the realm of personality, the opinions we are likely to hold are also inherited. Our minds and analytical abilities are based upon and attached to familial, tribal, and other forms of unconscious social conditioning. In this case, the individual believes that what he thinks is who he is. There is no sense of detachment from institutional or inherited views and prejudices. The thinking is separative in nature, with a general urge for exclusivity of perspective: "This is how I have been taught. This is how my forefathers thought. This is the way it is, and this is the way I am." Here the urge is toward a very fundamentalist perspective, with no room for disagreement or actual creative ideation (except relative to previously set, accepted parameters of communication). If the personal energies of the Moon and Mars interconnect with the mind (as they often do at this level), fanaticism is often the result.

At its most evolved state, the lower mind is a clearly focused and shining reflective lens for the expression of the Higher Mind and true intuition. This is when the Soul's Presence is linked to the rational expression of mind and an inclusive, insightful, wholistic, loving frame of reference emerges. You will notice that whenever the Soul's Presence enters the sphere of the personality, a distinct quality of love is expressed. This is only quite natural, as the Soul is the vehicle for the love aspect of Divinity. It is also the vehicle for consciousness, or "love in action." This is why it is said that love is consciousness and consciousness is love. There is no difference between the two in terms of the Ageless Wisdom. The more conscious a person becomes, the more loving. The more loving a person becomes, the more conscious. This has very little to do with any form of intellectual achievement. When we explore the esoteric planetary rulerships of the signs in part 2, we shall see that from the perspective of the Soul, Venus, "Goddess of Love," is the ruler of the sign Gemini. It is through Venus that polarities of analytic thought are brought to a loving harmony.

It is interesting to view the relationship between the Soul and the personality as a charioteer and his three horses. The chariot itself can be looked at as the synthesized personality energized by its three component parts (the horses): the physical, emotional, and lower mental bodies. When the three horses are working in unison, the chariot may be easily directed toward the accomplishment of its goals. It is then seen to be completely under the control of the charioteer. If, however, the three horses are left to travel without the guiding reins of the charioteer, the journey of the chariot is aimless, no matter how broad in scope, and eventually will fall short of any true purpose.

If the three horses try to move in different directions, as is the case in so many people's lives, one finds that in addition to aimlessness, there is the chaos of an unintegrated personality. Many of us can relate to the state in which our mind tells us one thing, our desires urge us in another direction, while our physical bodies are magnetized in yet a third area of expression. The net result is not only confusion, but a distinct loss of vitality and a disintegrated sense of self. Such a state of disorientation also has the disadvantage of becoming a vortex of negatively polarized or inverted energy. Such people act as human "black holes"—psychic drains on those around them as they constantly magnetize chaos into their lives.

Thus the first major step in attuning oneself to the charioteer is toward the integration of the body, emotions, and mind. This means taming, training, and even whipping those "horses" through the right use of will. This may be accomplished through proper diet and exercise, proper loving of oneself and others, and disciplined use of mental energy.

One of the greatest benefits of a psychologically oriented, personality-centered astrology is that it reveals which of these aspects of the lower self need integration. Such a psychologically based delineation of the natal horoscope reveals the roots of the personality in our early conditioning. It also shows the nature of those blocks to the harmonious interplay of the various personality components, as well as the potential paths of personality integration.

It is here that Soul-centered astrology may play one of its most useful roles in a person's life. It can expand the scope of the delineation of the horoscope in such a way that the linkage between the potentially or actually integrated personality and the Soul is revealed. Soul-centered astrology will also show those underlying karmic energy patterns that either work toward or inhibit such a linkage. The revelation of this information, along with the application of those counseling techniques pertinent to the chart in question, will unfold our understanding of the path of exteriorization of the Soul into the outer life.

Many people stop growing at the point of the integration and individualization of the lesser ego, without the attunement to the Higher Self, and this is very dangerous. At this point, the lower self is infused with the sensation (limited and temporal as it may be) of its uniqueness and separateness. When they reach this stage, people may seek to (e)go out into life and "push buttons"—exert their sense of personal power. It is often when such "buttons" are pushed back by the Law of Cause and Effect (karma) that the astrologer sees individuals for counseling and consultation! Such an integrated, nonattuned ego can create an even greater vortex of negative energy than the kind created by an unintegrated ego in chaos. The integrated ego, conscious of itself but unconscious of the greater Law and greater expression of the cohesive power of Love, can consciously or unconsciously focus a magnetic vortex which inverts creative harmony. Such an ego strives to pervert and subvert universal energies to the bidding of personal physical aims, thoughts, and desires. The stronger the ego in question, the greater the negative vortex, and more important, the greater the urge to create the universe in its own limited and exclusive image.

All too often during the history of humanity, this has resulted in the attempt to dominate the will, intelligence, and emotions of others. This is the intrinsic nature and structure of evil. Weaker and less developed egos at this stage may be relatively harmless to others. Their chief difficulty is the loneliness and desperation they engender in themselves by their separatist thoughts and feelings.

Until each individual member of humanity recognizes his or her wholeness and at-one-ment with the Soul (and eventually, the unity of these individual Souls into the Soul of Humanity), such a polarization of so-called good and evil will continue to exist. It is the goal of the Aquarian Age (and the New Group of World Servers) to plant the seeds of this process of individualization so that the Soul focus of humanity may eventually exteriorize. The aim of esoteric, Soul-centered astrology is to provide a distinct tool to monitor the energies and cycles of this process at this critical, transitional time in human history.

When one has finally become such an integrated personality, the issue of *sacrifice* becomes of paramount importance, and quickens the urge to consult the tables of celestial movements for answers. *Sacrifice* comes from the Latin *sacrificium,* which means "an offering to the gods." At the point of integration, one has the test of either continuing, with renewed strength, many of the old patterns of the ego structure, or sacrificing the ego to the life of the Soul, the life of the greater good, and the impersonal life. Such a sacrifice is very difficult to make, as the integrated ego will fight for its little existence.

Most of us come into incarnation as rough, unpolished, and certainly unconscious "stones." During the natural course of life, we are often forced to work on our stone—facet it, pressurize it with consciousness, and thus transform it into a jewel. The personality then shines brightly. It is creative, admired, magnetic, powerful—even sexy! And then, just at its peak of expression, many of us experience the need to place this jewel under the direction of the will of some higher force. The Soul may make demands on the shining, lesser self which the latter would prefer not to do. The Soul's Presence may tell you that in order for the real you to grow and develop, you must leave your present relationship. It may also tell you that it's time to change your profession, reorient your sex life, etc. The growing awareness of the Presence of the Higher Self may make these and many other demands upon the conditions of the outer life absolutely necessary. This results in those crises of reorientation which are so prevalent at the present time.

Many of the transits and progressions to the natal chart will be indicative of these kinds of crises of reorientation. An understanding of the relationship between the exoteric, personality-centered energies of the ruling planets, and the expression of these planets as viewed and experienced from the Soul-centered perspective, is most important. Such a comprehensive perspective will allow for the determination of the direction of one's life in such crises.

There is a focus of resolution which emerges from the tensions produced from such a distinctly polarized set of circumstances. This resolution is called "synthesis," and it is at the core of the essential meaning of the sign Virgo. (See chapter 9, p 192.) Synthesis—the Middle Way—is the Path by which one gradually fuses the lower and the Higher selves. It may be seen working out in life as the following process: Recognition-Polarization-Tension-Consciousness-Synthesis-Fusion-Resolution-Recognition-Polarization, etc. This is an ongoing procedure which underlies the weaving of the structure of the Rainbow Bridge, and results in what the Master, D. K., refers to as a "Soul-infused personality." (See diagram 5.)

The Soul is our individual link to the essential substance of the Creative Source. The various deaths and transformations which each of us has to undergo along the Path of Return are not all physical in nature. The focus of reorientation of the lower self requires the death of nonregenerative, emotional habit patterns, as well as the breakdown of outworn thought-forms. As painful as it may sometimes be, we have the opportunity to glean the lessons of our actions by remaining in the physical body during this process of transmutation. We can also rejoice in the releases from our blockages and our victories in overcoming them. This awareness is a great gift and an equally great responsibility. As consciousness grows and unfolds, so does the nature of the work we have before us. Our task is then seen to be one of making a way in the physical reality for the externalization of the Soul's energies, and thus for the defined and refined expression of our life's purpose.

The Soul is neither a theological speculation nor a philosophical reference point. Those individuals who demand intellectual proof of the Soul's existence are obviously not in touch with their own Higher

Self. They can never be while the intellect is used as the primary vehicle of approach to life. As we have just observed, the intellect has to be placed under the conscious direction of the Higher Self.

The Soul is a vital organism serving a number of distinct functions. It is very important to remember that we are Souls with physical bodies, rather than physical bodies with Souls. The physical body will have but one life, while the scope of the Soul's existence is much more permanent.

The Creative Source of life is unquestionably powerful, but at the same time incredibly subtle in Its essential nature. In this respect, It requires increasingly denser vehicles for Its expression as It descends through the various levels of manifestation. Such containers and conductors of the Life Force are created as they are needed. The process of this aspect of creation is at the center of the Ancient Wisdom Teachings.[1]

In this instance, it may be said that the descent into physical matter is analogous to the attenuation of the alternating current of electricity. Attenuation is the method by which the amplitude of AC current is reduced without causing any apparent distortion. Such a process calls for the stepping down of power so that the electrical current may flow properly and serve its purpose without destroying its conductor. Each of the vehicles of human consciousness conducts that current so that the stream of life may unfold at its particular level of expression. In addition, each of these vehicles of manifestation also insulates and protects the life energies of which it is composed.

The attenuation of the Life Force from the Soul to the physical body is a long journey. Unlike the attenuators created by modern science, which allow for a minimum of distortion in terms of the purity of the electrical current, the various bodies (vehicles) of the human organism have the propensity to severely alter this outpouring. The mental and emotional bodies are commonly so cluttered and clogged with karmic debris that the Presence of the Soul's energy is never perceived.[2]

Just as there are three bodies for the expression of the personality, there are also three vehicles which comprise the structure of the Soul. These two triads connect and correspond through the Antahkarana (Rainbow Bridge), and as a result, expand and develop consciousness. We may also assign certain planets to each of these three levels of

---

[1]There are three references which amplify this study. They are: *A Treatise on White Magic* and *A Treatise on Cosmic Fire*, by Alice A. Bailey, and *The Secret Doctrine*, by H. P. Blavatsky.

[2]At this period in human history, a tremendous "karmic cleansing" is taking place, both personally and collectively, so that more and more people will come to an awareness of this Presence, even though the crises that this necessitates may be quite painful. Yet the rewards of this process are equally great. The years 1983–1995 will be especially transformative in this respect, as Pluto transits its own sign, Scorpio.

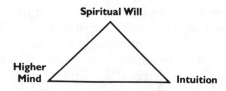

Diagram 3: **The Symbolic Structure of the Soul**

Soul expression, although the Soul's vehicles are certainly not limited by such assignations.

The Higher Mind is located in the upper levels of the mental plane. This is the abstract mind, as opposed to the concrete mind of logic and reason. We can also call these two divisions of the mind the formed and the formless. The Mercury-ruled formed mind of logic and reason is in a direct line of connection to the Jupiter-ruled, formless mind of abstraction. It is through the abstract mind that the Soul functions to universalize a person's world view, yet it is very important that the lower mind of concrete knowledge be trained and structured. It is this lower aspect of mind which allows for the discrimination of mental impulses and their correct application throughout our daily life. The Jupiter-influenced mental faculties seek expansion and universality, and as one might expect, lead one to search for a wider experience of life through philosophical and spiritual teachings. When the lower and Higher minds are properly aligned, a person can relate, in a logical and concrete way, his inner visions and insights into the Laws and Principles which underlie the greater metaphysical truths.

The intuitional aspect of the triad of the Soul is extremely important, as it is this faculty of contemporary humanity that is being, and will continue to be, emphasized in the Aquarian Age. The previous focus for the evolution of human consciousness was the development of intellect. This focus is rapidly changing, as the need to categorize, process, and assimilate a rapidly increasing amount of data is required by modern life.

The intellect must and will eventually be absorbed and synthesized into the intuitive faculty of our being. This will permit the sense of the collective, group life to steadily grow in importance in the consciousness of New Age humanity. Such an awareness will give rise to a distinct understanding of the relationship which exists between the individual and the various groups to which he or she may belong. The scope of such relationships will determine the important social and personal movements of the times to come.

Once this faculty of intuition is more fully developed, one will then be able to sustain a vision of the wholeness of life, and perform an individual task relative to the well-being of that whole at the same time.

The development of true intuition is a comprehensive faculty of perception. Once the linkage to true intuition is accomplished, a person has the ability to perceive that *quality of energy* which vitalizes any *form* of expression. This is the type of attunement, for example, which allows a person to perceive the consciousness of an author through his words. This is quite a bit more comprehensive than appreciating the writer's style and understanding his words. Intuition is that faculty of inner vision which permits an astrologer to place him- or herself at the point of another person's consciousness. It is from such a perspective that the correct level of interpretation of planetary energies may be accurately sensed as they play themselves out through a person's life. It is via the Jupiter-oriented Higher Mind that a particular world view and philosophical comprehension is added to this attunement. The Mercury-influenced lower mind will then allow the astrologer access to the right words and phrases to communicate his or her message.

In this respect, it is the cultivation and integration of intuition which allow a person *to see life as energy* and to be able to understand the relationship between energy and form. Another facet of intuitive perception is the ability to see the beginning, the end, and the probable pathways that the Life Force may take between the alpha and the omega of any of life's circumstances. The intuitive astrologer knows that (and this is not by conjecture, but through an instantaneous *identification with living intelligence*), given a certain situation, energy will move only in a limited number of specific directions. This use of consciously directed intuition in the delineation of a horoscope is a major indication of a New Age astrologer.[3]

When intuition on the level of the Soul is properly fused to the emotional vehicle of the personality, a wonderful alchemy takes place. An individual becomes aware of the needs of others, is supportive of those needs, and, relative to his individual talents and abilities, may choose to serve such needs. At this stage, a person has developed a loving detachment to most situations in life. He or she is then able to become a vehicle for healing and unification, without becoming involved in the complexities of a personal, emotional relationship. He feels, but is not attached or made compulsive by feelings. This frees him to love and be loved in a very real sense.

---

[3]The planet Uranus, in its rulership of Aquarius, its association with the faculty of intuition, and the evolution of so much that is of the New Age, is so very important that it occupies a major theme throughout this work. Chapter 4 is an essay on the significance this planet and its sign have on contemporary life, and their continuing influence in the coming Age.

This particular linkage is vital to one's individual Path of unfoldment as it aligns the heart (the center of love) with the brow (the Third Eye, or center of intuition). It is also, in terms of the Ancient Wisdom Teachings, the alignment of the Christ with the Buddha on an individual basis, and is thus a most potent focus for the exteriorization of one's life purpose. From yet another perspective, the joining of the heart with the center of intuition allows for perception into the collective purpose for humanity, as well as one's particular contribution within that much larger framework.

The third and highest aspect of the Soul's triad can be called the vehicle for the expression of the Spiritual Will. In esoteric terminology, this is called "Atma," and it is here that the Will of God individualizes and vivifies the Soul. At this point, the Soul is conscious of itself and its Source, just as we become aware of the presence of the Soul at the juncture of the Higher and lower minds. It is through awareness of the individualized Spiritual Will that one is attuned to the omniscience of life as a Conscious, Intelligent Entity.

This realization is the final phase of this process of linkage. As a result, the purpose for one's life becomes truly anchored and may be externalized through the physical plane. Thus, the highest and lowest vehicles of the Soul and the personality are fused and made one.

> Matter is Spirit at its lowest point of manifestation and spirit is matter at its highest.[4]

—H. P. Blavatsky

> As above, so below.

—Hermes Trismagestus

There are two planets which affect the expression of the Spiritual Will. The first is Neptune, at its most exalted level. The other is the Moon, when viewed symbolically as the Mother, the sustainer of all forms—in effect, as the Soul Herself. The Moon and Neptune are very closely related astrologically. We know that from a traditional perspective, Neptune is said to be exalted when found in the Moon's natural sign, Cancer. Yet, from the perspective of Soul-centered astrology, Neptune *is* the ruler of Cancer. (See chapter 9, p. 178.) It is when Neptune is found in this sign that the universal matrix, the waters of life, are at their most productive.

From the level of the personality, Neptune *is* the significator of illusion. It places a veil around true perception while substituting emotional glamour and mirage in the place of reality. Yet, when

---

[4]As quoted in Alice A. Bailey's *The Rays and the Initiations.*

viewed from its position at the apex of the Soul's triad, Neptune unveils the reality of spiritual truth and provides that matrix—that Essential Substance—through which the Spiritual Will may take eventual form in the outer life.

Taken as a whole, the Soul is the Middle Way, for it "stands" between Spirit and Matter. The Soul acts as the intermediary between Essence and material manifestation, provides the necessary channels through which consciousness may exteriorize and come to *know* itself. The grace of this knowing is that in the process, each of us comes to identify ourselves as Divinity in manifestation. We learn through the frequently painful processes of transformation and reorientation, as well as through our many births and rebirths, that the quality of our consciousness is Love Itself.

The concept of functioning on the material plane in an egoless state is not only completely unrealistic, but is totally incompatible with basic metaphysical law. On the contrary, the lower self should be seen and *trained* as a vehicle for the Soul's expression. The lesser self is an entity which can be "re-formed" and refined so that it may eventually correspond vibrationally with the Soul's rhythm and life purpose. This balance and attunement is an essential process. It is at the core of the Path of one's spiritual life, and the resultant externalization of that Path into one's practical life. One of the astrologer's most important tasks is to note how the lesser ego may be cultivated so that it may eventually harmonize with the energies of the Soul. Only then can Soul infusion take place and the basic human duality be resolved. When read exoterically, from the perspective of the personality, and then esoterically, from that of the Soul, the natal horoscope will reveal the unfoldment of this necessary process.

The personality itself is a tool for one's inner creative source. The better the tool, the more productive can be the "hand" which wields it. That "hand" is you! True creative intelligence does not originate within the structure of the lesser ego. Rational intelligence certainly exists and grows in its scope through one's participation in life. But true, creative intelligence comes from the Soul and is used to shape the ego as its instrument in the three worlds—physical, emotional, and rational—of its outer expression.

The world of the personality is vital. The material world is essential to our total unfolding. It is far easier to exist when we have the financial means to provide comfort for our children and ourselves. We may then pursue our spiritual awareness, free of the stress of poverty. Material poverty is an unnatural state, and is not a requirement for spiritual growth. It, like celibacy, is an *option*, but not a requirement.

What is required is the proper attitude toward the personal material, emotional, and mental life. It is the negative emotional attachment to the material plane, out of fear of loss, that creates those circumstances which inhibit our spiritual lives from flowering. A great deal of this fear is rooted in our biological karma and social conditioning. Once the personality is infused with the purpose of the Soul for the present incarnation, then one's true life work may be understood, and preparations undertaken to realize it. The quality of one's life reaches a more perfected and joy-filled state only when the inner purpose for that life is clearly envisioned. This awareness, and its accompanying strength and courage, come directly through Soul contact. Wealth and power are then "safe" commodities because they are grounded in higher values and clarity of vision. Such abundance may then be properly disseminated to others. This sharing of concentrated abundance is a major factor in the spiritual and social structures of the New Age. The Age of Aquarius is the Age of the dissemination of energy in all of its forms. It is for this reason that the concept and practice of networking, and the centralization and socialization of many economic and political systems, is on the increase. Abundance on all levels, on all planes of consciousness, is the natural order. Obsessive attachment either to abundance or its lack is unnatural and creates chaos.

A developed and usable personality requires an attitude of loving detachment. We must work to "watch our movie" (after all, whether consciously or unconsciously, we are writing and producing the script!) and not just be in the film. The development of the ability to witness ourselves (not to be confused with judging ourselves) is a very important step in actualizing our Soul's potential for its externalization in the outer world. The exercises and meditations provided at the end of this chapter may help to initiate and support such a perspective.

This self-witnessing will help us not only to individualize our egos, but to unite the ego of the lower self with the Soul. This process creates Soul-infused personalities who are capable of being consciously co-creative in the outworking of both the personal and the collective life of which we are a part. Once this Soul infusion takes place, a person begins to see life in a much different manner from one who is totally focused in the glamours of the lower self.

These glamours, illusions, and mirages lead to a disease which is at the core of both our materialistic confusion and many of our physical illnesses. It is called "me-my-mine-itis," and it is cured once we begin to live our lives from the heart and see with all "three" of our eyes. When the horoscope can be read from the Soul's perspective, the Path to the opening of the heart and our "other" eye becomes clearly revealed.

As Soul infusion takes place, one begins to perceive the world in increasingly more collective terms, without losing sight of its individual, component parts. One is thus able to see oneself, others, and all manner of interconnectedness clearly and simultaneously. In effect, Soul infusion allows for a vision of human networking, as well as an understanding of one's particular place within this huge collective. The quality of this comprehension is an expression of the Law of Attraction in action, which *is* the manifestation of the Love aspect of Divinity. It is thus that the relationship between the One and the many, the macrocosm and the microcosm, becomes increasingly self-evident—another gift from the cosmos!

The above is meant neither as a metaphor nor as a euphemism. These words are an attempt to give some indication of the frame of reference and actuality of perspective of a growing number of individuals at the present time. And the numbers are increasing geometrically! The process is called the "Path of Synthesis" or the "Path of Discipleship," and it is as much alive in this, the cusp of the New Age, as it was in ages past. Magic and magicians, initiates and initiations, have not disappeared—only their forms of expression have changed. The essential nature of the evolutionary scheme of life mutates minutely over the eons, as compared to the rapidity of its external transformations.

This is also true for astrology. The symbological archetypes upon which modern astrological science are based were set down in early Atlantean times. But the forms and applications of astrological interpretation are constantly changing in order to meet the needs of the civilizations and eras which birth both astrologers and their techniques of interpretation. A Soul-centered, esoteric astrology is emerging today because humanity is evolving rapidly enough to need and utilize such a system. The synthesis of the mental and intuitive faculties increases the ability to objectify our subjective reality. This development in human evolution is currently giving rise to a worldwide heightening of spiritual awareness. The net result of this movement of consciousness is the building of a link between the Soul and the personality, both on the individual and on a collective level—the Rainbow Bridge—which we discussed earlier.

Many of us are aware that there is such a bridge—such a Path to the alignment of our lower and Higher selves. Our crises of reorientation to the Soul (and the resultant expansion of personal consciousness) continue to reveal the nature of this Path to us, as well as our place within it. This causes us to question both the direction and the form of our true purpose. It is also the reason the contemporary astrologer is constantly asked to determine this purpose by the many people who also are seeking the inner meaning to their lives. The esoteric rendering of the chart will give the Soul-centered answer to this sincere quest.

Just as we build our physical bodies from the food substances in our material environment, we build the Rainbow Bridge from the substance on the mental plane of life. This construction becomes an increasingly more conscious process as the life of the Soul unfolds.

Diagram 4: **The Interchange of the Soul, the Personality, and the Rainbow Bridge**

The net result of the development of the Antahkarana/Rainbow Bridge is the linking of the three vehicles of the personality with the three of the Soul. In this respect we may say that the "weaving of the threads" of the Path (for the Rainbow Bridge is the Path) is occupying a great deal of our time and energy now. To become established, this linking requires several kinds of disciplines and experiences.

The connections which are required are:

1. The link between the lower mind and the Higher Mind.

2. The link between the personal emotional body and the intuition.

3. The link between the personal will and the will of the Higher Self.

These necessary contacts will bring three very common areas of crises and transformation into our lives:

1. A change of diet and attitude toward the physical body, leading to a healthier physical vehicle.

2. The transformation of personal desires and the way in which we express our personal, emotional, and sexual lives.

3. The training of the mind so that it is receptive to inclusive, philosophical perspectives, while breaking its attachment to limiting opinions and opening it to true intuitive perceptions.

When these "threads" are finally constructed, they facilitate the flow of consciousness from the Higher to the lower self. This produces a heightened awareness of life that eventually serves to negate all sense of separateness from the essential Oneness and Wholeness of Life's fundamental nature. Once a person senses his or her unity with the Creative Source, several wondrous things occur:

1. There is an absence of the fear of loss, extending from the most petty, materialistic concerns to man's greatest apprehension—that of physical death.

2. There is created, through the "brain" consciousness of a person, those impressions coming from higher realms. The latter lead to a definition of personal belonging extending into the universal. Such contact with these "lives supernal" gives the continuous inner guidance and direction for which we so yearn.

3. An identification occurs between oneself and the Universal Source so that one realizes in ever-increasing and expansive ways that he is the co-creator of his life and destiny. This is a most important realization to make, as it allows a person freedom to "move" within the circle of the horoscope, and releases him from an attachment to the biological karma of absolute predestination. A sense of inner freedom is achieved when the personal will is aligned to the Will of the Collective Source. The Path of Soul alignment is the process through which such a co-creation of personal destiny may be achieved.

The Antahkarana/Rainbow Bridge is that thread of consciousness which, through the Law of Attraction/the Law of Love in Action, reveals the interconnectedness and unity of all life. This is why we seek to tread the Path so that we may consciously recognize our unity with It. Such has been the Path of the mystic, the devoted student, and the seeker throughout the Ages. It is no different now, except through the forms that this Path takes in daily life in this century.

We build these threads of consciousness from our efforts in the exoteric, external world of the lower three aspects of our self. As we do so, we refine ourselves to a point at which we can magnetically attract the three corresponding aspects of our Higher Self to us. In this respect, we may see that many of our activities consist of working from the outside in. Once we realize that we have reversed this process—that we are identifying with our inner world and are working from the inside out—we may be said to be living as Souls, even if our efforts are those of fledglings at this eternal game. When this reversal has taken place, we may be sure that the anchoring of the Rainbow Bridge has occurred, and that we are indeed walking the Path.

Before a man can tread the Path, he must become that Path himself.[5]

—Alice A. Bailey

[5]*Discipleship in the New Age*, vol. 1, p. 715.

There are two other facets of the Rainbow Bridge and the Path that should be mentioned at this point. The first is that *the Path is the Rainbow Bridge* and is symbolically rendered through the diagrams and discussions presented herein. The function of this Path is linkage and communication, so that a person may be able to first identify with the Creative Essence of Life, and then, through serving It, become It. The Rainbow Bridge is created from the Love aspect of Divinity (governing cohesion in the universe), and through traveling upon its Way, that loving consciousness is consistently revealed to the traveler.

The second facet is that *the Path is the goal of life.* We in the Western world tend to be extremely goal-oriented as we move through our material world, with concepts of linear energy as our guidelines. We learn as we tread the Path that not all movements of the Life Force (in fact, relatively few) are linear. Nor are these movements all particularly logical in effect. We also come to realize that so-called "linear time" is but one small aspect of Time Itself. We eventually even manage to accept the above without having to *understand* it, which is no mean feat for the Western intellect!

It is this reorientation—from the linear to the transcendental, from the particular to the wholistic, and from the personal to the impersonal—that is conditioning a completely different set of personal and societal life circumstances. If the astrologer is to counsel other individuals seeking an interpretation of their life and events (as well as to comprehend one's own life and events), it is imperative that an understanding of the transformation of consciousness in our Age, as well as the structures of such transformations, be clearly delineated.

The Rainbow Bridge is built of mental substance, and as a result, is very much concerned with the realm of communication. Thus, its construction requires the creation of those kinds of relationships that allow the above-mentioned repolarization of energies to take place. As Gemini rules the basic dynamic of interrelatedness, and Mercury that of the energy of communicative linkages, this sign and planet will play a very important part in the building of the Rainbow Bridge. Two other planets are also vital to this process—Venus, which serves to harmonize polarities, and Saturn, which is the very force of consolidation and construction itself. Saturn is also the sphere most intimately connected to the mental plane. (These and many other astrological ramifications of the Rainbow Bridge are discussed in part 2.)

It is no wonder that, at this cusp of the Age of Aquarius—an Age oriented to Right Human Relations—there is so much focus and stress upon the material, emotional, structural, and sexual nature of human interchange.

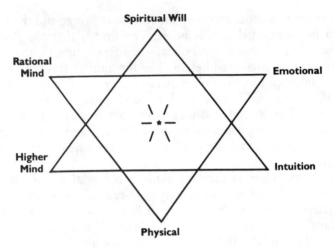

**Diagram 5: Symbolic Representation
of a Soul-Infused Personality**

The process of Soul infusion is expanding both our personal and collective consciousness. We are certainly experiencing this within ourselves through an increase in our sense of loving detachment and our urge to be of service to humanity. It is especially noticeable when we sense that our desires are becoming aspirations, and when the nature of our inner life increases our access to a sense of peace and strength, regardless of the nature of the external environments through which we function.

Diagram 5 represents the symbolic fusion of the Soul and the personality. It is, of course, the six-pointed Star of David, and is indicative of one who has trodden the Path of the Disciple and has achieved that inner and outer unity which is at the core of each of our quests. There is a seventh point to this star, which stands at its center. This is the Point of Light within the Mind of God—that quintessential unit both expressed and nonexpressed—which is simultaneously in and out of manifestation, and which is also our Self.

EXERCISES

The following selection of meditations, visualizations, mantra, and affirmations may prove to be of benefit in the alignment of the personality and the Soul. Please feel free to share them with friends and associates.

I. MANTRAM OF UNIFICATION

The sons and daughters of men and women
are one, and I am one with them.
I seek to love, not hate;
I seek to serve and not exact due service;
I seek to heal, not hurt.

Let pain bring due reward of light and love.
Let the Soul control the outer form
and life and all events,
And bring to light the love which underlies
the happenings of the time.

Let vision come and insight.
Let the future stand revealed.
Let inner union demonstrate and
outer cleavages be gone.
Let love prevail.
Let all people love.

II. THE GREAT INVOCATION

From the point of Light within the Mind of God
Let Light stream forth into the minds of men.
Let Light descend on Earth.

From the point of Love within the Heart of God
Let Love stream forth into the hearts of men.
May Christ return to Earth.

From the center where the Will of God is known
Let purpose guide the little wills of men—
The purpose which the Masters know and serve.

From the center which we call the race of men
Let the Plan of Love and Light work out.
And may it seal the door where evil dwells.

Let Light and Love and Power
restore the Plan on Earth.

III. VISUALIZATION EXERCISE

1. Find a quiet spot where you won't be interrupted.
2. Sit in any comfortable position with spine erect, ankles uncrossed, and hands either resting in your lap or upturned on your knees.

3. Breathe gently and deeply for two or three minutes and observe your breath while you quiet your mind.

4. Visualize the triangle of the personality in your mind's eye. Focus on the lowest point of that triangle, representing the physical body. See that point glowing with light and feel your own physical body, full of strength and vitality. Next, focus on the upper right-hand point of that triangle, representing the emotional body. See that point glow with light and still your emotions while affirming that you are love and are loved in return. It may help to imagine your emotional body as a clear, still pool of water reflecting the light of the sun. Finally, focus on the upper left-hand point of the triangle, which represents the lower mental body. See that point glow with light and still your mind so that there is no internal dialogue. It may help to envision the mind as a clear camera lens through which the sun's light radiates the prism of the seven colors of the rainbow.

5. See the three points of this lower triangle all aglow and connect these points with lines of their own light, so that the personality is seen as one unified, integrated whole.

6. Visualize the triangle of the Soul in your mind's eye. Focus on the lower left-hand point of that triangle, representing the Higher Mind. See that point glow with light and affirm that that place of knowing understanding is available to you and is you. Next, focus on the lower right-hand point of the triangle, representing the intuitive aspect of the Soul. See that point glow with light and affirm that that place of true perception is available to you and is you. Finally, focus on the apex point of the triangle, symbolizing the place where the Will of God is known within you. See that point glow with light and affirm that that place of revealed purpose is available to you and is you.

7. See all three points of this upper triangle aglow and connect these points with lines of their own light, so that the Soul is seen as a unified, integrated whole.

8. Now, view the upper triangle above the lower, with two parallel lines of force connecting them, as in diagram 4.

9. Continue to observe these two separate triangles, and watch as they begin to merge, taking the form of the Six-Pointed Star. When the two have become one, notice a brilliant Point of Light emerging at the center of the Six-Pointed Star and know that That is the Atom of the Life Force which is your Life. Observe and experience the energy of this seven-pointed image and be silent with it for as long as you wish.

10. Now, repeat the Mantram of the Soul:

> I am the Soul.
> I am the Light Divine.
> I am Love.
> I am Will.
> I am Fixed Design.

IV. AFFIRMATION

The following affirmation gives a very accurate picture of the relationship between the Soul and the personality. It also works to strengthen one's inner attitude and one's strength of resolve to tread the Middle Path.

> I am the Soul. I have a physical body, but I am not my physical body. My physical body is a part of me. I am the Soul. I have emotions, but I am not my emotions. My emotions are a part of me. I am the Soul. I have a mind, but I am not my thoughts and opinions. My thoughts and opinions are a part of me. I am the Soul. My body, emotions, and mind work harmoniously and in unison under my loving direction, for my highest good and for the highest good of all. I am the Soul.

3

The Evolution

of Consciousness in

the New Age

I recognize and affirm that I am a center of pure self-consciousness. I am a center of will, capable of observing, directing, and using all my psychological processes and my physical body.

—Roberto Assagioli
The Act of Will

As the wheel of the precession of the equinoxes turns, and we move from one World Age to another, the collective orientation of our ways of relating, the structures of our societies—indeed, the very fabric of our consciousness—is mutating accordingly. In her monumental work, *The Secret Doctrine,* H. P. Blavatsky speaks about a structure within that consciousness called the "ring-pass-not."

The "ring-pass-not" refers to the limit of the field of activity of any given organism—from an amoeba to the greatest of galaxies—in terms of the consciousness of that organism. Yet, as each organism evolves and, by so doing, creates extensions or vehicles for the continued expression of its particular type of consciousness, the "ring" expands. It moves to and creates other levels, thus increasing the ability of that organism to express its nascent, creative potentials. Each human being has his or her personal "ring-pass-not." You may confront this quite easily when certain life circumstances bring you to a point of crisis in which you say: "Beyond this, I cannot love any more. This is my ultimate point of giving." Then you are forced either into a situation of destruction or decomposition, or you are forced to widen your ability to love. This may still require the breakup of the *form* of the situation which focused this crisis, yet *essentially*, by expanding your ability to love in a given moment, you have extended your consciousness and grown. Consciousness is love and love is consciousness. Divinity is love in action and consciousness is the expression of that Love.

Humanity as a whole also has its "ring-pass-not." This "ring" is taking on another form of expression at the current time. As it does so, we are all involved in the many crises of the reorientation of our collective (and ultimately, our personal) consciousness which such a shift brings about.

One of the most important movements in the evolution of human consciousness at the present time is the requirement (and the impulse) that each individual be responsible for the direction of his or her own spiritual growth and development. This sense of personal responsibility, as expressed in the Age of Aquarius, is very different from the nature of personal and collective spiritual unfoldment during the past World Age. In the Age of Pisces, especially as it manifested in the Western world, we were dominated by a number of orthodox theologies administered by patriarchal authoritarianism. The majority of these theologies have been based upon a theory of transcendental dualism. What this means is that the sexes have been treated as unequal in nature, leading to a tremendous suppression of the feminine. Moreover, this dualism has led to a great division in the minds of most people between the material and the spiritual. It has also given rise to an erroneous and guilt-ridden concept of sin, based on the assumption that humanity and Divinity are separate in nature, as well as in manifestation. The degree of pain and social oppression which has arisen from such a socially sanctioned duality has been incredible in its scope. But pain will no longer be the vehicle of enlightenment and mystical revelation in the New Age!

We learn from the Ancient Wisdom Teachings that male and female are two equal polarities in a constant dance of creativity. The purpose of this interchange is to establish more and more avenues for the expression of that Whole within which these two polarities (and all of their manifestations) have their breath and being.

At the present time, the focus of this dance of polarities is *synthesis*. Here, synthesis means the ever-evolving focus of unity resulting from a *conscious* fusion of the various parts of this Whole. The Whole is transcendental in nature; that is, it manifests simultaneously on all levels of manifestation. The Whole is also immanent in nature; that is, present in its Oneness and undivided in its Wholeness no matter in what form or in the number of its manifestations. This is the underlying principle of "unity in diversity," and reveals to us that the Whole is always greater than the sum of Its parts.

We are discovering in this cusp of the New Age that each person, whether male or female, has to awaken his or her other inner half, and create an individual marriage of polarity. This means that many of the heretofore stereotypical and archetypical images, roles, and social dynamics based upon sexual duality (and all too often, the oppression of women) will have to end. The historical lineage of patriarchal authoritarianism will have to give way (and in spite of itself, is giving way) to a form of "co-parented self-determinism" based on a unanimity of purpose within a group context. As we outline "The Laws and Principles of the New Age," in chapter 4, the social and personal trends and movements within the scope of this transformation will become apparent.

We are also taught that "matter is Spirit at its lowest point of manifestation, and Spirit is matter at its highest." In their essence, matter and spirit are one, and only appear as an illusion of duality. This means that the material forms of Life are essentially created from spiritual substance. A human being can therefore honestly say: "I am God in human form. God and I are One." There are no differences between church and state. There are only differences in the degrees of self-realization and self-manifestation.

This focus of synthesis and unity, this resolution of dualities into greater, more inclusively loving wholes, is fundamental to the New Age. The New Age religions and the trend of the current transformations within the orthodox belief systems are growing ever more into this direction. In the short term, this evolutionary movement will produce an ever-widening schism between the fundamentalist views of the previous World Age, and the focus of synthesis as we move into the Age of Aquarius. This is only natural, although certainly not particularly comfortable, as we straddle the cusp of this great turning point in the evolution of human consciousness.

As we move forward, more of us are realizing that not only are we, as individuals, capable of continually realizing our own creative, Divinely centered potentials, but that no one else can give them to us. No one else can truly absolve us; no one else can save us. We may be inspired by others and may even be led to the door of wonderful, deep-seated spiritual revelations by others. But only we can open the door ourselves and go through it, and only we can live the revelations that we, individually, perceive as truth. This does not mean that we have to do this alone. On the contrary, the Age of Aquarius is an Age of humanism. It is an Age in which the Law of Right Human Relations and the Law of Group Endeavor are of the utmost importance. This is a time in which cooperation, companionship along the Way, and love between the sexes, races, nations, and all other groups of individuals will reveal itself as containing the highest living ideals of a spiritual life in the material world.

For many people, the notion of taking spiritual responsibility for themselves is bewildering and frightening. We have witnessed so many exclusive cults, some amazingly rich and powerful, which have amassed and wasted great financial and psychic resources. We have quite fortunately also seen how the centering of power in the lower selves of these cult leaders, whether from India or Indiana, has corrupted and perverted humanity's great spiritual aspirations. One reason why so much power has erroneously fallen into so few hands is that many people still believe in a world of gloom and doom. This world stimulates fear and provokes guilt and hysterical emotionalism. Indeed, we have seen such antics even among many so-called New Age groups. These are just "Old Age" groups in New Age clothing! As we examine the Laws and Principles of the New Age in the following chapter, we shall see just which qualities of consciousness are coming into manifestation at the present time and the kinds of crises (and victories) of reorientation they bring.

A baby is not born into life completely free and empty—a new entity, blemish-free, just waiting to receive its impressions from its parents and its environment. If you believe in reincarnation, you know that an individual comes into life complete with a history of personal karma. He or she is born to continue developing certain patterns of unfoldment and to complete others; to fulfill certain promises and to plant the seeds for future endeavors. Even if you doubt reincarnation, or are not sure of its validity—even if we discount reincarnation altogether—there is still not a baby born who does not carry an ancient history into life. This is the human history. It is carried in the genes. It is carried in the racial memory. It is certainly carried in the Soul, and the more conscious a person becomes during the course of his or her lifetime, the more the Soul reveals that history to the conscious mind. This is one of the factors of human evolution.

The ability, and even the concept of the freedom to empower oneself to direct the course of one's spiritual life, is completely contrary to human history up to the present time. If we examine the course of Western civilization for the past two thousand years (effectively, the Age of Pisces), we see that the vast majority of people have been dominated by two groups: a landowning aristocracy and a landowning church. The vast majority of all European or European-descended people come from antecedents who have been totally subservient to either one or both of these groups for at least fifteen hundred years. This means that their financial and spiritual directions were governed by others. The attempt to wield independent material or spiritual power meant the imminent threat of death, or worse! It is no wonder that part of our legacy as we enter the New Age is that so many people feel helpless financially, as well as spiritually. The elimination of a poverty consciousness, both from a material and spiritual level, is certainly an aspiration which we must plant and implement collectively at this time in our history.

All abundance comes from one Source. This Source is structured in mind and expressed through love; that is, through the Law of Attraction. The study of a more metaphysical astrology can help us to understand the cycles of the expression of this Source, as well as Its manifestations in our lives. The more we understand the Laws and Principles underlying such manifestations (and their specific applications in the New Age), the more we may attune ourselves to identifying with that one Source as our Self, and thus more consciously cooperate with Its cycles of unfoldment. As the number of Self-realized men and women of goodwill increase, humanity as a whole will progress to its natural state of abundance on all levels.

The above is a long-range project. In fact, I believe it to be one of the goals of the Aquarian Age—to prepare the world for the Messianic Age of Capricorn, two thousand years hence. Meanwhile, we shall be confronted by our own and other people's struggles to individualize their own centers of personal will in order to establish a sense of self-empowerment. This amounts to a concerted effort at finding and concentrating upon one's individual source of creativity. Once this is firmly established, the nature of the Age of Aquarius, its evolving social structures and values, will reveal to such individuals the collective nature of that creative Source. Then, Group Endeavor will truly flourish and another Law of the New Age will come into effect in its fullness.

To summarize the major transition in the evolution of human consciousness in our time, we could say that the "ring-pass-not" for humanity in the previous World Age was: "The Father in Heaven and I here on Earth are separate. I give my power unconsciously to others and suffer accordingly. This pain awakens me to my Self." The new "ring-pass-not" that is currently being developed by humanity during the Age of Aquarius might be stated as follows: "The Father/Mother, my Group of brothers and sisters and I, are One. I am a conscious expression of the Power of the Universe acting through the Will-to-Good. This enlightened understanding awakens me to my Self."

The astrologer of the New Age must be able to distinguish not only the shades of meaning inherent in the positions of the planets by signs, houses, and geometric aspects, but to "read" the level of consciousness through which the planetary energies are operating. In this way, the astrologer will be able to determine if the interpretation of the chart, or any of its specifics, should be based on the esoteric or the exoteric planetary rulers of the signs, or a combination of the two. (The definition of the esoteric planetary rulers is found in part 2 of this work, while the applications and interchanges between the traditional, exoteric planetary rulers and the esoteric ones form the basis of part 3.)

It would prove helpful to discuss the three broad stages through which human consciousness develops before actually examining these Laws and Principles of the New Age. It is important for us to keep in mind that each of these three stages is general in outline and is composed of many graduations of expression. For our purposes, let us call these three broad stages of consciousness unconscious unity, conscious duality, and conscious unity.

Unconscious unity: In this state, one is completely identified with the personality and the worlds of the lower self. In essence, one is tied completely to one's biological karma. One thinks and speaks like one's tribe, antecedents, and family. One's emotional reactions to the various situations of life are also very much in line with what has been established genetically and in terms of the accepted, collective behavioral patterns of one's particular biological group. This type of consciousness is still very much alive among the so-called civilized and developed nations of the world. For many people, it is a very safe and comfortable way of being. In fact, many conflicts arise when a person is evolving out of this state of consciousness and is beginning to quicken to the urge to individualize.

The state of unconscious unity reaches a point of danger on the collective level when it is reinforced by governmental policies or is established as a form of government. This has been the case with National Socialism in Germany, fundamental Islam as practiced by followers of Ayatollah Khomeini in Iran, or the more ultra-conformistic tendencies found in some forms of extreme communism.

On the personal level, another important characteristic of this state of unconscious unity is a person's inability to distinguish between energy and form. The expression, "what you see is what you get," is particularly descriptive in this respect. An individual who identifies completely with the personality is incapable of perceiving abstractions. He takes everything in his world personally. In effect, the environment and all of its events are seen through a reflective lens of personal thoughts and desires. Beyond certain socially conditioned and/or biologically inherited responses, there is very little, if any, connection with a sense of the human collective.

Conscious duality: This is the state in which most of us currently find ourselves. We have become aware that we are spiritual essence incarnating in physical form. We realize that spiritual aspiration is often apparently in conflict with material desires and biological habit patterns. There is often a seesaw effect, in which we move back and forth between concentrating our life resources for the will of the lower self, only to endure a crisis and then begin the reorientation toward the needs of the Higher Self.

Here, the good of the individual is constantly judged and balanced against the good of the collective. The two are seen as polarities, and as a result, there is often great conflict between our ideals and our previously established patterns of social interaction. In effect, the state of unconscious unity is one which we can compare to being in the movie of our life, yet unaware that it is a movie. Once the focus of individuation has begun in the early stages of conscious duality, we begin to be aware of the movie and are even able to observe it. We constantly move back and forth between starring in the film and being the critic, objectively watching the production unfold. The fullness of the perception (and the responsibility) that we are the producer, director, writer, *and* the star of the show has not dawned yet. When it does so (and eventually it does!), an incredible life crisis ensues, which is resolved through a much greater spiritual awakening.

The various stages of conscious duality are really the preparatory steps on the Path of Discipleship, for we now have to make those conscious choices of life-style and life values that will result in the creation of those more refined vehicles of consciousness.

Conscious unity: This is a state of being to which we are all aspiring. A few of us have already achieved this focus of consciousness. It stands as the goal of all our efforts at becoming. Conscious unity is another term for Soul infusion (see diagram 5). At this point in individual evolution, we know and live in the awareness of the Soul's reality. A synthesis has taken place between the lower self and the Higher. The three vehicles of consciousness of the personality are totally under the control and direction of the Soul. The outer life is constantly being molded to suit the Will and Purpose of the Higher Self. This Purpose is revealed in our daily life and the experience of our individuality is totally connected to the sense of our universality.

This principle concerning the relationship between the individualized sense of self and the universal wholeness of life begins to unfold during the later stages of conscious duality. At that point in our growth and development, we perceive the collective as often challenging to our lower ego structure, and it is! The struggles that ensue help us harmonize the fear of the loss of self experienced by the personality through the revealing vision of the Love of the Soul's reality. Thus, in the early stages of conscious unity, we perceive in no uncertain terms that the more individualized we become, the more universal. In effect, we perceive that that individualizing Self is the Self of the universe. The fears and apprehensions of the lower ego then begin to melt away as the inclusive wholeness of the Higher Self reveals Its true nature.

Now, the two most profound questions a person can ask may be answered: "Who am I? Why am I here?" And what is so very wonderful is that no one else has to answer these questions for us. The answers are self-revelatory and thus come from our individualized Truth. Totally believable, totally factual!

The state of conscious unity brings a great deal of responsibility into our lives, in addition to great joy. It reveals to the conscious co-worker (for by now, that is what we have become), that aspect of the Planetary Purpose, that facet of the One Work for humanity that is now our task to perform. At long last, our mission in life has been revealed and the sense of alienation and separation has now ceased. In its place is a distinct sense of purpose, an overwhelming sense of love, and a profound connection with an Inner Group of Teachers and an outer group of like-minded brothers and sisters who serve as our companions along the Path. I want to emphasize that what is described above actually occurs as we evolve our consciousness along the Way. It is the result of all the long efforts, sacrifices, tests, and trials. And still, it is but the beginning. . . .

4

The Laws and

Principles of

the New Age

Humanity itself is said to be the Hierarchy of Pisces, and this is the reason for Humanity's destiny, which is to fulfill the function of the World Savior. Think about the implications of that! Humanity must save itself! Humanity must save itself, must choose to manifest its own wholeness, its groupness, before it can save the world. . .

—Frances Adams Moore
Group Life—A New Age Reality

1. **The Law of Right Human Relations**
2. **The Principle of Goodwill**
3. **The Law of Group Endeavor**
4. **The Principle of Unanimity**
5. **The Law of Spiritual Approach**
6. **The Principle of Essential Divinity**

If we were to outline some of the most important themes underlying the sign Aquarius, we would unfold the basics of the Laws and Principles of the New Age. Foremost, Aquarius is a people sign, a human sign. Like Virgo, the Virgin; Libra, the Scales; and Gemini, the Twins; there is no animal associated with the Water Bearer. Aquarius signifies a state of being, a concept exemplified through a particularly human expression.

Aquarius relates to organizations, groups, and aspirations. It is more concerned with the relationships existing between the individual and the collective within which he or she functions, than with those relationships existing between individuals outside a group context. It is a fixed sign, insofar as adherence to principles is concerned, but its fixity also extends itself to that necessary focused link of common bonds that bind groups together through ideological union.

As an air sign, Aquarius is very concerned with the circulation of data, and unlike the watery Pisces, tends to be mentally rather than emotionally polarized. Aquarius seeks to communicate specific and often ideological information which it distributes through the structured networks it seeks to create. In this respect, individuals are seen as vehicles for the unfoldment of collective aims, the personal always yielding to the transpersonal for the purposes and betterment of the whole.

The two planets traditionally associated with Aquarius—Saturn and Uranus—further bear witness to the focus and importance of the mind. Saturn is very much the ruler of the mental plane. It is the planet most associated with structures, plans, and goals. In its methods of externalization, Saturn tends to be very logical and conceptual, yet we are not actually dealing with the intellect, per se—that is much more the province of Mercury and Gemini—we are dealing with the *structure of mental energy*. Indeed, Saturn is the force that endows the mind with the ability to structure its thoughts and construct its concepts. This is very different from the aspect of the thinking process that occurs once certain boundaries of the mind are anchored. In effect, Aquarius and Saturn say: "This is the reason for our reasoning. This is the cause for communication. This is the overriding structure and ideology within which we shall endeavor to achieve our goals of sharing information."

The energy of Uranus is very quick; it acts much faster than logic. Uranus is intuition which, as we have already discussed, functions to perceive the quality of the essential energy within any given form. Uranus endows the mind with the ability to comprehend the beginning, the end, and all stages in between the alpha and the omega of a given situation simultaneously. Uranus is the planet of true knowing and the true Uranian is the *Knower*. One of the major effects of Uranus is instantaneous and often telepathic communication. In fact, many words beginning with the Greek prefix *tele* (coming from *telos*, meaning "afar," "distant") are Uranian in nature. Telepathy means "to feel from afar"; television is "to see from afar"; telephone is "to hear from afar"; telegraph means "to write from afar"; and telescope means "to view from afar." These words are indeed Uranian in their activity as they seek to allow communication to occur from great distances. They are Aquarian in their essential nature as they serve to create channels and networks for the distribution of information and allow for group efforts to proceed more rapidly and efficiently.

There is another planet and several other factors associated with Aquarius which I would like to introduce at this point. From the perspective of the Soul, the planet most closely associated with Aquarius is Jupiter. In effect, we call Jupiter the esoteric ruler of Aquarius. As the "greater benefic," it tends to bestow abundance and expansive awareness on all it touches. It also brings the quality of joy into one's life—a quality which, along with courage, is very definitely Soul-centered. In fact, the more Soul-centered your reality and way of life, the more the qualities of joy and courage are present. Jupiter's position by house and sign in the natal chart will reveal where the quality of that *inner joy* is most likely to reveal itself.

The reason for this joy, and much of the reason for the hope that the Age of Aquarius will be characterized by an abundance of the Soul's Presence, is that Jupiter carries with it the energy of the Second Ray, which is the Ray of Love/Wisdom/Consciousness.[1] The New Age is ruled esoterically by Jupiter, and holds a great deal of promise for an abundance of joy for humanity. Finally, Aquarius itself is a sign of the Fifth Ray. This Ray has much to do with the concrete mind and technology, and the processing of data. The esoteric astrologer looks to the world of science and physics to be the vehicles through which the promises of the New Age and the Teachings of the Ageless Wisdom will be made manifest on the Earth.

Let us turn to these six major Laws and Principles of the New Age so that we may better understand the underlying themes which characterize the transitional nature of our times. We will see how these evolutionary currents affect us, both in terms of our personal lives and in the collective life which we share as Humanity. Such information can better help us to understand the astrological implications of both the natal horoscope and current planetary transits. In this respect, we will find ourselves in a much more objective position to counsel others (should we be professional astrologers, psychologists, teachers, or healers in other disciplines), or for that matter, to understand and counsel ourselves.

THE LAW OF RIGHT HUMAN RELATIONS

- **Keynote of the New Age**
- **Love and Intelligence working as a team**
- **Responsible group service for humanity**
- **Self-forgetfulness, harmlessness, and right speech**

[1]The nature and influence of the Seven Rays upon the signs, planets, World Ages, and human psychological characteristics is at the core of the teachings of Soul-centered astrology. We will be exploring the implications of the Seven Rays in parts 2 and 3, yet it is essential for the sake of a wider comprehension of the Laws and Principles of the New Age that they be mentioned here, since the nature of their influence is very appropriate in light of the present subject matter. After the reader has spent some time with the material contained in parts 2 and 3 about the Rays, he or she may then wish to go over these pages once again.

As Aquarius is the sign expressive of the focus of the collective creative outpouring of humanity, the urge for right human relationships is uppermost at the present time. This is as true for our personal relationships as it is for the major alliances between nations and national blocs. In fact, one of the main purposes in the outworking of the Law of Right Human Relations will be to unblock the blocs! It cannot be stressed strongly enough that our tendency as the Human Race is to move from a consciousness of the individual to a consciousness of the relationship between the individual and the collective. This will lead eventually (as we progress toward the end of the Age of Aquarius) to a greatly expanded awareness of the collective itself. We are watching humanity move from the personal to the impersonal and from the intellectual to the intuitive.

The seeds for such transformations are being anchored in today's world. Recent astrological transits of two of the outer planets have laid the foundation for this basic transformation. These were the transits of Uranus through Libra, which took place from the end of 1968 to the last months of 1975, and Pluto through Libra, which began in November of 1971 and ended in November of 1983.

Libra is the sign of personal relationships—of those rapports that concern themselves most specifically with one-on-one encounters. Uranus passing through this sign tended to revolutionize the nature of personal relationships. There was a birthing of an abundance of alternative life-styles which challenged the status quo of many forms of human interchanges.

When Uranus transited Libra, the ruling planet of Aquarius was housed in the sign of marriage. This was a clear indication not only of the unfolding of new social archetypes, but an infusion of the nature of collective purpose into the individual lives of hundreds of millions of people. This brought to mind the awareness that the Earth is our "planetary home" and our "global village." An entire generation of men and women of goodwill made sure that through their political, artistic, and spiritual activities, the idea of the One Humanity was clearly sounding during this period of the late 1960s and early 1970s. One of the greatest contributions that the generation of the "flower children" made was to bring to the forefront of human affairs this sense of a world community. The "We are all One" frame of reference, so much the ideological banner of the Love-and-Peace, Uranus-in-Libra generation, has indeed synthesized its way into the collective human orientation as we experience this cuspal period of the New Age. When we examine this transit from the esoteric perspective, we will see that Uranus *is* the esoteric ruler of Libra (see chapter 9, p. 199). From the point of view of the Soul, the unfolding of the Law of Right Human Relations into the collective consciousness is very much in right chronological order with the passage of Uranus through the sign of the Scales.

The simultaneous transit of Pluto through Libra is also worth our attention. Pluto is very much the significator of the process of death, transformation, and rebirth. It has a great deal to do with the release of the essential creative energy of life from its outworn or outmoded forms and containers. Pluto is at the core of the Law of Recycling—the facet of nature which continually transforms that which has died and decayed into new and evolving forms of expression. Pluto is thus a primary motivating energy of the Law of Reincarnation, whether this involves the rebirth of a person, a tree, or an idea. Its passage through Libra points to the regeneration, transformation, and re-creation of many different kinds of human relationships. Pluto in Libra thus brings into the area of human interchange an especially strong burst of creativity, as well as the end of an era and an outmoded way in which people have related and structured their lives.

From the esoteric perspective, the message contained in these transits is quite specific:

1. Uranus, as the ruler of Libra from the Soul level and the ruler of Aquarius from the outer, exoteric level, transits the Scales. This points to a beginning of the collectivization of human consciousness and the revolutionization of established structures of human relationships in order to allow the awareness of the individual's relationship to the whole to flourish.

2. Pluto from the Soul level is the ruler of the sign of the previous World Age, Pisces. The passage of Pluto through Libra, ruled esoterically by Uranus, planetary significator of the New Age, occurs simultaneously.

3. This is a clear, celestial indication of our entrance into the New Age and the implementation of the Laws and Principles (as well as the particular crises and victories) underlying this transition.

The need to establish Right Human Relations is paramount, as this process is the foundation for the flowering of the structures and forms of consciousness evolving in the New Age. The eventuation of a strong, unified, creative humanity requires that each one do his or her individual part in the One Work of human evolution. We are seeing a much heavier emphasis being placed on individual responsibility for the direction of creative and spiritual paths than ever before. The one great difference between the kind of individual responsibility that is demanded now and the kind of individual work that was required in the past has a great deal to do with this type of participation as an individualizing agent. In the past, one worked for one's lord, one's church, one's parents, or one's employer, and earned a living (or was allowed to keep on living!). The use of work—"Right Livelihood"—as a Path to the individuation of the creative Spirit in each one of us, was not an actualized concept. It is today. This means that people will be seeking more inherent *meaning* to the way they earn their livings so that who one is and what one does is balanced and integrated. This is yet another dimension to the urge for "wholism," which so characterizes our times. There is already an awareness of the need to create an inner sense of attunement—at-one-ment—with one's outer tasks. The urge for service to others is very much on the upswing, in terms of people's general orientation to life. Many people, no matter how fulfilling their professional interests may be, are finding an inner void that can only be filled through creating some focus of contribution to the greater whole of humanity. This urge to serve—this need to help heal the planet and its people—will require the implementation of the Law of Right Human Relations.

It is of vital importance that we become aware of the various levels upon and through which we participate in relationships. Then, we must strive to make the threads of such connections truly conscious and alive. In order to have right human relationships with anyone else, we must first have a right relationship with ourself. One of the names popularly given to a large segment of the current adult population is the "Me Generation." Indeed, there are a huge number of workshops, methodologies, teachers, teachings, diets, and an entire "spiritual supermarket" available to those wanting to know more about themselves. Some see this need for self-exploration as very self-indulgent. I can certainly understand how challenging it is for the millions of husbands and wives who have abandoned or semi-abandoned their traditional roles and ambitions for this search for self. This search is at its most frightening when people move forward without a "road map" to the Path of consciousness lying ahead. It also creates much pain, anger, and frustration for those who feel left behind and who may not be in tune with what they might tend to view as the foolishness of New Age fads—or worse.

But the search for self—the process of individuation—is not a fad. Certainly there are processes, weekend intensives, and specialized, spiritualized products which come and go. We could even say that a number of the outer forms of the search for self may be trendy or faddish—but that is the nature of forms in general. The essential search for the key to the expansion of our consciousness and the resultant transformations in our life-style are certainly *not* faddish. They are very much the manifestations of our intensely changing times and the resultant reorientations of our relationships.

It is of primary importance that we establish an inner sense of the right relationship with ourselves. This will require knowing, then harmonizing, and finally synthesizing the three vehicles of the personality. Fortunately, there are many fine methodologies and schools of healing and psychology that can be of real assistance in this worthwhile and very essential (and ever so long-lasting!) pursuit.

The Soul of Humanity, sometimes called the "Christ Consciousness," is the synthesis of all individual human Souls. This collective presence of Love is also unfolding, and It is unfolding *through* humanity. As It does so, It allows an ever-increasing possibility for love and abundance to enter both the individual and the collective life. Our job is to make the Way for It. The author believes that this will be done primarily through the six Laws and Principles outlined in these pages. When read both in the traditional and in the Soul-centered way, the natal horoscope will show how the individual may assist in this process of Higher Self-realization in and through the daily life.

Many people have reached a place in which their ideology concerning the Path and Its reality as a way of life are in conflict. Such people believe that once they have set foot on the Path, they can just glide through the problems of life. Nothing could be farther from the truth! In fact, for a while, the crises in life will appear to multiply after we have identified with the Way of the Soul. This is because there are now even more relationships and levels of relationships to consider than before.

Everyone on the planet has "horizontal" relationships. These consist of the ordinary interchanges which make up the personality life. We have our relationships with our family, lovers, employers, employees, or co-workers. We have our relationships with money, property, and other possessions, and the people involved in handling these matters. These "latitudinal" relationships also include those that deal with our church, social organizations, and educational institutions. This multitude of social interconnections is there for the seeker and the nonseeker alike. We could call these the relationships of the "single cross" we carry in handling the responsibilities of ordinary life.

Yet, those on the Soul's Path may find—initially, at least—that they feel "double-crossed." Not only must they deal with the rules, regulations, and structures of the horizontal life, but the additional and increasingly important code of behavior for the "vertical" or "longitudinal" life.[2]

Part of the process of infusing the Law of Right Human Relations into our awareness involves the alignment of the individual to those

---

[2]The happiness and delights of the life of the personality are many, as are the incredible Joys and Rewards of the life of the Soul. But many, many people have to struggle with the weight of their life before it becomes Light and Joy-filled. Indeed, one of the things we learn how to do on this Path of Self-discovery is to perceive, integrate, and then radiate such Joy 360 degrees around, above, and below us! Such is the nature of the Sun, the Creative Spirit in each of us.

"Higher Powers and Kingdoms" that exist simultaneously and cotangently with ourselves. This is accomplished through prayer, meditation, contemplation, visualization, invocation, and many other methods of approach. Another very important aspect of Right Human Relations on the vertical axis has to do with humanity's relationship to the lower kingdoms. We must take our proper responsibility—as individuals, and then as communities, nations, and the Human Race—to make sure that the well-being of the animals, vegetables, and minerals is secure. Thus the harmony of the planet is anchored, and life in all its forms and on all its levels of manifestation may proceed with conscious awareness of the evolutionary process. The continual monitoring of the right use of nuclear energy (another dynamic indicated by Pluto's passage through Libra), the intense awareness of ecological conditions on the parts of millions of activists, plus such organizations as Save the Whales, Greenpeace, and the Cousteau Foundation, are revealing humanity's consciousness of its vertical relationship to the lower kingdoms. The continued spiritual efforts we are making reveal our awareness of the Higher Kingdoms of life and our aspiration to be more closely linked with Them. Horizontally, too, there is a definite refinement and expansion in the way we understand our union as One Humanity. In recent years we have seen the initiation of a day for international meditation, December 31, as well as those humanitarian programs—Live Aid, Band Aid, Farm Aid, etc.—that focus on the charitable distribution of resources to groups, nations, and people in need. The latter could not be possible without the proper use of those Uranian inventions of global communications which bring what is distant so very close to home.

The following is a technique for the application of the Law of Right Human Relations. You may wish to use it and share it:

1. Visualize the Law of Right Human Relations as two clasped hands encircling a bright, glowing planet Earth.

2. Contemplate and consider the implications of Right Human Relations.

3. Make a plan as to how you may demonstrate Right Human Relations individually in the world.

4. Telepathically radiate the Law of Right Human Relations by repeating its name. Send forth your thoughts of Right Human Relations in all directions—north, south, east, west, above, and below.

5. Repeat the following afirmation: May everyone with whom I come in contact in any way be blessed in the universal brother- and sisterhood of the One Humanity.

THE PRINCIPLE OF GOODWILL.

- **Positive energy transforming the world**
- **Contagious inspiration to others**
- **Open door for communication and cooperation**
- **Cohesive force for good**

The need to be able to concentrate and focus upon a clearly defined creative direction is uppermost in the minds and hearts of a huge number of people. The reorientation to the reality of the Soul's Inner Presence, plus the relative freedom which Western and American society provides in the ability to choose one's field of endeavor, have allowed a choice of life direction which heretofore in human history has not been nearly so possible. Thus a multitude of people are restlessly seeking that focus of self-definition—and to those truly awakened by the Soul, a *focus of service*—which will further the process of individualization and dynamic social contribution. The attainment of self-actualization requires the right use of will, in no uncertain terms.

What this means is that another of the responsibilities currently confronting a consciously evolving person is the necessity of becoming self-empowered. The idea of being able to focus, hold, concentrate, and creatively use power is a very frightening prospect in the minds and hearts of many people. This is clearly the first time in human history when such a connection with the inner power of the Soul is not only available, but absolutely essential to successful living.

The polarity of the sign (and Age) of Aquarius is Leo, which exemplifies the flourishing of the individual creative spirit. It is very important for us to understand that the signs of the World Ages have to be considered as pairs, with the objective emphasis placed on the present Age. The subjective polarity is the sign opposite. The relationship between Leo and Aquarius will give rise to a clear-cut interchange between the individual and the collective. One will polarize and shape the other. We shall have more to say about this specific point very shortly when we discuss the Law of Group Endeavor.

The road to the proper path of individualization requires attunement and succinct development of the will. This process naturally serves to increase willpower. As will is the objective expression of causality, and thus creative impulse, it is very obvious that a person cannot co-create his own destiny and take an active, responsible role in the unfolding of the destiny of the collective, if personal willpower is not developed. And yet so many have been taught to shun any attempt at incorporating will into their lives. Once again, I would call the reader's attention to two major factors which are at the root of this particular frame of reference.

The first is evolutionary. Quite simply, the prevailing state of consciousness up until this time in human history has been tribal. The herd instinct of nonindividualized egos living under the primarily totalitarian political and/or theological social systems of the past Age has not allowed for the flourishing of true human potential. Certainly there have been many people over the course of the past two thousand years who, though often martyred, have been able to express the true dynamics of a self-actualized, and in rare cases, Christ-conscious individuality. But these have always been the exception. The majority of humanity has either been too unconscious, downtrodden, suppressed, frightened, or uneducated—purposely or otherwise—to move to any level of existence other than material survival. But this is dramatically changing! More and more people all over the world are recognizing the Aquarian/Uranian urge for the equality of self-expression, and the lowest common denominator of such an expression of self is actually getting higher and higher. We are seeing a definite increase in the number of people who are now expressing their consciousness through a state of conscious duality. And there are even a number of teachers and guides on the Earth at this time who inspire us through their focus of conscious unity. The latter are very definitely the "Points of Light" in the New Age.

The second factor is socially conditioned, and proceeds from the first reason why self-realized, right use of will has been incredibly inhibited up to this point in history. The majority of us have been taught not to express ourselves if, in that expression, we are perceived as being different from the majority of people around us. What we are finding out in this cusp of the New Age is that there is a unanimity of feeling, instinct, perception, and purpose among an incredible diversity of people. This awareness of subjective unity allows, fosters, and supports the outer differences in the expression of our various pursuits, interests, and inclinations.

One of the most prevalent crises that the astrological counselor encounters in the course of her daily work is the individual who finds herself with the need to break out of existing, often semiconscious tribal modes of behavior. Such a person is seeking to develop a pathway to her own, individualized use of will so that she may express her true focus of creativity. The establishment of this pathway allows her to come into contact with the current state of her own natural expression. This individual has perceived that her previous forms of self-expression are now quite unnatural to her newly expanding awareness. What is often required in such instances is the knowledge leading to the ability to construct or refine those vehicles of consciousness in the personality (body, emotions, and mind) that will allow for a greater expression of the Soul's Presence in her life. My conversations and communications with scores of other astrologers and co-workers around the world tell me that these themes are universally prevalent. Soul-centered, esoteric astrology is a definite aid to the revelation of this process of the refinement and integration of such vehicles of consciousness.

The Principle of Goodwill should be viewed from several perspectives in order to understand the scope of its origins and applications. Until about 1973, when I came into a profound contact with the Work of the Tibetan Master and a number of His students, I always had associated the word "goodwill" with Christmas carols. Goodwill for me was really nothing more than an aspiration, and quite an ideological one, at that. It never occurred to me that goodwill was a potency—a tremendous force that could be (and is) focused by the Souls of a multitude of men and women of actualized goodwill around the planet.

The more I meditated upon goodwill and associated with people whose strength of willpower was grounded in the Will-to-Good, the more I realized just how powerful and positive goodwill could be. It was of first and foremost importance to learn that power itself was something good. As my perception of the reality of willpower and its expressions in my daily life were gradually being centered in the reality of the Soul, this allowed me (as well as many others) to function from that place. I then realized that I was not going to abuse power, nor was power going to abuse me. In fact, the right use of will, as an expression of the Will-to-Love, could only be used as another healing device. This realization helped me to crumble my fears about the individualized use of my willpower and allowed will, goodwill, the Will-to-Good to be the force of creativity in my life.

The Ancient Wisdom Teachings tell us that our solar system is founded and is manifesting through the powers and energies emanating from Seven Rays. As we shall explore in part 2, the astrology of the Seven Rays forms the core of Soul-centered astrology. It is the Second Ray of Love/Wisdom that is the primary source of the life/consciousness of our particular solar system. Thus, will or power—the qualities of being of the First Ray—in our solar system and through this Humanity is actually the Will-to-Love, the Power-to-Love, the Will-to-Be-Wise, and the Power-of-Wisdom! Anything less is an inversion and a perversion of this reality. Those of us who are consciously aware that we are men and women of goodwill, are here on the planet at this time to establish firmly the essential truth of the Principle of Goodwill through our particular creative endeavors and various fields of service.

The natal horoscope is the blueprint which reveals what the natural scope of such creative endeavors may be. It also shows what blocks and natural affinities of energies exist in the life to either aid or inhibit the expression of those talents and abilities. The positions and interrelationships of the planets clearly indicate such circumstances. But we are not limited by our horoscopes, by any means. As the Path of repolarization to the Soul's Presence and Purpose is unfolding, one has the definite ability to envision and co-create one's destiny. This is free will in action and when, through the Soul, free will is connected to Love this becomes goodwill. This freedom permits the conscious attunement of oneself to the Divine Will. Free will is the voluntary creation of those vehicles of consciousness that can properly carry the Will and the Purpose of Life into the worlds of the lower kingdoms and from these levels back Home to the Soul once again. We are a part of the total creative expression of Life. The expansion of our consciousness reveals the Grace that lets us *know* that we are part of this purposeful, loving, and intelligent Being. Astrology—especially esoteric, Soul-centered astrology—is helpful in this gradual revelation as it bestows the ability to measure and delineate the rhythms of some of this cosmic and omniscient process.

As we work to align ourselves to the Soul's reality, and hopefully aid and counsel others toward this same orientation, we will be seeking ways to implement a greater measure of the Will-to-Good into our lives. One of these requires that we judge ourselves not too harshly, but that we nonetheless identify what in our personality inhibits a greater flowering of goodwill. A sense of separation and self-centeredness, expectations of how other people should or should not behave, especially toward ourselves, are several characteristics which must be transformed in order that the willpower be more fully expressed as a quality of love. Hostility, prejudice, and the intolerance of other people's differences are several other inhibitory factors against the manifestation of the strength and power of goodwill in our lives.

The above can be overcome by first implementing the Law of Right Human Relations to oneself—that is, the creation of a right relationship between our lower and Higher selves. This is aided through meditation and study, as well as right diet and a clear emotional life. In addition, we can work directly to cultivate those characteristics which serve to channel goodwill into our lives. These include, first and foremost, a spirit of service and generosity to others. In addition, and especially in our Age, it is important to foster a distinct awareness of our universal brother- and sisterhood.

Here is a technique for meditatively working on the Principle of Goodwill:

1. Visualize Goodwill as men and women happily and purposefully building and constructing the new City of Humanity.

2. Contemplate within yourself the implications of Goodwill as they are carried out by a conscious Humanity.

3. Make a plan as to how you may demonstrate Goodwill in your own way in the world.

4. Telepathically radiate the Principle of Goodwill by repeating its name. Send forth your thoughts of Goodwill as streams of light in all directions: north, south, east, west, above, and below.

5. Affirmation: Through the right use of will, goodwill, may I be guided to do my part in the One Work for Humanity.

THE LAW OF GROUP ENDEAVOR

- **Strength of many serving a common aim**
- **Mutual respect, love, and cooperation**
- **Wide range of effective relationships**
- **Creative energy inducing more light**

One of the most important avenues of social expression in the New Age is a unified focus of group purpose through which the individual may contribute and evolve. This means that group activities and the participation of the individual in collectively organized social structures is on the increase. We are thus finding that people are searching for a much more specific sense of belonging and a more intimate identification with a particular group or groups. For those who are awakened on the Soul level, such a reorientation from the more individualistic to the more pluralistic will require a great deal of self-definition so that the scope of their personal contribution and service to humanity may be consciously rendered.

Aquarius is, after all, the sign which exemplifies groups, associations, and organizations. Its urge for a collective, unified purpose is being demonstrated through the effects of its primary ruler, Uranus. The underlying need for structure and ceremonial formalism manifests through the effects of its secondary ruler, Saturn. In addition, much of this collective, structural orientation and formalism can be seen as coming from two other sources. As one of the four "fixed" signs of the Zodiac, there is a definite tendency toward a certain degree of group-oriented ritual inherent in the very nature of the Water Bearer. The other qualifying source, and the one most important to Soul-centered astrology, is the effect of the ruling Rays on the Aquarian Age.

On the outer, exoteric level, the New Age is ruled by Uranus, which in itself is the significator of the Seventh Ray of Ceremonial Order. It will be through the outer forms of social organization and aligned group purpose and endeavor that the inner, esoteric dynamics of the coming

World Age will flourish. These Soul-centered energies are indicated by the inclusive and benevolent Second Ray of Love/Wisdom inherent in Jupiter, the esoteric ruler of Aquarius.

One of the major contributing factors to today's personal and collective tensions is the fact that we have not fully entered into the New Age. We will not be completely anchored in it for several hundred years to come. Thus, ours is an epoch which clearly expresses the influences of both the Piscean and the Aquarian Ages. In terms of the nature of group endeavor, this juxtaposition and confusing confluence of tendencies has resulted in a plethora of illusion-based, glamour-filled, and even demented groups and cults.

Individuals who seek to devote themselves blindly to a group and its leaders do not have a clearly defined ego structure. Such people either cannot or do not seek to harness their personal willpower. It is much easier for them to give away their personal, financial, and psychic power to glamorous gurus, whether on television or in a tent. It is here that a great deal of spiritual deception and disappointment is currently taking place.

The very nature of the vast majority of these "Old Age/New Age" groups, their myriad martyr-blinded devotee adherents, plus the behavior and actions of their personality-cultist, demagogical leaders, "channels," and "facilitators," clearly reveals that the New Age has not fully manifested and an amazing hodgepodge of group "maya" reigns. Yet the Aquarian "urge to merge" within a group context of spiritual searching is very strong. Although this yearning has led a great many people to merge with those forms of "spiritual awareness" filled with deception, illusion, and glamour of all sorts, the actual need for group contribution and personal identity within the group is not wrong at all. In fact, this is one of the most natural urges on the planet at the present time. There are many groups who do indeed have a real "New Age Soul Force" at their center and who are working out the mandate of the times with a minimal amount of glamour and illusion. There are even some "channels" who, attuned to their souls, are able to serve others and are not mesmerized by media hype or astral-plane polarization. Yet I believe that ultimately, the only valid channel is "Channel You."

Since there are so many people involved in group processes at this time, we should examine some of the trends and characteristics underlying the formation of two major "groups of groups" during this cuspal period between the two World Ages. The first of these major tendencies concerns those organizations which are still primarily influenced by the Piscean Age of devotion and emotional polarization. This category of group affiliation is affected only in a superficial sense by the oncoming Aquarian Age. In essence, the major New Age influence is the ability for such groups to make use of modern technological achievements in communication in order to broadcast and proselytize their particular messages.

The nature of some of the fundamental energies manifesting through the more Piscean-Age-oriented groups may be listed as follows:

1. The planets Mars and Neptune predominate. Such a combination gives a need to carve out territories which combine the urges for terrestrial and spiritual power. The combination of the joined influences of Church and State is thus an extremely relevant theme in history (especially European history) during the preceding Age. The Inquisition is a very definite manifestation of the combination of Mars and Neptune in this respect. When we add Jupiter (as co-ruler of Pisces and exoteric significator of orthodox religions) to the influences of these other two planets, it is little wonder that religious warfare has been and still is a recurrent theme in our era.

2. Mars and Neptune are the planets most closely associated with the Sixth Ray of Devotion. When these two planets function through the lower self, the result is often fanaticism, as there is a tendency to exclusivistic belief systems: "My God is better than your God. My cause is sanctioned by heaven and yours is not. My religion is the only true faith," etc.

3. Group leaders at this very end of the Piscean Age tend to remain authoritarian and patriarchal in nature. They receive their authority—can *only* receive such authority—from the collective mass of blindly devoted individuals who, consciously or unconsciously, give away their *non-individualized, non-Soul-realized* willpower. This psychic transfer of energy has resulted in such mass movements as Hitlerism, Mao's Red Guards, Khomeini fundamentalism, the mass suicide at Jonestown, and a plethora of other blindnesses. It should be briefly mentioned at this point (and will be expanded in part 2) that Pluto is the esoteric ruler of the Piscean Age, which is why it is possible for the collective energies of the "underworld" to be brought into manifestation and harnessed through the focus of the personal will of such totalitarian group leaders during this cuspal time between the Ages. It is only through electricity, the airwaves, air warfare, broadcasting, and other Uranian/Aquarian inventions that such group phenomena and personalities as those mentioned above could exist and even briefly flourish.

4. Finally, it must be mentioned that there is much in the combination of Mars, Neptune, Jupiter, Pluto, and the Path of Devotion that is very kind and beneficial in nature. There are (and have been) many groups and collective functions on the planet which "serve and do not expect due service." Selflessness and harmlessness are distinct qualities of such an orientation which have been synthesized into the

collective consciousness of humanity. Certainly, the efforts of Mother Teresa and her international group of co-workers and supporters reveal this to us. The ideals governing the United Nations, the Peace Corps, Amnesty International, Greenpeace, and so many others are also examples of the linkings and joinings of energy between the end of the Piscean Age and the inception of the Aquarian Age.

The other major tendency, at the present time, in terms of current trends of group dynamics, concerns those collective efforts more dominated by the energies of the incoming Aquarian Age. The following paragraphs outline some of the predominating characteristics of this orientation. It should be noted that in the course of the next few generations, such themes will become increasingly more prevalent as the outer expression for group consciousness.

1. If devotion based on faith was a key theme of group endeavor in the Piscean Age, identification of purpose based on revealed knowledge will be the theme in the Aquarian. This means that the human race is being repolarized from an emotionally based orientation to one that is more mentally and intuitively anchored.

2. Groups which form under the New Age impulse are composed of individuals freely and consciously associating with one another. Such individuals are not held together either through ethnocentricity or separatist religious fervor. Emotional fervor of any sort, for that matter, is not and will no longer be the "psychic glue" which binds people together into negatively polarized Piscean Age groups. Guilt, fear, greed, and racism of any sort are no longer to be the instruments of group impulse, purpose, and identification. The promise of this potential (and a very real potential it is) has already crystallized in the minds and hearts of millions of men and women of goodwill everywhere. We are working now, each in our own field of service (with millions of others preparing such a personalized focus of social participation), to anchor these thought-forms into the daily life. Such activities will be brought about with more continuously integrated, mentally focused group endeavor and its resultant collective awareness.

3. One of the reasons it is so very important for each person to individualize his true nature is that the pattern for group interchange is changing. No longer will a nameless mass of "planetoids" be grouped around a central "star." Today's group leader has to personify the collective urgings of the group's energy. *Tomorrow's group leader will be the group itself.* Imagine then, if you will, a great galaxy of individualized stars revolving around a conscious common center, collectively and willingly moving toward a common purpose, idea, and focus of service. This is tomorrow's reality, and is why so many of today's personal crises involve the disappointments one encounters

when one compulsively, emotionally, and/or blindly gives away personal power to other people—be they gurus, lovers, or political leaders.

Love is the binding, cohesive force of Life. As we focus on our individualizing selves, our Soul-centered realities, and we mature accordingly, we do not have to fear that five billion separatist egos will result from our efforts at growth. We are One Organism by our very nature. Through those vehicles of world communication that are so much a part of the Aquarian Age, we will be able to realize this basic factor of our collective life. *Consciousness is love in action.* The increase of consciousness on both the personal and collective levels can only stimulate our cohesion and action as One Humanity.

4. A New Age teacher acts more as a brother or a sister than as a father or a mother. The New Age teacher, as well as the New Age group (functioning as the teacher from a collective perspective), seeks to guide a person toward an ever-increasing state of Self-realization. This can only lead to personal refinement and the Soul-focused urge to serve. The New Age teacher or group does not demand that you dress in the same kind of clothing, eat the same kind of food, have the same kind of sexual orientation, or act in any other way that accentuates an externalized, separatist exclusivity. The New Age group consists of individuals who are united through a subjective, inner orientation. Their particular disciplines and life-styles are stimulated from within and are not imposed from without by authoritarian figures claiming divine revelation.

5. Martyrdom and the giving up of a usually unintegrated and immature ego are two characteristics of the Piscean Age. *These are not the ways of the Age of Aquarius!* One no longer gains any spiritual merit through sacrificing oneself on the altar of any person or organization claiming spiritual authority over others. Our present goal is to create healthy, spiritually realized, integrated egos that allow for the merger with the Higher Self. This goal is accomplished through the polarization of the individual with the right focus of group endeavor.

The *Key Thought* in the implementation of the Law of Group Endeavor is "cooperation, not competition." Group cooperation is fostered through love, meditation, sharing, silent awareness, and communication. Criticism, devotion and attachment to personal ideals, and the assertion of dominating personal preferences create obstacles to cooperation and foster competition.

We can assist the proper unfoldment of Group Endeavor in ourselves and in others through the following exercise:

1. Sit back and reflect upon the various groups in which you are taking part. Observe your own role in these groups.

2. Contemplate the nature of each of these groups as a whole, and the contribution the group makes to its collective endeavors, outside

of either your own or anyone else's individual contribution. In effect, begin to view the group as the entity it is, and to see its function as an entity.

3. Focus on the Law of Right Human Relations and see its integration into the harmonizing of relationships within the group, as well as the relationship between groups.

4. Align yourself through the relaxation of your physical, emotional, and mental bodies. Lift yourself to the Soul level and link yourself with men and women of goodwill everywhere.

5. Dedicate yourself to group endeavor: "I dedicate myself, with all men and women of goodwill, to the building of the New City of Humanity."

And so it is. . . .

THE PRINCIPLE OF UNANIMITY

- **Unity transcending diversities**
- **Integrated group thinking**
- **Underlying common essence**
- **Balanced polarities for joyous living**

The Law of Group Endeavor can only externalize properly through the Principle of Unanimity. At the present time there is much confusion between "unanimity" and "uniformity." In fact, it will be the polarization between these two tendencies that will give rise to the potential duality inherent in the Aquarian Age. Duality as an underlying theme in all of manifestation is an essential quality of the universe. From the standpoint of the Ancient Wisdom Teachings, the fundamental duality is the one existing between manifested and unmanifested states of being. We will discuss this theme of duality again in greater detail in chapter 5, as well as in chapter 6, under the topic, "The Second Ray: The Ray of Love/Wisdom."

The esoteric, Soul-centered planetary ruler of the New Age is Jupiter—the planet most closely aligned to the Second Ray of Love/Wisdom. The cohesive, unifying power of Love underlies all the manifestations of the Age of Aquarius. But from the exoteric, external perspective, there are two other planetary rulers of this Era: Uranus, as primary ruler, and Saturn. The influence of Uranus manifests the tendency toward collectivity, in general, and *unanimity* as the higher aspect of this collective urging. Saturn inclines the times toward certain characteristics of *uniformity*.

The word *unanimity* comes from two Latin roots—"Uni," meaning one, and "anima," meaning soul. Thus *unanimity* means "(the state) of being one soul." *Uniform*, however, is defined as "one form"

(Latin: "forma"). It is very interesting to note that unanimity speaks directly to the level of the Soul and its collective orientation from the perspective of love, while uniformity speaks about union from the more material levels of expression of the personality.

Saturnian uniformity within the collective framework has been pointed out as an underlying theme of the so-called "Old Age/New Age" groups with authoritarian figureheads at their centers. It is the type of social structure clearly outlined in Orwell's *1984*—one in which the collective orientation of the Aquarian Age manifests through the conformistic, hierarchical structure which is so much an externalization of Saturn's energy patterns. This type of social manifestation was in evidence both in Maoist China and Stalinist Russia. The Saturn-dominated, Aquarian Age orientation is currently in evidence within those religious groups, organizations, and societies that demand complete adherence to exclusivistic creeds of theological or ethnic superiority. Yet, on a more positive level, Saturn can also supply those underlying *structures of unification* (rather than strictures of doctrinal limitation), which allow for a unanimously functioning group or society to operate.

Uranus is the planetary link to the faculty of intuition. Intuition gives the ability to be conscious of archetypes—those great, collective ideas from which innumerable divergencies of expression may flower and flow. A society or other group based on unanimity is one in which the focus of *purpose,* the consciousness of the *inner goal* for any outer endeavor, is the common denominator of awareness at the core of each person in that group. As individual alignment of the Soul and the personality takes place, each individual learns to create his or her outer field of expression, so that a multiform potential of creativity is available to that group purpose. In effect, the group helps to support and define the individual, refining and strengthening one's sense of self and personal creativity. Diversity, as an expression of essential unity, is thus made into a practical reality of life. Is this not a paradigm of the Universe? Does this not speak to us of the primary relationship of the Macrocosm to the microcosm? Does this not recall to us the "unified duality" of the transcendental and immanent natures of Divinity? What a wonderful potential awaits humanity if we can endeavor collectively to manifest the Laws and Principles of this New Age!

Uranus and the sign of Aquarius are associated with the concept of freedom: the freedom to be the archetype of oneself. So many people are fighting a contemporary battle of self-definition as they work to liberate themselves from the constraints of the previous Age. In fact, the first step for many along their Path is realizing the nature of these restraints. During the Piscean Age, there were no accepted alternatives to patterns of established behavior. But at this cuspal period, people are becoming increasingly receptive to the incoming thought-forms and their potential externalizations in the New Age. It is here that so many conflicts arise.

We have been raised, nurtured, and conditioned by the concepts and social structures of Piscean Age energy. This, added to the primarily tribal unity of most consciousness, has made ignorance tolerable, if not blissful. Suddenly, within the past twenty-five years, a tremendous wave of new possibilities has "descended" upon human consciousness, liberating some, threatening others, and placing a great many more in a state of conscious duality.

The polarity to the Uranian urge for the creation of new and liberating thought-forms is the fundamentalism of Saturn. This is manifesting today in Islamic, Christian, Victorian, and other forms. As we have just noted, energy tends to polarize itself into dualistic expressions—that is part of the very fabric of manifestation. The cusp of a World Age—any Age—is particularly chaotic as one set of two-thousand-year-old, anchored thought-forms (and the physical social structures which result) comes to be replaced by another. Just look at what happened in the world at the birth of Jesus and the advent of the Piscean Age two thousand years ago! The movement from the previous Age of Aries to the era of the Fish was equally transformational in its scope of expression as is the current world period. (See part 7 of *Alan Oken's Complete Astrology*.) The Age of Aries externalized the quality of *will* into the collective consciousness. The Piscean Age externalized *love*, although *pain and martyrdom* became the archetypical vehicles for the outward expression of such love. The Age of Aquarius is a synthetic period in which will and love are to be joined and harmonized through a particularly human—and hopefully humane—form of expression. To me, this is in preparation for the Messianic Age of Capricorn some two thousand years hence.

At this particular time in human history, we are seeing both in ourselves, and in the struggles for personal and group liberation around us, a tremendous effort at freeing ourselves from those previous thought-forms and structures which in the Piscean Era were integrated aspects of daily life, but which are seen today as restraints on personal and group freedom.

One of the strongest of all collective mind-set, thought-form patterns in the Piscean Age is martyrdom and the idea of victimization. This is especially strong within the scope of marriage and relationships. It was thought (and is still widely practiced) that to be a martyr to one's spouse, children, or lover was something that was either commendable or at least an absolute facet of loving them. The Aquarian Age frame of reference is quite different in this regard. We are realizing that each of us is responsible for the co-creation of our own destiny (one's partner in this respect being the Life Force). I am not a victim of anyone's unconscious conditioning but my own! I can be and indeed aspire to be a *server*, as serving humanity and world service are definite aspects of the New Age paradigm. I am not a *servant*, especially to those whom I love and who state that they love me. Servants and slavery (both physical and emotional) are aspects of the previous Age.

The difficulty and fear that so many people are currently experiencing is based on yet another juxtaposition of forces. The new thought-forms and the resultant crystallization of social structures have not happened, as yet, while the old thought-forms have lost much of their meaning and strength. We are still in a period of "cuspal limbo," so that people are caught between these two orientations, one of which is nonregenerative, and the other of which is yet to be fully generated! It is little wonder that in terms of consciousness, many of us may feel like the Hebrews at the end of the Age of Taurus, wandering in what appears to be a desert of confusion, while waiting to arrive at the Promised Land. The New Age Eden is the New City of Humanity, a place in which the Principle of Unanimity (as well as all the other Laws and Principles) is grounded firmly in the collective consciousness, and the Soul's reality is made known to the vast majority of humanity as a living Presence.

The New Age is indeed one of liberation, but before we can touch the freedom of the creative process inherent in the manifestation of new thought-forms, we must free ourselves from unconscious adherence to the past. In terms of the perspective of the outer, collective personality life, the urge for freedom is taking place through the *self-declared* liberation of those groups of individuals who have been bound and fettered during this previous world period. Thus we have been seeing the appearance of those sociopolitical movements of women, gays, blacks, and other oppressed groups who will continue to be at the forefront of the transformational activities of the times. Such activities have ideological overtones, for social psychology and politics are very much within the province of Aquarius and Uranus.

In addition to the above, one other "group of groups" has to be mentioned. This is perhaps the largest and most synthetic of such units. It is certainly among the most important, as it contains many members of the aforementioned collectives. This is the virtual legion of New Age Light Workers who, coming from all backgrounds and ethnic origins, are crystallizing the energies of the Aquarian Age. Their common purpose—their focus of unanimity—is the urge to serve. One of the primary (and one of the most joyous) struggles facing humanity today is the need to be able to differentiate one's particular field of service while integrating oneself into the consciousness of the whole. It is thus that the process of individuation is advanced in our time.

The combined energies of Saturn and Uranus lead to a manifestation which is becoming very typical of the Aquarian Age—networking. Networking exemplifies the Principle of Unanimity and the Law of Group Endeavor very clearly. The underlying structural organization of Saturn, plus the communicational faculties of Uranus, bring about a global network of connections forming the basis of New Age work. It is a work of people and for people and the planet. The tremendous efforts that are being made at networking are only made possible through our awareness of our unified purpose and the expression of goodwill. People are discovering their essential unity at an ever-increasing rate and are helping one another to utilize their respective differences for the sake of the whole. This can only be possible when there is an alignment to the Soul. This alignment is the dispensation and great gift of the New Age to all of those ready to accept it.[3]

Many astrologers and counselors in other disciplines are being confronted by individuals struggling to find their Path toward greater self-definition and awareness. This is very much like having a multitude of adults simultaneously asking, "What should I be when I grow up?" One "is" already "something," and yet that "something" is not leading to a more enlightened and love-filled state.

I believe that the resolution of many of these quests of self-searching rests in both an attitude of and the actual practice of service. It is through some form of service—some outer focus of collective awareness—that "me-my-mine-itis" can be cured, and the polarized personality may then be transformed into the unified individual. Service to humanity and the Path leading us to it is very definitely a fundamental paradigm for human evolution in the New Age. It is when the newly emerging individual attunes him or herself to the Principle of Unanimity that a sense of belonging to the Whole is created and we are "home" once again. Inner peace, joy, and courage then accompany the "traveler" on the Way. An examination of the natal horoscope from the Soul-centered perspective can reveal just where such service lies and the Path through which one may become integrated into this global network of New Age servers.

There are naturally certain obstacles to achieving an inner sense of unanimity which have to be confronted and transformed. These in-

[3]The New Group of World Servers is the result of such efforts at individualizing, connecting, and networking on a global level. One's participation in the NGWS is an attitude, and is characterized by the active and practically expressed urge to be of service to humanity. For more about the New Group of World Servers, the reader is advised to consult the book (and a most important volume it is) *Serving Humanity—A Compilation*, by Alice A. Bailey (edited by Aart Jurriaanse).

clude: attachment to the personal will; pride; fanaticism; undue attachment to detail; and assuming the responsibilities of others. All of
the above interfere with the Law of Group Endeavor and do not
allow for the establishment of a focus of Unanimity. The balancing
forces to these obstacles are: acknowledgement of unity in diversity;
an awareness of common purpose; a focus on united intent and
unified group desire; and the blending of the various components of
group activity—that is the individuals involved.

The following is a meditative technique for attuning oneself to the
Principle of Unanimity:

1. Align your lower vehicles (physical, emotional, and mental)
through relaxation and deep breathing. Lift the united lower self to
the Higher, the Soul, and experience the two as One.

2. Identify yourself as a man or woman of Goodwill and dedicate
yourself to serving humanity.

3. Visualize the Principle of Unanimity as people from all different
ethnic and social backgrounds, yourself included, all with hands
linked together, forming a great circle around the planet Earth.

4. Reflect upon the meanings and implications of Unanimity.

5. Contemplate your own contribution to this collective effort.

6. Send your thoughts of Unanimity out in all directions around
you and affirm that Unanimity can manifest and triumph in the world.

THE LAW OF SPIRITUAL APPROACH

• **Stairway to the Soul and to inner revelation**
• **Light resulting in greater Light**
• **Elevation to higher purpose**
• **Evocation of divine energy**

> . . . "Spiritual" refers not only to experiences traditionally
> considered religious, but to *all* states of awareness, all the
> human functions and activities which have as the common
> denominator the possession of *values* higher than average
> —values such as the ethical, the aesthetic, the heroic, the
> humanitarian, and the altruistic.
>
> —Roberto Assagioli
> Synthesis—the Realization of the Self

As the New Era unfolds, humanity is becoming less polarized to the
emotional appeal and methods of expression of the religions of the
Piscean Age, and more attracted to the intuitive focus and spirituality
of the Age of Aquarius. That which was based on separatist dogmas
of exclusivity is now being replaced with spiritual insights into those
underlying Laws and Principles of inclusive awareness.

Uranus, governing planet of the externalization of the coming world period, is very much the vehicle of expression for intuitive perceptions. We are leaving behind that which dualistically separates us from our fellows—apartheid, extremes of wealth and poverty, the oppression of women, the concept of God and sinner, etc.—and accepting that which unites us into a focus of greater acceptance and universal equality. Although it is true that the primary religions of the Piscean Era teach that God is Love and that we should "love our neighbor as we love ourselves," the application of this Golden Rule has not been too successful. Yet the potential for the positive transformation of this duality into a greater synthesis is very near at hand.

There is within the human being a tremendous urge for self-betterment. Not only is this applicable in the material sense, but it is at the very foundation of the need for greater self-fulfillment. Such an urge can be called "divine discontent." It is certainly the force which pushes us on and on to create and to live in a more harmonious and spiritually anchored world. The Law of Spiritual Approach governs this basic impulse. In this period, we are finding that there are an incredible number of techniques, methodologies, and practices which can help us fulfill our goal. There seems to be a great freedom of spiritual expression available to us insofar as the pursuit of our spiritual aspirations are concerned.

People are finding that they are inventing new vocabularies for their experiences—words and phrases which convey their particular perceptions into the heretofore hidden world of spiritual presence. This perception is the result of the awakening of the intuitive faculty of their being. There is almost an instinctive awareness now that we are indeed one humanity, one global village, one revolving and evolving organism. As our inner eye awakens, it sees with ever-increasing clarity the relationship between the visible and the invisible, and that the two are drawing closer and closer together.

The evolution of humanity proceeds on a spiral from one state of increased awareness to another. The forms of such growth differ from individual to individual, based on personal and biological karma. Yet the stages of this unfoldment—the "initiations" into the Greater Life—are constant, and progress the same for all. This is why there is so much identification between all people who call themselves "New Agers." They look different, speak all the languages in the world, come from various socioeconomic backgrounds, but all are united in the mutual awareness that spiritual growth and evolution is the inspiring force and focus of their lives. Never before has the Law of Spiritual Approach been so omnipresent in its concept, as well as in its practical application.

The technological advances at this cusp of the Aquarian Age, especially in communication, have made it possible for people to acknowledge the universality of the times and their collective participation in an amazing and rapid state of the evolution of consciousness. This creates both personal and collective conflicts as the reorientation from the personal, materialistic frame of reference becomes replaced by a collective spiritual service orientation. It is this schism that has created so much in the way of divorce and domestic and professional discord. It is very difficult to be in a relationship, whether it is personal or professional, when one of the partners is continuously invoking the Law of Spiritual Return, while the other equally invokes the "law of material return." This conflict, however, may bring about a greater synthesis as we learn how to integrate the spiritual into the material, thus impressing the life around us with ever-greater possibilities for evolutionary expression. As many of us can attest, this process can be rather painful, but the results of such successful transformations lead to a definite increase in the quality and joy of life.

It is important to realize that the methods and practices that are available to us are just processes. We must be very careful not to attach ourselves so emotionally that we lose perspective on the difference between the essential spiritual quality of life and the vehicles which express it. The need for belonging, especially at a time when society is being conceptually uprooted, is so strong that many will cling fervently to anything that gives them a sense of anchorage and a haven in the outer chaos. This is one of the reasons why cult groups and fundamentalist religious movements are so popular. A person can say: "I can stop here. I am saved. I've found it." But as the constant scandals surrounding such cult figures and "religious" leaders reveal, there is no safety, except in the unfolding inclusivity of one's own Soul—a Path that accepts and does not judge, and loves not by a love which "passeth all understanding," but with one that *is* all-understanding. Acceptance through knowing, discrimination through intuitive perception, and loving through conscious awareness are some of the more important methods through which the Law of Spiritual Approach is being expressed by humanity at the present time.

As we have seen in diagram 2, there is a dual stream for the manifestation of the Life Force. This is the scheme of the evolutionary and involutionary pathways. The Law of Spiritual Approach is also a two-way movement, as it is intimately linked to another important metaphysical principle—the Law of Magnetic Attraction. In this respect, the Law of Spiritual Approach is applied through the dual pathways of Right Human Relations: the vertical and the horizontal. The initial step is the linkage between the Soul and the personality, which forms the foundation to the Path of Discipleship. This need for linkage is at the heart of the evolutionary urge within each of us. At its most fundamental, this inner need to grow is actually the Will-to-Be of the Life Force. As the Soul-personality union increases in its magnetism and aligns in its mutual approach, the Light, Love, and Intelligence of the Divinity within each of us begins to radiate outward horizontally, touching all beings with whom we may come in contact. This brings into our lives those people and those tests, experiences, and opportunities to serve which further our own and other people's movement into Light.

The Laws of Spiritual Approach and Magnetic Attraction reveal that the force, power, and love of Divinity and the Spiritual Presence are always available to us. They reach us in a direct and more individualized way through the Soul. They express themselves outwardly, horizontally in life, through the pathway and field of service we create by the refinement and alignment of the personality. This particular linkage is revealed to us astrologically, as we shall see in part 3, through the juxtaposition of the horoscope as read exoterically and esoterically. As a person aspires to a greater and more refined truth, the energies of that truth unfold. Thus, a person wishing to know more about the truth of personal loving, for example—who sincerely asks that such truth dispel his personal illusions and mirages—will invoke those experiences that will make this truth a reality.

So many of us think that once we consciously walk the Spiritual Path, life will immediately become easier for us. This is far from the truth. Life immediately becomes more *joyous* for us, for joy is the nature of the quality of the Soul's unfoldment, but not necessarily easier. It says in the Bible (Matthew 7:7): "Ask and ye shall receive; knock and the door shall be opened unto you." This is the Law of Magnetic Attraction in action. But to receive a great gift, you must be in a place within yourself that permits reception. This can only be accomplished through the sometimes painful process of elimination, which is accelerated through spiritual aspiration and practices: meditation, affirmation, visualization, right diet, etc. You asked for it, and now you are getting it! The joy and the Soul's second great quality of expression (and one of Its most profound gifts)—courage—sustain us during this period of transformative reorientation.

We turn to Soul-centered astrologers and healers to help us delineate the timing and nature of this Path. The healers are the priests and priestesses of the New Age. They help us to link ourselves once again to our wholeness as human beings. This is the meaning of the very word *religion*. It comes from the Latin, *religare*, "to link up once again." Astrology reveals our links to the cosmic Whole. It does this as a science, but also as a healing technique. In this respect, astrology is very much a tool of the Law of Spiritual Approach.

The anchoring of the Law of Spiritual Approach in your life may be facilitated through the practice of the following technique:

1. Align yourself by relaxing your physical body. Still the emotions through an inner affirmation that all is peaceful within you and around you. Give yourself the mental image of a still, clear, beautiful lake and identify this lake as your emotions. Focus your mind and quiet any extraneous thoughts. It might help to repeat the words, "the Law of Spiritual Approach." Link up and affirm the integration of your physical, emotional, and mental vehicles. Breathe deeply and normally while you accomplish this.

2. Link yourself through the heart and through your inner eye of perception to all men and women of goodwill all over the world. Affirm your unity with them.

3. Dedicate yourself to the building of the New City of Humanity with all your New Age brothers and sisters.

4. Open yourself to Soul linkage and say the Mantram of the Soul:

> I am the Soul.
> I am the Light Divine.
> I am Love.
> I am Will.
> I am Fixed Design.

5. Visualize the Law of Spiritual Approach as humanity reaching up as one group to the Sun, and the Sun shining its rays of Light, Love, and Intelligence down into and encompassing humanity.

6. Reflect and meditate upon the unity of Spirit and Humanity and its implications in terms of World Goodwill.

7. Contemplate your own contribution to this collective effort.

8. Telepathically radiate the Law of Spiritual Approach in all directions around you.

THE PRINCIPLE OF ESSENTIAL DIVINITY

- **The spark of God in every being**
- **The need of people and God for each other**
- **Connection of all life, large and small**
- **The very synthesis of life**

In the beginning, the scientists tell us, there was the Big Bang. From this divine Act of Will, the manifested universe came into being—once again! The Law of Cyclic Return tells us that this Big Bang could be one of an infinite number of expressions of the manifestation of the Cosmic Life in outer form. The alterations of the "inbreathing" and the "outbreathing" of God, the rhythmic movements of the unmanifest

to the manifested and then back to the unmanifest again, the alterna-
tions of this process of inherent cosmic duality, known in Sanskrit as
Manvantara (manifestation) and *Pralaya* (rest/unmanifested), are continuous and never-ending. In effect, our Big Bang is just one in an
infinite series!

Yet this beginning of our manifested universe did indeed come from
One Source; in this, both physicist and metaphysicist agree. All forms
birthed and developed from this One Source are of the same matter—
the Divine "primordial broth" of Creation. The metaphysician and
the mystic would also say that these forms are the *body* of the
Creator, as well. But in this next point, physicist and metaphysicist
disagree—at least, for the present. The metaphysicist and student of
the Ancient Wisdom Teachings would state that this matter of the
universe is alive and intelligent. We would say that this Life and this
Intelligence can be and is experienced by those sensitive enough to
recognize Its Presence. We would also say that this Life "inhabits" all
matter, and that we are also that Life, incarnating in human form.

The Principle of Essential Divinity expresses itself through three
primary concepts: unification, synthesis, and universality. In effect,
when an individual or a group identifies itself with its Essential
Divinity, all three of these dynamics of spiritual awareness become
conscious and integrated aspects of that person's or group's self-
expression. The awareness then of our collective Origin moves us
from a place of mere intellectual conjecture into one which acts as
part of our living consciousness. Life is then being led from the Soul's
perspective through the personality, and one's true purpose in being
becomes actualized. Synthesizing the Principle of Essential Divinity
into one's active, creative life is a major step of personal and/or group
initiation.

The words "essential divinity" contain in their derivations a profound meaning. Essential comes from the Latin *essere*, meaning "to
be," while divinity can be traced from the Latin *dius* back to the
Sanskrit *devas*. Both the Latin and more ancient Sanskrit words
mean, of course, "god." "Essential divinity" means the state of being
a god, and thus all matter, originating as it does from its One Source,
is essentially divine. That Divinity impregnates itself as a conscious
expression within us when we identify ourselves *as* It. As we continuously expand this reality of ourselves into the world around us, the
nature of the omnipresence of divinity becomes increasingly self-
evident to our expanding (and loving) vision.

It is the nature of synthesis that focuses the essential life quality and
expresses it as love. This is the function of the Soul. A Soul-centered
life, whether on the group or individual level, is one that fosters and
expands the world synthesis of humankind. This type of collective

focus is taking place on the planet at the present time. And as we shall soon discover, it is the combination of the energies of Uranus (as exoteric ruler of the Age of Aquarius), Jupiter (as its esoteric ruler), the Seventh Ray (as the Ray energy of Uranus), and the Second Ray (as that of Jupiter) that are the prime significators of the transformation of human consciousness in the New Age.

Love is the quality of consciousness as expressed through the Soul. In the Age of Aquarius, love on the personal level will manifest quite differently from the way it did in the preceding World Age. In the present era, the two forms of the expression of personalized love are both quite prevalent, which is why there is so much confusion today about the nature and direction of personal love, sex, and commitment. It is, after all, in the realm of human relations that most people find their major tests (and interest) in life.

The basic duality at the present time is that personal love for those people still polarized by the energies of the Piscean Age is profoundly emotional, idealistic, devotional, and exclusive in nature. The Aquarian Age archetype for the expression of personal love is quite different. In the first place, friendship and like-mindedness tend to be at the basis of relationships, rather than passion. This does not mean that there is no passion—just that relationships are increasingly becoming more mentally rather than emotionally polarized. Love will tend (and is tending) to be more altruistic, humanitarian, and functional and— sorry to say for those still in the Piscean modality—much less romantic than the nineteenth- and early twentieth-century varieties.

Romanticism, with all of its poetry, artistry, beauty, sacrifice, passion, fun, and foolishness, was invented as a framework for personal relationships by the French and the Italians. This occurred between the twelfth and fourteenth centuries, midway through the Piscean Era. Before that time, Western romanticism as a way of life wasn't nearly as developed. The Greeks had a certain sense of the romantic, and a great focus on the idealistic and heroic, but they weren't true Piscean Age romantics. The Romans thought that they had some romantic sensibilities, but in the finer things of life, they were always copying the Greeks.

This French and Italian romanticism was greatly enhanced in the eighteenth and nineteenth centuries, and then was strongly embellished and regenerated by twentieth-century Hollywood—needless to say, Pisces rules the movies! This Neptunian legacy has contributed much to people floating through life, searching for an ultimately personalized, one-on-one, *From Here to Eternity* romance. Loving on the personal level is one of life's greatest gifts. Yet that personalized love, when successful, becomes the vehicle for a more transpersonal, loving reality.

For so many, the compulsive and insistent urge to love someone exclusively and forever has led to a tremendous amount of disappointment, the sale of an enormous number of records, tapes, and movie tickets, plus, in our era, a great deal of (often forced) awareness about the difference between the real and the ideal! The generation born with Neptune in Libra (1943–1957) has been especially affected (and afflicted) by the Age change in this respect, as Neptune (in addition to ruling films) can be either the great illuminator or the great veiler of reality, depending on whether the love it embodies is either transpersonal or personal in nature. Libra, of course, is the sign of partnership, marriage, and personal relationships par excellence.

Love on the personal level in the New Age will tend to move toward a group focus, insofar as the purpose of one's devotion is concerned. Thus there will be a transition from devotion to a one-on-one situation to attachments more firmly anchored by group affinities and collective belief systems. As evolution proceeds, devotion will gradually give way to loving detachment, so that the functions of group service and group dynamics can be more successfully accomplished. This aspect of social reorientation will definitely be an important part of the nature of the unfolding of human consciousness as the Age of Aquarius progresses. The purpose of this orientation away from devotion is to move the individual from a primarily exclusivistic way of expression of the love force to an ever-expanding inclusivity. This is how the universality aspect of the Law of Essential Divinity will be expressed in the coming World Age.

The success of personal relationships in our era is based on the ability of the people concerned to find a synthetic focus for their love for each other. That is, they must create and identify with a third, transcendental focus of expression for their personal relationship in order for it to continue to be creatively and socially prosperous. This third has to be able to take the two individuals out of their polarizing focus of interchange, or else the relationship will either stagnate or disintegrate. If the nature of the third is collective in orientation and brings out a greater identification with the essential divinity of the two people, they and their relationship will grow. The struggle for so many people who are in relationships at the present time has much to do with the reorientation and integration of an intense focus of personal exclusivity into a less intense, less passionate, and more collectively oriented expression of love.

One of the most important vehicles for the objectification of the Principle of Essential Divinity is the right use of will. In the Ancient Wisdom Teachings, we are told that the distinctive quality of Divinity is Will. This expresses itself primarily and in all forms of life as the Will-to-Be. In the New Age, we are being required to recapture the sense of our personal will and personal creative dynamic (as well as the personal responsibility for its right use), that was so sacrificed in the Piscean Era. Yet this sense of will can only be used rightly in the Aquarian Age when it is consciously united with the collective will of the group. This represents another set of problems for the emerging individual in our times.

As the restraints and restrictions of the thought-forms (and their externalizations as social norms and collective morality) of the past Age gradually dissolve, many people will find themselves with a greater, wholistic sense of themselves than ever before. Yet as stated in chapter 3, when the individualizing ego is not consciously integrated within the framework of a (loving) collective, there is a great danger that the will can be used incorrectly. The next few generations will provide the testing ground for humanity so that people may properly learn how to temper the creative potential of the individualized ego into a harmonious vehicle for the collective will of the group.

The astrologer should keep in mind the nature of the polarity of this Aquarius-Leo Age. Leo is the sign of the expression of the individualized ego and its focus of outward creativity. Aquarius is the socialized expression of Leo, and thus represents the nature of the will of the collective and its focus as a creative force in life. Both Aquarius and Leo are signs of the Fifth Ray of Concrete Knowledge. It is under the influence of this great Ray that science and technology are developed. Thus it is through the sciences that the Principle of Essential Divinity and its components of unification, synthesis, and universality will be most clearly manifested in the New Age.

Another great challenge to humanity at the present time comes from this great outpouring of scientific discovery. In addition to the geometric progression of the mind's revelations, the rate of human intuitive perception is also growing. There is thus a very definite polarity between intellect and intuition. This should be contrasted with the fundamental polarity of the Piscean Age—that of believers and nonbelievers. This duality will resolve itself in the New Age through the Law of Spiritual Approach, as the universality of Essential Divinity is perceived through the many pathways that try to "link us up again" to that of which we are already a part.

The current Aquarian Polarity could be said to be one existing between "knowers" and "non-knowers." Currently the scientists think that they know and place the metaphysicians in the other category, while for many metaphysicians, the reverse is seen as true! The Law of Group Endeavor and the Principle of Unanimity should, in time, resolve this particular opposition. In the meantime, this polarity is very healthy as we gradually learn and share in one another's knowledge. The purpose of this particular Aquarian Age duality is to help join the collective mental body of humanity's personality with the intuitive vehicle of humanity's Soul. This fusion is part of the process involved in the creation of the Group Antahkarana (Rainbow Bridge), and will eventuate into the emergence of the Coming One during the Messianic Age of Capricorn.

The following is an exercise to help us invoke the Principle of Essential Divinity into our lives:

1. Align your physical, emotional, and mental bodies in much the same way as was outlined in the first step of the technique for anchoring the Law of Spiritual Approach.

2. Contemplate each of the three expressions of the Law of Essential Divinity and some of their qualities:

   a. Unification—right human relations, loving detachment, readiness to adjust personal opinions for the good of the many.
   b. Synthesis—goodwill, compassion, love for humanity, service.
   c. Universality—the sense of being one with the cosmic whole, recognition of universal unity.

3. Link yourself through the heart and through your inner eye of perception to all men and women of goodwill all over the world and affirm your unity with them.

4. Visualize the Principle of Essential Divinity as a brilliant Ray of Light connecting all people, uniting all people, and being the Life of all people.

5. Affirm with love in your heart that a living consciousness of unification, synthesis, and universality is the crystallizing focus of human evolution in our time and in the time to come.

6. Contemplate your own contribution to this collective effort.

7. Telepathically radiate these thoughts in all directions around you.

8. Say the Great Invocation on page 37.

5

Ten Postulates

of the Ancient

Wisdom Teachings

We are living in one of the great crisis eras in all human history. Issues of peace and war, poverty and abundance, of racial, political, and industrial conflict face us on every side. Religious divisions and the clash between age and youth are likewise prominent, and underlying all is the basic conflict between material and spiritual values, between self-interest and world service.

And yet there is a universal recognition that mankind is entering a New Age. Science has made the world one, and human knowledge and intelligence are greater than ever before. Countless movements based on goodwill are attempting to create a better world, and there is a growing recognition of humanity's essential unity.[1]

The Ancient Wisdom Teachings are a great compendium of factors which comprise the structure of the unfolding of the manifested universe.[2] As we endeavor to utilize astrology as a tool of intuitive perception into the essential nature and life purpose of a given individual, it is absolutely necessary that we attune ourselves to some of the more important of these factors. Thus the esoteric, Soul-centered astrologer may apply the insights gleaned from these Teachings to the astrological information revealed from the natal horoscope. The scope of vision thus attained will not only allow for a more accurate and profound treatment of the natal chart, but will also facilitate the astrolo-

[1]These two paragraphs appeared in "World Service through the Power of Thought." Published by the Lucis Trust, New York, 1974.
[2]See Bibliography for further information on this subject.

ger's own life Path. It is this scope of reference, plus a focus of service, an attunement to Truth and the Teachers, an orientation to the Soul, as well as the skills inherent in mastering certain techniques of delineation, which all contribute to preparing the astrologer and student for participation in the Greater Life.

The following are ten important postulates of the Ancient Wisdom Teachings. I believe that once they are studied and contemplated, they will be most helpful in the delineation of the horoscope and in counseling others. There are many more such postulates, laws, and principles, some of which we have already discussed. Through the study and consideration of these postulates, the reader will have a wider approach to those factors and techniques of esoteric interpretation which comprise the rest of the present work.

Postulate 1: Hylozoism—All substances and organisms, either organic or inorganic, are imbued with life. This is true from the most microscopic atomic particle to the Galaxy of galaxies.

The word *hylozoism* comes from two Greek roots: *hylo,* meaning "wood," and hence referring to the material out of which something is created; and *zoe* meaning "life." This term signifies that there is life in all matter. The majority of today's scientific community will say that anything that is inorganic is not alive, but this is a matter of perception and measurement. If the rational mind is doing the perceiving (which it cannot—it can only observe and judge, analyze and communicate) and measuring, then most certainly, a rock or a quantity of lead will appear lifeless. If one is experiencing the energy of that stone or mineral through the intuitive focus of the Soul, then the Life within—the Life that *is* those substances—will be very clearly seen, as well as felt, sensed, and to a certain extent, even communicated to the consciousness of the perceiver.

The rock or the piece of lead will send out an emission—an emanation that can be easily experienced by one who has either not developed a strong rational, mental body, or by one who has synthesized the mental vehicle into the intuitive.

The religion of Bali, Indonesia, is a form of animistic Hinduism. A Balinese will find a stone whose shape and resonance "speaks" to the finder. It would be very common to see that rock enshrined thereafter on a pillar, with daily offerings made to its Living Presence. The rock is perceived as an embodiment of Divine Energy, and so it is. This rock does not know that it is alive, but it lives, and in some alchemical way, it gives life to its finder and his family. An animal doesn't know that it is alive, but try to capture or kill it, and see how quickly it runs!

What differentiates humans from beings of the lower kingdoms in nature is that we know that we're alive; some of us also know that we are filled with Life. Those Beings Who live on planes of consciousness and manifestation more highly evolved than our own human kingdom know something else. They know that They *are* Life. We know that we are alive; They know that They are Life Itself. As the Tibetan Master would say, "Ponder on this."

The greater a person's ability to perceive and experience the life which embodies all forms, the greater the Presence of the Soul in actuality. The healthy and whole person is one who can see with the rational mind and perceive with the intuition simultaneously. This indicates that a great degree of fusion between the Soul and the personality has already taken place. The esoteric planetary rulers of the signs may then be said to be operative in the life, and the horoscope can be interpreted accordingly. (See chapter 9.)

Postulate 2: What we identify as matter and spirit are the same thing vibrating at different intensities. Matter is spirit expressing in its densest form, and spirit is matter vibrating in its most subtle. The solidity and tangibility of the material world around us is illusionary.

Thus we can state, as Einstein did in his theory of relativity, that energy and matter are interchangeable. We also know that all life is energy, that all the energy which is life is in motion. The rate of the vibration of that motion determines the form of the manifestation of that energy. This is of primary concern to the metaphysician. It is also one of the basic principles which explains the differences in the effects of planetary and sign vibrations upon individuals, relative to their evolutionary level. A more evolved, Soul-oriented individual will vibrate at a much higher frequency than a more materially attached, personality-centered one. The nature of the frequency of the vibratory rate will very much determine if an individual will respond to the exoteric or the esoteric planetary rulers. Additionally, the vibratory rate will also indicate which of the three levels of the zodiacal sign expression will predominate in the life. (See chapter 9.)

The energy we perceive as a rock is moving at a much slower rate than that of a human being. We perceive the rock as solid stone, but the rock "perceives" us as light. We see our dog as our pet. Our dog sees us as its god. As a person evolves and the Path of the Soul unfolds to the awakening consciousness, he begins to see the things and people in his life more as energy and less as tangible forms by themselves. Such a person's perception and struggle involve the consideration of the constant interrelationship between the two. The development of this kind of intuitive vision is absolutely essential to the Soul-centered astrologer. In order to read the horoscope correctly, the astrologer must be in tune with the level of consciousness of the individual for whom he is reading, and not just with the patterns of planetary arrangement. Such an attunement justifies the astrologer's focus of delineation and level of interpretation of the celestial energy sources to their terrestrial counterparts. The more that an individual is able to perceive people, places, things, and especially *ideas* as combinations of various frequencies and intensities of energy, the greater the Soul attunement, and consequently the greater the ability to love impersonally and universally.

One of the benefits of not having any planets in the element of earth in the natal chart is the potential for just this kind of "energized" perception. When Soul-centered, a person without any (or with very little) earth in the natal horoscope is apt to see "through" things, situations, people, and ideas rather than experiencing the magnetizing, confrontational, or confining qualities of their various forms. Such individuals may easily know themselves to be vehicles through whom higher energies work and externalize. On the personality level, the situation will manifest very differently. In this case, a natal horoscope without the element of earth either at the Ascendant or in any planet/sign combination would give the individual very little practical focus to his life. A certain naïveté would be present, and there would be a distinct need to learn the lessons of a materially grounded life. One of his needs in the present incarnation would be to integrate and synthesize the rest of his life energy with the physical plane.

If there are many planets in the earth element, two tendencies are likely. On the personality level, the individual would tend to see everything as form. Intuition would become extremely limited and he would tend to become stuck, trapped, and totally attached to form *as* essence. If the level of evolution is especially developed, the "earthy" individual has been trained through previous karmic experiences to be able to perceive the relationship between form and essence very clearly. Thus he may not only be able to see the plan within the form and the form as an extension of the plan, but to effect some sort of transformative action on the Earth as a result of these perceptions. The person without any earth in the chart may indeed have the same perception, but be less likely to create such terrestrial transformations materially. Such an individual would tend to work more on the mental, intuitive, or emotional planes, depending on the elemental emphasis of air, fire, or water in the chart. By "plan," I am referring to the focus of *essential divinity*—the Will, as It seeks to express Itself through the given form of Its creation. This latter is, as previously indicated, the primary Spirit-Soul relationship inherent in all of life.

There are some people who will prepare their oatmeal in the morning, sit down to eat it, and that is that—they are eating their oatmeal. There are others who will make this same oatmeal, but as they recognize the Divinity present in all things and in all acts, they will make it differently. They know that God is making that oatmeal, that God is that oatmeal, and that God will sit down at the table and begin eating Itself. The form is the same: "I am eating my oatmeal." The difference is the focus of perception, and that focus is created through a variance in the vibrational rate of the consciousness of the individual.

Postulates three, four, and five are actually three facets of a very great Law. This is the fundamental principle upon which the entire science of astrology—both exoteric and esoteric—is based. It is called the Law of Correspondences, and may also be expressed by the phrase, "As Above, So Below." These three postulates and this Law are so very interconnected that we will first list the three and then discuss them together.

Postulate 3: Space is not empty. What appears to be space is the field of consciousness, the "body" of a great Cosmic Life within which all manifestation lives, moves, and has its being.

Postulate 4: All of the infinite number of parts of this great Life are interconnected through an energy substance called aether. Thus the smallest cell does not pulsate, nor the largest sun emanate, without their vibrations and energies being felt throughout the Cosmos.

Postulate 5: Each and every one of these "lesser lives" lives within the body and consciousness of a Greater Life.

To the student of the Ancient Wisdom Teachings, and to the Soul-centered astrologer in particular, the planets are perceived as individual living Entities within that Greater Organism we call the Solar System. The electromagnetic force fields existing between these globes are viewed as the vehicles for the expression of the interrelating consciousnesses of these planetary Beings. The modifications by cosmic geometry of these force fields (which the astrologer calls the "planetary aspects") are viewed as the outworking of the ordered Plan of Divine Intelligence as revealed through the planets. And as we shall soon observe, the natures of the Seven Rays also play a very important part in the unfolding of the Creative Consciousness. All of this interplay of Forces and Lives is conscious and alive. All of the apparent "space" that exists between the planets in our solar system— indeed, in the Universe—is occupied and is the very fabric of the body of that Divine Organism within which we live, move, and have our being. Astrology, in both its esoteric and exoteric modes, is an evolving system which works to measure and define some of the facets of this cosmic drama.

As a person strives to increase his or her own conscious awareness, the expansive nature of such efforts at individual growth brings him ever closer to the awareness of his own inclusion within the scheme of this universal Plan. We begin to see that what may appear to be an empty space in our own lives—left there perhaps by a lost lover, the abandonment of an intellectual frame of reference that has outworn its usefulness, the change in our professional creative focus, or any other facet of our human lives—is not an empty space at all. *The true nature of such apparent emptiness consists of the energy of process and transformation.* That process does not consist of empty space! The previous form of the manifestation of the life energy may have dissolved, but what remains are the particles and pieces that have to be transformed and reassembled. This often requires substantial concentration and inner work on emotional, mental, and higher levels in order to bring forth another lover, another mental structure of related thought-forms, or another focus of professional interest. The spaces required to do this work are filled with the energy of the Life Force which we bring into conscious manifestation through the joining of our own creative energy—our own right use of will; our own Will-to-Be. The Law of Correspondences tells us that just as such spaces exist in our own lives for the creative purposes we may bring to manifestation, so too the Life of Lives has Its enormous, but creatively pregnant spaces in the universe, for Its creative furtherance.

All of Life comes from the One Life. There is thus an essential affinity between all forms of that Life. In our solar system, the quality of the consciousness of that affinity—that which underlies the nature of the Law of Attraction—is Love. The structure of Divine Intelligence at work (which in our solar system is embodied by the planet Saturn) is the vehicle of the interconnectedness of these natural affinities. These structures are created from various densities of cosmic aether, the primordial building substance of the universe—the "threads of manifestation" which are woven together into the various "cloths and fabrics" of life. Metaphysics speaks to us about this process of weaving, while astrology reveals much about the nature and purpose of the cloth, as well as the time needed to create it.

The nature of the interconnectedness of life, as well as the inherent magnetic affinities between all forms of manifestation, are major facets of the Law of Correspondences. This allows the personality to link with the Soul, as well as for the Soul to link with its Source, the Monad—our Spiritual Self (see diagram 6). It is through the Law of Correspondences that we are able to become One with our own Spiritual Essence. This linkage is made possible through several dynamic processes of spiritual growth: meditation, prayer, and invocation. Briefly stated, meditation fosters the focus of magnetic attraction between the Soul and the personality. Prayer acknowledges Divine Presence in our life and *as* our Life, while invocation (which is actually a science in itself) brings Power into manifestation. Affirmation is a technique of invocation which is becoming increasingly popular in terms of the New Age approach to spiritual responsibility.

The human Monad is the originating Source of all of our incarnations. It is that individualized "Point of Light in the Mind of God" which links us directly to the Universal-Creative-Mind-Spirit and which is that Spirit. This Monad is Divinity eventuating and incarnating into human form. As the following diagram shows, the Monad is also triune in nature, and each of the three parts of this Trinity corresponds to one of the three parts of the other two. Together, the

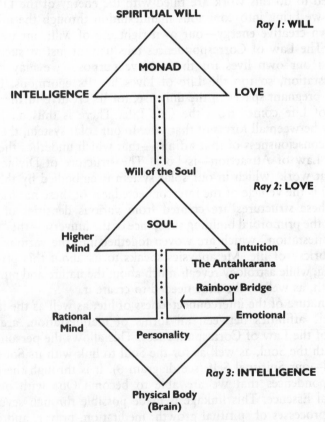

Diagram 6: The Triune Nature of Man

Personality-Soul-Monad comprise the Holy Trinity of Man, and are the archetype for Creative Expression as we know It to be. These three triangles, their nine component parts, and the Ray Energies which correspond to them, form essential facets of Soul-centered astrology.

Postulate 6: Each of these "lesser lives" is made in the image of God.

Each of us has a direct line of correspondence and intimacy between ourself and our Divinity. In this respect, a human being is made in the image of God. Postulates seven, eight, and nine will further outline the structure of this Divine imprinting. Yet even though Man is a god and one with God, God is not a man, except when incarnating in human form. There is a quote from that incredibly beautiful and ancient Hindu text, the *Bhagavad Gita,* which may clarify this statement. It is spoken by Brahma, God the Creator, to His Disciple, Arjuna. The Lord Brahma says: "After having pervaded the universe with a fragment of myself, I remain."

This statement is a succinct expression of all that is contained within postulates three, four, and five, as well as the great Law of Correspondences itself. The meaning of this phrase is that Divinity is always whole, even though It may manifest Itself through Its infinity of parts. Even in parts, It is whole, and It is whole *beyond* Its parts. Divinity is immanently Whole and transcendentally Whole. It is greater than the sum of Its parts and it is the sum of Its parts.

The duality of the Age of Pisces was based primarily on the transcendental nature of Divinity. This emphasized God as being "above," and humanity as being "below." In effect, this paradigm diminished humanity's ability to use and take responsibility for its creative will. The duality of the Aquarian Age is focused on the unity of the two natures of Divine Expression: the transcendental as well as the immanent. The essential unified focus of the manifested universe is becoming more and more the frame of spiritual reference for the New Era. It is thus that an individual recognizes his or her inherent spiritual creative will as well as his link with all of humanity. This will in time eventuate into the Group Consciousness that will mark our Age.

Postulate 7: All of manifestation is energy in differentiating forms. This energy emanates from a Source which reabsorbs it after it has expressed itself through its forms and cycles.

Postulate 8: There is no absolute death. There is only change of form and state. The cycle of birth and rebirth is endless until the Law of Cause and Effect (karma) is satisfied. It is then that unity is reached and reincarnation ceases.

All of the creative substance in any one cycle of manifestation was birthed at the same time, during its Big Bang. The Law of Rebirth and the Law of the Recycling of Matter tell us that there have been and will be many such Big Bangs. The Universe began from this cyclic inception and unfolds through the creation of the myriad forms of its expression, yet it always remains essentially One. All of its forms emanate from the same Source and are created from the same primordial aether as its fundamental building material. Just as we alternate our breathing through a lifelong cycle of inhalations and exhalations, the present cycle of universal manifestation will once again be "inhaled" into its Source after it has passed through its cycle of incarnation. Then, after a certain interlude, the Universe will birth itself again into yet another expression of manifestation. The Ancient Wisdom Teachings tell us that cosmic reincarnation is an infinite process.

The above process has its definite parallel in terms of human existence. Each of us is born through a process by which an aspect of the Soul "cloaks" itself in the bodies of mental, astral/emotional, and physical matter. Each of us has a life span through which the opportunity for Soul infusion and evolutionary growth is made possible on both the individual and collective levels. At the appropriate time in this cycle, the Soul begins to remove itself from its three lower vehicles and absorbs the information of its experiences in that incarnation back into Itself. Then, at yet another proper moment, It comes forth again through the various densities of the three "lower worlds" which are appropriate to karma. The natal horoscope is, of course, based upon these "appropriate" and karmically induced moments. The interpretation by exoteric methodology reveals the nature of the interplay of the energies as they manifest in and through these three densest vehicles. The delineation of the horoscope through the Soul-centered approach reveals the purpose of the incarnating Soul, as well as its relationship to the trinity of the personality.

There is another facet to this cycling of births. The process of birth, life span, what we call death, and the synthesizing, absorbative process which occurs after the Life Force is removed from the physical body, is the essential key to the rhythm of evolution. It also reveals the essential quality of Love which is at the root of all manifestation in our particular solar system.

The purpose of involution is to allow Spirit to penetrate deeper and deeper into matter; for matter and all things of matter to realize their spiritual essence. Evolution is the process by which this increasingly spiritual, self-realizing matter is reabsorbed back into the Source of its creation. Yet as each of us "returns Home," we come back with more than what we were when we left. The Path of Return is such that the closer we get to our spiritual Self, the greater our realization of our own Divinity. This realization comes through our expanding consciousness, and the development of consciousness is a function of the Soul—the Love aspect of Divinity.

The Grace of God is contained within this ever-expanding Self-realization. Divinity as Spiritual Will continues to manifest Itself while Soul as Love continues to create the vehicles for Its expression. The more we realize ourselves as Souls, the more we come to identify the Spiritual Will which is our essential being. The personality provides the vehicle for the Intelligence or linking aspects of Life to mix and interplay, thus creating new opportunities for the expression of Spirit in form. Thus, as Divinity comes to "know Itself" through the creation of Its forms of manifestation, we (as Its forms) come to know ourselves as It. This is the essential purpose for being alive—to know through our consciousness that we are Life Itself. In the Aquarian Age, this realization will come to each individual through service to humanity and through the application of the Laws and Principles of the New Age.

The next two postulates outline a very major occult principle—the Law of Sevens.

Postulate 9: Our solar system has a septenary nature. It responds and interplays with seven cosmic emanating sources within our immediate universe. The energy radiations of these sources are called the Seven Rays, each of which has specific qualities of vibration and manifestation.

The number seven was called "worthy of veneration" by the Pythagoreans. These students of esoteric mathematics knew that the number seven was highly significant to the Sacred Teachings. It represents the creative powers of the Seven Spirits before the Throne of God, also known as the Archangels. Seven is thus the number of Cosmic Law, for it is through these seven primary forces that the One creates and builds the primary structures of the manifested universe. This heptad of forces is essential to Soul-centered astrology, and is here known as the Seven Rays.

There are many sevens, both in the Ancient Wisdom Teachings and in Soul-centered astrology. Primary among these are:
1. the Seven Planes of Manifestation
2. the Seven Kingdoms in Nature
3. the Seven Levels of Consciousness
4. the Seven Chakras, or Centers of Force
5. the Seven Sacred Planets
6. the Seven Root Races of Man
7. the Seven Rays

The Ancient Wisdom Teachings tell us that our solar system is one of seven related star systems. Each of these is a tremendous center or vortex of life energy in the body of a Great Entity. This Divinity is called the "One About Whom Naught May Be Said," so vast is Its consciousness and scope of Being. Each of these systems is also the primary vehicle for the expression of one or the other of the Seven Rays. Our particular solar system is said to be the Heart Center of the "One," and is thus the vehicle of expression for the Second of the Seven Rays—the Ray of Love/Wisdom. This endows the consciousness of our Solar System (for It, too, is alive and is the immediate Divinity within Whom we "live, move, and have our being") with Love/Wisdom as the primary quality of the expression of Its Life Force. Thus the more conscious a person becomes, the more loving, and the more loving, the more conscious. In our solar system, the words "love" and "consciousness" mean and are the same thing. *All the problems of the individual and of humanity have to do with a block in (and most important, may be resolved by) the flow of love/consciousness.* Once this block is freed—once a channel is opened up to the flow of love/consciousness—the needed healing takes place. Then abundance replaces lack on any level and balance is restored.

Human beings have seven vortices of life energy; so does each planet and solar system. The occult term for these centers of force is *chakra,* from the Sanskrit word for "wheel." In our solar system the seven chakras, or expressions for the Second Ray of Love/Wisdom, are: Vulcan, Mercury, Venus, Jupiter, Saturn, Uranus, and Neptune. Each of these planets also corresponds to one or the other of the Seven Rays. Finally, each of these seven planets, Rays, and chakras corresponds to an endocrine gland and/or a part of the human body. Thus there is a direct linkage from the human heart into the Heart of the One About Whom Naught May Be Said. This relationship is based on the Law of Correspondences, and is expressed through the Law of Sevens. Nothing happens in the universe that doesn't have its correspondence on all the planes of manifestation. The Law of Cause and Effect (karma) intimately interrelates and interconnects all of these structures. It is the extension of our awareness that perceives that reality, and it is the realization of Love which allows us to be conscious of this unity. The interplay of planets, Rays, chakras, and physical organs is vital to the nature of the structure of those laws, energies, and methods of horoscope delineation fundamental to the outworking of Soul-centered astrology. (See tabulation 3 on p. 155.)

Postulate 10: This sevenfold nature is, for the purposes of manifestation, divided into the three (symbolized by the triangle) and the four (symbolized by the square and the equal-armed cross).

The three is always the Trinity. In its most fundamental, this Trinity may be expressed as Spirit, Soul, Matter. We have also discussed the outworking of the three as Monad, Soul, and Personality. We shall shortly discuss the three as the Trinity of the major Rays: Ray One of Will, Ray Two of Love, and Ray Three of Intelligence.

As the One, Spirit is the Divine Father as Creator. As the Two, Spirit is the Great Mother, the Sustainer of Life. But as the Three, we see Divinity giving birth to the forms of Itself out of Itself, and it is thus that the Triad represents the expression of the interplay of Spirit and Soul, Male and Female. The three can thus be said to be the Creative Force of Life in the action of manifestation.

Four is representative of the crystallization of manifestation into all of its myriad and infinite forms. Four is Spirit, Soul, and Matter concretized, birthed. It is also the number of foundation, structure, and roots. Four is halfway between one and seven, and as such, it is always representative of a turning point in a cycle, as well as the point of sustained tension in any given equilibrium. The Fourth Ray, for example, is called Harmony through Conflict. The Fourth Kingdom of the Seven is the Human, standing as it does halfway between the three lower kingdoms of nature and the three higher. As we shall soon discover, the fourth chakra is the heart center, and it, like humanity itself, rests halfway between the three centers of personality expression and the three centers of the Soul.

When we add three and four together—when Spirit interplays through the birth of Its forms—we have a cycle of manifestation, a seven. But should we multiply three times four, we have another very important number (especially to astrologers), the twelve. Multiplication allows for a greater differentiation of energy than does addition. Thus twelve is indicative of all the potential which comes through the distribution and dissemination of energy. Yet when we add the two numbers which comprise the twelve, we get $(1 + 2) = 3$. Thus twelve is a direct extension of the powers inherent in three when multiplied by four, the number of the concretization of matter. Twelve allows for a wide range of building to occur and for a multiplicity of life expressions to manifest through it. Some of the more important twelves are:

1. The twelve signs of the zodiac (based on the three qualities of the motion of energy: cardinal, fixed, and mutable; and the four basic elements: fire, earth, air, and water).

2. The twelve tribes of Israel (as well as the twelve Prophets and the twelve Patriarchs).

3. The twelve Gates of Heaven.

4. The twelve Apostles of Jesus.

Finally, let us mention another number that, from an astrological and metaphysical perspective, is very interesting. This is the number eighty-four, produced by multiplying seven times twelve. This number is also reached by adding three cycles of seven times four, or twenty-eight. Eighty-four years is the length of the orbit of Uranus around the Sun. It thus takes this planet seven years to pass through each of the twelve signs. The passage of Uranus through four signs takes twenty-eight years $(2 + 8 = 10; 1 + 0 = 1)$; eight signs take fifty-six years $(5 + 6 = 11; 1 + 1 = 2)$; while the entire orbit takes the full eighty-four years $(8 + 4 = 12; 1 + 2 = 3)$.

Uranus is closely associated with the functions of the Collective Mind which, by permeating all of humanity, creates those connective links between the individual and Mankind. The length of its orbit and its passage of seven years through each of the twelve signs is highly significant in this respect. The orbit of Uranus reveals the cycle of common human development.

Since seven is indicative of the entirety of a cycle of manifestation, when it is multiplied by four, the resulting number—twenty-eight—reveals an anchoring, a concretization, and a readiness to move on through some major turning point or crisis of completion into a new phase of life. The astrologer will note that the twenty-eighth, fifty-sixth, and eighty-fourth years of life coincide with major phases of the progressed lunar and transiting Saturn cycles. These two planetary passages are representative of the nature of the psychological, developmental growth of an individual in his or her relationship to tribe, family, society, and eventually, his participation in the planetary life.

These three twenty-eight-year periods of life may be viewed as follows:

1. *Years 1–28:* the period for the establishment and potential integration of the personality. The anchoring of self-awareness through tribal and family associations; the unfoldment of the biological karma.

2. *Years 29–56:* the period of the expansion of the personality into the dynamics of its social roles. The unfolding of self-awareness through societal karma. The awakening to the presence of the Soul is quickened by the tensions produced through one's social responsibilities, as well as through the urge for recognition by one's society.

3. *Years 57–84:* the period of the lessening of the hold of the personality on the three lower vehicles and the increase of their control by the Soul. The detachment of responsibilities on the personal level and the increase of awareness of the need to contribute with developing impersonality to the collective. The assumption of responsibility for a greater role in the planetary life.

PART TWO

A SOUL-CENTERED ALPHABET: THE ASTROLOGICAL BUILDING BLOCKS

6

The Nature and

Influence of the

Seven Rays

The seven brothers are all the children of the same Father, but the elder three partake of the Father's nature. The younger four resemble the Mother. The three elder sons go forth into the universe of stars, and there they represent the Father. The younger four go forth into the universe of stars and show the nature of the one the Father loved.

—Alice Bailey, *Esoteric Psychology*, Volume I

The First Ray: **The Ray of Will/Power**
The Second Ray: **The Ray of Love/Wisdom**
The Third Ray: **The Ray of Active Intelligence**
The Fourth Ray: **The Ray of Harmony Through Conflict**
The Fifth Ray: **The Ray of Concrete Knowledge and Science**
The Sixth Ray: **The Ray of Devotion and Idealism**
The Seventh Ray: **The Ray of Ceremonial Order and Magic**

One of the most universal beliefs associated with traditional astrology infers that the planets and signs *cause* terrestrial events and personality characteristics. As such, there is the tendency to view the zodiac and the heavenly spheres as instigators of a fated causality. This idea of predestination implies that humanity has little hope for escape from its beleaguered condition. For the Soul-centered, this is a misconception. Yet for those individuals totally focused and identified with the three worlds of the personality, this is not altogether incorrect.

The vast majority of personality-centered human beings are swept along unconsciously by the rhythms, movements, and patterns of their biological karma, instinctive desires, and national orientation. There is very little actual sense of self-consciousness, and what little there may be is too easily suffused by the nonindividualized, collective herd instinct. They are incapable of actuating and integrating into daily life the kind of self-actualization and self-realization that characterizes one in whom Soul-consciousness has been developed. It is only when Spiritual Will expressed through the Soul connects, via the Rainbow Bridge, to the personal will that such a focus of self-actualization is possible. Then, a person may recognize him- or herself as a co-creator of his own destiny, along with the Plan of the Creator. At a later and more evolved stage of individual development, he begins to recognize and accept the responsibility for being a co-creator of the collective destiny of humanity.

Popularistic, personality-centered astrology has historically mirrored this fatalistic, causal relationship between the planets and the signs and humanity, and as a result, has strengthened this thought-form of dependency and helplessness. It should be said, however, that in the past twenty-five years, much has been done by the Humanistic Movement among professional astrologers to alter this widely accepted view. Yet the distinction has to be made that personality-centered people—the vast majority of people in the world—identify themselves with the materialization of events and attach themselves to the *forms and effects* of manifestation. The Soul-centered identify themselves much more with the *relationship* between cause and effect, and respond to the quality aspect or consciousness inherent in manifestation. An increasing number of us are currently developing along this latter line of approach to life and are dealing with ourselves, our brothers and sisters, and the world, accordingly. The very few Spirit- or God-centered individuals *are* the factors and direct vehicles of causality in our world, and identify themselves with Life Itself.

The Science of Relationship is intimately involved with the expression of consciousness. The nature of Soul-centered astrology concerns itself primarily with the karma, patterns, and timing of the cycles of those relationships which unfold the consciousness of the One Life through all Its infinite forms of manifestation. The Seven Rays are the basic building energies of manifestation and are the keynotes of this relationship between cause and effect. It is the interplay between the Seven Rays and the twelve zodiacal signs, each operating through three basic levels of expression (see chapter 7); the seven sacred and the five non-sacred planets (creating thus another twelve); the seven major vital life centers and their corresponding endocrine glands; and, in an associative sense, the major planetary aspects and the twelve houses of the natal chart, that form the basis for the astrology of the New Age.

In chapter 5, postulates nine and ten, we mentioned the importance of the number seven and the septenary nature of the structure of our manifested universe. We are taught that our solar system, with its seven sacred planets, is one of seven such solar systems, the stars and planets of which comprise the "Body" of the Great One—the Divinity, About Whom Naught May Be Said. Each of these seven systems is the primary expression for one of the Seven Rays. The seven stars in the constellation of the Great Bear (or the Big Dipper, as it is also called) are the Source and emanating vehicles of the Seven Rays. These seven stars collectively focus the causal First Ray of Will/Power. The constellation of the Great Bear is the primary solar system of these seven and is a Solar System in the truest sense of the term. The Great Bear is not composed of one star with a family of circling planets; it is composed completely of stars. The central focus of this System is the star which commands the energy of the Will/Power of the One.

One of two primary stellar vehicles for the Second Ray of Love/ Wisdom is our Sun, which represents the Heart of this Great One. The other is the great star, Sirius. This means that all the Seven Rays function in our solar system *through* the Second Ray, making It and the quality of Its energy of Love/Wisdom the most vital to us. The importance of this statement cannot be underestimated, as it indicates a great Absolute Truth: Love and the Wisdom which leads and proceeds from Love are the primary qualities of consciousness in our solar system, and hence, of life here on Earth. All of the other six Rays work through Love/Wisdom and are subject to it.

The Law of Correspondences and the Law of Sevens tell us that each of the great Seven Cosmic Rays is divided into seven subrays, each connected to and having the influence of its Cosmic Ray Parent. Yet these seven subrays are tinged with and are a part of the influence of the one Ray of which they are seven parts. As I have mentioned, our Solar System, our solar Life Force, is of the Second of these Cosmic Rays. The Second Ray is the energy of Love in Action, and is expressed primarily through the forces of the Soul, the quality of consciousness on any plane of manifestation, and the Christ Consciousness in Humankind.

It is most important to clarify this terminology, for following the Path which leads to the unfoldment of the Christ Consciousness in a person is not necessarily the same as following one of the various religions of Christianity. The way of unfoldment leading to this State is more rightly called the Path of Discipleship, and Christianity is but one of many roads leading to the one "Noble Path." The Christ Consciousness is the revelation of the Soul's reality. The Soul does not have a religion; It is the synthesis of all religions. The Soul does not have an exclusive Path; It is the synthesis of all Paths leading to It. The Lord Jesus was the Christed Self of the Piscean Age, and He remains a Beloved Brother in the Brotherhood and Sisterhood of the Planetary Hierarchy. The Lord Jesus occupies a position relative to the Christ in the same way that the Lord Gautama occupies a position relative to the Buddha. Indeed, in terms of the dual nature of the Second Ray, it is the Christ Who is the Love aspect and the Buddha Who is the Wisdom aspect.

The Path of the fusion of these two aspects of the Second Ray within each of us is at the core of the evolution of human consciousness. There is only the One Divinity and *all* else is an expression of Its Life, Love, Intelligence, and Body. In this respect, *the purpose of our solar system is the unfolding of consciousness on all levels. The purpose for humanity, both collectively and individually, is the revelation of the Soul's reality—the Love which is at the center of all forms and manifestations of Life.*

We should thus consider the Seven Rays as they pertain to our planetary life as:

Ray One: **The Will and Power to Love**
Ray Two: **The Essential Love Energy**
Ray Three: **The Active, Intelligent Expression of Love**
Ray Four: **Love Expressed Through the Fusion of Opposites**
Ray Five: **Love Expressed Through Concrete Knowledge and Science**
Ray Six: **Love Expressed Through Devotion and Idealism**
Ray Seven: **Love Expressed Through Ritual, Order, and Synthesis**

Let us use color as an example to carry this illustration of the Seven Rays and their subrays a bit further. As the primary color of the spectrum representing the Second Ray is indigo (see tabulation 2, p. 140), we can say that the actual First Ray energy, as manifesting through our Second Ray solar system, is indigo/scarlet. In the same way, the Second Ray color is indigo/indigo; the Third Ray (in reality, the third subray of the Second Ray) is indigo/green; likewise, the Fourth Ray is indigo/yellow. The Fifth Ray color is indigo/orange; while the Sixth Ray is indigo/blue-rose; and the Seventh Ray is indigo/violet.

The Earth has an indigo sky. As a planet, we are under the primary influence of the Fourth Ray of Harmony through Conflict. Perhaps the presence of the true Second Ray color gives us a protective and helping hand as we struggle through the conflicts which seem to characterize our Earthly and human-oriented drive for harmony.

The relationship between one-three-seven-twelve is very important to our understanding of the relationship of the Seven Rays to the signs, planets, and houses of the horoscope. The processes and forms of creation are endless, and yet they serve to enhance Divinity's consciousness of Itself and subsequently, our own consciousness of our own Self. In this process of manifestation, the One (while all the time remaining Whole) divides Itself first into two: positive and negative, masculine and feminine. These two combine to produce a third. These three aspects of the One unite, and from their various combinations, the seven are produced. All the forms of manifestation are thus outpourings of this initial Trinity and these four further differentiations. The Seven Rays are divided into two groupings. Rays One, Two, and Three are the Primary Rays or *Rays of Aspect;* that is, the three essential aspects of Divinity. Rays Four through Seven are called the *Rays of Attribute,* as they express the attributes of the first three Rays in greater detail of manifestation, and are combinations of the qualities of the Primary Rays. In actuality, Rays Four through Seven emanate from the Third Ray of Active Intelligence, while this Third Ray is actually a product of the energies of Rays One and Two. These seven energies enter our solar system through the Twelve Gates of the Zodiac, and each one of the seven is primarily focused through three of the signs. Thus the twelve signs are the vehicles for the sevenfold energies of manifestation representing the Trinity of Life, which is essentially and ever One.

ASTROLOGICAL SIGNIFICANCE OF THE SEVEN RAYS

In the pages which follow, you will be given relatively brief yet thorough descriptions of the powers, characteristics, contributing forces, and keywords inherent in the meanings of the Seven Rays as they are best suited for use in astrological work. I would very much like to give the reader some suggestions on how to best incorporate this material about the Seven Rays into his or her own method of approach to the delineation of the natal chart.[1]

The Seven Rays should be seen as being much closer to the basic energies of life than their expressions through the archetypes of the twelve signs. The latter are further differentiations of expression of

---

[1] Alice A. Bailey wrote a definitive, five-volume Treatise on the Seven Rays. These books, and especially the third in this series, *Esoteric Astrology,* comprise the theoretical basis of all the work now being conducted internationally in order to process and develop these themes into an astrology for the New Age. Please refer to the Bibliography for further reference guides.

the Seven Rays. It is for this reason that a greater understanding of the seven will lead the astrological student to a deeper and more penetrating attunement to the twelve.

1. First, study the nature of the energies of the Seven Rays, and then see how they interplay with the nature of the twelve signs as they express through the three quadruplicities or crosses of cardinality, fixity, and mutability.² Then, examine the Rays and the signs through each of the triplicities of fire, earth, air, and water. This will allow you to integrate and synthesize the nature of the Rays into your accepted astrological knowledge.³

2. Meditate on the symbol for each of the Rays. This will give you an intuitive and nonverbal connection to the Ray force itself. Meditating on the symbols of astrology and the Ancient Wisdom Teachings is strongly recommended so that you develop a link between intellect and intuition—a link that is vital to the Soul-centered astrologer.

3. Make your own lists of keywords relative to your understanding of the Ray energies. One of the gifts bestowed by Uranus, the planet ruling the practice of astrology both exoterically and esoterically, is the ability to view the infinite numbers of forms of life by their categories and archetypes. This allows a fusion of the relationship between the one and the many, and between the macrocosm and the microcosm. Extend this process into your studies and observations of the Ray energies in the life around you.

4. Do not think of the planets as causal factors or "energy-source" bodies, as they are in exoteric astrology and the horoscope of the personality. They should be seen more as lenses, or focalizers, through which the Seven Rays express themselves in the solar system. As we shall see in chapter 9, the planets are divided into two fundamental groups: sacred and non-sacred. These will be contrasted with the more traditional and exoteric subdivisions of the planets: higher and lower octaves.

5. It is very important to recognize that each person is simultaneously under the influence of several Rays. These influences act both individually and collectively. The nature of this multiple Ray influence is as follows:

    a. The Ray of the Solar Logos/Solar System—Ray Two

    b. The Ray of the Planetary Logos/Earth—Ray Three

    c. The Rays of Humanity—Ray Four (the Soul Ray); Ray Five (the current personality Ray)

    d. The Rays of one's nation—Ray Two (United States' Soul Ray); Ray Six (United States' Personality Ray)

---

²Chapter 7 contrasts the three crosses from both the esoteric and exoteric perspectives.
³A list of the keywords and concepts relative to the twelve signs, three crosses, and four elements is provided in *Alan Oken's Complete Astrology*.

RAYS OF THE NATIONS

Nation	Soul Ray	Personality Ray
Great Britain	Two	One
France	Five	Three
U.S.S.R.	Seven	Six
China	One	Three
India	One	Four

Information for Australia, Canada, and New Zealand, and several other nations is not available. It may be of interest to the reader, especially those not born or living in the United States, to list some of the Soul and personality Rays of other nations.[4]

6. The following is a list of Ray influences which are more individual in their expression than the ones listed above.

    a. The Ray of the Monad (one of the three Rays of Aspect)
    b. The Ray of the Soul (any one of the Seven Rays)
    c. The Ray of the Personality (any one of the Seven Rays)
       The Ray of the mental body
       The Ray of the emotional body
       The Ray of the physical body

Although a person's mental, emotional, or physical Ray may be found on any one of the Seven, the Tibetan asserts that certain of the Rays tend to dominate in this respect. Thus the majority of people would tend to find that their mental body was either of the First, Fourth, or Fifth Ray; their emotional body would express either the Second or the Sixth Ray; and their physical body would be an expression of either the Third or the Seventh Ray.[5] We will be discussing the nature of these Ray influences on the natal horoscope in part 3.

---

[4]See *The Destiny of the Nations*, by Alice A. Bailey, for a more complete listing.
[5]For further information, see Bailey's *Esoteric Psychology*, vol. 1, p. 321.

THE THREE RAYS OF ASPECT

The First Ray: The Ray of Will/Power

SIGNS: *Aries, Leo, Capricorn*   PLANETS: *Vulcan, Pluto*

SYMBOL:

From the One who is the seven goes forth a word. That word reverberates along the line of fiery essence, and when it sounds within the circle of human lives it takes the form of affirmation, an uttered fiat or word of power.... Why this blind power? Why death? Why this decay of forms? ... Faintly the answer comes: I hold the keys of life and death. I bind and loose again. I, the Destroyer, am.

—Alice A Bailey[6]

The First Ray is the causal focus of life. It is the Will-to-Be, and as it acts through the Second Ray energy of our solar system, it may also be called the "Will-to-Be-Love." And yet the First Ray is also known as the Lord of Death, the Destroyer of Forms, and the Lord of the Burning Ground. Its planetary vehicles for expression are the two spheres most associated with decomposition, regeneration, and rebirth: Vulcan and Pluto. And of the Hindu Trinity of Brahma the Creator, Vishnu the Sustainer, and Shiva the Destroyer, it is Shiva which is most closely associated as Lord of the First Ray. The purpose behind this facet of First Ray activity is clearly brought forth by the Tibetan when He speaks of the function of the First Ray as the Finger of God:

Through the application of the Finger of God in its directing and forceful work, we have the cyclic destruction of forms, so that the manifestation of Deity may grow in power and beauty. Thus the Lord of Power or Will performs the task of destruction, thereby bringing beauty into being and the revelation of God's will and His beneficent purpose.[7]

This tells us much about the nature of First Ray energy and, as we shall soon discover, about the people who embody it in terms of their

[6]*Esoteric Psychology*, vol. 1, p. 63.
[7]In Bailey's *Esoteric Psychology*, vol. 1, p. 133.

Soul and/or personality life. We can see that out of the chaos of destruction is birthed the Will-to-Create. It is this powerful Will that is the energy behind the Big Bang, which initiates all cycles of creative expression, whether in terms of the birth of a universe, or the orgasmic movement leading to the conception of a child. This is certainly the energy working through the planet Pluto, and represented by its regenerative and destructive modes of expression.

From a purely pragmatic, astrological perspective, we have a hint here relative to the functioning of the Yod or Finger of God geometric angle in the natal chart. The Yod is created when three planets relate to each other by two 150-degree angles (inconjunctions) and one 60-degree (sextile) angle. This is illustrated in diagram 7, in which planet A signifies the apex point of the Finger of God. I believe that we should look at planet A and the house position it occupies as a point through which First Ray energy will be expressed in the natal map. The forms of expression of planet A are constantly challenged by life, especially by those circumstances indicated by planets B and C and their house positions. The natural habitual and karmic patterns of planet A, when expressed, lead to continuous disruptance in the life. There is the need to establish some new focus of release for that planet's energy so that new forms for its expression may be birthed into the life. The nature of the harmonious interchange between planets B and C (as indicated by the sextile between them) as well as the two house positions and their interconnections, will point the way to this rebirthing and regeneration of form.

The energy of the First Ray acts as a catalyst, breaking up old and existing conditions so that new ones may eventuate. It is indeed the power behind the Phoenix who rises from the ashes of destruction to create itself anew more gloriously. The First Ray stands behind the

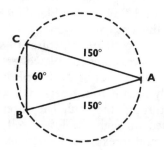

Diagram 7: The Finger of God or Yod
Multiple-Aspect Pattern

other Six to shatter the forms They have created so that new worlds may emerge. The Kingdom of the First Ray is Shamballa, "the Place where the Will of God is known." The purpose of the Great Lord of Death is to allow for the entrance of Light, for the First Ray is indeed the dynamic Idea in the Mind of God which initiates all the work in any cycle of Creation.

Aries, Leo, and Capricorn are the signs of the First Ray, with Aries predominating this triad. It is quite obvious from what we know about these signs that First Ray types of people are going to display natural leadership qualities or, at the very least, the urge to give direction. The First is the Ray of government and politics. If you will look at tabulation 2 on p. 140, you will see that two of the three First Ray signs are also connected with the Seventh Ray of Order and Ceremony. The combination of the influences of these two Rays, Aries, and Capricorn, makes it clear that the structured and orderly expression of power, and its wielding and application, are very important traits of these two astrological signs. This is one reason why when Mars, exoteric ruler of Aries, is found in Capricorn in the natal chart, it is said to be in its exaltation. It is the exaltation of the expression of First Ray energy—Power and Will!

People who are strongly influenced by this Ray of Will/Power find that they move into positions of leadership quite easily. In this respect, they display a very natural positive drive, a directness in personal relationships, and the ability to carry out their often self-appointed tasks and assignments with self-confidence and responsibility. Other First Ray attributes include the courage to persist against all odds, as well as the ability to inspire others to new heights of personal daring and expression. There is a special zeal and enthusiasm in the face of challenge while they continually motivate others.

As leaders, First Ray people often have to make decisions about the direction others have to take in their lives. They frequently have to pass judgment and, when highly developed, tend to have the ability to join mercy with justice. This particular trait is very much the evidence of the presence of Second Ray energy blending with First. First Ray individuals are very diligent, not given to asking for support and praise. They much prefer to create structures of support for others so that a project may be successfully completed.

All of the above characteristics of the First Ray are quite positive in nature. They can apply equally to the personality level and the expression of the First Ray through the Soul. The difference to keep in mind is that when expressed through the lower self, the urge will be to wield personal power and to express the personal will on (or perhaps over) others. A loving personality can do this quite effectively in a firm but gentle manner, but the purpose will be for the expression of the personal will, its aims and ambitions. When the First Ray is being focused through a Soul-centered individual, the expression of Will and Power is collective and impersonal in nature. Thus, when the Soul is in full possession of the lower self, none of the following characteristics, illustrating the negative expression of the First Ray, can ever be possible.

Some of the pitfalls associated with the negative polarity of the expression of First Ray energy have to do with the misuse of will. There may easily be an inclination toward unbridled ambition and dominance. The Disciple on the Path is taught to "work ambitiously, but without attachment to ambition." This is not true for the personality-centered First Ray type, who tends to attach himself to the forms of the goals he has in mind, and to move forward with all the power the ego may be able to manifest. This can often lead to impatience and arrogance when dealing with others. Courage can give way to foolhardiness, and the urge to support other people's efforts is transformed into the need to dominate through sheer use of force. When expressing First Ray energy through the mental plane, this type of individual may come across as cold, aloof, and detached—a know-it-all who's here to tell you what to do without question.

A First Ray physical body tends to be ectomorphic. The person is usually wiry, self-projective, and alive with nervous energy. A chubby person could never be a First Ray body type—that is much more a Second or Sixth Ray tendency. Now, why is that? If you check tabulation 2 on p. 140 once again, you will see that protein is ruled by the First Ray. Fat is a Second Ray substance, while water is ruled by the Sixth. Thus, a lean body that tends to metabolize protein is First Ray, while those body types (and many of the personality traits associated with them) that tend to retain water and fat display much more traits of the Second and Sixth Rays.

Keywords and Key Phrases
of the First Ray

1. *Concept*: Will, power, destroyer of form, the urge to rule, the vehicle for creative initiation on all levels.

2. *Soul Level*: The use of spiritual will for the benefit of the collective; power utilized for the purpose of enhancing unity and beauty; the expression of will for the purposes and well-being of the group.

3. *Personality Level*: Ray of soldier, statesman, ruler, explorer, leader; government, politics, and administration.

a. *General Positive Traits:* Courage, diligence, quick discernment, leadership abilities, inspires others, adventurous, not dismayed by initial failures, but remains persistent until goal is achieved.

b. *General Character Difficulties:* Limitless ambition, uses will for selfish purposes, manipulative of others through personal power, easy to anger, cannot take criticism, strong sense of personal pride.

c. *To Be Cultivated:* Compassion, humility, tolerance, caring, sympathy.

d. *Mental:* Strong, one-pointed mind with very individual opinions and points of view which can lead to a sense of isolation; need to dominate the thinking of others, or at least to lead the direction of thought; thinking is purposeful, as is the choice of intellectual interests.

e. *Emotional:* Can be very detached and cold; sometimes emotions are very deep-seated, and may explode volcanically; shy and reserved emotionally most of the time.

f. *Physical:* Ectomorph—lean, medium-tall to tall.

The Second Ray: The Ray of Love/Wisdom

SIGNS: *Gemini, Virgo, Pisces*   PLANETS: *Jupiter, Sun*

SYMBOL:

The Word is issuing from the heart of God, emerging from a central point of love. That Word is love itself. . . . The Word in the beginning was. The Word hath dwelt and dwells with God.

—Alice A. Bailey[8]

The Second Ray is called the Master Builder, as it acts as the primary vehicle for the expression of the many forms of the primary, creative urge. It occupies the second aspect of Divinity, the Soul, and is the mode for the expression of consciousness, the quality of Life. As we have mentioned, the Second Ray is the most important to us, as it is the Ray for the expression of the Life of our solar system. Our solar system is essentially dualistic, as there are two forces which work through it: Love and Wisdom—Ray Two. It should come as no surprise that the theme of the duality of life is absolutely fundamental for us all. The urge to reconcile all duality and to create synthesis out

[8]*Esoteric Psychology,* vol. 1, p. 65.

of polarization is at the core of much of our individual and collective self-development. In this respect, the basic duality with which we are all dealing is the relationship between the Soul and the personality. Their eventual fusion and synthesis is what constitutes the state of the Initiate in humankind and is the goal of our individual evolution. The consciousness which results from these efforts is the Grace of God and reveals the essential Love/Wisdom, Second Ray energy of Life. The importance of Gemini and its esoteric ruler, Venus, as the vehicle for the fusion of the pairs of opposites into a greater expression of harmony and beauty, is most important in this respect. (See chapter 9, p. 172.)

The Second Ray represents the cohesive force in the universe. It is this energy which unites and binds and allows all the building of Creativity to take place. The Second is thus the Ray of Lord Vishnu, the Sustainer of all the forms of Life, and is known as the Ray of the Soul—the Ray of the Hidden Christ. It is the Ray of the female principle because the Soul (female essential nature) embodies and gives form to the Spirit (male essential nature). The Soul (Second Ray) is the matrix from which all other forms are built. As we shall shortly discover, much of the differentiation into the myriad forms of Life is accomplished through the work of the Third Ray. The Second Ray supplies the matrix so that the work of Creation may be carried forth into manifestation.

Love is that matrix, that Mother Force, which births those forms that house the essential Spirit of Life. Love is the healing dynamic which, through its cohesiveness, eventuates the process of evolution into greater and more highly evolved wholes. Love and the energy of the Second Ray unites, binds, and holds all of the manifestations of Creation together. This is the power of the female energy in the universe, while the male force continues to instill and inspire. (It is a wonderful function of the synthetic nature of the Seventh Ray, the primary Ray energy of the New Age, that these male and female qualities are expressing themselves simultaneously through all men and women of goodwill. This united function of the energy of life can only enhance the quality of the love present in our world, creating men and women who are more synthesized and less polarized in their ways of interrelating. This is a definite aspect of Soul orientation in the Aquarian Era.)

The Second Ray is the energy behind what we can call "universal love." It is very definitely connected to the powers of intuition, as once intuition is developed, one attains a very focused awareness of the wholistic quality of life. The Second Ray instills cooperation between people, philanthropy, and the urge to serve. It is the Ray of the teacher and the Ray of the Planetary Hierarchy, the Illuminati of any World Age. The Second is very connected to the Sixth Ray of religion, but unlike the Sixth, which has the tendency to promote and develop exclusivistic pathways of belief, the Second Ray is totally inclusive in nature.

Another facet of Second Ray energy is its healing quality. It is the Ray most associated with the plant kingdom, and is especially linked to flowers and perfumes. It might interest many to know that those distillations from flowers known as the Bach Flower Remedies are Second Ray in nature and intent. This healing function of the Second Ray is most important, as it is through the attunement to the Soul that the healing properties of the Life Force emanate and produce a greater wholeness. The Christ is often referred to as the Healer of Mankind, as this Great Initiate is, in essence, the Soul force for Humanity and is, along with His Hierarchy, the personification of Love/Wisdom. However, Christianity, as it has been practiced for the most part during the past two thousand years, in much more closely linked to the Sixth Ray.

Virgo is the "controlling factor," or primary sign of the Second Ray at this time. Its function has much to do with the increase in the activity of the Christ; that is, the expansion of Love/Wisdom in the hearts of humanity. This is often most effectively accomplished through those outer activities which we have come to associate with this sign: service, healing, and methods of self-improvement. Another interesting factor is the relationship of the Virgin Mother with this sign. It is within the womb of the Mother that the embryonic Christ is nurtured. Nine months later (if we count precessionally), we reach the sign of the Initiate, Capricorn, and the Christ is born at the winter solstice. Some other names associated with the Second Ray clearly demonstrate its relationship to healing, love, and the Christ. These are: the Lord of Eternal Love, the Giver of Wisdom, the Son of God Incarnate, the Cosmic Christ, and the Radiance in the Form.

The Second Ray is primarily the Ray of Consciousness, the second aspect of Divinity (Life and Form being the other two). Consciousness relates life and form, and through it, the indwelling principle of love is revealed. The strong Second Ray person is always seeking to establish Right Human Relationships by evoking the higher consciousness existing between people; that is, the consciousness of the Soul's reality. It is thus that the Second Ray is the energy of Universal Brother- and Sisterhood, and most expressive of the inclusive quality of Love Incarnate.

All the signs connected to the Second Ray are dual, although Virgo goes one step further and is considered, due to its relationship with the Mother, and thus the birther of all forms, as multiplistic in nature. It is for this reason of dualism and multiplicity that on a practical level, people who tend to be strongly Second Ray in nature have the tendency to vacillate. Their views often change relative to the people in their surroundings. The urge is for universality, so that in their need to be all-embracing, they lose their focus and steadiness. Second Ray people tend to mix well with others, and when they are developed, their radiance makes them loved and admired for their compassion and nurturing qualities. As the Second Ray is one of Wisdom as well as Love, Second Ray people tend to be teachers by nature. Yet it should be noted that if the Wisdom aspect of the Ray is emphasized, and is not balanced by Love, there is a tendency toward aloofness. They may then appear indifferent to others and lacking in the compassion that is at the very heart of this Ray's life quality.

Second Ray individuals are the peacemakers of the Earth. Since they are able to see all sides to a given situation, as well as the whole, all simultaneously (a gift of intuition), they often find themselves in diplomatic roles. The "go-between" nature of the "shuttle diplomacy" initiated by Dr. Henry Kissinger (himself a Gemini) illustrates the kind of movement particular to Second Ray energy when acting in the cause of governmental diplomacy.

Some of the more difficult and negative traits associated with Second Ray personalities revolve around misplaced and overemphasized sensitivity. Magnetism is especially associated with the Second Ray. As a consequence, a person may become too responsive to the needs of others, with the resulting sense of feeling overburdened by the pains of the world. This is an example of picking up or absorbing negativity from the collective level, and then unconsciously transforming it into some form of personal life situation. This is a definite pathway to depression, anxiety, and a very poor self-image. Inertia, helplessness, and a sense of ineffectiveness are other traits which may characterize such a negatively polarized Second Ray type of person.

The above speaks about the misplaced direction of the Love aspect of the Second Ray. If the Wisdom quality is not being properly directed, that which could be viewed as a universality of mind may degenerate into contempt of others perhaps more limited (or so one thinks) in their mental capabilities. This type of Second Ray person has to be very careful not to become so overly absorbed in his own philosophical views that he mistakes his personal opinions and perceptions for universal truths.

Keywords and Key Phrases
of the Second Ray

1. *Concept:* Universal love and truth, philanthropy, brotherhood; the urge to inclusiveness, consciousness; the nurturing quality which supports all life; the expression of the Soul.

2. *Soul Level:* The urge to bring about a sustaining, loving wholeness to any group or life situation; the ability, through magnetic attraction, to bring about healing; the focus for the stimulation of consciousness, and hence for greater love/wisdom; the ability to see beyond differences into unifying principles.

3. *Personality Level:* Ray of teachers; people in the healing and service professions.

    a. *General Positive Traits:* Naturally sympathetic and compassionate; eager to be of assistance; generous and philanthropic; calm, strong, and patient when dealing with the daily situations of life; faithful and reliable; lovers of truth who are very intuitive by nature.

    b. *General Character Difficulties:* Coldness, if Wisdom aspect is overemphasized; indifference to others; misplaced affection— always feeling sorry for things; a negative, "why is it always happening to me" outlook to life; rarely satisfied with personal accomplishments.

    c. *To Be Cultivated:* Faith in love as the healing force in life.

    d. *Mental:* A love of knowledge that may lead to learning things for the sake of learning, rather than for any practical reason; tendency to become absorbed in specialized field of study; can be profoundly universal in philosophical outlook, or a mere dilettante, with too many interests.

    e. *Emotional:* Calm and serene; more involved with sustaining feelings than with giant shows of passionate emotionalism; can become overly attached to others, and have a difficult time releasing them; is the peace initiator in any given set of conflicts.

    f. *Physical:* Delicate and gentle physical body, with a tendency toward a small stature.

The Third Ray: The Ray of Active Intelligence

SIGNS: *Cancer, Libra, Capricorn*   PLANETS: *Earth, Saturn*

SYMBOL:

Let mind control. Let the clear shining of the sun of life reveal the mind of God, and set the shining one upon his way. . . . Let the two paths converge. Balance the pairs of opposites and let the path appear between the two. God and the Path and man are one. . . . Let the Researcher of the past uncover the thought of God, hidden deep within the mind of the (Lords) of Love. . . .

—Alice A. Bailey[9]

The energy of the Third Ray, like the third aspect of the Christian Trinity—the Holy Ghost—permeates into every form of life. The Third is the Active Intelligence of Divinity, and represents the inherent intelligence within all matter. This can be the ability to relate to the world—to know, in fact, that "I am that I am." It can also be the much simpler expression of intelligence found, for example, in the phototropism of a one-celled animal who, as a result of that intelligence, is attracted to a source of light. On the mineral level, Active Intelligence acts magnotropically, and results in the attraction that certain minerals have for magnetic substances. Plants display the action of the Third Ray as they find their way to the soil in which they must root, or to the sunlight from which they also absorb life-giving nourishment. All animal intelligence is especially connected to the Third Ray.

The energy of the Third Ray is synthesizing in nature. It works to effectuate the Plan of Creation by blending the energies of Rays One and Two, bringing them into objectivity through intelligence and the mind. In this respect, the Third Ray is very much involved with matter and the creation of forms. Two of its names reveal this purpose: the Great Architect of the Universe, and the Builder of the Foundation. The Third Ray extends the matrix of the Second Ray into those channels of activity which result in the infinite forms of life. And as we shall see in the next few pages, the Four Rays of Attribute—Rays Four, Five, Six, and Seven—are all emanations of this great, synthetic Ray Three.

Yet all of the three Rays of Aspect are in constant synthetic activity on all levels—cosmic, solar, planetary, human, and atomic. The movements and rhythms of the interplay of Will-Love-Intelligence constitute the essential Cosmic Dance of the Universe. These three Rays are "as much a unity as is a human being who conceives an idea, uses his mind and brain to bring his idea into manifestation, and employs his hands and all his natural forces to perfect his concept" and bring it out into form.[10]

[9]*Esoteric Psychology*, vol. 1, p. 67, 69–70.
[10]Bailey, *Esoteric Psychology*, vol. 1, p. 159.

The Third Ray is said in the Ancient Wisdom Teachings to be the Ray of the Personality of the Planetary Logos—the Divinity that is the Earth. In this respect, no matter what the individual Rays of each person may be, all of humanity is strongly governed by the Third Ray, and intimately linked to the energies of the two planets most closely associated with it: Earth and Saturn. It is under the influence of the Third Ray that we learn to create, making our mistakes and earning our victories, until we become conscious co-creators with the Creator Itself. The Third Ray corresponds to the personality—that vehicle of expression of the Soul through which we come to know ourselves as active, intelligent expressions of the One Life. Some of the other names used in connection with the Third Ray are: the Lord of Memory, the Three-Sided Triangle, the Dispenser of Time, the Keeper of the Records, and the Universal Mind.

> This Ray brings in the factor of discrimination through mental activity, and this, in its turn, balances the so-called love nature, and it is in truth the cause of our evolutionary growth. The life in forms passes through discriminative and selective activity from one experience to another in an ever-widening scale of contacts.

—Alice A. Bailey[11]

Of the many Laws of Life, some of which we have already discussed, the Law of Economy is connected to the work and energy of the Third Ray. This Law is very much involved with the distribution of material atoms, as well as their connections and relationship through vibrational rhythm. This Law is fundamental to the creation of form, and works with the principle that matter always follows the line of least resistance. In this respect, we will see creation often operating in our Universe in a rotary motion, as worlds within worlds within worlds orbit each other in ever-connecting links of manifestation.

There is another very important principle conditioning the movement of energy. It may be summarized as: Energy Follows Thought. This is a metaphysical axiom at the foundation of creativity, and one which totally expresses the nature of the Third Ray as applied through the activities of humanity. It is very important for those of us actively working on the expansion and evolution of our consciousness to pay special attention to how we use the mind. As the mind is the vehicle for the expression of the Third Ray in action, it is the focusing lens for the creation of forms. Saturn is the force of the crystallization of matter, as well as the planet most closely linked with the entire mental plane. It is through the mind that we have the option of either creating incredible limitations for our self-expression, or creating those conscious parameters for the limitless expression of our creative, loving will. (I have found the work of the Church of Religious Science, and the writings of its founder, Dr. Ernest Holmes, to be of incredible positive value in the application and understanding of the right use of mental energy.)

The Third Ray reaches our solar system through the signs Cancer, Libra, and Capricorn. Cancer is the predominant sign of this Ray at the present time, as it is intimately linked with the consciousness of the masses of humanity and the collective urge toward self-expression in the world of form. If you will refer to tabulation 2, you will see that Cancer and Capricorn are also two of the three astrological expressions for the action of the Seventh Ray—the Ray of the Aquarian Age. In this respect, the activity of mind and Ray Three are fundamental to individualized expression in the New Age. This requires each of us to be the co-creator of our daily lives through the expression of Will and Love in the outer world of forms.

Since the Third is the Ray of the mental plane, people who are expressing its qualities in their life tend to be the creators of ideas. They are abstract thinkers—scholars, mathematicians, and inventors. In this respect, the Third is very related to the Fifth Ray of science and the concrete mind, where mental energy is applied practically. Those people whose personalities resonate closely to the Third Ray are often good at business, and can handle money wisely, as they see it not merely as numbers, but as form representing energy. They are usually able to plan ahead and make the best use of their time. The relationship with time is very important to Third Ray individuals, and no wonder, as the ruling planet of this Ray is Saturn/Chronos, which is the planet most closely linked with temporality, its cycles and karma.

The Third Ray is, by definition, the Ray of activity. People who are closely connected to the Third Ray are very much on the go. This is due to the emphasis on the mind and those relationships created by the ideas which occupy so much of their activity. Third Ray-dominated individuals enjoy those teaching methods which utilize and appeal to the Higher Mind, and there is a tendency to be preoccupied with abstract philosophical questions. They are attracted to mass communications, so that the information and ideas they wish to share may be easily related to large numbers of people. This is especially true when the Third Ray is operative on the Soul level, and the frame of reference is the collective.

When the Third Ray is expressed by someone through his personality, and that person is not grounded in the Soul's reality, there is a tendency toward craftiness and the manipulation of matter. This results in the unscrupulous businessman. Contrast this to one who is working in the world of business and finance, but from the Soul level. Such an individual would be designing those projects that would tend to distribute material supply so that all of humanity might benefit. In this case, the attitude of service underlies his activities, and the reality of the Third Ray (the third subray of the Second) would become truly manifested.

One of the major difficulties encountered by Third Ray people is the tendency to worry about time. They may easily find themselves overly concerned about trifles and details. This is really the fear of not being in control of those life situations that they have not planned or calculated. They may also express a definite intellectual pride, and as a result, find themselves falling into patterns of isolation. Such individuals may also exhibit a very critical attitude, as well as a certain absentmindedness—the "absentminded professor" syndrome is very common among them.

A Third Ray delusion is the attitude that a person has to be constantly busy. In one horoscope, the individual had many planets and positions relating to the Third Ray, one of the most significant of which was a tenth house Capricorn Moon. He related that when he was a younger man, he thought that if he looked busy all the time, people would think that he was important. This type of "masquerade in motion" is very typical of a Third Ray "glamour." Yet there are many Third Ray individuals who relax through abundant physical activities of all sorts. This is not a glamour, but the correct way to channel abundant mental energy.

Keywords and Key Phrases of the Third Ray

1. *Concept:* Mental illumination; the power to produce synthesis on the physical plane; the blending of will/power and love/wisdom to produce the forms of life.

2. *Soul Level:* The birthing of ideas to benefit humanity; the structuring of time and activities to allow for group energies to flourish; inherent, objective intelligence ready to be used in service to humanity in all ways.

3. *Personality Level:* Ray of the astrologer, scholar, judge, banker, economist, chess master, abstract thinker.

    a. *General Positive Traits:* Adaptability, clear intellect, articulate speech, and ease in communicating ideas; business skills; ability to plan in advance in logical ways; a fine capacity not to worry oneself or others about insignificant matters.

b. *General Character Difficulties:* The tendency to be overly active and nervous; too much pride in one's intellectual capabilities; selfishness through a sense of isolation; the manipulation of others, especially in terms of the use of other people's resources; mind games; overly strong attachment to materialism.

c. *To Be Cultivated:* Tolerance, sympathy, devotion, accuracy in detail, open-mindedness to other people's ideas.

d. *Mental:* The Third Ray mind at its highest is the vehicle for pure abstract thinking, and is thus the mind of the theoretical mathematician. Other mental traits include: the ability to sustain long periods of concentration in intellectual or philosophical pursuits; a wide view on all abstract questions; and the ability to communicate one's thoughts very clearly and powerfully. On a much lower level, it is the mind of the propagandist, who is able to manipulate the mental energies of others for his own purposes. Notice that one can be extremely intelligent but not necessarily Soul-centered.

e. *Emotional:* More involved with the love of nature and animals than with interpersonal "affairs of the heart"; objectification and analysis of feelings more prevalent than deep passions. When asked how he feels about something or someone, the Third Ray person will most likely begin his response by saying, "I think."

f. *Physical:* Mesomorphic, very well coordinated, good at sports and gymnastics; bodies tend to be able to carry out all the tasks demanded of them; active physical types who are eager to follow through physically on what they think.

The following Table of Correspondences of the three Rays of Aspect may prove to be helpful in understanding their interrelationships:

TABULATION 1:
TABLE OF CORRESPONDENCES

Ray One	Ray Two	Ray Three
Spirit	Soul	Matter
Monad	Soul	Personality
Life	Quality/Consciousness	Form
Father	Son	Holy Ghost
Shiva	Vishnu	Brahma
Male	Female	Androgyn
Will	Wisdom	Intelligence
Power	Love	Activity
Energy	Focus	Experience
Shamballa	Hierarchy	Humanity
Head	Heart	Throat
Vulcan	Jupiter	Saturn
Pluto	Sun	Earth
Cardinal	Fixed	Mutable
Initiate	Disciple	Ordinary Individual
Great Bear	Sirius	Pleiades

To summarize our brief examination of the three Rays of Aspect, we can say that Ray One is the reflection of the Father aspect, the Monad, the Ray of Will or Power, the One Who conceives the original Plan of creation on any plane or level of manifestation. Ray Two, the Love Ray, is the second aspect of the Trinity of Life. This is the aspect of the Son, Who is very closely connected to the Mother, the source/

matrix for all form. This second aspect represents the Soul, or factor of the Consciousness in Life. The Soul is the Master Builder Who works out the blueprint for creation. Ray Three of Active Intelligence connotes the actual builders and materializers of the Divine Plan of Creation. It is through the workers on the Third Ray and the plane of Mind that the Plan is brought into objective manifestation through the detailed activities of the Four Rays of Attribute.

THE FOUR RAYS OF ATTRIBUTE

In our solar system, the four Rays of Attribute express in much greater detail the various characteristics, traits, purposes, and activities of the three Rays of Aspect. They work in effect to broaden, distribute, and define the three major Rays. These four are all synthesized through the Third Ray of Active Intelligence.

There are certain major affinities between the Three and the Four which we should examine:

1. Rays One, Three, Five, and Seven are connected through the evolutionary movement of the power of life made manifest through concrete forms of expression. These great Forces are very involved with the functioning of intelligence and the structuring of matter into objective appearances. They are closely associated with the Laws underlying the movement of the Plan of creativity. Within these four Rays, there are two pairs which have an even closer affinity with one another:

   a. *Rays One and Seven* reveal in their interchange and connection the originating Power of Life as it is organized and expressed throughout the physical world of matter. As Ray One corresponds to the highest expression of Life on its most subtle (yet most powerful) plane of origination, Ray Seven corresponds to the densest—the physical plane—and is thus the plane of destination. Thus the two planes which correspond to the First and Seventh Rays anchor the entire scheme of the involutionary/evolutionary expression of creation.

   b. *Rays Three and Five* are the two Rays of the mind through which an originating idea or archetype becomes differentiated into the world of form. It is here that the "one becomes the many," expressed through the various factors of communication of intelligent activity. In effect, Ray Three can be considered the Higher Mind, while Ray Five corresponds to the lower mind. There are also two Sanskrit terms that can define the difference and relationship between the two major divisions of the mind as they work in connection with Rays Three and Five. One of these terms is *rupa manas,* which means "the mind of forms," and naturally corresponds to the activities of Ray Five. The other is *arupa manas,* meaning "the formless mind," or the mind of pure ideation, which is the correspondence of the working of the Third Ray.

2. Rays Two, Four, and Six are related to each other through the inner life, and deal with the abstract and spiritual nature. They relate to aspiration, the various forms of expression of love and devotion to ideals, as well as to the philosophically abstract. These three Rays are also very involved with the inspiration which leads to the artistic expressions of life, to beauty, and to the interconnection between the real and the ideal. These three Rays correspond to the quality or conscious aspect of Life, as they find their source in the Soul aspect. Here, too, is a pair of Rays that bear a very close affinity for one another:

   a. *Rays Two and Six* primarily govern the emotional life of a person, and have a great deal to do with the nature of his emotional or astral body. Rays Two and Six endow traits and characteristics to a person's desire nature, and point to the types of emotional situations that are magnetized into his life. It is through the work of these two Rays that aspiration to the reality of the Soul's Life is made possible. In this respect, Rays Two and Six are aided by the Ray most strongly connected to the Path of Discipleship—Ray Four. As we shall soon discover, the Fourth Ray functions to harmonize and balance the inner world and the outer—the world of Soul and the world of personality.

3. In terms of *the life of the personality,* the following Ray relationships predominate:

   a. *Rays One, Four, and Five* are strongly connected with a person's *mental* life, and have a great deal to do with the nature and quality of his mental body.
   b. *Rays Two and Six,* as mentioned above, govern the *emotional* life and the emotional or astral body.
   c. *Rays Three and Seven* apply to the nature of the vital, *physical* life and are closely connected to the physical body.

4. The four Rays of Attribute are also seen as "blended Rays"— expressions of the interrelationships between the three major Rays of Aspect. These blendings work out as follows:

   a. *Ray Four, Harmony through Conflict,* also known as the "Ray of Harmony, Beauty and Art," is a blending of Rays One and Two.
   b. *Ray Five, Concrete Knowledge,* is a blending of Rays One and Three.

c. *Ray Six, Devotion and Idealism,* is a blending of Rays Two and Three.

d. *Ray Seven, Ceremonial Order,* is also known as the "Ray of Synthesis," as it is a blending of Rays One, Two, and Three.

A very important note: As a person evolves from a personality-centered life to a Soul-centered one, the Ray of the Soul gradually absorbs the Ray energies involved with the personality, and then proceeds to dominate the life. This process of absorption is a major aspect of the evolutionary process of the unfolding of consciousness. As the Soul *is* consciousness, its gradual externalization through the absorption and synthesis of the personality and its Rays is very much the foundation of individual development.

The Fourth Ray:
The Ray of Harmony through Conflict

SIGNS: **Taurus, Scorpio, Sagittarius**   PLANETS: **Mercury, Moon**

SYMBOL:

Form and its Soul are merged. The inner vision watches o'er the fusion, knows the divine relation and sees the two as one. But from that point of high attainment, a higher vision blazes forth before the opened inner eye. The three are one, and not alone the two. Pass on, O pilgrim on the Way.

—Alice A. Bailey[12]

The Fourth Ray is especially connected to humanity as it corresponds to the Fourth Kingdom of Man, and represents the struggle inherent in the human nature: that between the instinctual, animal life of the Third Kingdom, and the conscious life of the Soul— the Fifth Kingdom, wherein dwells the Planetary Hierarchy, the Illuminati of the Age. The fourth center of energy (chakra) in a human being is the one at the heart. Its placement between the three lower centers and the three higher (and their corresponding kingdoms and planes of manifestation) clearly reveals the purpose of the Fourth Ray as an agent of balance. (The chakras form an essential aspect of the occult study of human anatomy. They are most important to the study of esoteric psychology, the relationship of the psychological interchange between the Soul and the personality.

---

[12]*Esoteric Psychology,* vol. 1, p. 70.

Their function in terms of Soul-centered astrology is found in chapter 8.)

The Fourth Ray is often referred to as the Ray of the "art of living," as it is in our daily human lives that we find those crises of reorientation that contrast our lower self with our Higher, leading us eventually to the Path. It is little wonder then that the Fourth Ray is the Ray of the Disciple, and that the primary sign associated with its expression is Scorpio, the sign of death, transformation, and rebirth.

Sagittarius, the sign of the Centaur, is also connected to the Fourth Ray and to the Path of Discipleship. This particular sign of duality personifies the struggle to align the Higher Mind and its philosophical aspirations with the very human urge to explore the sensory nature of our physical world. The resolution of this conflict (indeed, this is one of the main purposes of Fourth Ray energy and its accompanying life experiences) produces the "one-pointed Disciple." This is a person who has been able to integrate the personality into the life of the Soul and emerge victorious.

Taurus, the third sign connected to the Fourth Ray, is preeminently the one of beauty and the arts. It is primarily a sign of form, and yet its planetary ruler from the Soul level is Vulcan, the Destroyer of Form—the planet which most strongly releases the energy of the First Ray of Will/Power. It is the creation of the various forms of life and the ultimate release of consciousness from them that constitutes the lessons of daily living. It is from these conflicts that the individual learns the proper relationship between energy and form. As the Fourth Ray is a blend of Rays One and Two, this lesson is not only most appropriate, but is also inherent to its nature.

The Fourth Ray, through its connection to the fourth plane of Buddhi or Intuition, allows humankind to evolve to a place in which the intellect is transcended by a far deeper attunement and understanding of life. It is, after all, the development of intuition that allows the individual to perceive the essential energy of life contained within appearance, so that he is not blinded by the material manifestations in front of his eyes. This quality of perception can only come through his struggles to grow. In terms of human life, such struggles have a great deal to do with death and loss.

The passion of the Crucifixion of Jesus is very much the Cosmic Drama of the Fourth Ray. This act of sacrifice (the word itself coming from Latin roots meaning "to make holy") is, in effect, the objectification of the Path of Discipleship. It is here that the lower self is given up to its Higher Vehicle of expression, the Soul. Yet in the New Age, physical crucifixion is not the way of the seeker on the Path of Eternal Knowledge. The transformation of the lower self into the Higher will be through the direct revelation of that knowledge which comes through the seeker's efforts at growth and transformation.

The Fourth Ray leads to that type of discrimination required for the life of the Soul and the way of service. It brings to us those conflicts which work to release us from the illusions and glamours that inhibit our perception of right and wrong, in terms of our own karmic patterns. It is thus the Ray of trial and error, so that we may move from the unreal to the real.

The Fourth Ray is the energy behind what we may call "Divine Discontent." Since the Fourth is the Ray of humanity itself, and fully 60 percent of all people have a Fourth Ray mental body, this kind of discontent, of never feeling fully satisfied, of the urge for better and better ways for self-expression, is a typical one for the majority of us. From the esoteric perspective, divine discontent is actually the difficulty one experiences when the outer life does not allow for the fullest expression of the inner life; when the lower self is not in alignment or harmony with the Higher.

There is a common rhythm for those crises brought on through the urgency of Fourth Ray energy. It may be outlined as follows: A person finds herself in a relative state of *harmony,* but then a certain *change* enters her life, shifting the status quo. Such a change brings on the tensions of *struggle* between the past and the unfolding future, between the urge for things to stay the same and the inevitability of transformation. A *battle* ensues between the two opposing forces, which leads to a passing and a *death of the form* of the situation. She is left with the struggle to *reconstruct a new form* out of the experiences of the battle that has just taken place. This new form consolidates and settles, and once again there is *harmony*—until the entrance of the next change! Is this not the rhythm and movement of Scorpio? The Fourth Ray, the human state, forces the resolution of conflict, the harmonizing of the pairs of opposites, and the eventual evolution from the focus of instinct and desire to the release into consciousness and pure, essential love.

As the Ray of beauty and art, the Fourth Ray is also essentially the refiner—the urge for an ever-more-perfect representation of the Will of God in the many forms of Its expression. The true artist is constantly struggling to present through painting, sculpture, music, film, and the written word, a clarification of an idea or a feeling which may properly express his inner aspirations or life urgings. Anyone who has ever stood before an empty canvas, a formless lump of clay, a quiet piano, a case of unused film, or a ream of unmarked paper, and struggled with that need to bring form out of or to any of the above, has surely confronted the energies of the Fourth Ray. The Tibetan Master shares the balance, harmony, and struggle which is fostered by the Fourth Ray in the following words:

Colour, and yet no colour now is seen. Sound and the soundless One meet in an infinite point of peace. Time and the timeless One negate the thoughts of men. . . . Form is there found, and yet the psychic sense reveals that which the form is powerless to hide, the inner synthesis . . . that point of unity which—when it is duly reached—reveals a further point where all the three are one, and not the two alone.[13]

Some of the other names associated with the Fourth Ray are: the Link between the Three and the Three; the Divine Intermediary; the Corrector of the Form; and the Master.

The Fourth is the Ray of struggle, and those people who are especially connected to it will find a very special duality appearing in their lives. The qualities of activity and inertia are here so equally in proportion that Fourth Ray individuals may find themselves torn between the love of ease and pleasure and the need to take consistent action. This is one conflict shared by both Taurean and Sagittarian individuals. As the Ray of the artist, the Fourth is especially connected to color. People who are closely associated with this Ray may find themselves with tremendous gifts. They may also find it extremely difficult to focus and externalize their talents, due to the aspect of inertia which is so much a characteristic of this Ray type. It is through courage and sustained vision that the Fourth Ray type overcomes inertia, and once this occurs, is extremely and dynamically creative. Although the Fourth is not the easiest Ray of expression, the resulting awareness which comes from living out its struggles creates the pathway of intimate contact to the resolution of all crises—the love which is the consciousness of the Soul. Indeed, as the Fourth is the Ray of the Human Kingdom in nature, it is one which we all share.

Keywords and Key Phrases of the Fourth Ray

1. *Concept:* The principle of beauty existing in all things; the urge to balance opposing tendencies in order to bring about a greater harmony; the art of living; the urge to achieve perfection.

2. *Soul Level:* The "Divine Artist"—one who seeks to raise humanity's consciousness through the realization of the beauty and harmony existing in nature and in the world of forms; the mediator between heaven and earth, God and man; the Priest.

[13]In Bailey's *Esoteric Psychology*, vol. 1, p. 70.

3. *Personality Level:* Ray of the mediator, interpreter, artist, and those healers whose treatments involve the harmonizing and balancing of the body's energies and polarities—acupuncture, certain techniques of massage, color therapy.

    a. *General Positive Traits:* Strong sense of equilibrium and symmetry; a poetic sensibility, especially about nature; imaginative and creative in the formation of one's life-style; can sustain struggle and conflict until desired aims are achieved.

    b. *General Character Difficulties:* Indolence, self-indulgence; may be overly passionate; may initiate conflicts unnecessarily; restlessness and a tendency to depression when goals cannot be accomplished. (Since the Fourth is very much a blend of Rays One and Two, when the energy of the First Ray of Will/Power is not in balance with the Second Ray, the resulting lack of direction for the expression of Will is clearly marked. This demonstrates as a poorly focused sense of personal orientation to life and a resultant lack of willpower.)

    c. *To Be Cultivated:* Serenity, emotional balance, confidence, self-control, truth, clarity of purpose.

    d. *Mental:* Urge to understand the underlying meaning which can resolve opposing ideas and philosophies; need to construct new forms of ideas out of existing ones; may sustain opposing ideas and opinions indefinitely, thus producing perpetual inner conflicts; ideas are visualized as forms in the mind.

    e. *Emotional:* Mood swings with great highs and lows; strong passions; can be compulsive, and is prone to exaggerate feelings; strong and loyal affections; sympathy for the struggles of others; generous and courageous.

    f. *Physical:* Tendency for balanced, well-proportioned bodies; will like to adorn themselves, as the need to express physical beauty is very strong.

The Fifth Ray:
The Ray of Concrete Knowledge

SIGNS: *Leo, Sagittarius, Aquarius*   **PLANET: *Venus***

SYMBOL:

A beam of light illuminates the form; the hidden now appears. Knowledge of God and how He veils Himself finds consummation in the thoughts of man . . . and this—the love which maketh all things new—must stand revealed. This is the purpose back of all the acts of this great Lord of Knowledge.

—Alice A. Bailey[14]

Just as the Fourth Ray prepares for the expression of Love/Wisdom through attunement to intuition via the struggles of daily life, the Fifth Ray is the expression of Love/Wisdom through the intellect. This occurs through scientific research and experimentation in order that the Plan of Divinity may be revealed through the mind of man. It will be at that point that Knowledge will eventually express Wisdom. It is thus that the Fifth Ray is connected to the Second, but it is also very closely linked to the Third Ray of Active Intelligence. It is the purpose of the Higher Mind to penetrate and purify the lower so that humanity may perceive, identify, and know the Mind of God behind all the forms of manifestation. This is the great work of the Fifth Ray from the esoteric perspective, and *the reason for the development of the intellect*. By obtaining right knowledge, the Fourth Kingdom of humanity will achieve complete balance, and thus be ready for its entry into the world of the Fifth Kingdom—the realm of the Soul.

As the sign Aquarius is on the Fifth Ray and on no other, the scientist and researcher will lead the way into the esoteric realities in our time, and reveal through their work those metaphysical Laws and Principles which underlie the Ancient Wisdom Teachings. The work of such men as Albert Einstein, Fritz Capra, Nikola Tesla, Albert Szent-Gyorgyi, Stephen Hawkins, and others are examples of this type of Fifth Ray scientist. We should recall that Uranus, planet of experimentation, is the exoteric planetary ruler of this sign, while Jupiter, which is the vehicle for the Second Ray, stands behind Aquarius and the Age from the perspective of the Soul. Both Uranus and Jupiter work to unite—Uranus from the place of Mind, and Jupiter from the place of the Heart.

Venus, the natural harmonizer of the solar system, is the planet most closely associated with the Fifth Ray. As the esoteric ruler of Gemini, it works to link the energies of the Higher and the lower mental worlds. (See tabulation 3, p. 155.) She is the unifying factor behind duality. In terms of the exoteric interpretation of the natal horoscope, a person with Venus in Gemini at birth would most likely have two relationships occurring simultaneously, setting up a conflict of interest. Yet the purpose of such a situation, when viewed esoterically, is to find the synthesis between the two kinds of loving which these relationships tend to represent as archetypes. The lessons learned through this struggle of duality often work to allow this individual to

[14]*Esoteric Psychology*, vol. 1, p. 75.

become a vehicle for harmonious human relationships in general. Thus Venus in Gemini gives the potential to raise a person's consciousness about the nature of love—not just on the personal level, but in terms of the collective, as well.

Sagittarius is the embodiment of the duality existent between the lower mind of the personality and the Higher Mind of the Soul, the resolution and harmonizing of which leads to the "one-pointed Disciple." Yet it is Leo which is the controlling factor of this Ray. The development of mind leads to the development of individuality. It is this sense of "self-creation," this sense of self-identification through the dynamics of one's own creativity, that is essentially Leonian in nature. Present-day humanity is very much influenced by the Fifth Ray and its expression through education, science, technology, and psychology. There is a science behind the use of the mind which, if learned and understood, brings about that necessary step of self-knowing and self-actualization which is absolutely essential to the process of the expansion of human consciousness. The Fifth Ray is "in reality, that on which a man learns to use all acquired knowledge of the 'form divine' in such a way that the inner life is served and the outer form becomes the magnetic expression of the divine life."[15]

The Fifth Ray, through this influence of Venus, also brings into life the energies of the sign Libra as they work out in the outer, daily life. This evokes a point of balance or equilibrium, making possible the next step in the course of the evolution of Right Human Relations. The Tibetan Master teaches that Libra will be active in a most potent way during the last part of the current century. This is most interesting for the astrologer, as both Pluto and Uranus transited this sign during the 1970s, which was a time of incredible social change in our society. This was the period of intense activity in terms of women's liberation and the repolarization of the roles inherent in sexual relations, leading to many forms of alternative life-styles.

Some of the other names used in association with the Fifth Ray are: the Revealer of Truth, the Door into the Mind of God, the Guardian of the Door, the Dispenser of Knowledge, the Keeper of the Secret, and the Master of the Hierophants. These names let us see the clear connection between the Third Ray and the distribution of its energies through the activities of the Fifth. People who are very closely linked to the influence of the Ray of Concrete Knowledge are very analytical by nature. They insist upon logic in all things, and will not tolerate woolly or undisciplined thinking. They need to see everything that is conjectural proved through measurement and the scientific method.

[15]Bailey, *Discipleship in the New Age*, vol. 1, p. 542.

In this respect, they do not readily get along with abstract philosophers or those more intuitively inclined.

As the scientists and technicians of the world, people of the Fifth Ray have keen intellects and tend to be very accurate in detail. These are the computer whizzes and the programmers, processors, and categorizers of information and data. With their great love of knowledge, this type of individual is strongly attracted to mental games and intellectual gymnastics. The subjective world of metaphysical inquiry does not draw them, and they will challenge spiritual assertions at every turn, always seeking to reduce or destroy (and in the case of the more evolved, prove) the more intuitively experiential by the weight of sheer logic and mental domination. Their attitude is usually one of: "If it can't be seen or 'realistically' proven, it does not exist." Since the mind so completely dominates the life, many Fifth Ray people can be said to be very judgmental, critical, and rather separatist in their outlooks. Yet the more evolved of Fifth Ray-influenced people will, through the scientific method, seek to prove the validity of metaphysical inquiry.

The contributions they make to the well-being of society are limitless. It is this group that produces all the lifesaving devices of medicine (thereby revealing the Fifth as a subray of the Second Ray of Love/Wisdom and healing). It is the Concrete Mind that produces the rockets that will take mankind to the other planets and solar systems, and by so doing, create those reorientations of consciousness that allow mankind to view the universe as the creation of the Divine. The Fifth Ray is especially involved with the communication sciences, and most specifically, with light and electricity. In this respect, laser technology is under its domain. Mankind is constantly seeking ways to enhance the domination and control of the environment. This requires an ever-increasing understanding and deeper penetration into the Laws of Matter.

Scientific investigation is the primary vehicle for these discoveries, yet this particular scenario presents some inherent dangers. We have tremendous evidence in our century of the Fifth Ray personality or mind becoming detached from its Second Ray parent. It is then that science goes astray, the mind separating itself from the orientation toward unity stimulated by Venus and Love. The technology of death then becomes the focal point for the expression of Fifth Ray energy, and science is perverted by the economic or power urgings of the personality-based and -abased groups of individuals seeking the exploitation of others. In this respect, the reader should examine the relationship that exists between the First, Third, Fifth, and Seventh Rays to see how such circumstances eventuate. Humanity achieves its highest manifestation when, as an agent of the Fourth Ray, it stands as a balance between the two great "lines of energy" of One-Three-Five-Seven and Two-Four-Six. It is through the influence of the Fifth, as the collective personality Ray of humanity, that the battle to integrate these Forces is played out in our century.

Keywords and Key Phrases of the Fifth Ray

1. *Concept:* The vehicle of expression for the Ideas in the Mind of God; the urge to reveal Law through intellect; the power to express Divinity through deep penetration into matter.

2. *Soul Level:* Those who work to be connecting links of intelligence between the abstract world of pure ideation and the concrete world of practical application; precision and exactitude in creating those forms and inventions which allow for the outpouring of Higher-Mind Intelligence.

3. *Personality Level:* Ray of the scientist, technician, lawyer, engineer, researcher, computer expert, and logician.

   a. *General Positive Traits:* Power to master a chosen field of expertise; detached observer in quest for truth; accuracy in speech; precise mental perceptions and vision for the application of knowledge; love of scientific inquiry.

   b. *General Character Difficulties:* Lacking in compassion and sympathy; an overly narrow perspective; constant analysis and the splitting of hairs; pedantic; overemphasis on the form aspect of life; materialism; harsh criticism, mental pride, prejudice.

   c. *To Be Cultivated:* Intellectual tolerance; devotion, active love, nurturing, reverence, and sympathy.

   d. *Mental:* Primary vehicle of expression; the direction of logic has to be taken to its conclusion; works with precision and detail in structuring the externalization of ideas; great need for specialization of interest; thirst for knowledge accomplished through seeking, searching, probing, and experimentation; urge to determine the cause and effect of things through verifiable proofs.

   e. *Emotional:* Although the Fifth Ray is rarely, if ever, seen as the vehicle for the expression of the astral body, its strength as the Ray of the personality or the mind can overshadow an individual's emotional Ray energy. In this case, feelings always become subordinate to thoughts, leading to a certain sense of personal isolation and emotional defensiveness.

   f. *Physical:* The Fifth Ray is rarely, if ever, the Ray of the physical body.

The Sixth Ray:
The Ray of Devotion and Idealism

SIGNS: *Virgo, Sagittarius, Pisces*   PLANETS: *Mars, Neptune*

SYMBOL:

The Crusade is on. The warriors march upon their way. They crush and kill. . . . March toward the light. The work goes forward. The workers veil their eyes from pity as from fear. . . . The form must disappear so that the loving spirit may enter into rest. The cross is reared on high; the form is laid thereon. . . . They mount upon the cross. Through war, through work, through pain and toil, the purpose is achieved.

—Alice A. Bailey[16]

The Sixth has been the primary Ray of the Piscean Age. It is foremost the stimulator of religious devotion and idealism, but since A.D. 1625, its effects, as well as the energies of the Age which it inspired, have been gradually withdrawing from manifestation. At the same time, the Seventh Ray energies of the Aquarian Age have been growing stronger, as they imprint their messages upon the collective consciousness of humanity.

The Sixth is on the same line of force as the Second and Fourth Rays. In this respect, we see in its expression the outpouring of the urge for Love/Wisdom in connection with the Ray energy of Harmony through Conflict. Mars and Neptune are the two planets most closely associated with the Ray of Devotion and Idealism. Mars is the exoteric focus, while Neptune serves as the esoteric, Soul-level one. This indicates that the movement toward the revelation of the universal love which is so much a part of the highest, transcendental influence of Neptune, is often masked and colored by the exclusivistic and warlike nature of Mars. The devotional qualities of the Sixth Ray have often been expressed in the world through the vehicle of religious wars. When we add to the above influences the energies of Virgo's urge to be of service, the idealistic adventurism so closely associated with Sagittarius, and the need for self-sacrifice so characteristic of Pisces, we can also see the roots for the fanatical facets of the Sixth Ray when expressed through Mars and the personality.

The Crusades and the Inquisition are manifestations of this dynamic of Sixth-Ray activity, as well as outpourings from the height

[16]*Esoteric Psychology*, vol. 1, p. 79–80.

(or depth, if you will) of the Piscean Age. On its Soul level, the Catholic church is also very much an expression of the Sixth Ray, as the martyrdom and self-sacrifice of Lord Jesus are so much the founding archetypes for spiritual aspirations. On the personality level, this religion is much more closely connected to the Seventh Ray of hierarchical and ceremonial order.

The Sixth Ray is closely associated with the astral plane, and during the Piscean Age, people were far more sensitive to this level of manifestation than they are today. This meant that such lower astral entities as ghosts and goblins, some types of fairies and elves, plus a host of other creatures and entities, were quite accessible to the everyday consciousness of ordinary men and women. The often loathsome creatures which decorate the Gothic churches of Europe were very much a part of daily awareness. Mystical visions, interchanges with saints and demonic forces, were all realities to the astrally sensitive consciousness prevalent during the Dark and Middle Ages.

The fear and persecution of cats (who, as "psychic batteries," are very attuned to the astral plane), the suppression of women, and the superstitions associated with witchcraft (more often than not, forms of nature worship and herbal healing methods), are also manifestations of the urge to control and limit the outpourings of psychic or astral energy. This was also the time of sexual prohibitions and the enforcement (as well as the religious idealization) of chastity. From an astrological perspective, the latter (as applied and practiced during the Piscean Era) were lower manifestations of the Sixth Ray; that is, Neptune and Mars combining to veil and mystify the natural expression of sexuality and its associative release of emotional and psychic energy.

The other, brighter side of the Sixth Ray during the Piscean Age is personified by the legends of King Arthur, the Knights of the Round Table, and the Search for the Holy Grail. This was romanticism at its highest, exemplified through the code of chivalry, which is still the basis for manners and etiquette in most Western societies. The idealism of the Sixth Ray, and its connection to the signs Virgo and Sagittarius, have impressed and influenced male-female relationships for the past thousand years. It has given rise to the archetype of the "white knight" on his Arabian charger (or in his German sports car) always coming to the rescue of the beautiful maiden in virginal white, who is ever eager to receive him!

People and groups which are strongly influenced by the Sixth Ray will indeed lay down their lives for the object or concept of their devotion. Yet this orientation is so exclusive that people with different beliefs are considered pariahs, or worse! The crusading, spiritual warrior with a sword in the shape of the cross is a typical illustration of the Sixth Ray orientation.

This single-mindedness is clearly illustrated by the way in which the Spanish laity and church conquered the New World. There was total slaughter and destruction, and absolute disregard for any existing spiritual belief systems. And yet, the Sixth Ray heart could sincerely believe that the burning of thousands of bodies would "save" thousands of souls. This kind of extreme dualism was very expressive of the dominance of the Sixth Ray during the Age of Pisces. It was further exaggerated by the influence of Mars and the primary controlling sign, Sagittarius, as it unfolded through the personality level.

The religious creeds and ideals connected to martyrdom are still influential wherever Sixth Ray energy predominates. We must keep in mind that the Seventh Ray, Aquarian Age energies and archetypes are very new and have not supplanted the previous Ray/Age energies yet. "Holy War" is very much an integrated and highly respected aspect of fundamental Islam. Islamic martyrs achieve an instantaneous place in Heaven, very much as do those Christians who die for the defense or propagation of their faith. This Sixth Ray attitude was also present in the Japanese "Code of Bushido," when devotion to the emperor during World War II was the underlying inspiration for institutionalized suicide. Terrorism, suicide, and all other urges for self-annihilation based on religious and/or philosophical idealism are very much under the influence of the Sixth Ray.

In terms of religious wars, the influence of the Sixth Ray is still quite active in the Holy Land, Northern Ireland, and in South Africa. Not only are there wars in these countries between Moslem and Jew, Catholic and Protestant, white and black, respectively, but in all of these sorrowful situations, there is an abundance of fanatical terrorism on both sides. There are, of course, additional economic reasons for these conflicts, but all holy wars are, in reality, a cornerstone of racial and tribal religious sects.

It can easily be deduced from the above that the Sixth Ray, in its lower, personality-focused expression, tends toward an extreme narrowness of belief, as well as a one-pointed, self-righteous approach to religion. The current surge in fundamental, evangelical Christianity, with its inherent dualism and strongly emotional message of pain, suffering, sin, and redemption, is also archetypical of the influences of the Sixth Ray at the end of the Piscean Era.

It should not be inferred from all that has been said above that the Sixth is the "Bad Ray"! This is not true. One finds in its expression those devotional qualities that keep families together, instill great and small philanthropic gestures, and denote such saintly people as Mother Teresa and St. Francis of Assisi. It was the Sixth Ray (in connection with the First, and certainly the Second) that characterized the Passion of Lord Jesus. The Sixth Ray is also the inspiring force of people for whom the principles of Love, Goodness, Purity of Heart, and Selflessness are living energies and form their way of life.

> Each individual person has been created to love, and to be loved. Doesn't matter race, doesn't matter religion—every single man, woman, child is a child of God, in the image of God, and that is what we look at.
>
> —Mother Teresa

The Sixth Ray is, however, primarily connected to the solar plexus center and the astral plane, which are locations for the expression of emotion and personal desire. On the level of the personality, focused through Mars, emotion and desire have the tendency to take on selfish and exclusivistic expressions. But when these two qualities of human expression are transformed (through the lessons of Scorpio and the energies of the Fourth Ray) and reoriented to the Soul level, they become instead Intuition and Spiritual Will, and are then ready to be utilized in an individualistic way for the good of the collective. It is then that the Sixth Ray is functioning through Neptune at its highest, and becomes a tremendous vehicle for the loving focus of the Christ Consciousness.

Some of the names associated with the Sixth Ray and its forces and energies are: the Negator of Desire, the Warrior on the March, the Crucifier and the Crucified, the Devotee of Life, and the Sword Bearer of the Logos.

In order for us to have a more personal connection to the energies of the Rays, let us examine the influence of each of the seven as they work through the astral body. The astral plane, as mentioned, is primarily governed by the Sixth Ray, as it is the sixth plane of manifestation (see tabulation 2, p. 140).

The Influence of the Rays Expressing Through the Astral Body

First Ray: A person with a First Ray astral body can give the impression of being cold, distant, and aloof. Such an individual considers many of the emotional ups and downs of relationships to be quite trivial and not too worthy of attention. Yet the emotions can be very deep, and are usually evoked through some form of noble sentiment, such as love of country and attachment to family tradition.

Second Ray: A highly developed Second Ray astral body expresses the purest kind of love. It is gentle, never separatist, and totally supportive in nature. An individual with such an astral body tends to love all and be loved by everybody in return. A person with a less developed Second Ray astral body can be too full of sentimentality and emotional expectations for his own welfare.

Third Ray: As the primary mental Ray, people who express their emotions through the Third Ray are not overly romantic, nor are they geared to deep emotional responses. Since the Third Ray corresponds to the animal kingdom, one usually finds that individuals who are in the forefront of animal protectionism and natural conservation are highly affected by a Third Ray astral body.

Fourth Ray: This influence tends to express itself through the arts. The emotions exhibited by a person with a Fourth Ray astral vehicle would most likely be through a love for art, music, and dance. There is a deep appreciation of beauty, although on a personal level, the emotions may be quite self-disciplined. This is so that the person may express a balanced presentation of his feelings. A person with a less developed Fourth Ray astral body would tend to be compulsive, and would need to learn how to channel his emotions correctly so that they are properly integrated into the whole of the personality.

Fifth Ray: This is very rarely a vehicle for the astral body. When there is an emotional expression of the Fifth Ray, it would tend to manifest as a love of knowledge—especially in a very specific area of expertise.

Sixth Ray: As one would expect, Sixth Ray emotional bodies tend to produce people who are very devotional and idealistic by nature. When not highly evolved, this can lead to the type of blind devotion most commonly demonstrated by members of exclusivistic religious cults and sects. A collective expression of Sixth Ray "emotional madness" was the mass suicide at Jonestown. On an individual basis, such an undeveloped emotional vehicle can lead to involvements in very abusive relationships, where devotion and loyalty at any price are underlying motivations. On a higher level, a Sixth Ray emotional body can lead to the vision and faith of the mystic, the altruism of a server of humanity, and the selfless devotion and caring expressed by so many nurses and religious workers (not to mention an "army" of mothers!).

Seventh Ray: As this is the Ray of Ceremonial Order, people with Seventh Ray emotional bodies tend to manifest those feelings which are right and appropriate for the set of circumstances in which they find themselves. A less evolved Seventh Ray astral body would tend to produce an individual who may be particularly socially inept, whose responses are always out of sync with what is expected of him. As Uranus is the primary planetary expression of the Seventh Ray, this behavior is most typical when the Moon is afflicted by Uranus in the natal chart, or when she is in Aquarius with difficult aspects, especially from Mars (Sixth Ray ruler). Finally, a Seventh Ray astral body may indicate a person who is a lover of pomp and circumstance of all kinds.

Keywords and Key Phrases of the Sixth Ray

1. *Concept:* Intense focus of one-pointed devotion to ideals or beliefs; the purification of the emotions by the mind (Ray Six is a blending of Rays Two and Three).

2. *Soul Level:* The urge to transform selfish and personal motivation into selfless, impersonal devotion for the good of all; the bringing about of circumstances which reorient the exclusive to the inclusive for the greater expression of Love/Wisdom.

3. *Personality Level:* Ray of the saint, martyr, evangelist/preacher, religious workers of all kinds, psychics, mediums, many kinds of healers, theologians, poets, etc.

   a. *General Positive Traits:* Reverence and devotion; single-mindedness when attached to a cause; courage to fight for beliefs; love, tenderness, loyalty, sincerity, self-sacrifice.

   b. *General Character Difficulties:* Fanaticism; blind devotion; bigotry and prejudice; exclusive attitudes; hero worship; overly dependent on others for emotional support.

   c. *To Be Cultivated:* Tolerance; truth; common sense and practicality; flexibility to be supportive of other people's views; balance of one's feelings.

   d. *Mental:* Devotion to beliefs and opinions; can be narrow-minded or very universal, depending on level of development; much more intuitive and sensitive than logical or precise; can shape thoughts and ideas to suit personal ideals and creeds.

   e. *Emotional:* Please refer to previous paragraphs about Sixth Ray astral body.

   f. *Physical:* Distinct tendency to be overweight; large and bulky frame with a leaning toward water retention; very sensitive to alcohol and other drugs; endomorph.

The Seventh Ray:
The Ray of Ceremonial Order and Magic

SIGNS: *Aries, Cancer, Capricorn*   PLANET: *Uranus*

SYMBOL:[17]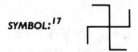

"Let the Temple of the Lord be built," the seventh great Angel cried ... seven great sons of God moved with measured pace. ... The work of building thus began. ... The temple grew in beauty. ... Thus shall the temple of the light be carried from heaven to earth ... God has created in the light. His sons can now create. ... "Let the work proceed. Let the sons of God create."

—Alice A. Bailey[18]

The Seventh Ray, and the energies of the Aquarian Age which it stimulates, began coming into manifestation in the current world cycle in the year A.D. 1675, while the influences of the Sixth Ray and the Piscean Era were just beginning to wane. As the New Age energies gain in the strength of their expression, the characteristics of the Seventh Ray will become increasingly apparent to us all.[19]

The Seventh Ray is essentially an agent of fusion, blending, and coordination. Its main function is to work for the infusion of the energies of spirit with the substance of matter. "Matter and energy are interchangeable" is the message contained within Einstein's formula of relativity: $E = mc^2$. "Matter is Spirit at its lowest point of manifestation, and Spirit is matter at its highest," said Madame Blavatsky.

---

[17]The right-hand swastika is an ancient symbol of the Sun. It demonstrates, through the rotation of its arms, the course taken by the Sun in the Northern Hemisphere, which appears to travel from the east and then move south to the west. It is an incredibly ancient symbol consistent with good fortune and prosperity. The name "swastika" is derived from the Sanskrit *svastika*, meaning "conducive to well-being." This name in turn comes from two Sanskrit roots, *su* or "well" and *asti*, from the verb "to be," indicating "it is." This right-handed swastika has been used as a symbol for the positive expression of life by the ancient Mesopotamians, the early Christians and Byzantines, the Mayans, as well as the Navajos. Today it is still used in Bali among the Hindu Indonesians, as well as in India itself, with Jains and Buddhists also employing it as a harbinger of good fortune. This swastika should therefore not be confused with the "sauvastika" or left-handed, black swastika, which was used during World War II. The latter is a symbol of the night, and the demonic Hindu goddess of death, Kali.

[18]Bailey, *Esoteric Psychology*, vol. 1, pp. 83–84.

[19]Chapter 4: "The Laws and Principles of the New Age," outlined several of the more apparent Seventh Ray influences. Other points of interest in this respect which specifically contrast the effects of the Sixth and Seventh Rays in terms of the World Ages may be found on pp. 357–375 of Alice A. Bailey's *Esoteric Psychology*, vol. 1.

"When matter and spirit vibrate at the same rate, evolution and involution will cease," say the Ancient Wisdom Teachings. Thus the Seventh Ray demonstrates itself most clearly through the transformation of matter. In this respect, it is the working of the Seventh Ray which aids in the fusion of the Soul and the personality, and the resulting reorientation of an individual's life purpose and direction. It is this process of Soul infusion that can be symbolically rendered by the Seventh Ray alchemist as the process of changing lead into gold. The hope for the Aquarian Age, the Age of the Seventh Ray, is for such a "golden," collective transformation and reorientation to take place for humanity. Certainly the opportunities are there for us to do so.

The Seventh Ray is particularly associated with the seventh plane of manifestation—the physical. Its purpose, therefore, in terms of physical reality, is to bring out into objective appearance all the latent spiritual qualities contained within a given form. An individual who has actively integrated his or her lower and Higher selves and is living the life of a spiritually realized human being reveals it in the special radiation he exudes.

The Seventh also brings its quality of radiation into the mineral kingdom, to which it is especially connected. It is this Seventh Ray influence which stimulates the intense qualities of attractiveness and potency in gemstones, as well as the inherent radioactivity of certain elements. The Seventh is most particularly the Ray of crystals. The current interest in crystals as focalizers of energy and as talismans of all sorts testifies to this increase in experimentation with Seventh Ray energy for the purposes of transmutation and transformation. The fads and glamour currently associated with crystals (such as the creation and promotion of occultly meaningless crystal jewelry) will fade. But the recognition of the esoteric value of crystals in terms of their healing properties has been reawakened from its origin in ancient, magical traditions. One should also take note of the fact that the color particularly associated with the Seventh Ray is violet. Of all the many kinds of crystals available at the present time, the amethyst variety seems to be especially popular.

This connection with the physical plane is most important, as it reveals the Seventh as the outer reflection of the potencies of the First Ray of Will/Power. The structuring, crystallizing effects of the Seventh Ray show the relationship between these two Rays as the externalization of Will and Power through the agency of Law and Order. The function of the Seventh Ray is to change those forms, both physical and mental, which are no longer of service to the Plan of the unfolding evolution of creativity. In this respect, we can see the deeper significance of Capricorn as the controlling sign of this Ray, and Uranus as its planetary focalizer.

It is the energy of Capricorn which coordinates and structures matter for the unfolding of higher purposes. Capricorn is the sign of the Initiate, indicating a person whose consciousness has been released from the thrall and desires of materialism. As such, the energy of life is freed to shape itself again and again, according to the needs and exigencies of the Soul.

Mind serves as the lens which brings the archetypical ideas created through the work of the Third Ray of Active Intelligence out into our daily life. This is accomplished through the many fields of Fifth Ray mental activity of concrete knowledge and research. This combination of the will to manifest (Ray One), essential idea (Ray Three), and form of idea (Ray Five), crystallizes in the materialization and presence of the will in the world of outer appearances (Ray Seven). The importance of Capricorn in this respect (as well as its planetary ruler, Saturn) should be noted, since three of the above-mentioned Rays (One, Three, and Seven) manifest their potencies through it.

Thought-forms are the building blocks of manifestation. The creation, continual adjustment and transformation, release, and material expression of thought-forms constitute much of the work of the interconnections between these Ray energies. The particular function of the Seventh Ray, in this respect, is the fusing and blending mechanism. As the Seventh Ray is the synthesis of the First, Second, and Third Rays (in reality, three subrays of the Second Ray), the presence of Second Ray energy within the essential make-up of the Seventh allows for this sustaining, harmonizing, and cohesive synthetic quality to express itself. (Further research into the nature of thought-forms and the wider functioning of the Seventh Ray may be found by a study of *A Treatise on White Magic,* by Alice A. Bailey.)

Uranus has a very important role to play in the outworking of the Seventh Ray. In both esoteric and exoteric astrology, Uranus acts as the higher octave for the expression of Mercury. The latter, as we know, is connected to the processes of communication, logic, and the functions of the rational mind. Uranus is much more connected to intuition and the birthplace of those archetypes and great Ideas which gradually filter down, through the process of involution, into the collective and individual consciousness.

The astrology student will recall that Uranus finds its exaltation in Scorpio and its fall in Taurus. This is equally true for both personality- and Soul-centered astrology. Yet the esoteric implications expand this concept. The nature of Taurus tends to fixate energy, binding it to matter and desire. This tends to inhibit the outworking of Uranian energy and the expression of new, evolutionary archetypes and thought-forms. Scorpio is the sign of death, transformation, and rebirth, and is particularly suited to the kind of activity which is associated with

Uranus—the revolutionary transformation of social concepts and ideals. It is through Scorpio that the personal values inherent in Taurus undergo certain necessary transmutations. This process allows these values to fuse and become part of the collective orientation of Aquarius, the sign of Uranus's exoteric rulership. The interchange between Uranus and Capricorn indicates the great potential social and personal conflicts of the New Age and the outworking of the Seventh Ray on the material plane. If more of the Second Ray energy contained within the Seventh is invoked by the massed intent and group endeavor of men and women of goodwill, we will see an era in which consistent originality of ideas will birth those products and services that will be of benefit to all. Clear lines of communication will be made possible through advanced technology, and the blending and cohesion of humanitarian purposefulness can give rise to world cooperation as it has never been seen before.

This will require an enormous amount of harmonious fusion and blending, as the two energies—Uranus and Capricorn—are essentially opposite in the way they externalize. Therefore, there is a potential conflict from their interchange if they are not properly anchored through the encompassing Ray of Love/Wisdom. This would most likely manifest as a polarization between the forces of innovation and social reformation (Uranus) and those structures of established thought-forms of law and order (Capricorn, when externalizing from the personality level). The years 1988 and 1989 are most important in this respect. It is during this time—the time that this book is being written and produced—that the great Saturn (ruler of Capricorn) and Uranus (ruler of Aquarius) conjunctions are taking place. These conjunctions in Sagittarius (and the very close approximations of these two planets in Capricorn) are the complementary aspects to the conjunctions that took place in late Taurus and early Gemini in the 1940s. Those were the years when the great war between fascism (Saturn/Capricorn) and democracy (Uranus/Aquarius) took place. I believe that the transformations in the structuring of world power alliances, and the birthing of the new social archetypes that occurred as a result (and others that will result) of these two series of conjunctions (as well as the next Saturn-Uranus conjunction forty-five years hence), will create the basic structural framework for the evolution of global social direction for the New Age.

The Seventh Ray unifies, but it also contains the potential for conformity. This can be the emotional conformity of Cancer, where everyone shares the same feelings in order to lend security to the whole. It may also be the social conformity of etiquette and collective social behavioral patterns expressed through Libra. This is most notably demonstrated by Japan and the Japanese, who are a nation and a people strongly influenced by Libra and the Seventh Ray. And it can, of course, be the structual conformity of governmental organization, as exemplified by communism—that system of government most closely associated with the Seventh Ray. Although the sign Aquarius is associated exoterically with Uranus, and thus many of the externalized manifestations during the New Age will be closely associated with its influence, the energy *behind* the New Age is Jupiter, esoteric ruler of Aquarius, and the planet most closely associated with the Ray of Love/Wisdom. *It is this factor that is the great hope for the future of humanity.*

Like the other six Rays, the Seventh also has several other names associated with it. Some of these are: the Unveiled Magician; the Bestower of Light from the Second Lord; the Custodian of the Seventh Plane; the Builder of the Square; the Expression of the Will; and the Revealer of Beauty.

People who are especially connected to the Seventh Ray are lovers of ceremony. They delight when things are done properly and in order. This is the Ray of the impeccable maitre d', the infallible nurse, the organizational genius, and the designer of all sorts of beautiful forms. In the world of the arts, the latter would be especially true if there were also a strong Fourth Ray influence in one's character and makeup. Seventh Ray individuals love precision, and as a result may sometimes be overly concerned with details.

Seventh Ray personalities, for example, are given to working with organizations on both personal and professional levels. They enjoy forms and procedure and are very happy when they are clear about the "Upstairs and Downstairs" of things. They may find themselves interested in communications, but are usually more drawn to the style of presentation than the content of what is presented.

Healing of the shamanistic or ritualistic variety is also of the Seventh Ray, as are all outer trappings of religious ceremony and belief. The function of rites and ceremonies in terms of a tribe or society is to assure each person a place in the larger social order. It allows everyone the opportunity to serve some useful function and to know that he or she is part of the larger whole. In the Aquarian Age, this unifying ceremony will be facilitated through mass communications and the collective sharing of similar thought-forms. A recent example of this took place on December 31, 1986, when hundreds of millions of people around the world joined together at noon GMT for an international (and no doubt multidimensional) meditation.

Keywords and Key Phrases
of the Seventh Ray

1. *Concept:* The coordination and unification of the inner life principle and its expression in form; the reflection of Will through Order; fusion, blending, coordination.

2. *Soul Level:* The urge to gather, formulate, and harmonize various aspects of a given set of life circumstances into an ordered expression for the Will of God; the urge to make "heaven on earth."

3. *Personality Level:* Ray of the master of ceremonies of any event; film or stage producer; ritualist and shaman; organizational bureaucrat.

  a. *General Positive Traits:* Care in detail, perseverance, strength, and self-reliance; the ability to bring forth order out of chaos; often able to merge the powers of will (Ray One) with cohesiveness (Ray Two) to produce material results (Ray Three).

  b. *General Character Difficulties:* Too rigidly adheres to rules and regulations; may sacrifice self-determination to follow orders set down by superiors; may be very interested in omens and superstitions (especially if the Sixth Ray is also strong); pretentious, formal, follows ceremony mechanically.

  c. *To be Cultivated:* Humility, gentleness, tolerance, open-mindedness, greater realization of world unity.

  d. *Mental:* Tends toward an orderly mind; puts ideas, opinions, and facts in neat categories for future use; looks for opportunities to make the most out of things, and can thus be very innovative; may also, on the other hand, find himself bogged down by old methodologies and the inability to adapt to new circumstances.

  e. *Emotional:* Tendency to manifest the "right and appropriate" feelings for the circumstances in which he finds himself.

  f. *Physical:* Usually very adept at dealing with the physical environment; will like to organize his surroundings in neat and precise ways so that he may function at his optimum; usually of middle stature, with healthy body weight and evenly developed musculature; is often very well coordinated.

... Only when this (fusion, unity, blending) is intelligently realised can the disciple begin to weave the threads into a bridge of light (the Rainbow Bridge/Antahkarana) which eventually becomes the Lighted Way across which he can pass into the higher worlds of being. Thus he liberates himself from the three (lower) worlds. It is—in this world cycle—pre-eminently a question of fusion and expressing (in full waking awareness) three major states of consciousness: Shamballa (Will) ... Hierarchical (Love) ... Human (Intelligence) ...

—Alice A. Bailey[20]

---

[20]*The Rays and the Initiations*, p. 466.

TABULATION 2: SOME MAJOR INFLUENCES AND CORRESPONDENCES OF THE SEVEN RAYS

RAY	I	II	III	IV	V	VI	VII
NAME	Will/Power	Love/Wisdom	Active Intelligence	Harmony through Conflict	Concrete Knowledge	Devotion/ Idealism	Ceremonial Order
SIGNS	Aries Leo Capricorn	Gemini Virgo Pisces	Cancer Libra Capricorn	Taurus Scorpio Sagittarius	Leo Sagittarius Aquarius	Virgo Sagittarius Pisces	Aries Cancer Capricorn
PLANETS	Vulcan Pluto	Jupiter Sun	Saturn Earth	Mercury Moon	Venus	Neptune Mars	Uranus
KINGDOM	Shamballa	Hierarchy	Animal	Human	Current Humanity	Vegetable	Mineral
CHAKRA	Crown	Heart	Throat	Root	Brow	Solar Plexus	Sacral
GLAND	Pineal	Thymus	Thyroid	Adrenals	Pituitary	Pancreas	Gonads
SENSE	Touch	Intuition	Sight	Smell	Intellect	Taste	Hearing
FOOD	Protein	Fat	Carbohydrate	—	Vitamins	Water	Salts
POLITICS	Fascism	Democracy	Socialism	Citystate	Oligarchy	Theocracy	Communism
STONES	Diamond Crystal	Sapphire Turquoise	Emerald Jade	Jasper Agate	Topaz Citrine	Ruby Garnet	Amethyst
SHAPE	Circle	Triangle	Square	Circle squared	Sphere (lens)	Cube	Pyramid
PLANE	Pure Spirit	Monadic	Atmic	Buddhic	Mental	Astral	Physical
COLORS	Scarlet White	Indigo	Green	Yellow	Orange	Blue-rose	Violet

7

The Path of

Incarnation and

the Three Crosses

What we are witnessing today is the gradual emergence of a picture of the universe which presents us with a special problem, for it demands the acceptance of a new dimension of reality. This "fourth dimension" can be defined by the elusive, yet revealing word: Interpenetration. What is implied by it is that the universe and our total beings interpenetrate. The era of isolated, irreducible, and quasi-absolute individualities . . . is passing away.

—Dane Rudhyar
The Sun Is Also a Star

Incarnation takes place via a process of involution. The Soul, through its contact with its higher aspect, the Monadic-Spiritual-Self, becomes increasingly aware of its mandate to manifest. It thus sends downward into the three lower worlds—the rational mind, emotions, and physical reality—an aspect of itself. This becomes the personality—the lower self. As this lower self grows in consciousness, it awakens to its source of life in the Soul and the evolutionary process—the Path of Return—begins in earnest. This Path is also known as the Path of Discipleship.

The vast majority of people are at work building a "landing base" for the Soul to anchor on the Earth, and hence the intense attachment to the material plane. Others, a bit farther along the Path, are consciously at work shaping their physical, emotional, and mental vehicles for a purpose sensed but as yet unseen. This is the stage in our lives in which many of us currently find ourselves. It is that time in our lives when we take on certain disciplines of diet, exercise, study, and aspiration to love in ways that are new but essential to us. And we often do not know the *reasons*; our inner voice, our intuitive self, just reveals that this is the way for us at the present time—and we listen.

Then there is a third group of us—the New Group of World Servers. This group, numbering in the millions at the present time and growing, consists of men and women of goodwill who, through tremendous work and effort, have been able to forge a conscious link between the Soul and the personality. Each of these individuals has his own particular field of expression—his own particular focus of the creative dynamic which permits him to manifest the Soul purpose for the present incarnation. This purpose is always connected to the service of humanity, in one form or another. It is a healing work, in that it seeks to create a greater awareness of the collective whole in which we all live and have our being.

The path of human evolution and the movement of the Soul and the personality through their various cycles of incarnation can be seen through the Soul-centered approach to astrology. Both the Soul and the lower self mature through their contacts with the material world and the various kinds of Earthly experiences which occur, lifetime after lifetime. There is a pattern both to this cycle and to those underlying impulses which give rise to any of the varieties of life orientation a person may express. The unfolding of this pattern, and the kinds of events one creates or precipitates during a lifetime, are very much connected to the level of Soul growth or consciousness, relative to the degree of material attachment or personality awareness.

The Soul-centered astrologer views the Ascendant as the focus of the Soul and the Sun as the vehicle of personality expression in the natal horoscope. (See part 3, "A Guide to the Soul-Centered Delineation of the Natal Chart," for more complete details of this process and perspective.)

In the natal chart of the totally personality-centered individual, the unfoldment of both the Soul and the personality revolve astrologically in a clockwise direction. Thus the movement of signs shifts from incarnation to incarnation, from Aries to Taurus via Pisces, along the design of the precession of the equinoxes. This is called the "ordinary wheel of the Great Illusion." The focus of awareness and the underlying life motivation are underscored by *desire*—desire for the material life; desire for incarnation (the word itself meaning "to enter into the flesh"). This passage of many lifetimes is related to the Mutable Cross, and serves to give the Soul the necessary *knowledge of earthly experiences*. In this respect, desire serves the purpose of gathering in the lessons of life gleaned from the multifaceted experiences of the four mutable signs.

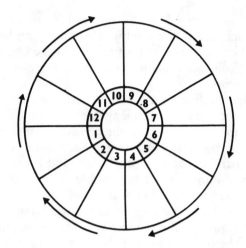

Diagram 8: Direction of the Ordinary Wheel for:
a) the totally desire- and personality-centered individual;
b) the Mutable Cross and the urge for experience.

Desire takes four different forms relative to the astrological elements. In the earth signs, desire manifests as the urge for material security, the acquisition of material possessions, and the achievement of social prestige. The desire for experience itself and the excitement of being in many places with many different kinds of people characterizes this level of life expression for the air signs. The desire for sensual response and pleasure, as well as the desire for emotional stimulation, characterize people of the water signs at this point of evolution. In terms of the fire signs, it is one's urge for personal recognition—"Look at me, I'm here!"—that underlies the desire to be.

When reincarnation is proceeding on this avenue of expression, and it does so for many lifetimes, the movement of the signs, as I mentioned, is clockwise. This means that the Soul sign (rising sign) would go from Aries in one lifetime to Pisces in the next. On the personality level, a person born with the Sun in Sagittarius would find him or herself with a Scorpio Sun the "next time down."

The "circling of the wheel" (which may consist of many cycles of incarnation) brings us to the stage of evolution for the more consciously advanced person. This is the point in which one has become more refined and defined in the use of life energy. This is, in its uppermost reaches, also the level in which a person begins to experience the quickening of the Soul's presence in the life, and enters into that state of "conscious duality" to which we referred earlier on in part 1 of this work.

At this stage of human evolution, desire mutates to *aspiration*. Once again, one may spend many lifetimes at this level, for the refinement of the lower vehicles (the physical, emotional, and mental bodies) is a long process. The increasing tension of duality "between heaven and earth" becomes strongly felt, and a choice is eventually made as to the nature of one's path in life. As we shall soon see, once the choice is made for the "life of the Soul" and the resultant service to humanity, a third "turning of the wheel" takes place. At this second point, however, the individual is said to be moving onto the Fixed Cross. The purpose of lifetimes spent here is the revelation of *the true nature of Love*. The rising and the Sun signs are still moving clockwise, and once again, the differences in the life expression are strongly conditioned by the astrological element in which these signs are placed.

When the earth signs predominate, the experiences emerging from those aspirations which lead to the unfolding of Love (that is, the consciousness of the Soul) take place through the professions, business, and the arts. When the air signs predominate, one holds the aspiration to link and join people so that some increasingly unifying message may be shared which is helpful to humanity. Idealistic, life-supporting, nourishing sentiments and their resultant acts are the vehicles used by the watery signs at this evolutionary level. Finally, the fire signs focus their aspirations through inspirational and stimulating creative ideas and projects.

Once a person has become fully anchored in his or her Soul's orientation, and Love has merged with knowledge to become Love/Wisdom, evolution takes on a very distinct focus, and the direction of the "turning of the wheel" mutates accordingly. The individual is then said to mount the Cardinal Cross, and the wheel reverses, moving counterclockwise, from Aries to Pisces via Taurus. Thus a person born with Cancer rising and a Pisces Sun who has reached this level of Soul direction would find that the next incarnation would most likely begin with Leo rising and the Sun in Aries.

The nature of the movement between the three crosses should be clarified. The three crosses indicate the three basic levels of human development: unconscious unity (totally personality-centered); conscious duality (initial to advanced stages of conscious personality-Soul relationship); conscious unity (total Soul-centeredness). A person can have the cardinal sign of Aries rising and be on the Mutable Cross.

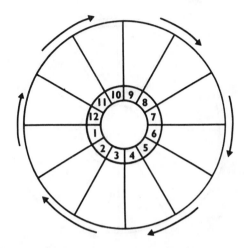

Diagram 9: Direction of the Ordinary Wheel for:
the re-orienting, aspiring individual; the Fixed Cross and the
urge for spiritual orientation; the circle will reverse as
Soul-centerednes is achieved.

Likewise, a mutable Gemini can be on the Fixed Cross of Disciple-ship. It is also very important to note that in a given incarnation you can change Crosses, as well as the direction of the wheel.

A person may find that he came into this lifetime on the Mutable Cross, and through certain circumstances (usually the failure of desire and the increase of aspiration), he is now hard at work on the Fixed Cross. Some others of us may have found ourselves experiencing the tensions of duality inherent in the Fixed Cross, only to discover that our Spiritual Approach to life has created a complete reversal of this dualistic orientation and that we are now very one-pointed in our urge for World Service in the Aquarian Age.

Once the expression of the life urge is motivated by pure *Spiritual Attraction* and intent, and having passed the necessary tests and trials inherent on the Fixed Cross, one may then proceed to mount the Cardinal Cross. It is here that a person (finally!) gets his "job"—his planetary purpose in terms of service to the collective humanity. It is at this point that the personality has become the total vehicle for the Soul, and the orientation of the life has transformed itself from a personal to an impersonal one. This is called the Path of Sacrifice. Such a Path leads to one of three directions: Initiation through

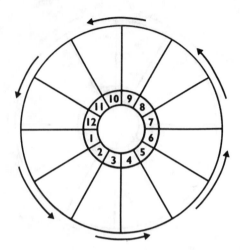

Diagram 10: Direction of the Reversed Wheel for:
a) the Disciple and the Initiate; b) the Cardinal Cross of Spiritual Activity.

Capricorn; World Service through Aquarius; or the Work of the World Savior through Pisces.

The reader might wish to tune into him- or herself at this point. Is your life moving backward, toward the preceding signs of your Ascendant or Sun, or forward, toward the orientation of the following signs? Is your life motivated by desire? By aspiration? By the urge for Initiation, World Service, or conscious Self-sacrifice? Or—and this is very likely—is your life being motivated by some combination of these tendencies, revealing movement in this lifetime from one wheel to the next?

The Cardinal Cross is very much related to the First Ray of Will/ Power and to the urge for sacrifice. In this case, sacrifice means the will to manifest, the "leaving of the Father's House" and the descent into matter. This Will-to-Be, coming from the Will-to-Good, characterizes the signs of the Cardinal Cross and aligns them most strongly with the First Ray.

The initiating urge to manifest (Aries) finds a home and is able to root (Cancer). It is through the latter sign, "the Gate into Incarnation," that the Soul takes incarnation for the first time. A point of balance is reached in Libra when the Soul and the personality work in harmonious relationship. It is in the sign of Capricorn, "the Gate of Initiation," that the Will-to-Be culminates and the goal envisioned by the incarnating Soul is finally achieved.

If we examine the Ray qualities of the four cardinal signs, we will see the direct unfolding of the First Ray:

Aries expresses itself on Rays One and Seven.

Cancer expresses itself on Rays Three and Seven.

Libra expresses itself on Ray Three.

Capricorn expresses itself on Rays One, Three, and Seven.

We can see from the above that the One-Three-Seven line of the Rays reveals, more clearly in this Cross than in any other, the distinct movement from Will to Mind to the world of many Forms. This is, esoterically, the reason why the Cardinal signs are known in traditional astrology as the signs of Motivation, as they harness the Will toward manifestation.

On the wheel of the personality-centered individual, an incarnation in Aries is going to precede one in Capricorn by only two stages: Pisces and Aquarius. This means that one will arrive at the summit— the sign of culmination—prematurely. On the Soul level, there will be eight incarnations (or major testing grounds) between one in Aries and one in Capricorn. This will give the kind of experience that will allow a Soul-centered Capricorn individual the *evolutionary maturity* that such an incarnation brings into life. Those Capricorns who are abusing power, whose center of Will/Power is based on a level of immature personality expression, have taken the "short route" of the ordinary wheel. Through the desire for power, they have assumed a place of personal responsibility without the proper balance of wisdom, love, and sacrifice. In effect, such individuals have become "short-circuited," for once they awaken to the futility of this unbalanced state, they have to start all over again.

It is very important to remember the underlying Presence of the Second Ray—the Lord of Love. This Ray energy contains within it the factor of redemption. This means that we do have the power of choice; we can reverse the wheel. Usually, this process of reversal begins on the Fixed Cross when the experiences of life begin to teach us about the true nature of desire, and we begin to aspire to those life circumstances that take us out of our lower centers. It is through the sign of Scorpio that such experiences come about, but we are capable of learning the lessons concerning the transmutation of desire when we incarnate in any one of the signs. It is just that the lesson of reorientation is most concentrated in the sign of the Eagle, which allows us to soar to new heights of creative expression as we leave the desires of material attachment behind.

I am of the opinion, in any event, that there are ways to "move around" the wheel. I think that the lessons of several signs can be learned in one lifetime (although there is no rush!). Perhaps this has something to do with the experiences gleaned through the progressions of the Sun and Ascendant as they pass through the zodiac. We are just beginning to explore the avenues open to esoteric experimen-

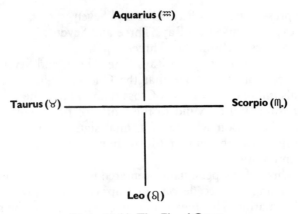

Diagram 11: The Fixed Cross

tation, research, and conjecture. The field is wide open for those
empiric judgments and contributions made from keen observations.
That's what the scientific aspect of astrology is all about in the first
place.

And then there is always the mystery that transcends all of my own
or anyone else's knowledge, which continually reveals to me that the
use of mind and the creation of intelligence are but vehicles for the
expression of Love. It is this connection to the Second Ray energy of
the Lord of our Universe that is absolutely the most important thing
of all, and the true reason for the creation of any system of astrological delineation. For in the final analysis, what the astrologer is seeking
to perceive is the functioning of the Mind of God, and I believe that
after all possible efforts at this task, we will discover that such mental
systems are there as channels for the Love which *is* the Divine Essence.

The Fixed Cross is especially related to the Second Ray. It is
through the energies of these four signs, more than any of the others,
that an individual undergoes those experiences which reorient the life
of the personality to the life of the Soul. Just as the cardinal signs
indicate lessons of motivation and direction—that is, Will in Action—
the fixed signs are very closely aligned to the *establishment of right
values*. Thus a life emerges based on the fundamental Soul qualities of
inclusivity and unselfishness; that is, Love in Action.

The two pairs of signs which make up the arms of the Fixed
Cross—Leo-Aquarius and Taurus-Scorpio—indicate the pathways by
which such transformations occur. For the personality-centered, the
Leo-Aquarius polarity will express itself with the desire to extend

personal influence over others. The Leo personality will tend to dominate the environment with its need to rule. Thus the "little Leo" will try to fix his mark upon others, imposing not only his personal will, but his personal values as well. The Aquarian personality will tend toward an exclusivity of belief systems in which he will seek to extend his personal values over as large a group of people as possible. In both cases, the achievement of personal objectives is very definitely the aim of the activities.

When the reorientation of values takes place through this polarity, the Soul-centered Leo uses the strength and force of his personality as a vehicle for the good of the whole. He then shines brightly with true spiritual radiance, using will and determination for impersonal, creative purposes. The Soul-centered Aquarian also becomes a World Server, and uses his wide-reaching visions and abundant social connections to create links for the purposes of unification and wholeness.

In terms of Taurus and Scorpio, the personality-centered individual will use the great magnetism of these two signs to bring about an increase in the desire for unbalanced sensuality and material possessions. Nothing will satisfy—the more he has, the more he will want. It will be in the wanting even more, rather than in the having, that the urge-to-be will express itself in an increasingly tense and more frustrated manner. At the very best, the experiences gleaned from the personality expressions of these signs lead a person to the awareness that he is trapped in the lower nature. It is then that he has the opportunity to transmute this orientation and reverse the wheel.

The death of the personality to the life of the Soul, when taking place through the signs of this polarity, knows no greater strength of expression. Freedom from attachment to matter (Taurus) and the establishment of one's true, spiritual identity and direction, are the results of the often painful process of transformation (Scorpio) which occurs through this arm of the Fixed Cross. Yet it should be clearly stated that the measure of the darkness which often accompanies these changes is also, in much greater measure, the expression of the Light when the wheel reverses.

The Mutable Cross relates very strongly to the Third Ray of Active Intelligence. It is the purpose of the four signs of this Cross to provide the ever-widening fields of experience through which consciousness may expand. The four signs are connected to four major stages of the evolution of human consciousness.

Gemini is very much the sign of humanity. It is the quintessential symbol of duality—the essential duality that creates the tensions (and eventual awareness) in the relationship between the Soul and the personality. Virgo is the place of purification, and thus a stage of testing and elimination. It is here that the individual prepares to do

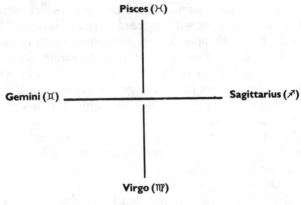

Diagram 12: The Mutable Cross

battle for the Soul and cleanses himself accordingly. In the sign of Sagittarius, the Disciple emerges in the one-pointed focus of the Higher Mind. This is what the arrow in the bow of the archer symbolizes. Last, the sign Pisces represents the Initiate, the World Savior, the most inclusive and synthesized expression of the Soul in human form.

On the ordinary wheel, the energies of Gemini and Sagittarius often point to those expansive activities that are completely involved with self-interest. The gaining of knowledge, the urge for a multiplicity of experiences, the need to teach and share information, are all vehicles for the expression of the lower mind and the dominance of the lower self in the environment. Such individuals believe that everyone should think and hold the same intellectual, religious, or philosophical creeds as they do. It is within this frame of reference that we find people who are much more "do-ers" than "be-ers," and whose relationship with the outside world of phenomena takes on far more importance than the inner world of causality. Eventually, the lifetimes within such a frame of reference lead to the focused, one-pointed drive of the personality. The latter is a preliminary step to the reversal of the wheel.

When reversal has taken place, the life of the Soul naturally intensifies. In terms of Gemini-Sagittarius, all activities are geared with complete awareness toward the expansion and evolution of consciousness. Such individuals usually create those communicative links and transformations in the educational process that increase the quality of life for many people. They are very involved with harmonizing, blending, and sharing knowledge for higher purposes.

The activities of the Virgo-Pisces arm of the Mutable Cross on the ordinary wheel often point to diffusion and lack of discrimination. The relationship between Soul and substance is not perceived, so that the individual is unable to attune to the quality of the life force within a given form. This is especially true for Virgo. The same set of circumstances is also quite correct for the personality-centered Pisces, but the nature of the diffusion often manifests more in terms of indiscriminate emotional or sensual responsiveness.

Once the wheel has reversed, the nature of the expression of this arm of the Mutable Cross changes accordingly. The nurturing qualities of the Mother (Virgo) focus and expand to include all forms of life, and cohesion is brought to the places where chaos once reigned. The urge to serve takes on extraordinary power, as old and nonregenerating forms of life are washed away so that the resurrection and evolution of the life force may proceed (Pisces). These signs, when manifesting through individuals on the Cardinal Cross, produce the true planetary healers.

8

An Initial

View of

the Chakras

*In the human kingdom, consciousness develops in cycles and unfolds spirally from individualization to the fully developed, self-conscious personality. From there it moves through the path of initiation to full Soul-consciousness, and finally, to identification with the **ONE** or God.*

—Helen Burmester
The Seven Rays Made Visual

The seven major chakras, or centers of vital force, are very important factors in terms of the esoteric physiognomy of men and women. They correspond to planets, as well as to the major endocrine glands and organs in the physical body. The science of the interrelationship between these "wheels of prana," or life energy, is quite complex and amazingly revealing in terms of the process of the circulation of vitality, both in the three vehicles of the personality and in the Soul. It is beyond the scope of the present work to advance the theories and results of research done in this area by esotericists.[1] I would like to present, however, certain information concerning the basic nature and correspondences of the chakras in terms of their relationship to Soul-centered astrology.

As we have seen, the First Ray represents the fiery Will-to-Be of Divinity, First Cause, Spirit. The expression of this Life Principle in the human organism is called the Monad. The roots of the seven major chakras are found along the vertical axis of the cerebrospinal column. They are actually seven streams of the life force originating

[1]See the Bibliography for further information on this subject.

from this Monadic source. These streams are like rays of sunshine, constantly pouring out the life-giving vitality of the Will-to-Be. The structure inherent in the Law of Correspondences reveals that the individual Monad is to our total organism what the Sun is to our solar system, while the Sun is but one of countless Monads to its solar parent: As Above, So Below.

The etheric body is also called the "etheric double," and constitutes the densest part of the aura, extending about a half inch or so from the physical body. Among its many functions, this etheric sheath acts as a protector, much like the atmosphere of the Earth serves to shield our planet from harmful radiations. The etheric double helps to protect us from psychic and physical intrusions. Just like our atmosphere, the etheric body is very sensitive and can be harmed.

The Monadic "pulse of life" is transmitted to the Soul, and from there it further descends through the involutionary stream into the vehicles of the personality. The "etheric body" surrounds and interpenetrates the dense physical organism and is contiguous to it. This etheric vehicle is composed entirely of the "threads" of this Monadic vitality. The energy of these lines of force activates the power of the nervous system and anchors itself through the major chakras to the endocrine glands and other organs within the physical body. The etheric threads also form channels along which the more subtle forces flow, affecting our physical and psychic conditions. These channels relate very closely to the meridians used in acupuncture and other forms of Oriental medicine.

We are all aware that the ozone layer of the atmosphere has become imperiled through the extensive use of chemical pollutants, thus increasing the risk of cancer and other ailments. Pollutants also affect the etheric double. Many drugs, for example, including and especially alcohol, burn through the etheric sheath and weaken it, exposing the individual to various psychological and physical dysfunctions. Tobacco has the opposite effect, tending to tighten or shrink the etheric organism, thereby lessening a person's sensitivity to others and to the environment. One of the primary reasons people smoke is to "calm the nerves," thus lessening the impact of the environment upon them. The smoke acts as an insulator and psychic protector, but also reduces the sense of personal responsibility for an individual's position in a given social situation. Excessive smoking also enhances a subjective approach to life, thus inhibiting the "working out" of cancerous thoughts and feelings, as the smoke blocks the free expression of these areas. Circulation and purification is thus inhibited, contributing to nonregeneration and consequent illness.

The threads of etheric energy cross at certain points. Where a large number of these crossings occur, a vortex of energy is created. This vortex is a chakra. In addition to the seven major centers, there are twenty-nine lesser centers and forty-nine smaller ones.[2] Some of the more important of these minor centers can be found in the palms of the hands, at the shoulders and hips, and in the soles of the feet. The spleenic and alta major chakras are two of the most important of these other centers. (Some of the early theosophists writing about the chakras totally substituted the sacral or sexual chakra with the spleenic. My feeling is that this was done not so much for esoteric differences of opinion, but as a result of the influence of Victorian morality on esoteric studies. The goodly nineteenth-century esotericists were no doubt trying to prevent the erstwhile student from the overdevelopment of this particular "center of force"!)

Diagram 13 shows the relative position of the "flowers" of the chakras—that portion of each of these centers that expands outward into the etheric body. As mentioned earlier, the "roots" of these centers are located tangentially to the cerebrospinal column.

The Seven Chakras

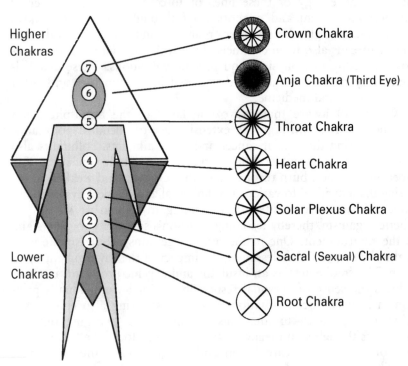

[2]Bailey, *Esoteric Healing*, p. 72.

TABULATION 3: RAYS, CHAKRAS, ENDOCRINE GLANDS, PHYSICAL ORGANS, AND PLANETS

Ray	Chakra	Gland	Organ	Planet
1	Crown	Pineal	Brain	Vulcan Pluto
2	Heart	Thymus	Heart	Jupiter Sun
3	Throat	Thyroid	Vocal cords, lungs	Saturn Earth
4	Root	Adrenals	Spinal column	Mercury Moon
5	Brow	Pituitary	Eyes, ears, nose	Venus
6	Solar plexus	Pancreas	Stomach, liver, gall bladder	Mars Neptune
7	Sacral	Gonads, ovaries	Reproductive systems	Uranus

The location of the planets in the natal horoscope, as well as their sign positions and geometric aspects, will tell us a great deal about the relationship of the chakras, glands, and physical organs to one another. The development of the energies working through the vital centers may also be viewed from the perspective of progressions and transits. The manifestations in the life of an individual are, of course, all relative to the level of consciousness of the person in question. We will be exploring these astrological points of reference through the delineations offered in part 3 of the text, but for the purposes of our current discussion, let us look at a few examples.

1. The natal trine from the Sun to Jupiter stimulates the heart (both from the physical and etheric perspectives). This offers great potential for the development of the heart chakra. If either if these planets is in Leo, the emphasis is even stronger. On the personality level, this influence gives a jovial personality and a tendency to excess. On the

Soul level, such a trine reveals an individual who is very much a vehicle for the expression of Second Ray energy.

2. When Pluto is in the tenth house, the use of Will/Power will be a very potent tool for the furtherance of a person's goals. On a personality level, this can be interpreted merely as great ambition and the urge to control and dominate others. On the Soul level, this brings about crises and destruction so that beneficial new forms of power may emerge for the use of humanity. The sign that Pluto is in will tell us much about the quality of the Ray through which this planet will be working.

3. Pluto square to Mercury will overstimulate the adrenals. On the personality level, this will give a fiery speaker—one who will use all the powers of the mind to influence and dominate others. On the Soul level, the individual will find him- or herself in the midst of many verbal and mental quarrels and differences of opinion. The task will be to bring about harmony through conflict (Mercury as Fourth Ray Ruler) through the right use of will (Pluto's relationship to Ray One). This may not be particularly easy (square) and could be an essential test of the personality (if Scorpio is rising) or the Soul (if Pisces is rising, as Pluto is the ruler of Pisces on the Soul level).

4. Uranus is making a long-lasting conjunction to natal Venus by transit. The individual in question is on the Fixed Cross, as he is hard at work harmonizing his inner and outer lives. This is a combination of the Fifth and Seventh Ray influences leading to the birth (conjunction) of a new cycle in the relationship of these two planets. Venus is the ruler of Gemini, and Uranus the ruler of Libra on the Soul level. This individual's higher impulse will lead him to create some new forms of communication that will bring forth a deeper understanding of life. This is seen through the combination of the Fifth Ray of Concrete Knowledge and the Seventh Ray of the Organization of Form. The signs Gemini and Libra bring in the social and communication elements. The joining of the energies of the gonads and the pituitary gland, when stimulated from the Soul level, leads to the birthing of creative fire for the advancement of knowledge. If this transit were to be viewed only from the personality-centered approach, we would see that the person in question is about to meet a new group of individuals who would most likely lead him to some form of social experimentation. Should any kind of creativity emerge from these encounters, the results would most likely be for the benefit of the individual involved, and not extend through a collective orientation.

There are several points I would like to share regarding the nature of the relationship between the Soul, the chakras, and the physical body, which may prove to be of interest. The crown chakra is the most important from the perspective of the Soul, as it is Its point of "entry and exit." When the crown center is fully open and operative, an individual is said to be awakened to the Soul's reality, and those processes resulting in a Soul-infused personality have been accomplished. Thus the "thread of consciousness"—the pathway of the Soul into the personality—is focused in the region of the pineal gland. It is through the Ray line of Will/Power (Rays One-Three-Five-Seven) that the Soul is able to regulate physical plane activities through the nervous system and the brain.

The "thread of life" is anchored in the heart, as it is there that the Sun rules in terms of the Second Ray "Life" of the Divinity of our solar system. The life force in the individual is distributed in the physical organism through the circulation of the blood. From the perspective of the Rays, this corresponds to the Ray line of Love/ Wisdom (Rays Two-Four-Six).

As the expansion and development of consciousness takes place and the link between the Higher and lower selves occurs, the unfolding of one's personal evolutionary direction manifests. An individual then finds that there is a definite reorientation to his or her life direction. This occurs simultaneously with the increased activation of the various chakric centers.

The life of a person on the Mutable Cross (one who is totally personality-centered) is only expressing itself through the lower three chakras. Thus the life is spent focused on:

1. Survival in the material world—root chakra (instinctive intelligence)

2. Survival of the species through the expression of personal desire— sacral chakra (instinctive sexuality)

3. Survival through the power of the expression of personal emotions—solar plexus chakra (instinctive territorial dominance).

Very often, as one transforms the nature and direction of consciousness, certain changes also occur in the physical body. This means that a person mounting another Cross may find himself inexplicably ill for certain periods of time. Just as the mental and emotional bodies have to be purified as alignment to the Soul progresses, so, frequently, does the physical body. Ordinary, allopathic medicine may not be able to find the cause of these symptoms. Yet through an esoteric medical diagnosis, the planetary and chakric correspondences may be ascertained. My own experience is that these subtle imbalances are corrected more efficiently by the use of Oriental and herbal medicine, when practiced by a highly trained healer.

As consciousness expands and a shift is made to the Fixed Cross, and then eventually to the Cardinal Cross, there is a corresponding shift of the expression of the life energies to the higher centers. Thus an individual who is Soul-centering would find the following changes taking place in his life:

1. Instead of vacillating between an intermittent emphasis on the mental, the emotional, and the physical life, an integration of these three facets of the personality would be taking place. This would result in a synthesized, strongly focused lower self.

2. The values, needs, and desires of this lower self would begin to give way to the sensing of higher, more inclusive, and less personality-focused values, needs, and desires.

3. The awakening to the world of true spiritual realities and perceptions would be accompanied by the urge for wider and more selfless service, and the need to be joined in a group dynamic by others of like mind. This is the arena and world view of the Soul-centered individual.

The process described above has its correlation in terms of the reorientation of the energies of the lower centers and their absorption by those centers located above the diaphragm. There is a pattern to this reorientation:

1. The center of the personal will, located in the root chakra, becomes magnetized and is "drawn under" the influence of the center of Spiritual Will located in the crown center.

2. The energies of the sacral center likewise come under the control of the throat center. (The astrologer might find it interesting to note here the relationship of Mars/Scorpio, traditional rulers of the sexual organs and functions, and Venus/Taurus, significators in exoteric astrology of the throat and speech.) The Third Eye (brow center) begins to open, and the combination of the energies of the throat and the brow gives rise to a tremendous creative potential.

3. As the heart center awakens, it draws the energies of the solar plexus to it. This eliminates the tremendous confusion that many people have about their ways of loving. If the solar plexus is functioning and the heart is closed, one is likely to interpret personal emotional needs and lust as love. When the heart center has opened and the energies of the solar plexus have become integrated within it, then one becomes the vehicle for the cohesive, healing, and uplifting joy which is at Love's core. This Love may also be expressed while making love!

When the four higher centers are opened and one has become Soul-centered, the focus of existence moves from survival to life:

1. Life as expressed through Love—heart chakra (true Consciousness)

2. Life as expressed through Creative Activity—throat chakra (true Intelligence)

3. Life as expressed through Perception of Reality—brow chakra (true Spiritual Awakening)

4. Life as expressed through Identification—crown chakra (true Spiritual Will).

In recent years, many methods for the stimulation and opening of the centers have appeared. Much has been said about the "opening of the Third Eye" and the generation of .psychic powers which such development allegedly brings about. Many classes, especially for those people "training" to be psychics and/or channels, have stressed the need to "sit for development," and as a result, to stimulate the seven vital centers. Spiritual development comes with the development of spiritual responsibility. The evolution of a Soul-centered individual is not witnessed by attachment to glamour-ridden phenomenology. The externalization of the Higher Self requires, more than anything else, an inner attitude of service and a clear method of training; the opening of the higher centers may then safely take place, along with the accompanying perception of spiritual reality, and as the result of a great deal of dedicated work.

I teach no mode of awakening the centers, because right impulse, steady reaction to higher impulsions, and the practical recognition of the sources of inspiration, will automatically and safely swing the centers into needed and appropriate activity. This is the sound method of development. It is slower, but leads to no premature development, and produces a rounded unfoldment; it enables the aspirant to become truly the Observer and to know with surety what he is doing: it brings the centers, one by one, to a point of spiritual responsiveness, and then establishes the ordered and cyclic rhythm of a controlled lower nature.[3]

—Alice A. Bailey

[3] *Glamour: A World Problem*, pp. 261–2.

TABULATION 4: THE SIGNS, PERSONALITY-CENTERED RULERS AND RAYS, SOUL-CENTERED RULERS AND RAYS

Sign	Ray	Traditional Ruler	Ray	Soul-centered Ruler	Ray
Aries	First Seventh	Mars	Sixth	Mercury	Fourth
Taurus	Fourth	Venus	Fifth	Vulcan	First
Gemini	Second	Mercury	Fourth	Venus	Fifth
Cancer	Third Seventh	Moon	Fourth	Neptune	Sixth
Leo	First Fifth	Sun	Second	Sun	Second
Virgo	Second Sixth	Mercury	Fourth	Moon	Fourth
Libra	Third	Venus	Fifth	Uranus	Seventh
Scorpio	Fourth	Mars Pluto	Sixth First	Mars	Sixth
Sagittarius	Fourth Fifth Sixth	Jupiter	Second	Earth	Third
Capricorn	First Third Seventh	Saturn	Third	Saturn	Third
Aquarius	Fifth	Saturn Uranus	Third Seventh	Jupiter	Second
Pisces	Second Sixth	Jupiter Neptune	Second Sixth	Pluto	First

9

The Twelve Astrological

Signs and Their

Soul-Centered

Planetary Rulers

The horoscope is a blueprint of our character. Character is destiny. There is nothing static in this universe in which we dwell. We can change by changing our attitudes and patterns of behavior. In so doing, we change our destiny. . . . An understanding of planetary influences allows you to take your life into your own hands and intelligently utilize the planetary influences that will help you in your evolution if you but will.

—Isabel Hickey,
Astrology—A Cosmic Science

ARIES
The Light of Life Itself.

This is the dim point of light found at the center of the cycle of manifestation, faint and flickering. It is the "searchlight of the Logos, seeking that which can be used" for divine expression.[1]

Rays of manifestation:

First ⊙ *and Seventh* 卍

---

[1]This quote and the eleven that follow are found in Alice Bailey's *Esoteric Astrology* (pp. 329–330).

Planetary rulers and their Rays:

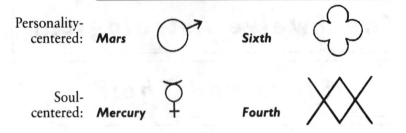

Personality-
centered: **Mars**   **Sixth**

Soul-
centered: **Mercury**   **Fourth**

Aries is the initiating Will-to-Be, the continuous pulse of the Life Force as it emerges through the creative, fiery aethers and moves through the various planes of the evolutionary scheme, until It anchors Itself in the world of forms. It is this connection between the alpha and the omega of the unfolding Life which reveals Aries as a vehicle for both the transcendental and immanent Presence of Spirit. Spirit is transcendental because the fiery nature of the Divine Will interpenetrates Itself as It moves through the Soul of any entity into the body of any form. It is immanent due to its omnipresence at the fiery core of every atom, Monad, and star.

As an expression of the Will/Power of Divinity, Aries is the embodiment of the First Ray. As the directing, controlling urge for the expression of that Will in the world of forms, it is also endowed with the energies of the Seventh Ray. And there is one other vitally important factor which distinguishes Aries from all of the other signs on the First and Seventh lines of Ray energy.

As the "Light of Life Itself," Aries is a pure emanation from the Mind of God—that place "where the Will of God is known." This initiating focus of life makes Aries the *birthplace of ideas,* according to the Ancient Wisdom Teachings, as all of manifestation has its beginnings as Divine Ideas. It is through Aries that the Plan of the Logos, the Divine Will, descends to us either individually, or collectively as humanity, via the plane of the Soul.

In this respect, the esoteric, Soul-centered planetary ruler of this sign is Mercury, known traditionally as the "Messenger of the Gods." When operating through a Soul-centered individual, Mercury brings forth from the plane of causality some aspect of the evolutionary Plan for humanity and our Earth.

Mercury acts primarily as an intermediary. He is the messenger between the Fifth Kingdom of the Souls and the Fourth Kingdom of Humanity. Mercury also functions to link the Higher Mind with the lower so that the inner realization of one's place in the Plan of Life may be recognized and then, through the use of applied logic, externalized into the three lower worlds of the personality. Mercury thus aligns the energies of the Third Ray of abstract ideas with the Fifth Ray activities of the concrete mind. It is the concrete mind as an aspect of the personality which allows a person to analyze and distinguish the differences between "you and me"; the self and the not-self. Mercury also acts as the intermediary between the Soul and the connecting nervous impulses of the brain. It is Mercury's task to coordinate the relationship between the Higher and lower selves, and as we shall shortly discuss, it is Venus which harmonizes and blends the two.

In traditional, personality-centered astrology, Mercury is always viewed as a planet expressive of duality, and indicative of a certain conflicting tension. Yet from the Soul-centered perspective, Mercury is a vehicle for creativity *as it serves to relate opposites or opposing forces* so that they may eventually fuse. In this respect, Mercury is seen as the planet through which the Fourth Ray of Harmony through Conflict is said to operate. The Fourth Kingdom in nature is the Human, and it is through the Human that the evolutionary scheme of the seven Kingdoms is held in balance. It is the Human Kingdom which is expressive of the greatest tension of all, as it is placed right at the center of this evolutionary structure (see diagram 2).

The fourth plane of manifestation is the intuitive, and it is on this plane that the advanced Aries individual works. The Soul-centered Aries also functions as an intermediary. It is through his Soul-directed actions and speech that he inspires others to forge their own connections between their Higher and lower selves. He shows the way, reveals the Plan, and instills courage into his environment. It is also to be noted that a person with Mercury in Aries who is functioning on the Cardinal Cross is a highly intuitive, rather than a highly mental, person. The Fourth Ray, which stands midway between the Three Rays of Aspect and the Fifth, Sixth, and Seventh Rays of Attribute, holds the same kind of tension in terms of the Seven Rays as the Fourth Kingdom holds in nature. Thus it is Mercury, the Fourth Ray, and the Fourth Kingdom of Humanity which are the intermediaries between the upper and lower worlds, planes, and kingdoms. Mercury and the Fourth Ray work to fuse and blend the great dualities of human nature into one cooperative whole, thus advancing the evolutionary Plan for life on Earth.

The following paragraphs in this chapter, from Aries to Pisces, relate to the Sun as well as to the rising sign:

ARIES on the Mutable Cross (totally personality-centered individual). The personality-centered Aries is usually quite unconscious of him- or herself. The urge to project the desires of the lower self is very instinctual. The "mutable" Aries moves through life with a "me first" attitude that is usually undirected in terms of any focus of objectivity. This doesn't make for a "bad" person as much as it does for one who is rather naive and unaware.

The gathering of knowledge is completely confrontational in nature. The lessons of life are learned through emotional and physical victories and defeats. Mars is the ruling planet in this case, and the attachment to the sense of territoriality is thus very strong. Aries on this level is the sign of "I am my urges." Undirected impulsiveness is very definitely the modus operandi of the unevolved Aries, and all the pushy, headstrong qualities associated with the Ram in traditional astrology are very much in evidence. As Mars rules, the life is far more influenced by the sexual organs and the Sixth Ray than anything else. Although the Aries person is fiery by element, he is thus much more watery-emotional in his way of self-expression. His life is totally governed by the desire for dominance and the need for personal recognition.

ARIES on the Fixed Cross (awakening to the Soul-personality relationship). As the relationship between the Soul and the personality becomes more evident, the life energies of Aries take on a much more consciously directed orientation. The effects of Mars become more focused, and the individual begins to fight for those causes which involve not only his own well-being (a predominant motivation for all his personal actions), but also the well-being of others. The anger and moral outrage which is often seen as one of the major conditioning factors behind Aries' actions begins to lose its instinctual overtones, and becomes more closely aligned with conscious purpose.

The Aries individual at this level is not just going to strike out blindly into life—he is going to create some sort of plan of action. In his urge to conquer any opposition, the Aries mind (Mercury) begins to come into play and personal aggression (Mars) is going to be seen as a vehicle for bringing about a balance to an inharmonious situation (Fourth Ray). Instead of fighting as an instinctual response to territorial infringement, Aries now views himself as an instrument to correct injustices and, if necessary, as an instrument of sacrifice for some high ideal. This is the idealism of the Sixth Ray at work, expressing Aries as the "Sacrificial Lamb." The real soldier is not afraid of death, but sees himself at his most noble—as a vehicle for harmony through conflict. It is in such circumstances that an Aries on the Fixed Cross discovers the meaning of Love.

ARIES on the Cardinal Cross (the Soul-centered individual). The Aries who has mounted the Cardinal Cross has assimilated and synthesized all the previous levels of experience. He has taken on the conscious responsibility for the right use of will (First Ray) in the organization and direction of daily life (Seventh Ray). Such a person is in constant touch with the plane of intuition, and is able to perceive the essential quality of life within any given form of its expression. Such an Aries recognizes and works with the Plan of evolution and is in touch with his role for its unfoldment. Aries is now a conscious personification of the Will-to-Good.

There are four keynotes for such an individual:[2]

1. Express the *will* to be and do. (First Ray)
2. Unfold the *power* to manifest. (First-Seventh Rays)
3. Enter into *battle* for the Lord. (Mars and the Sixth Ray)
4. Arrive at *unity* through effort. (Mercury and the Fourth Ray).

The Soul-centered, Mercury-ruled Aries is able to arouse, stimulate, and infuse new spiritual awareness into any activity. His is the fire of divine impulse that can penetrate into any form and bring forth the spiritual will at its center. Through the energies of Pluto and Vulcan (rulers of the First Ray), and Scorpio (ruled on the Soul level by Mars—the same planet which rules Aries on the personality level), Aries has the will and the power to transform the lower into the higher. This transformational ability is expressed through the mind. (Scorpio is also a sign of the Fourth Ray, and hence related to Mercury.) It is this intuitively based mind that is the "weapon" of the highest unfoldment of Aries. Aries is the fiery channel that provides for Mercury's expression, allowing for the birthing of a true Idea coming from the Mind of God. Such an Idea is, in actuality, a spiritual impulse taking form. Perhaps this is the reason for Victor Hugo's comment that "Nothing is as powerful as an idea whose time has come."

ARIES KEYWORDS

Mutable	Fixed	Cardinal
Instinctual	Directed	Inspired
I am (you are not)	I am and You are	I and You and We are One
Immediate	Planned	Unified
Fire of desire	Fire of aspiration	Fire of identification
Pulse	Glow	Radiance

[2]Bailey, *Esoteric Astrology*, p. 93. (Emphasis and notes added.)

Mutable	Fixed	Cardinal
Urge to overpower	Urge to focus power	Vehicle for the Power
Blind will	Struggle with will	Purposeful use of Will
Private	Officer	General

Aries Keyword Phrases[3]

Let form again be sought. This is the orientation for humanity on the ordinary wheel. It shows that the energies of Mars and the focus of the creative fire of Aries are used to anchor the incarnation for the purpose of material expression and personality dominance.

I come forth and from the plane of mind, I rule. This is the orientation for those individuals who have worked to express their life through the direction of the reversed wheel. This phrase indicates the influence of Mercury and the plane of the intuition on the life.

TAURUS
The penetrating Light of the Path.

This is a beam of light, streaming forth from the point in Aries, and revealing the area of light control.

Ray of manifestation:

Fourth

Planetary rulers and their Rays:

Personality-centered: *Venus*   *Fifth*

---

[3]A total of twenty-four such phrases will be used in this chapter. All of them were adopted by the Tibetan Master Djwhal Khul, from a very ancient and unpublished text which He calls the *Old Commentary*. They can be found in Bailey's *Esoteric Astrology*, pp. 653–4. The comments which follow all of the phrases are mine.

Soul-
centered: *Vulcan* ∨ *First* ⊙

The work for the spiritually oriented person whose Sun, or especially whose rising sign, is Taurus has to do with the principle of illumination. The task is to irradiate the physical world and uplift the physical plane. This is accomplished through the penetrating Light of the Divine Will. The testing ground has to do with not becoming trapped by the very same physical plane which Taurus seeks to enLighten. This is no easy task, by any means! The Ancient Wisdom Teachings tell us that Taurus is the sign which embodies the major incentive of life. This is due to the fact that *Taurus is the embodiment of desire* in all its forms—not just the desire for physical goods and pleasures. The latter is desire in the life of the personality-centered individual. It is in this realm of expression that the traditional keyword phrase for Taurus, "I have, therefore I am," predominates the existence.

In the life of one attempting to walk the Path of Light, this desire is transmuted into the spiritual aspiration which surfaces in the urge to liberate oneself and others from the attachment to matter. The person who has achieved and integrated this aspiration finds that his "planetary task," and the nature of his contribution to humanity, is based on his ability to be determined and steadfast in the application of will/power in furthering the evolutionary Plan for mankind.

Taurus is especially connected to the Buddha, for just as the passion of the Christ takes place through Pisces, the Buddha is said to have been born, reached enlightenment, and died in the sign of the Bull. These events are celebrated each year at the Wesak Festival, the time of the Full Moon when the Sun is in Taurus. The Buddha taught that the path of detachment from desire is the vehicle for the entrance of Light; that is, the Creative Will—the energies of the First Ray. He did this through those methods which imparted the means to awaken the Third Eye—the "Eye of the Bull." This awakening brings into one's daily life a consciousness in which the expression of the Soul is centered in the intuitive or "Buddhic" plane. Such an awakening brings forth the potential for the fullest expression of our humanness. In this respect, the dual horns of the Bull become the single horn of the one-pointed spiritualized being, as symbolized by the Unicorn.

Taurus is only found on the Fourth Ray; the Buddhic is the Fourth plane, and the Human is the Fourth Kingdom. The fourth chakra (through which the Second Ray emanates) is the heart. This is the very center of human expression, while the externalization of the use of intuition comes through the Third Eye point, or the brow center. The latter is related to Venus, the exoteric ruler of Taurus. As the heart is the Christ center and the brow the Buddhic one, there is a very special relationship here. The heart is Love and the brow is Wisdom. When the two centers merge (as they eventually do on the evolutionary Path of the spirtually awakening), the Ray of Love/ Wisdom unfolds completely.

It is always important to recognize the Law of Correspondence at work. As we open our hearts and Higher Minds, we externalize those aspects of ourself which correspond to the Christ and the Buddha. *This opening is at the core of all of our efforts at self-realization; this is the realization of the Self.* The work to free ourselves from possessiveness and materiality so that through these lessons true Wisdom may emerge is very definitely at the center of the Taurean phase of the turning of the wheel.

Taurus is the sign of our Earthly life. As such it embodies a great conflict—one which can be seen in the Ray which operates through it. The Fourth Ray—of Harmony through Conflict—is the most "human" of the Rays. It is very much the factor behind the "art of living," and presents those tests, trials, and victories which give rise to the spiritualization of humanity. It is this Ray of Art and Beauty which so attracts these "sons and daughters of Venus." It is the Fifth Ray of the lower mind, ruled by Venus, that stimulates the Taurean toward the acquisition of more "gold," in all of its forms.

On the Soul level, the ruling planet of this sign is Vulcan, which is primarily a planet of First Ray energy. Thus it is that on the Soul level, a life in Taurus is chosen to teach an individual how to transmute material desire into Spiritual Will. With Vulcan we enter upon one of the most esoteric aspects of Soul-centered astrology. Modern astronomers have not been able to ascertain its exact placement in the solar system, although Vulcan has often been cited throughout the past few centuries and always in the same general area—between the orbit of Mercury and the position of the Sun.

Dr. Douglas Baker, in section three of his book, *Esoteric Astrology,* states:

> The truth of the matter is that Mercury, the next planet closest to the Sun, captured Vulcan and took it into its own gravitational field (within that of the Sun). Vulcan moves very, very slowly around Mercury and occasionally, when all conditions are favorable (and these are extremely rare), Vulcan could be seen against the solar disc from the viewpoint of the Earth. But always, Mercury would be very close, certainly within three degrees of Vulcan.

Dr. Baker gives no astronomical data to support this statement.[4]

Vulcan is a constant factor in the astrology of the Ancient Wisdom Teachings, and its rulership and relationship to Taurus and the First Ray is consistent. The Tibetan Master, in Bailey's *Esoteric Astrology,* states (italics are mine):

> You will note also that the First Ray influence, expressing through Pluto and Vulcan, is only felt in a positive manner upon the Path of Discipleship. This First Ray potency has only *lately* been experienced by humanity. . . . Hence the recent discovery of Pluto and *the sensed power of Vulcan, veiled by the potency of Mercury and hidden behind the planet.*

The general consensus among astrologers, and one which my own work has shown to be valid, is that Vulcan can always be found within 8 degrees, 30 minutes of the Sun's natal position, and as a result, using a 10-degree orb, is often conjunct with Mercury (although this is not always the case). Unless the Sun is in the early or late degrees of its sign, Vulcan will always be in the same sign as the Sun. If this is not the case, and until an ephemeris is available, the astrologer can determine its position through the careful investigation of the client's life. The proper use of intuition, so absolutely essential to the Soul-centered astrologer, will be required in this case. It is not such a difficult factor to determine if, let us say, Vulcan is in either Aries or Taurus in the horoscope of a Taurean, when one is familiar with the different effects of these two signs on the life.

One of the fundamental precepts common to all astrological teachings, and relative to the discovery of the "new" planets, is that such celestial bodies are revealed when human consciousness has evolved to the point where response to their energies is possible. The astrologer has only to study this statement in relation to the eras in which Uranus, Neptune, and Pluto were discovered to appreciate its validity. As humanity evolves to the place where more and more of its members can use the Will as the Will-to-Good, Vulcan's physical presence will be made known to us. We are still struggling along with the other First Ray planet, Pluto, and its rulership over atomic energy (with its resulting byproducts of destruction and potential for good).

Fortunately, thanks to the efforts of David Walters of Cincinnati, Ohio, an ephemeris may soon be available for Vulcan. He has recently done a great deal of research and solid work to locate Vulcan's orbit and create an ephemeris for it. (Mr. Walters disagrees with the

---

[4]Two of the most available texts relating to Vulcan, its position and meaning are: *The Planet Vulcan: History, Nature and Tables,* by L. H. Weston, and *Vulcan: The Intra-Mercurial Planet,* by Carl W. Stahl. See Bibliography.

orbital movements as outlined by Weston.) This effort is part of the
international focus on the astrology of the Soul (combining esoteric
astrology with esoteric psychology) by many students of the Ancient
Wisdom Teachings.[5]

On p. 374 of Bailey's *Esoteric Astrology,* the Tibetan Master says:
"Taurus forges the instruments of constructive living, or of destruction. It forges the chains which bind, or creates the key which unlocks
the mystery of life." Vulcan is the forger, known to us as the "Blacksmith of the Gods." Vulcan creates those tools and weapons that
allow one to forge Light into Matter and which transform Matter
back into Light. Mercury, as the Messenger of the Gods, reveals the
direction for what is needed (Aries), how to go about getting it
(Gemini), and how and where to use what is gotten (Virgo). The
relationship between Vulcan and Taurus also involves Mercury. Vulcan is the transmitter of the energies of the First Ray, while Taurus
and Mercury relate to the Fourth, which operates through the base of
the spine and deals with the "root of matter." A clear channel has to
be forged, lower energies have to be transmuted to higher, so that the
First Cause of the Will may be properly externalized into the world of
forms. This process of transformation, in terms of humanity, is almost always expressed through tests of detachment from desire. Vulcan, on the Soul level, is the vehicle through which the Power of
transformation descends into the very Matter of our outer world. By
forging new weapons and tools for the use of consciousness/love,
Humankind and the Taurean individual are freed from the chains
which limit the greater expression of life.

*TAURUS on the Mutable Cross (totally personality-centered
individual).* On the level of the personality, Venus rules the earthbound Bull. Venus also expresses herself through the Soul (in the sign
of Gemini, where she predominates), but when acting through the
triad of the lesser self, Venus tends to bring into life the urge to
acquire things of beauty and to have those experiences which serve to
heighten physical pleasures. Taurus is the most magnetic of signs on
the Earth plane, and possesses an instinctive urge to acquire physical
objects and emotional sensations. In this pursuit, Taurus is most
stubbornly determined. It is well said that the son or daughter of the
Bull never lacks for anything. The sense of lack which Taureans often
feel comes through the great desire to always have more of everything. This is one reason why there is often a tendency to clutter and
to accumulate physical weight. The Taurean always views her cup as

[5]As of this writing, Mr. Walters is preparing a paper on the subject for publication, which
should be ready for general distribution during 1989. He may be contacted about his
research at the Seven Ray Institute, 128 Manhattan Ave., Jersey City Heights, NJ 07307.

half empty—never half full. Will is used for the attainment of personal desire, and the life, rooted in the lowest chakra, is completely captured by the magnetism of matter.

TAURUS on the Fixed Cross (awakening to the Soul-personality relationship). Taurus is connected to the whole concept of values. Indeed, often the Taurean's values regulate the direction of the will. The primary test at this level has to do with the active transformation of desire. The Taurean on the Mutable Cross learns about desire through her direct experiences. The Fixed Cross Taurean has already gathered in such experiences and is now faced with the urge to release her attachment from desires. She now struggles this way and that between her envisioned aspirations to nourish, supply, and give of herself freely, and the equally strong urge to possess.

The Scorpio-Taurus polarity is at its most powerful at this stage. It is now that the energies of the sacral center have to be lifted to the throat. The potential which comes about from this evolutionary process endows the Taurean with a great artistic and creative potency, thus expressing some of the higher qualities of the Fourth Ray of Beauty. Right speech and right livelihood (two streams of the Eightfold Noble Path taught by the Buddha) become paramount at this point, leading to the right use of the Will.

TAURUS on the Cardinal Cross (the Soul-centered individual). Once freed from attachment to matter and the chains of desire, the Taurean can stimulate the presence of Light in any form which matter may take. This is the true white magician; the true healer. Here, dominance over form has been won through one of the most difficult battles faced by any of the twelve signs. The "Eye of the Bull" radiates forth like the strongest of beams, clearly pointing the way to the reality of spiritual presence and Divine Will. The "art of living" takes on new meaning, as such an individual's artistic or professional expression is transformative by its very nature—freeing, uplifting, and healing everything in its environment.

TAURUS KEYWORDS

Mutable	Fixed	Cardinal
Instinctual possession	Directed possession	Released possession
I have	You and I share	It is all ours
Blind will	Focused will	Transcendental Will

Mutable	Fixed	Cardinal
Basic form	Refined form	Released from form
Earthly desire	Aspiration	Embodiment of Will
Conflict	Harmony through conflict	Resolution of conflict
Stubborn	Resolute	Will-filled
Horns of desire	Horns of struggle	Horns of plenty
Selfish will	Dualistic will	Goodwill

Taurus Keyword Phrases

Let struggle be undismayed. This is the phrase for Taurus on the ordinary wheel, and reveals the influence of the Fourth Ray. It indicates the urge to move forward into matter so that all lessons are learned about the nature of form. It is then that the conscious duality can take place, so that Taurus may learn how to use discrimination in the physical world.

I see, and when the Eye is opened, all is Light. The Soul's vision is through the cosmic eye of the Bull of God, demonstrating the presence of the First Ray. Once this vision of spiritual reality is developed, the Light which shines through Taurus serves to transform and uplift everything and everyone with whom she may come in contact.

As the individual descends into incarnation and when he takes an astral shell (emotional body), he definitely comes into a Taurian cycle, for it is desire which impels to rebirth and it takes the potency of Taurus to bring this about.

—Alice A. Bailey[6]

GEMINI
The Light of Interplay.

This is a line of light beams, revealing that which opposes or the basic duality of manifestation, the relationship of spirit and of form. It is the conscious light of that relationship.

[6]*Esoteric Astrology*, p. 380.

Ray of manifestation:

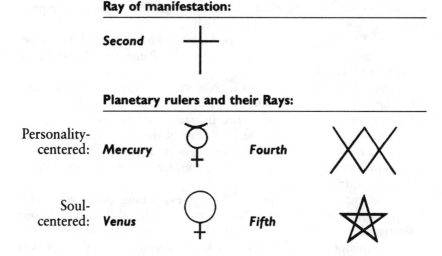

Second

Planetary rulers and their Rays:

Personality-
centered: **Mercury**   **Fourth**

Soul-
centered: **Venus**   **Fifth**

Aries is the beginning of a cycle of incarnation for the impulse of the Will-to-Be. The form responding to that fiery impulse is Taurus, evoking the Desire-to-Be, and corresponding most closely to the astral body. The relationship between this primordial urge and its response in desire is governed by the sign of Gemini.

The primary function of all the mutable signs is to produce a constant flux—a periodic, cyclic movement of time and space—in order to provide an adequate field of expression for the life of the Soul. It is the gathering of life experiences, based on the movement of relatedness and relationship, that is fundamental to Gemini, in particular. Gemini relates. Our previous discussion about the nature of the Soul has shown that It is primarily concerned with connectedness—that is, the Soul is the Way through which Spirit becomes Matter and Matter, Spirit. The Soul stands in the middle; It is the Middle Way. In this respect, it is the aspect of the Soul which represents the principle of the Christ; that is, the quality of Love which is the Second Aspect of the Divine Triad of Will-Love-Intelligence.

As the sign most significant of relatedness, Gemini appears most strongly through the Second Ray, and has as its Soul-centered ruler hat planet considered by esoteric astrologers to embody the most highly evolved of all planetary energies, Venus. Venus seeks to unite and blend, merge and harmonize all of the dualities in life. Venus takes these conflicts of duality (as indicated by Mercury, personality ruler of Gemini and planetary ruler of the Fourth Ray of Harmony through Conflict) and transforms them into a higher octave of expression. She does this through the creative expression of the mind and her relationship to the Fifth Kingdom of the Soul. In this respect, three correspondences should be noted:

1. The Second Ray influence of Gemini, and the relationship between the Second Ray, the Soul, and the Planetary Hierarchy of Masters and Teachers;

2. The rulership of Jupiter as it connects with the Second Ray, and the relationship which Venus holds with Jupiter as the Lesser and Greater Benefics, as they are called in traditional astrology;

3. Venus's connection to the Fifth Ray of the Concrete Mind. The latter, on the personality level, often works out through the logical aspects of Mercury's influence. This is another linkage between Venus, Mercury, and Gemini.

Gemini changes, mutates, and adjusts everything that is necessary for the evolution of the Soul, both in our individual lives, and in our collective life as humanity. From the Soul-centered approach, the house cusp upon which Gemini is located in your natal chart will reveal where these Soul-unfolding changes are most likely to come about, as well as the areas in your life where a great deal of Second Ray energy will be found. If you will note this carefully and then apply this method to the other signs, their Rays, and the houses they occupy in your chart, you will have a great deal of information regarding the nature of the Ray energies in your horoscope.

Venus, as ruler of Gemini, balances and harmonizes these movements and brings into the life the quality of Grace. Gemini reveals the relationship between any pair of opposites. When this polarization is expressed through Mercury, the Fourth Ray of Harmony through Conflict emerges. The purpose of polarization is to create a greater awareness of the pair of opposites, so that a more harmonious relationship may evolve. Mercury serves to create this awareness, but often through the focus of conflicting opposites inherent in the Fourth Ray nature of that planet. But Venus is an agent of synthesis because it is her function to blend and harmonize opposites into more creatively evolved wholes.

One of the most fundamental and important of Earthly polarities is the one which exists between male and female. When these two are brought into harmonious union through the positive influence of Venus, the human race advances. One doesn't have to be an esoteric astrologer to know this—it is exotericism at its most romantic! Yet the functioning of Venus as she works to blend and unite is very definitely geared to the purposes of creative procreation. This is the case whether the resulting creation is a child, a work of art, a political idea, or wherever else the Spirit may move. Eros himself is but Mercury imbued by the spirit of Venus!

The combination of Venus and Gemini also brings in another very important relationship between the Rays. It is here that we have the connection between the Second Ray of Love/Wisdom (Gemini) and the Fifth Ray of Science and Technology (Venus). When properly blended, and this is most certainly the responsibility of the men and women of goodwill, we will find that the great advances made by the scientific community will only be used for the betterment of mankind. It is in the adjustment and sharing of knowledge that Gemini and Venus play such an important role. We should also note that Aquarius is only found on the Fifth Ray line of Venus's rulership. This is yet another reason why the Aquarian Age holds the promise not only of amazing technological advances, but also of the expression of the Second Ray, through Venus's connection to Gemini and the Law of Right Human Relations. One should also note that Gemini is the vehicle for the transmission of the energy of that great Second Ray star, Sirius, into our solar system.

There is another relationship under the rulership of Venus and Gemini which is very important to the spiritually oriented individual. In effect, this entire work is dedicated to the unfolding of the understanding of the relationship between the Soul and the personality. Gemini and Venus rule the Rainbow Bridge, or Antahkarana—the vehicle through which this relationship occurs. It is only through the harmonious blending of the energies of this primary pair of opposites that the evolution of the individual may take place on spiritual, as well as material levels. The scope of one's objective/Earthly and subjective/Soul-focused experiences, and the adjustments needed to reconcile these with one's level of consciousness, are also part of the Gemini-Venus task.

Another facet of Gemini's rulership is its connection to the etheric double, the nature of which we discussed in chapter 8. It should be noted that the etheric double stands between the astral plane and the dense physical body. The chakras are located here, and it is through the etheric double and its various components that the vital energy of life (solar prana) is distributed, through the etheric network, into the nervous system of the physical vehicle. These connective links and circulatory systems are very much under the direction of Gemini. Venus helps them all to connect, so that there is a harmonious linkage between the visible and invisible bodies and vehicles of consciousness which constitute the true "Human Body."

GEMINI on the Mutable Cross (totally personality-centered individual). The urge for movement, and its external stimulation without plan or purpose, is very definitely a characteristic of the most basic kind of Gemini. The life is neither consciously connected to the cohesive energies of the Second Ray nor to the harmonious blending and synthetic rhythm of Venus. The instinctual mind rules. The totally personality-centered Gemini is often unaware of what he thinks. He moves to the dictates of mind motivated by the desire for experience.

The focus of relationship here is how everything and everyone relates to oneself. The sense of shared interchange is totally missing. Every movement, every person is "viewed" (if such a subjective perspective can be related to "seeing" in any form) as a means of furthering one's own particular ends. The lessons in life will begin to teach the Gemini on this level the true nature of interrelatedness. For the most part, however, the personality-centered Gemini will tend to view life through a "me versus them" perspective, at best becoming aware of the nature of opposites, but as yet having absolutely no idea that mutual harmony can exist or that anything else but duality is possible.

GEMINI *on the Fixed Cross (awakening to the Soul-personality relationship)*. Orientation of relationship is the important factor to be learned and expressed at this level. There is a very definite awareness of others, even extending to an understanding of relationships that do not involve the self. The mind seeks to expand its comprehension of relatedness, and the desire to accumulate knowledge presents itself. Intelligence moves from instinctual to creative, and from subjective to objective. A Gemini on this level will move beyond the concept that his or her opinions constitute an absolute philosophy of the world. (This is also what I like to refer to as "a Gemini impersonating a Sagittarian!") The urge to share what it is possible to know will be fundamental to Gemini's movements and interests at this stage of development.

As the Rainbow Bridge actually begins to unfold, the duality in one's life is seen to manifest through the nature of one's relationships. Unless there is a solid anchoring of consciousness on the Soul level, there will be a diffusion and scattering of interests, desires, and aspirations. Many of the crises in life now appear to come through the mixed intent and crossed purposes in these interpersonal exchanges, as one tries to harmonize oneself with people on various levels and stages of evolution. This is, of course, a reflection of the inherent dual quality of the Fixed Cross. One is apt to find oneself moving between two sets of people all the time: one group which represents the desires and the nature of the lower self, and another that represents the frame of reference of the Higher. Vacillation is likely to take place until a greater focus of Venus comes into play, replacing the Fourth Ray influence of Mercury in the life.

GEMINI *on the Cardinal Cross (the Soul-centered individual)*. At this level, the Gemini individual is being used as a conscious vehicle for creating harmonious linkages in the world. The work for such a person may have to do with aligning and blending various conflicting political and social forces; acting as an agent for harmony in terms of group interrelations; becoming a diplomat for peace and mutual understanding; inventing technological advances for the benefit of humanity, etc. It should be clearly understood that a Gemini expressing himself at this level is completely conscious of the spiritual implications of his activities. He is, in effect, acting as an agent for Hierarchy— an "intermediary of Light and Love"—which is the highest expression of the combination of Gemini and Venus in the Human Kingdom.

GEMINI KEYWORDS

Mutable	Fixed	Cardinal
Mutation of relations	Orientation of relations	Right Human Relations[7]
Lower mind serving instincts	Lower mind serving knowledge	Lower mind serving Higher Mind
Relating others to self	Relating self with others	Relating the One to self and others
Subjective mind	Subjective/objective mind	Wholistic mind
Polarizing/ subjectifying	Polarizing/ objectifying	Synthesizing/ harmonizing
Tossed by the wind	Circulates the wind	Co-directs the wind
Nonpurposeful movement	Related movement	Directed movement

Gemini Keyword Phrases

Let instability do its work. This phrase embodies within it all the vicissitudes of ordinary life: unpredictable changes, instability in human relationships, and the lack of cohesion in the lives of a huge

[7]That is, carrying forth the Plan for humanity as a messenger for Right Human Relations, backed by the power of the Will-to-Good.

multitude of people. Such instability serves to bring about the need to find the focus of harmony which comes with Soul awareness.

I recognize my other self, and in the waning of that self, I grow and glow. The individual knows himself to be the Soul. As the personality releases its hold upon the life energies, the Soul is able to relate to the lower self and the material world with greater direction and clarity. The lower self then becomes the disciplined extension of the Higher, creating whatever adjustments may be needed to bring forth the Soul's presence.

 CANCER
The Light within the form.

This is the diffused light of substance itself, the "dark light" of matter. . . . It is the light awaiting the stimulation coming from the soul light.

Rays of manifestation:

Third   △   *and Seventh*

Planetary rulers and their Rays:

Personality-
centered: *Moon* ☾   *Fourth* ✕✕

Soul-
centered: *Neptune* ♆   *Sixth*

The progression of the signs through the Zodiac is actually a representation of the scheme for the evolution of the incarnating human being. The first three signs are the most subjective in nature:

Aries: The fiery urge to be; the birth of the seed for incarnation on the mental plane.

Taurus: The response to this outpouring through Aries; the solidification of the urge to take form manifesting on the emotional plane as the Desire-to-Be.

Gemini: The movement of interchange between cause and effect, mind and emotion, primal beingness and its response; the activity of the vital life force.

Cancer can be seen as the resulting synthesis of these three previous stages of unfoldment. It is the integrating culmination for the expression of the urge to incarnate—not just as mind or desire or movement, but in an actual form containing all three. Cancer is known in the Ancient Wisdom Teachings as "the Gate In"—the place where a physical incarnation is taken for the first time. This should not be mistakenly construed to mean that every person born with Cancer rising or a Cancer Sun is incarnating for the first time on Earth. There are many cycles of incarnation, many turnings of the wheel, many mountings on and off the various Crosses. It is rather that an incarnation in Cancer indicates that this is the first cohesive anchoring of the Soul in a physical body for a particular cycle of unfoldment. This is one reason why Cancers are always so busy looking for a home, a place to root, a foundation upon which to build future incarnations, and a point on the material plane to which the Soul may polarize its presence, thus creating a line of movement for the Antahkarana. Likewise, an incarnation in Aries reveals the sowing of seeds on the mental plane that will be the "atomic nuclei" for future incarnations of that individual. Or, if the Aries is a more highly evolved being, his seeds will be sown for collective impregnation on the mental plane of future generations.

Cancer is a watery sign, but the Crab inhabits both land and sea. It comes forth from the collective matrix of the ocean, gains its nourishment from her plants and creatures, yet keeps a strong relationship to the sandy beach. The Cancer individual is just the same. Intimately in tune with the forces of psychic currents which play in and out of her reality, the Crab nonetheless reaches out to the earth for its security and breath. It exists in a psychic sense within the watery matrix, but it cannot survive when exclusively in this element. It can be nourished and protected by water, but it cannot evolve if continually submerged within the ocean's waves. So Cancer moves in and out of the psychic sea, bringing its alternating rhythms to the earth as she seeks her port of Earthly anchorage.

Like an embryo, Cancer lives in the protective waters of the mother, and yet derives her life through the oxygen in the air that we all breathe. This air, of course, comes to it through the umbilical cord. The process of the Soul's connection to its physical form does not complete itself until the infant has left the mother and is able to breathe on its own. This breath anchors the Soul force into the body, and the process of evolutionary and physical growth continues. Until the force of the personality fully individualizes in Leo, Cancer will find that the urge to retreat back into the watery protectiveness of the mother's womb will be as strong, if not stronger than, the urge to be born into the light of individualized self-definition.

Rays Three and Seven work through Cancer. The Third Ray of Active Intelligence acts to bring about a primordial matrix of life energy that eventuates into all the forms of external life. The latter finds its expression through the Seventh Ray. Cancer and its polarity, Capricorn, are both on these two Rays, and their relationship is most essential for us to understand from a Soul-centered perspective. We shall explore the details of the dynamics of Capricorn in its appropriate place, but let us share at this point three very significant correspondences between the two:

1. Cancer, as we have mentioned, is called "the Gate In," while Capricorn is known as "the Gate Out." This is the place on the human evolutionary path in which a great initiation takes place, freeing the individual from the rigors and repetitions of the Mutable and Fixed Crosses.

2. Capricorn, and its ruler Saturn (both on the personality and Soul levels), provide the structured ordering of the Laws of Manifestation which give rise to the multitudinous forms of life.

3. The Cardinal qualities of earth and water, as embodied by these two signs, hold the *motivation for manifestation*, clearly anchoring the energies of the Seventh Ray on Earth.

Cancer represents the mass consciousness. This is instinctual, and is based on desire and the automatic response to the form life. *Desire is humanity's initial response to form*: "I want. I need. Give me." One feels hunger on all three levels of the personality: mental, emotional, and physical. And one needs to be nourished in all three lower vehicles in order to develop into a fully healthy and integrated organism. The particular relationship existing between desire and form has been part of this mass consciousness for eons. The current wave of human evolution is adding another quality to this primordial duality— the need to know. It is not enough for us just to desire and to have those desires fulfilled. We are not satisfied by this primitive response to life. Ours is a quest for identification with the light contained within the form through the direct revelation of the Higher Mind. The Aquarian Age embodies this quest and has been called the sign of "I Know, therefore I Am," for centuries. *The mandate and the promise for humanity in the Aquarian Age is the transformation of mass consciousness into group consciousness*. This takes place as a result of the process of individuation; that is, the externalization of the Soul force contained within each of us. Once this group consciousness emerges, humanity will itself become the "Prince of Peace" and the Second Ray of Love/Wisdom will emerge through Jupiter (Aquarius) and the Sun (Leo) in much greater fullness.

The primary expression of the potencies of the Moon and Neptune through Cancer is very appropriate. The relationship between these two planets is symbolic of the rapport between the Moon, Mother of All Forms, and Neptune, the God of the Waters—"The Spirit of God moving upon the face of the waters," to paraphrase Genesis. The Spirit of God enlivens this primordial life matrix, placing therein the seeds for the creation of all forms. All life originated in the sea, the forms gradually evolving from the amorphic to a greater solidity and definiteness as the creatures of the waters moved out onto the land. The natural, shifting rhythm of the way Cancerians swim, glide, dance, and often evasively meander through life, is expressive of those tidal currents which still connect the Crab (and hence the Family of Man) to the liquidity of its origins.

Through the Fourth Ray, the Moon is very much an essential aspect of the collective expression of the Human Kingdom. From the level of the personality, the Moon rules many major facets of our ordinary life:

1. The attachment to forms and basic self-preservation;
2. The physical mother, her womb, the birth process;
3. The early psychological factors; the home and family life;
4. The tribe; that is, one's national and/or racial roots;
5. The genetic and biological karma;
6. The ability (or inability) to bring cohesion and integration into the world around us on both emotional and physical levels;
7. The sense of psychological "belongingness," as expressed by such thoughts and feelings as: "This is my country, my family, my home, my mother—me as a psychological unit."

One of the fundamental conflicts of this personality-centered orientation to life is its exclusivity. The waters of the Soul/Neptune wish to pull the individual into the ocean of the collective life experience. Yet the individual cannot "swim" safely in these universal waters without first having anchored its own sense of psychological independence and particular focus of self-expression. It is here that we come to understand that the more individualized a person becomes, the more universal he can be. Through the expanding consciousness, the many is seen as a reflection of the One, and the One is seen as whole in each of Its parts. This revelation (which some would rightly call "mystical") is the gift of Neptune, as well as the product of a Soul-centered consciousness.

The Moon relinquishes its control to Neptune when attachment is released from those facets of life ruled by the Moon on the personality level. Then the root chakra—the center wherein dwells the unconscious urge for self-preservation, which is, like the Moon, a vehicle for the Fourth Ray—loosens its dominance as the driving force behind life. The removal—or, at the very least, the objectification—of the desire to be attached to form frees the individual in increasing stages toward the identification with the Will-to-Be at the crown center. It is thus that the First and the Fourth Rays connect. The root center can then be utilized for the externalization of matter which has become consciously linked to Divine Cause, allowing for a direct "breathing upon the waters of life" by the Creator Spirit.

The connection to Neptune as the Soul-centered ruler of Cancer is very profound. Neptune "unveiled" is not the same influence as it is when masked by the unconscious waters of the emotional life. It is by her actions on the unredeemed lower self that Neptune earns her reputation as the primary force behind self-destructive addictions. If the personality is not safely anchored through a strong, integrated, and *aligned* ego structure, the magnetic force of the waters of the psyche will indeed try to pull the struggling individual back into unconscious and undifferentiated beingness. One has to work incredibly hard to unmask the mirages of Neptune (as focused through the Moon) to arrive at the illumination of Neptune as a vehicle for the Sun!

The totally Soul-centered individual does not react to ordinary feelings or sentiments. He or she is no longer attached to those personality responses which we could either characterize as being painful or pleasurable. One is only aware of the universal Love which underlies the Soul's expression of Life, and is thereby a server of that Love in conscious devotion to humanity. Thus the Sixth Ray, working through Neptune on the Soul level, reveals its highest function and purpose.

CANCER on the Mutable Cross (totally personality-centered individual). The sense of conscious individuality is totally absent. The Cancerian on this level is completely identified with her parental, tribal, and genetic background. Unknowingly, she is constantly activating and responding to the genetic strings which bind her to the physical life and, through her own particular form of expression, perpetuates them and her karma into the environment. Self-preservation is at the very core of her being, and there is usually a tremendous instinct to hoard, possess, and attach. Life is felt both sensually and psychically, but this is not an evolved type of psychism through which she can "see" and "know." This is more the type of psychism by which the effects of the phases of the Moon, and the emotional currents of her surroundings, move in and out of her psyche, leaving impressions which she has difficulty differentiating and distinguishing. The line between what are "her" impressions and what constitute the influences of other people is blurred. She unconsciously struggles to retain a faint glimmer of self, which often manifests through the collection of objects and the attachment to money and food.

CANCER *on the Fixed Cross (awakening to the Soul-personality relationship)*. At this point in evolution, the individual awakens to her surroundings in order to establish a clearer relationship with them. In effect, the Crab has come out of the unconscious but pregnant waters and is exploring life on Earth. There is a growing sense of separateness which, at an early stage, can be very frightening. When a path of personal, creative self-expression is chosen, this fear diminishes as she finds her "niche" in life and from this nest, can then create those objective contacts allowing the nourishing aspect of Cancer's nature to come forward. This stage demonstrates the difference between the mother who instinctively protects her child from any and all outside influences, and one who intelligently guides her child toward a more discriminating perspective on life. In a personal sense, this discrimination extends to the psyche, as well. Aware that certain influences are impressing themselves upon her, the Fixed Cross Cancer develops the kind of perceptive intelligence which allows her to differentiate among them. There is still the need to separate that which is "mine" from that which is someone else's, for the conscious fluidity of the universal expression of love has yet to emerge. The early stages of Cancers on the Mutable Cross only feel "at home" among their own tribe and within the most familiar of surroundings. On the Fixed Cross, however, Cancers may feel more at home no matter where they go, as the inner anchor to life on Earth has been integrated to a much greater extent within the psychological mechanism of the personality. At later stages, the concept and glimmer of the Love of the Mother begins to take root. Soon the world will be Cancer's home.

CANCER *on the Cardinal Cross (the Soul-centered individual)*. The Moon relates Cancer to the sign of Virgo as, esoterically, the Moon is the ruler of this sign. (See p. 195 for further details regarding this important relationship.) On the Soul level, the quality of the Mother as harbinger of the Christ Consciousness is embodied in the Soul-centered Cancer. The Cancerian has now developed into an individual of limitless compassion and tremendous inner reserves of nurturing energy (that is, the higher expressions of Neptune and the Sixth Ray). This is an advanced human being who is selflessly creating those forms and structures on the Earth for the betterment of humanity. Such an individual would be found hard at work trying to feed the homeless, creating projects for the best use of agricultural lands, and generally devoting his life to the cohesive networking of men and women of goodwill. He is also a vehicle of the highest expression of Third, Sixth, and Seventh Ray energies, which pour through him into a hungry environment.

CANCER KEYWORDS

Mutable	Fixed	Cardinal
Totally subjective	Awakening to environment	Identifies with the Whole
Selfish desire	Shared desire	Selfless desire
Waters of womb	Waters of earth	Waters of Life
Self-preserving	Self-nurturing	*Self*-serving
Instinctual mother	Worldly mother	Universal Mother

Cancer Keyword Phrases

Let isolation be the rule, and yet—the crowd exists. When a person's life is centered in the personality as its total expression, his eventual destiny will be isolation and loneliness. He is so fundamentally subjective that it becomes impossible to connect with others, no matter how close the biological or karmic attachment. Without the tension of the personality-Soul relationship, he becomes imprisoned by the shell of the lower self.

I build a lighted house and therein dwell. The illusion of separateness eventually gives way to the illumination of universality. It is then that the Soul-centered individual becomes the channel for the "Light of the World" which, when expressed through Cancer, is unlimited nourishment to all the forms and creatures of life.

LEO
The Light of the Soul.

A reflected point of light logoic or divine. The light diffused in Cancer focuses and reveals eventually a point.

Rays of manifestation:

First　　*and Fifth*

Planetary rulers and their Rays:

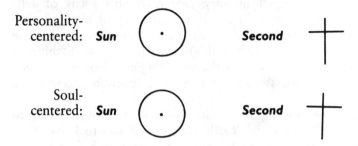

Personality-
centered: **Sun** ⊙   **Second** ✝

Soul-
centered: **Sun** ⊙   **Second** ✝

The purpose of this solar system is the unfolding of consciousness. In the life of a human being, this translates as the activation of self-consciousness. Once we know that we are a self—self-demonstrating and self-creating—we then come to know ourselves as an extension of universal creativity. The quality of that revelation comes to us as unconditional love.

In order to comprehend the dynamics of that love as it operates in an individually focused way, evolution proceeds out of the mass consciousness of Cancer and into the intense self-consciousness of Leo. This doesn't mean, of course, that people born with the Sun or rising sign in Cancer are lacking the evolutionary "equipment" to stabilize an individualized sense of self. We go through many rounds and cycles of incarnation, and for many Cancers (or for any of the other signs, for that matter), the anchoring of this sense of self has already been accomplished. Such a self-realized person would be inclined to have a highly stabilized point of release for the externalization of the nurturing and form-giving energies of the Crab. It is in Leo, however, that the inherent creativity of such self-awareness begins to manifest outwardly in some individualized manner.

Leo is a fixed, fiery sign. The "Sons and Daughters of Mind" are "Children of Fire" because our Divinity is a creating and consuming flame.[8] This is also the flame of purification, and as it expresses itself through the First Ray, where Leo is also found, it burns and destroys anything which hinders the progress of the creative will. In this respect, Leo is also related to the two planets of the First Ray: Pluto and Vulcan.

One of the most celebrated of First Ray Leos is Napoleon, whose

---

[8]In the Ancient Wisdom Teachings, humanity is sometimes referred to as the "Sons and Daughters of Mind," as it is understood that the origin of our being is a fiery atomic spark in the Mind of God. A wider comprehension of this concept may be obtained if one considers the relationship of the energies of Aries and the First Ray, the Will-to-Be, and its connection to Mercury and the Fourth Ray of Humanity.

highly developed will, coupled with Leo's Fifth Ray mental qualities, characterized his imperial military career. As his focus of self-consciousness was centered in the Leo personality of his Sun, such self-glorification did not last long and, as the history books reveal, he had an ignominious end. Pluto and Vulcan will destroy anything or anyone that stands in the way of the unfolding evolutionary Plan, be it a person or the solar system, for theirs is a function of Shiva, the Destroyer.

Leo is of paramount importance in the life of a person aspiring to the Path of Discipleship and World Service. He has to know himself through the tests leading to true self-awareness before he can come to the realization of his essential divinity. The tests which accompany this quest for self-consciousness often take the form of extremely intense challenges to the personality, the primary nature of which are embodied in the sign of Scorpio and will be discussed under that heading.

Once this sense of self becomes fixed, a center of self-actualization is established through which the foundation of a cycle of incarnations, as expressed in Cancer, may begin to grow and develop. Leo is polarized to Aquarius, the sign of group consciousness. If Leo is the heart, Aquarius is the circulatory system. That which is centered in the fixed, fiery sign of the Lion has to be distributed through the airy networking of the Water Bearer.

I think that a strong personality-centered Leo may find himself confronting a great deal of social tension in the Age of Aquarius. In effect, the forces of the Age are saying: "Okay, you can be a star, you can assert your creative will and focused mental energy, but only as it relates and is of benefit to the collective. Whatever you do and no matter how strong the urge to leave your own particular mark on your creations, your efforts must have some group relevance." In the New Age, Napoleons are no longer appreciated except as pastries, and even then, they have to be shared with friends!

Yet the fixed, fiery nature of Leo operating on the Soul level in the Aquarian Age acts as a loving center and source for the creative focus of the heart (Second Ray) as it externalizes through the mind (Fifth Ray). This centralized emergence of creative/loving ideation can then be distributed throughout the collective via the social networks established by Aquarian Age humanity. The Fifth Ray energies of Leo and Aquarius, working through the forms of science and technology, will produce those inventions which are to be circulated throughout society. It is for this reason that Alice Bailey and the Tibetan Master tell us that in the Aquarian Age, the scientific community will be the primary vehicle for the expression of the Love/Wisdom of the Second Ray. I do not doubt that this statement will come as a shock to the metaphysical community, which looks very warily upon the imposed and projected limitations of those who have created a "religion" out of the rational mind. Such words would also challenge the scientific community, most of whom associate the Ancient Wisdom Teachings with the library of the Massachusetts Institute of Technology!

If we examine the Leo-Aquarius polarity, we will find that it is totally on a Fifth Ray/Second Ray line of expression. Both these signs are found on the Fifth Ray, while the Soul-centered planetary rulers of these signs—the Sun and Jupiter—focus the energy of the Second Ray of Love/Wisdom. In regard to a planet/sign relationship, the reader should keep in mind that it is the Ray, acting through a planet, that is the energy source of a manifesting stream of Life. The latter is externalized through the "field of expression" of a particular sign or signs. The Age of Aquarius is thus primarily one of Love/Wisdom, which is expressed in the outer world through the products of the concrete mind behind science and technology. In this respect, the essential *Life of Humanity* will come to know itself through the consciousness inherent in the *Soul of Humanity*, as expressed in the outer world through those communicative inventions and social systems which link all of us together as the *Body of Humanity*. These three facets of our collective beingness are all enlivened by the Sun and the Second Ray. (In terms of current social evolution, we should note, for example, that the "United States of Europe" is a current reality. One can obtain a "European Passport," to live, work, travel, and remain in almost all of the countries of Western Europe without special visas or permits, provided that one is a citizen of a nation in this community. The European Common Market is another prototype of such a unified focus, as is the United Nations, from a planetary level.)

Leo produces the growth of individualism out of the collective matrix of Cancer. This sense of self-consciousness is being strongly fostered in the evolutionary progression of the current generations of humanity. The urge for such self-development is especially prevalent for those people who have Pluto in Leo in their natal charts (1939–1957). This Pluto-in-Leo group has been called the "Me Generation," and with good reason. Pluto, a First Ray planet, acting through the Fifth and First Ray qualities of Leo, produces an energy which shatters the thought-forms of the past and births, in a most intense way, a new dynamic of self-consciousness. That "self"—that concept of "me"—has been and will continue to be strongly challenged with the passage of Pluto in Scorpio (1982–1994). During this twelve-year period, individuals born between 1939–1957 will encounter some major crises of reorientation in their lives.

Scorpio is the sign through which the process of transformation reorients personal values into social ones, and personality-centered, self-conscious identity into an understanding of the relationship between the individual and the whole. It is in Aquarius that full participation in this collective, via service to humanity, takes place. While natal Pluto in Leo is being squared by transiting Pluto in Scorpio, there will be a great challenge to realign and redefine one's personal life values into those which are better suited for the expression of a wider and more comprehensive participation in life. In this sense, the individualization which took place in Leo evolves toward a universal inclusivity. In order that this process may take place, certain aspects of the personality (as signified by the houses which Pluto rules and tenants natally) will be focused upon for change and transmutation. In effect, a First Ray planet is square to a First Ray planet, which can only lead to death and rebirth. People with the Sun or rising sign in Leo or Scorpio should take special note of this great opportunity for growth. After all, "the heavens" are taking special note of you!

This book is primarily concerned with the relationship of the Soul to the personality. That is, we are studying the relationship of the quality of Life to the form of Life, as revealed in esoteric astrological symbolism. There is another relationship—the one existing between the Light of Life Itself (which is embodied in the existence of the Monad) and Its expression through the Soul. This is the relationship between Life and the Quality of Its expression; that is, consciousness. The astrology of this interchange is beyond our scope, and for the vast majority of us, also beyond our life experience. Yet I do want to point out that the Sun is the ruler of Leo on all three of these levels: Monadic, Soul, and personality. It is thus that the Second Ray externalizes on all of the three major levels of Being in our solar system. As a result, we can begin to grasp the importance of the Lion as the vehicle for the creative potency of Divinity in manifestation. It is the only one of the celestial spheres which has this triple relationship to the signs.[9] The Sun is the primary focus and center of the creative life force, and reveals its nature as:

1. The Life of the Sun on the Monadic level;
2. The Heart of the Sun on the Soul level;
3. The Physical Body of the Sun on the personality level.

There are three types of fire, which correspond to the three levels of Being mentioned above. These are Cosmic Fire, symbolized by Aries;

[9]Those who wish to pursue studies into this little-known aspect of esoteric astrology, which we call "Hierarchical," would be well advised to follow the hints and indications offered in *Esoteric Astrology*, by Alice A. Bailey. Madame Blavatsky, in *The Secret Doctrine*, also shares some information in this area. Although this is the most esoteric of astrologies, there are some correlations regarding the Hierarchical Planetary Rulers and the signs well worth investigating.

Solar Fire, as indicated by Leo; and Planetary Fire, signified by the third of the fiery signs, Sagittarius. Each of these fires, working on Will, Soul, and Personality respectively, purifies a path for the expression of Divinity. As our will, love, and relationship to the material world are continually tested, many of us have experienced and will continue to experience the "burning ground" in our individual lives. It is only through such tests that our lower vehicles come to be transformed and refined so that the process of Soul union may continue to unfold.

The functions of Leo and the purifying fire of the Soul may be summed up by the word "sensitivity"—that is, the integration of the personality apparatus leading to the sensitivity to Self. This occurs in four stages:

1. Sensitivity to the influences and impacts coming from the external environment of the physical senses. As consciousness begins to objectify and "fix" itself as "a point of Light," one begins to view the sensory impact of the environment upon the physical body, emotions, and mind from a place of detachment. Leo at this stage serves to solidify, "fixate," and bring such responses together.

2. Sensitivity to the will, wishes, and urgings of this integrated, self-conscious lower self. In essence, it is here that the ego is fixed as a self-motivating entity.

3. Sensitivity to the Soul as the conditioning factor of response to life. At this stage, the Soul has become "fixed" as a point of mediation between the creative fire of the Spiritual Self and the physical world of the lower self.

4. Sensitivity to Spiritual Will. As Leo is a sign of the First Ray, response to the right use of will is of paramount importance. When Leo has developed to a point of being a "liberated" person—that is, free from the thrall and karma of the lower self—then he can begin to transform the outer environment into the proper vehicle for the expression of the Inner Plan and Purpose of Divinity. This is accomplished through World Service, as indicated by Leo's polarity, Aquarius.

LEO on the Mutable Cross (totally personality-centered individual). The true fire of Spiritual Will is masked by the shadow of the personality at this stage. This is the typical show-off—a person quite full of a sense of himself, but with no foundation in true creative potency. The need to dominate the environment by the sheer weight of the personality is very apparent, yet there is a distinct inability for any sustaining or lasting impact. Usually the personality is marked by a tremendous need for attention, especially to things of a physical nature such as clothing, and those material possessions which are reflective of his sense of personal taste and self-esteem. This is why jewelry, one's house and children tend to take on a great deal of importance. Here Leo needs the reflection of admiration, a sense of being a "shining star," and in the case of children, the assurance of physical continuity. The court of Louis XIV of France could be said to be the epitome of this type of Leonian orientation. It was Louis, dressed resplendently as "the Sun King," who said "L'Etat, c'est moi! I am the State!"

LEO on the Fixed Cross (awakening to the Soul-personality relationship). At this stage of self-unfoldment, the Fixed Cross Leo develops an increasing awareness of the dynamics of creative self-expression. He has to make his mark on the environment, but is also becoming more and more aware of the conscious rather than instinctive use of will, and the need for continuity of purpose in order to be effective. In this respect, he has a growing consciousness of himself, not just as an entity living on the planet, but as a co-creator of and within his environment. His struggle and battleground at this phase has a great deal to do with "getting out of the Way." His attachment to the personality is still very strong, and he has the impression that his ego is the doer, the creator, the person ultimately responsible, or the one to whom others are ultimately responsible. The sense of the transcendental, in which he acts as a *conscious vehicle or mediator* of the creative Will-to-Be, has yet to fully crystallize. He has a tremendous need to orient himself to the larger collective. In the case of the totally personality-centered Leo, the urge is for the collective to surround him, much like planets revolving around a sun. When on the Fixed Cross, however, the lesson being learned is one of *relationship to the collective.* This requires a greater sense of integration and assimilation of the personality into the larger will of the group. When on the Mutable Cross, the nature of the lower self is so insecure and immature that he constantly attempts to dominate the collective. The Fixed Cross Leo has, to one degree or another, fixated and blended the personality, thus allowing a group experience to be less threatening to this process of self-integration and eventual Soul infusion.

LEO on the Cardinal Cross (the Soul-centered individual). There are two very important underlying factors about the Leo person which constitute the "heart of the Lion." These are:

1. The Will-to-Illumine, which comprises the deep urge toward self-knowledge, self-awareness, and the development of a positive intellect, electrically potent so that it may fire the minds of others. This Will-to-Illumine is an aspect of the workings of the Fifth Ray.

2. The Will-to-Rule, which in the early stages expresses itself as the dictatorial power of the ego. Yet at later stages, it is this Will-to-Rule that leads a person to achieve control over that very same personality, and in its mastery, achieve Soul control. This is one of the primary

functions of the First Ray as it expresses itself in our Second Ray solar system.

When Leo has mounted the Cardinal Cross, these two facets of the will—rulership and illumination—emanate from the Soul. The individual is now able to instill and inspire the group within which he serves a central role and function. This service is focused on cohesive direction and the expression of those creative fires that keep the movements of the collective in motion. Leo becomes a vehicle for the centripetal force of the creative will as it functions to hold any group together. Yet the Cardinal Cross Leo does not see himself as *the* center, but as an integrating, fixating expression of the collective will.

> Yet the only truly self-conscious person is the man who is aware of purpose, of a self-directed life and of a developed and definite life plan and programme. . . . In the truly developed self-conscious man not only is direction, purpose, and plan present, but also a consciousness of the active agent of the plan and action. Ponder on this.

—Alice A. Bailey[10]

LEO KEYWORDS

Mutable	Fixed	Cardinal
Physical Sun	Heart of the Sun	Spiritual Sun
Lower self	Higher Self	The One Self
Reflecting light	Emanating Light	Source of Light
Rule by instinct	Rule by intelligence	Rule by Love
Self-centered	Self-centering	Center of Self
Instinctual use of will	Intelligent use of will	Right Use of Will
Domineering	Focused	Purposeful
Roar of the beast	Voice of man	Call of Divinity
Birth of individuality	Fixation of individuality	Consecration of individuality

[10] *Esoteric Astrology*, pp. 288–9.

Leo Keyword Phrases

Let other forms exist. I rule because I am. This phrase characterizes the "benevolent dictorship" which is often the form of expression for the personality-centered Leo. The "other forms" are seen as extensions of the undeveloped self over which "young" Leo takes control in an instinctual and unconscious manner. "I rule as a right of my presence in any situation" would also be a proper way to state this type of Leonian frame of reference.

I am That and That I am. This phrase shows that the individual has identified with the Soul and that the two—the Soul and the personality—have reached a relationship of fusion and integration. Now Leo is prepared to rule as a conscious extension of Divine Will.

VIRGO
The blended dual Light.

Two lights are seen—one bright and strong, the light of form; one faint and dim, the light of God. This light is distinguished by a waxing of one and the waning of the other. It differs from the light in Gemini.

Rays of manifestation:

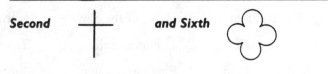

Second   and Sixth

Planetary rulers and their Rays:

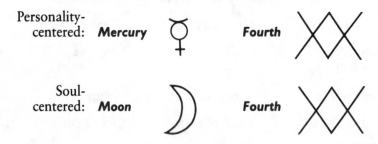

Personality-centered: Mercury   Fourth

Soul-centered: Moon   Fourth

In Leo, humanity anchors the sensitivity to the Higher Self through the intense focus of the multileveled self-awareness which characterizes this sign. It is in Virgo that those processes of externalization of the Soul onto the physical plane are undertaken. In this respect, Virgo is seen as the sign of the "Hidden Christ," as it represents the inner gestation and growth of the Soul force within each of us. This is the sign of pregnancy, and it is ruled by the Moon, symbolizing the Mother of All Forms. These forms and the Mother Principle shield and nurture, protect and conceal, swelling with all the potential of birth. The Mother gathers all the nutrients necessary to feed her unborn child and allows them to pass through her in a blended and distilled form to the embryo in her womb. Then, at the right cycle of evolution, the Mother births her "Child," revealing the hidden spiritual reality. This process of gestation is the function of Virgo.

Gemini and Virgo are very closely related, especially on the personality level, as they are both ruled by Mercury. In the expression of the rational faculties of the mind, which are so much the province of the Messenger, Gemini rules the process of analysis, while Virgo is more concerned with synthesis. This relationship is also reflected esoterically. The primary difference from this perspective is that in Gemini the Soul and the personality are separate entities constantly relating and balancing one another. In Virgo, the personality and the Soul are blended, but this blending has yet to take on its objective manifestation. In effect, Virgo represents the statement "the Christ *within* you, the hope of Glory." Thus the evolutionary stage of human development indicated by Virgo is the stirring of the subjective life within each of us. This is the quickening urge of the Soul's Presence, but the consciousness of the Soul is yet to be born. This birth into objective life, and the responsibility which such a birthing entails, will take nine more months, or astrological signs, to culminate. Therefore, if we were to count nine signs on the reversed wheel (the Wheel of Man), the birth of a living Soul in the form of a human being would appear in the sign of the Initiate, Capricorn.

Virgo the Virgin is intimately connected to this process of the birthing of the Christ, the Savior—the Grace of Divinity which dwells within. It is in the externalization of this inner Grace that each man or woman finds his rightful place in the material world, and is thus able to fulfill his or her appropriate life task. Virgo is, after all, the sign of one's "job"—one's place in the practical world. This may explain why Virgos are so preoccupied with finding their right livelihood, and why work, and the often compulsive need to perform the proper function in the larger scheme of things, is so much a part of people who are strongly influenced by this sign.

The above paragraph may seem to contain a very strong Christian statement and may seem out of place coming from a nonreligionist esotericist and student of the Ancient Wisdom Teachings. So, in this respect, a word of explanation is required. The Christ, coming from the Greek word *Cristos,* or "Anointed One," is an Office of a very high degree. It is held by different Great Ones in cyclic succession. The Christ in the previous Piscean Age came as Lord Jesus, Whose name (as he was a Jewish man) comes from the Hebrew word for "savior"—*Yahweh*. In our esoteric tradition, we speak of the next Cristos as being the Lord Maitreya. No matter Who may occupy the Office of the Christ, the energy of this Great One is the synthesis of all Human Souls. The Christ is, in effect, the Soul of Humanity, Whose Gift is Love Incarnate. It is thus quite true that it is through the Christ (Love, the Soul), but not necessarily or exclusively through the Christian churches (for these churches represent just one of the many "Noble Paths" for people to tread upon their search toward Light), that we reach the Light of the Monad, the Spirit, the God-Self. Although the forms of the various churches and religions have proven to be a very important ingredient of humanity's approach to Divinity, we must take great care not to worship these forms (which is difficult, as the forms tend to worship themselves!), but to see them as the respected vehicles for the Divine Light which they contain. *Virgo is thus a lesson in the discrimination of form.* Those individuals born into this sign or with Virgo rising will often find that such tests of material discrimination are at the very core of their lives.

The Ancient Wisdom Teachings tell us that the name Virgo is a corruption of an Atlantean name that was applied to the Mother Principle. Lilith, the dark moon of astrology, was the name of the last Virgin Goddess of Atlantis. There are three other names for the Virgin that we should examine, as they will reveal more about the esoteric nature of this sign: Eve, Isis, and Mary.

Eve is the symbol of the mental nature of humanity, and represents the desire for knowledge. She symbolizes the eating of "the fruit of the tree," or the information gained by the Soul from physical incarnation. Isis has two forms: veiled and unveiled. She also represents the gathering of such information, but her domain is the realm of the emotions. The veil of Isis has to do with the illusions of the astral plane, while the unveiling of the Goddess reveals the perception of hidden truth. The root of the name Mary is very ancient. It is constantly associated with water, whether it is from the Sanskrit root *maya*, the Hebrew *mayam*, or the Latin *mare*. Mary is the maternal matrix of form, originating in the sea. It is from the physical body of Mary that the "Heavenly Fish" was born, Jesus, the Anointed Savior of the Age of Pisces. Virgo, in her three aspects of mind, emotion, and body, represents the synthetic qualities of the Mother Principle, which is blending the proper nutrients for her unborn offspring; she is always gathering in the proper information for the growth of the Soul.

Virgo symbolizes the depth and darkness in which the Light is protected. Hers is the "womb of time," in which God's Plan slowly gestates and is brought into manifestation. We are currently at the "eighth month" of this gestation period, for that is the number of signs from Virgo to Aquarius on the reversed wheel. We are thus beginning the last phase of a great preparation. It is a phase that will take another 2,160 years, but will lead inevitably to the Age of Capricorn—the "ninth sign," and the birth of the Initiate/Christ/ Messiah. The Age of Aquarius is thus an Age of preparation for the Coming One. It is a time when the process of Leonian individuation will give rise to the necessary group consciousness of the One Humanity, and the externalization of the One Soul which is the inner life of that Humanity.

Let us examine some of the Ray relationships of Gemini, Virgo, Mercury, and the Moon, so that some of the deeper meanings inherent in these signs and planets may reveal themselves. Gemini and Virgo are both vehicles for the externalization of the Second Ray of Love/Wisdom. Virgo also manifests the Sixth Ray of Devotion. The blending and relating qualities of these two signs give all forms of life the opportunity to express the essential Love quality which is the consciousness of the Divinity of our solar system.

The Moon, "Mother of All Forms," manifests on the same Ray as Mercury, the Fourth Ray of Harmony through Conflict, which has as its function the balancing of Spirit and Love (and is, as a result, a blending of Rays One and Two). The Fourth is also a Ray of Attribute, as it is an emanation of Ray Three. It is this Third which stands behind physical forms as the coordinating Ray, so that the Ideas of the Creator may be expressed throughout the lower kingdoms. The Fourth is also called "the Ray of Essential Living." This means that in our daily lives we are always at work trying to balance will with love, and essential ideas with the forms they take. This also requires our continual attempts to integrate and blend our sense of personal power (One) with the wisdom (Two) and intelligence (Three) to evoke harmony out of the conflicts of life. The Fourth is also named the "Ray of Beauty," and the quest for same is a primary factor in the "divine discontent" which motivates Humanity, the Fourth Kingdom. In view of these Ray factors, we can see that Virgo is totally connected to the cohesive power of the Mother and the force of Love/ Wisdom, as the Virgin is intimately related to the Second, Fourth, and Sixth Rays by virtue of the planetary energies which play through her.

Through the Moon, Virgo relates to Cancer, and the more we study these two signs, the more this relationship reveals itself. Cancer, as we have seen, is the watery matrix of primordial life. She represents the diffused energy of the mass consciousness, capable of moving in any direction when impulsed by the Will of the Father/Spirit. Cancer is the amniotic sac and the nutrients in the amniotic fluid. In this respect, Cancer is representative of the potential abundance that surrounds us in our daily life if we but learn how to use our willpower correctly to tap into it. Virgo, a sign of the earth element, and analytical Mercury, Virgo's exoteric ruler, differentiate the potential wholeness of Mother Cancer into the myriad forms needed by all of the Mother's children in our daily lives. Cancer, the Third Ray matrix, thus connects with Virgo through the Fourth Ray qualities of the Moon, and brings into life the necessities required by each of us to do our part in the One Work.

The Tibetan summarizes the interchange between Virgo and Cancer, Mercury and the Moon, very clearly:

When Mercury, the Divine Messenger, the principle of illusion, and the expression of the active higher mind, has performed his mission and "led humanity into the light" and the Christ-child out of the womb of time and of the flesh into the light of day and of manifestation, then the task of that great center we call humanity will be accomplished.[11]

VIRGO on the Mutable Cross (totally personality-centered individual.) At this stage of evolution, the urge to gather resources is instinctive. This can easily result in a cluttered life in which both the outer physical environment and the subjective thought world are filled with items and ideas that are both necessary and unnecessary. It is very difficult for Virgo at this level to be able to differentiate "the baby from the bathwater," and as a result, the individual is often lacking in both physical and mental discrimination. Form and attachment to form are of primary consideration, resulting in compulsive acquisition. This type of Virgo has a horror of empty spaces, and will fill the air with excessive words, her closets with superfluous clothing, and her mind with needless thoughts. Behind all of this activity is the fear of the void, of not having, and of the subjective darkness in which Virgo, if she would just relax long enough, would discover that spark of cohesive and healing Love. As the fear of introspection predominates to such a large extent, there is the tendency for Virgo to exteriorize a protective wall of materiality and excessive attention to outer details. In this way, Virgo can protect herself from yet another deep anxiety—that other people may also perceive her lack of cohesion and the apparent void at her center. Yet it is within this very void that she may find her salvation and peace.

[11]Bailey, *Esoteric Astrology*, p. 273. If we contemplate the relationship existing between Mercury, the Moon, and Humanity, and the Fourth Ray (which predominates in the expression of all three), much will be learned relative to the fundamentals of human nature. Take the time to "ponder on this."

VIRGO on the Fixed Cross (awakening to the Soul-personality relationship). Here is where we find the typically critical Virgo—the perfectionist in search of the exact and proper synthesis for all situations. The process of discernment is at work in earnest as Virgo moves from instinctive gathering to the refined objectification of herself in the outer world of forms. Her collecting and self-preservation take on much more clarity as her sense of self becomes stronger and more defined. She is discriminating and analytical. Virgo, at this stage of personal development, is likely to be just the opposite of the cluttered, personality-centered kind. Her world is ordered and given over to the conscious blending of influences. In this respect, she is often found cleansing and purging herself from previous encounters, collections, ideologies, and experiences. She is eager to retain what is valuable and to release that which serves no practical function in her life, whether this is a relationship, a job, an idea, or a kitchen appliance. If it doesn't work, toss it out or pass it on! In the previous stage, Virgo cannot usually make such objective assessments, stuck as she is in the need to indiscriminately gather and store.

Service now comes into Virgo's frame of reference. The Mutable Cross Virgo will state to the world: "I'll fit in anywhere, do anything, function and *survive* under any circumstances." This is the effect of the Moon and Mercury working through the Fourth Ray on the personality level of the root chakra. The Fixed Cross Virgo is much more likely to state: "I would like to do something which allows me a certain form of creative self-expression—one which benefits and serves others in the process—so that I may have a clearer understanding of my function and role in society." The earlier frame of reference is one in which Virgo seeks relationships and occupations in order to sustain personal survival at a very basic physical and/or emotional level. This means that the personality-centered Virgo is much more likely to have indiscriminate relationships. This provides at a basic level the form of physical intimacy, creating the illusion that she does not have to deal with the void on the emotional level.

This is, of course, not the case for the Virgo who is awakening to the Light within. Virgo on the Fixed Cross moves back and forth in a rhythm of fullness and emptiness. She is constantly experimenting physically, emotionally, and mentally, all the while gathering those experiences that will bring her to a stage in which she feels ready to birth her true mission and perform her true task of work and service.

VIRGO on the Cardinal Cross (the Soul-centered individual). Service and the activity of the Soul totally dominate the life of a Virgo who has reached the level of the Cardinal Cross. The necessary experiences of the three worlds of the personality have been accomplished, and a perfect blending and synthesis has taken place. Virgo can take from all of her gathered resources and give them out to a world in need of nourishment and caring. It is here that the Second and Sixth Rays of Love/Wisdom and Devotion come into play at their strongest, in terms of their human expression. *Life is led as an act of love.* Devotion to the universality of humankind is at the core of her being, and that core is now enlivened and enlightened by the radiance of the Soul.

Virgo is the sign of the six-pointed star of the Soul-infused personality. It is through the loving and magnetic force field of the inner Soul/Christ Presence that the Law of Attraction operates and the three vehicles of the personality fuse and blend, aligning themselves with the corresponding three vehicles of the Soul (see diagram 5). The Cardinal Cross Virgo has accomplished this process in herself and furthers it in the world around her through her focus on healing and world service.

VIRGO KEYWORDS

Mutable	Fixed	Cardinal
Self-serving	Serving others	Serving the One
Indiscriminate	Discriminate	Inclusive
Unordered	Search for order	Order out of chaos
Fear of emptiness	Sense of resources	Totally resourceful
Hiding from self	Working on self	Self-realized as Love
Physical	Mental	Philosophical
Survivalist	Discriminately creative	Vehicle of the Creator
Trapped by form	Co-creator of form	Form of the Creator

Virgo Keyword Phrases

Let matter reign. Matter is form and comes from the Latin word *mater*, which means "mother." On the ordinary wheel, Virgo is so intimately connected with the form life that the consciousness has not, as yet, developed the necessary objectification for its release as Light. Yet it is through the lessons of matter that Virgo, at a later stage, comes to regard that precious inner purity which, at an earlier stage, was regarded with dread and fear, as the embryo of the Soul's presence.

I am the Mother and the Child. I, God, I Matter am. These are the words of the Soul, recognizing Its function as a vehicle for the Father's Light. This is also a statement of perfected, blended unity in which Spirit (God), Soul (Christ), and Body (Matter/Mother) are all unified. In effect, this lesson of Virgo reveals to us that Matter and its Creator are but one continuous line of cosmic expression. It is through consciousness (that quality of the Soul) that humanity comes to this realization. It is through service to humanity that such an awareness of the Eternal Life and all of Its Forms is quickened into physical reality.

LIBRA

The Light that moves to rest.

This is the light that oscillates until a point of balance is achieved. It is the light which is distinguished by a moving up and down.

Rays of manifestation:

Third △ *and Seventh*

Planetary rulers and their Rays:

Personality-centered: *Venus* ♀ *Fifth* ☆

Soul-centered: *Uranus* ⛢ *Seventh*

Libra's tendency to be noncommittal and rather blasé—which on the surface indicates a lack of passion, an impartiality, an "it's all okay with me" attitude—can be very disconcerting to a person of a more martial nature. Try this out too often with a Mars-ruled Aries or Scorpio partner, and see how a war ensues! When Mars is also in Libra, a person of Balance tends to tip the scales. It is assured that should the Sun and Mars be conjoined in this sign, then whatever "you" may like, "I" am going to dislike. "I" will also make sure to attract someone into my life with whom there will be such consistent dissent that "I" will always be on one side or the other of any dispute. Such confrontations of personality continue for Libra (Mars notwithstanding) until ultimate peace is achieved through marriage with the Higher Self.

From the Soul-centered perspective, Libra represents a pause, an interlude, a place of assessment, a point of contemplation, a hiatus between two activities. Soul-centering people incarnating in Libra may take this "karmic hiatus" as they prepare for the great conflict awaiting them (and everyone else, for that matter) in Scorpio. Libra provides that seesaw experience which can be very confusing both to the Libran and to those with whom he may be in relationship. This consists of the dualistic rhythm of a person who has perceived something much deeper than the material aspects of the form life. This individual has experienced the Presence of the Soul but is not fully anchored in Its consciousness. He is thus polarized, and tends to waver back and forth between the desires of the personality and the service orientation and transpersonality of the Soul. Such is the great duality and testing ground of people born on the Scales. This rhythm is often alternating, for at certain times of his life, Libra is much more Soul-oriented, while at other times, his personality may predominate. Librans are thus in flux between these two major polarities of life, but for a very good reason—they are supposed to learn the nature of the energies and experiences of this polarity very intimately. Their job is to harmonize these two currents, as a result of experiencing the two contrasting but related sides.

In this respect, we should recall that Venus, the exoteric ruler of Libra, is the esoteric ruler of Gemini, the sign of the relating and harmonizing of opposites. In addition to creating a state of balance between the two "abutments" of the Rainbow Bridge—the Soul and the personality—Libra prepares the Way for the Disciple to do open warfare in Scorpio: here is one side of the battle; there's the other. But the real fight (leading to the Soul infusion of the personality) has not, as yet, commenced. Libra is not ready for such intense turmoil, but draws out the battle lines, taking alternating positions.

As Uranus is the esoteric ruler of Libra and the exoteric ruler of Aquarius, sign of human relationships, Libran evolution unfolds through the interplay of interpersonal dynamics. In earlier stages, especially when on the Fixed Cross, Librans engage in those relationships which clearly define the differences between loving a person from the Soul level *as opposed to* loving someone from the focus of the personality. A bit farther down the Path, Libra will work to integrate and balance these two expressions of loving.

This dilemma will be finally resolved through Scorpio. Libra is the sign of the balancing of desires: the desires of the threefold lower nature and the desire for a Soul-centered way of dealing with life. This is often idealistically expressed as the search for one's "Soul mate." Scorpio represents the eventual mastery of spiritual and material desires, and gives rise to the "Victorious Disciple." Its polarity is found in Taurus, which on the personality level is the sign of the rulership of the physical desires over life. Pisces, perhaps the most mystical of all the signs, is the embodiment of the consummation of "the desire of all the nations," the result of divine desire: the World Savior, the Coming One, the Messiah. In terms of the natural and normal focus of human desires in relationships, the Tibetan Master says that Libra is more associated with sex than any of the other signs. This is due to Libra's expression as the balancing agent between the basic polarities of life—the male and the female. The very nature of Libran tension sustains another essential duality—one which characterizes the polarization of the life energies passing between the two sexes: attraction, on the one hand, and competition and combativeness on the other.

Walking the Path requires that a person develop the ability to perceive right values and perfect judgment in dealing with others. This is embodied in the Law of Right Human Relations, the keynote of the Age of Aquarius. Such perceptions are the result of the correct balancing of mental energies. This process is very much involved with the interplay of Mercury, Venus, and Uranus; Gemini, Libra, and Aquarius; and the Third, Fifth, and Seventh Rays. Naturally, the Second Ray of Love/Wisdom, as the primary Ray of our solar system, is always involved in any focus for the expression of Life. But certainly the Second Ray must play a vital function in the expression of Love on the human level, as the Second emanates through the heart chakra.

Libra is found on the Third and Seventh Rays. The Third has Saturn as its planetary ruler, and it is while expressing itself through Libra that Saturn finds its exaltation. It is when on the Scales that the Lord of Karma acts at its most just. Saturn, as we know, is also called "The Great Judge." It is very severe when the Laws of Life are broken, but is equally rewarding when the Laws are followed with love and justice.

There are four additional keywords that we can use for the Cardinal signs: Aries—creation; Cancer—manifestation; Libra—legislation;

and Capricorn—initiation. Libra, and the multitude of forces which play through it, have a great deal to do with the administration of the Laws of the Cosmos, especially as they express themselves through human interchanges. This sense of structuring is a direct expression of the Seventh Ray of Ceremonial Order. We can note, therefore, that the sign of Capricorn (ruled by Saturn both exoterically and esoterically) is also on the same two Ray lines as Libra—the Third and Seventh—revealing the close association between these two signs and their planetary rulers. Libra is intimately connected with legislation, as it represents the field of expression through which the plan of manifestation (impulsed by Aries and formulated through Cancer) works itself out according to spiritual and natural law. It is through Right Human Relations that Libra creates a balance between the laws of humanity and the Laws of Divinity. The Third is the Ray of the primary fusion of Spirit and matter, leading to the eventual manifestation of all the forms of life.

Sex is also considered a Third Ray phenomenon because it is the sexual process that produces the physical forms for humankind. Venus, the exoteric ruler of Libra, is the planetary significator of the interplay of human sexuality. The Fifth Ray quality of Venus expresses itself as the synthesizing focus of mind which serves to bring any pair of opposites into a balanced harmony. This results in those ideas, inventions, and products that may benefit humanity. The Second Ray is brought into expression through Venus's esoteric rulership over Gemini, a sign preeminently of the Ray of Love/Wisdom.

The three air signs are brought into alignment as follows:

Gemini is ruled by Venus on the Soul level.

Libra is ruled by Venus on the personality level and by Uranus on the Soul level.

Aquarius is ruled by Uranus on the personality level.

We can see from the above that Libra connects the two other air signs, bringing them into a harmony of relationship. On the Soul level, Gemini and Aquarius merge with Libra through the interchange of their planetary rulers. Libra becomes a centering and blending place for these energies. A more evolved balance is achieved by transcending personal differences and focusing on collective interrelatedness. This is one of the primary functions of Uranus, as the Soul-centered ruler of this sign. *Uranus through Libra is able to distill new social archetypes out of the conflicting dualities (inherent in the polarization of energies) contained within the personal and sexual aspects of relationship.* This is synthesis at its highest level of expression, and provides a vehicle for the birthing of new Ideas out of the experiments created by Life through Its manifold forms.

We should keep in mind that Uranus is the planetary ruler of the most synthetic of the Rays, the Seventh, and that there is thus a direct line of communication between the First Ray of Will/Power and the Seventh of the Ordering of that Will into the structures of physical life.[12] The reason many people are unable to reorder and reorient their lives has to do with the right use of willpower. Uranus has its planetary exaltation in Scorpio and is thus a vehicle for the transformation of the personal into the Spiritual Will. This transformation often occurs in life through the area—that is, house position—Uranus occupies in the natal horoscope. This house position will show where the restructuring of human relationships is necessary to bring about such a refocusing of the personal willpower. Wherever Uranus is, so is Libra, insofar as the Soul level is concerned. It's an irony of human life that we often have to become a bit "unbalanced" in our personal relationships in order to learn certain fundamental lessons and finally emerge as Soul-centered beings.

If, in the natal chart, there is a square or opposition aspect between Uranus and Venus, there will be some difficulty in making the transition from the personal to the transpersonal, in terms of interpersonal relationships. From the exoteric level, one would say that such an individual would have "surprises in relationship"—he would be attracted to unusual people, unreliable individuals, or to those people completely different from himself. The urge for unusual and, at times, socially censured relationships would be quite strong. All this, in terms of the personality, is most likely to manifest as a certain "irregularity" in his personal life. If either Uranus or Venus were the rulers of the fifth or seventh or eleventh houses in the personality-centered natal chart, such tendencies would be even more strongly emphasized.

As the Soul-centered meaning of such a square or opposition, we would find that one of the reasons the Soul incarnated was to express balance and harmony in those houses which Uranus and Venus tenant and rule. The difficult encounters in the personality life would be the

---

[12]The reader will recall that earlier in this chapter I mentioned that there was an aspect of esoteric astrology which examined the planets and signs from yet a higher or "Hierarchical" level. In this respect, it should be noted that Uranus is the ruling planet of Aries, and is thus involved with the Birthing of Ideas from the perspective of a much greater cosmic collectivity. This relationship ties the First and Seventh Rays into a much stronger bond and also further explains the presence of Aries on both the First and Seventh Ray lines. I have purposely eliminated most references to Hierarchical planetary rulers and their various functions, as they have almost no relevance to the information contained here. Familiarity with this subject will have almost no practical reward for the vast majority of us. Even for those who are active on Soul-centered levels in the expression of their lives, the integration of this Hierarchical information will do little good toward understanding the delineation of the natal horoscope. For the interested student, there is always much joy in the accumulation of and intuitive attunement to esoteric knowledge. Thus, if one is so inclined, please refer to the Bibliography for further references and study guides.

means through which such lessons could be learned. Once mastered and integrated, the results of such experiences may be shared with others through Right Human Relations. People with these aspects of Uranus and Venus are trying to bridge the personality's way of dealing with others and the Soul's way of interrelating and merging with others. The ensuing struggles are there in order to resolve any dualities about human relationships. Once the Soul level has been fully anchored, the Seventh Ray qualities of Libra and Uranus emerge in their fullest, encouraging the individual's ability for social organization to benefit humanity.

LIBRA on the Mutable Cross (totally personality-centered individual). This person has relationships for the sake of having them. The need for experience, in terms of the projected personality and external response to the lesser ego, is paramount. The attitude of stronger personalities of this type is, "Be cooperative and do things my way!" Other people may find themselves often used as an audience as the Mutable Cross Libra plays and parries his egocentricity against his or her "(in)significant other." There is thus an awareness of others only as vehicles of response for personal self-expression. The drama and passion of personality-centered human "love affairs" is absolutely at the core of this individual's way of moving through life.

If Venus is in Scorpio with the Sun or rising sign in Libra at this level, the individual is very likely to try to take advantage of any social situation in which he finds himself. The only balance is one in which the lion's share of any encounter is gained; otherwise, this Scale feels that an injustice has been committed. The bright and often gracious (or ingratiating) personality can be very much a mask for trying to emerge victorious from any relationship. At this stage, Libra is definitely the sign of open warfare, and personal competition is very fierce, as well as deeply and instinctively rooted. Libra and Aries are polarities, but while the Mutable Cross Aries will be individually combative and aggressive, the Libran at this level has to engage another person in this drama of "point and counterpoint."

LIBRA on the Fixed Cross (awakening to the Soul-personality relationship). Libra on the Mutable Cross is an instinctual response to action-reaction. There is no objectification of the relationship between any two forces who oppose each other. Once mounted on the Fixed Cross, however, Libra becomes aware of the true meaning of oppositional energies: the growing awareness of the other outside of any subjective, instinctual response pattern. The urge to be victorious over another person gradually gives way to the need to bring a balanced rapport into any focus of human relationship. This urge for harmony also extends itself into the arts, business, and politics, as well as the more abstract philosophical domains.

The purpose for mounting the Fixed Cross is to gain an increased association with love. Love is, of course, the quality of consciousness of the Soul, and it is through Libra that this focus of love takes on an idealized romanticism. The duality so inherent in the rhythm of Libra's movements between the lower and the Higher selves is heightened at this stage of evolution. There is much less tension in the life of a Libra on the Mutable Cross: one "loves" passionately for the purpose of the fulfillment of personal desires. Once on the Fixed Cross, however, the search for the ideal partner, for the specific complement to one's goals and aspirations in life, begins to dominate one's personal attitude toward relationships. A refinement toward all things of beauty and a sincere interest in fair play, regardless of winners or losers, begins to emerge through his relationships. Libra on the Fixed Cross is very aware of the increase of tension which occurs when his life is not in a state of harmony, when he is living unfairly or unjustly, when he is not being equal in all things.

Libra on the Fixed Cross moves back and forth between the world of the personality and the visions of the Soul. This is a life based upon oppositions and the need to consciously select those opposing forces which can be correctly polarized to give rise to yet a greater harmony. Until Libra mounts the Cardinal Cross, this remains the stage of the weighing of the opposites.

LIBRA on the Cardinal Cross (the Soul-centered individual). Libra achieves his place on the Cardinal Cross when the vehicles of the lower self are totally balanced with those of the Higher. It is then that the personality and the Soul are in harmonious alignment and the Libra individual has become an active and conscious worker for the benefit of humanity. Libra is then the personification of the Law of Right Human Relations, and is active in furthering the unity between all peoples. Such a person may be very busy in the outer world, bridging and fusing ideas and social structures in order to birth new archetypes for the advancement of the Plan of evolution. This is the action of Uranus and the Seventh Ray, and Librans on the Cardinal Cross are the very embodiment of such activities.

Always at the center, Libra on the Cardinal Cross is quite able to deal with the apparent chaos of many opposing forces, and to perceive the common thread which merges and unites them. Working through Venus in the world of forms, and through Uranus in the world of ideas, Libra is able to harmonize one with the other so that the shared vision of group endeavor predominates. These Librans are not so much peacemakers as they are social innovators and cohesive factors in the delicate worlds of finance, politics, and diplomacy. Their ultimate focus is on creating a proper balance of Will, Love, and Intelligence in every situation in which they find themselves. The Seventh is, after all, a synthesis of the Three Rays of Aspect, brought into the world of daily life through the socially integrating factors of Uranus and Libra.

LIBRA KEYWORDS

Mutable	Fixed	Cardinal
Imbalance	Urge for equilibrium	Perfect balance
Lust	Lust vs. love	Perfected love
Need for dominance	Winners and losers	Perfection of Sacrifice
Personal relations	Interpersonal relations	Transpersonal relations
Totally egocentric	Myself vs. others	The One Humanity
Eye for an eye	Eye to eye	The Third Eye
Materialistic	Idealistic	Realistic

Libra Keyword Phrases

Let choice be made. This statement reveals the consistent tension which exists for Libra on the ordinary wheel. It is the tension of opposing forces needing harmony and balance. This is the battle between the lower and the Higher selves as it plays itself out through the personality. It is here that Libra is tested, and right judgment and proper use of love are cultivated.

I choose the way which leads between the two great lines of force. Right choice is always made when one is aligned with the Will-to-Good. This statement reflects the relationship between the First and the Seventh Rays, as well as between Aries and Libra. The battle lines are drawn, and yet Libra's goal is on the focus of world service through the unfolding of expanded consciousness and the resulting responsibilities such visions entail. This is symbolized for us through Saturn's exaltation in the Scales.

SCORPIO
The Light of Day.

This is the place where three lights meet—the light of form, the light of soul, and the light of life. They meet; they blend; they rise.

Ray of manifestation:

Fourth

Planetary rulers and their Rays:

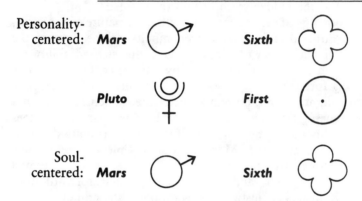

Personality-centered:　*Mars*　　　*Sixth*

　　　　　　　　Pluto　　　*First*

Soul-centered:　*Mars*　　　*Sixth*

As the preeminent Ray of humanity, the nature of the Fourth Ray and its corresponding planet and sign relationships is fundamental to each of our struggles as we work to move from "darkness into Light and from death to Immortality." As the primary sign of the Fourth Ray, Scorpio is most closely involved with this struggle in human evolution. Scorpio is thus the sign of the Path of Discipleship. It is through Scorpio that the personality enters into battle with the Soul and eventually emerges as the "Victorious Disciple"—the Soul-infused personality. But as we all know, the Way is not easy, and the Path is filled with many—often self-created—obstacles. When an individual is born with Scorpio rising or the Sun in this sign, he has committed himself to battle in the present incarnation. The lower self has to be redeemed by the Higher; the awareness of the relationship between the two has been established through Libra; a choice has been made to fight; and the war ensues. This will be especially the case, in the most objective sense, when the Scorpio individual has also mounted the Fixed Cross—the stage in personal evolution in which this particular battle is the strongest.

The goal and the Path of Scorpio is not just to do battle. It is not enough that the pairs of opposites, once polarized in Libra, now meet in an intense urge to absorb each other. Scorpio does, after all, embody the Fourth Ray—the path of Harmony through Conflict. And conflict there must be! The processes of transformation inherent in the Scorpion will go beyond the battle as they proceed into fusion and blending—two other characteristics of the Fourth Ray.

"The light of form, the light of soul, the light of life" represent the personality, the Soul, and the Monad (permanent spiritual atom of one's being). Scorpio's great task after the battle is over is to reintegrate these three major human aspects (corresponding to the Three Rays of Aspect: Monad—First, Soul—Second, Personality—Third) into a blended, conscious whole. This is the secret of the "Fourth Way," as well as the hidden truth of rebirth revealed.

There is another great secret contained within the nature of Scorpio— the secret of directed energy. The fixed quality of the "eye of the eagle," added to the power of Mars, gives to this sign an ability for focused direction of purpose unequaled by any other. Once desire is brought to the forefront of consciousness (and this can be the desire for spiritual enlightenment and human betterment), Scorpio loses not one atom of energy through diffusion: the Path is clear and he goes for it! The rhythm of the movement in this "going" is quite different from that of Aries, the other Mars-ruled sign. Unless there is some immediate response by the form aspect of life, Aries' fire will diminish, subjectify itself, and then suddenly burst forward once again as the Ram pushes instinctually (although sometimes naively) ahead. Aries does not have to keep the same goal; it is not a fixed sign. Aries just has to move forward and express itself. It is the fiery matrix of life, as opposed to Cancer, which is the watery matrix.

As a fixed water sign, Scorpio is undeterred in its orientation. It has a firm and envisioned goal at all times. That goal is found in Capricorn, the sign of the Initiate. Aries has to rekindle its fire, but the water of Scorpio is always flowing down a fixed course, moving resolutely toward its delta. Should the course be blocked, the water will flow around, wear away, or seep through any obstacle. The current is fixed, the will is set, the waters of the personality (especially the emotional body) will be irradiated by the fire of the Monad/Spirit and blended in the loving consciousness of the Soul.

Three of the most important collective archetypes for humanity are the Christ, Whose Passion is embodied in the sign Pisces; the Buddha, Whose Path of Enlightenment is laid out for us in Taurus; and Hercules, the Hero-Disciple, whose tests and trials are portrayed most vividly in Scorpio. In *The Labours of Hercules*[13], we find that in order to achieve victory over the dominance of the lower self, Hercules (a Son of God) has to fight the three-stemmed, nine-headed Hydra/ Serpent. This battle is representative of the three major tests a person encounters when his Sun or rising sign is in Scorpio. The goals of these important trials for Scorpio, as well as for anyone else who treads the Path, are as follows:

1. The need to transform his attachment and orientation to the desires of the personality to the goals and purposes of the Soul.
2. To show, through his actions, values, and "Field of Service," that he is prepared for the tests of Initiation to be taken in Capricorn.
3. To reveal his responsiveness and sensitivity to the Will-to-Good of the evolutionary Plan for humanity.

Each of the above tests have three component parts, which correspond to the three aspects of the personality: physical, emotional, and mental. On the physical plane, the tests have to do with sex, physical comforts, and money. On the emotional level, these necessary transformations deal with fears, hatred, and personal ambitions. In terms of the lower mind, thoughts (and their resulting actions) of pride, separativeness, and cruelty constitute the nature of these trials. Scorpio is tested and retested to make sure that he is ready to become the "One-Pointed Disciple" personified by the sign of Sagittarius.

As we have seen, the duality of the battle lines are drawn in Libra—the Soul on one side of the Rainbow Bridge, and the personality on the other. From the ranks of the personality, an "entity" emerges as its champion. The Ancient Wisdom Teachings call this "Black Knight" the "Dweller on the Threshold." The champion of the Soul also emerges, known as the "Angel of the Presence." The Dweller can be said to represent the sum total of all the personality characteristics that have remained unconquered and unredeemed. Such traits and energies must be transformed before one may continue to take the next step on the path, and certainly before any further initiation is possible.

The Angel of the Presence and the Dweller stand facing one another; the battle between the two must commence. In the course of that battle one either succumbs to the personality and moves back into an incarnation in Libran duality, or the Dweller is transformed and absorbed by the Angel of the Presence, the battle is won, and the One-Pointed Disciple emerges in Sagittarius. This may only happen when the ego first recognizes itself as the Dweller. This occurs when a

---

[13]For a fascinating and beautifully written description of all of the twelve tests, see *The Labours of Hercules*, by Alice A. Bailey.

person says to himself: "I'm standing in the way of my own progress. It is neither something nor someone outside of myself that is preventing my evolutionary growth, it's me—my lower self. I must now find the way, bring on the tests, and engage in the necessary battles that will free me from my Dweller and allow Soul alignment to take place." The person treading the Path continues the war between the pairs of opposites, but this time with much greater objective, conscious awareness. He is now ready to give himself to the tests of Scorpio. *These tests and trials are self-initiating,* for this is the way of the Path: we knowingly and lovingly (that is, consciously) place ourselves in those environments wherein our tests and trials are unavoidable and inevitable. It is thus that the third element of each step on the Path emerges—sacrifice. We work and struggle to be tested so that we may sacrifice the lower to the Higher, the personality to the Soul. This is the primary and fundamental purpose of Scorpio.

At a further turning of the wheel, the Disciple becomes the World Server in Aquarius. This is one of the reasons why Uranus, exoteric ruler of the Water Bearer, has its exaltation in Scorpio. Uranus and Aquarius work to condition and create a new order of life. In this respect, the work of the Rays of this planet/sign combination—the Seventh and the Fifth—serve to transform scientific invention and technical knowledge into those products and social systems that will unite and benefit mankind. The desire to change the status quo—to bring a new orientation into life out of the synthesis of the old order and previous, collective (as well as individual) experiences—is very much the expression of Uranus. Scorpio is the perfect vehicle of expression for this transformation and birthing of new archetypes. The battleground in which the old order and the new idea struggle for synthetic rebirth into yet another form of expression is very much a Fourth Ray encounter. Such a struggle, in terms of human evolution, *leads to the reversal of the wheel*—an occurrence very much centered in Scorpio. It should therefore not surprise us that so much turmoil in human sexual behavior, the establishment of Right Human Relations, the changing social dynamics of humanity on a global level, and the relatively recent introduction of inventions involving nuclear energy, are so much a part of the cusp of the Aquarian Age. Astrology teaches that all of the above-mentioned innovations and directions in human behavior are under the individual or combined influence of Uranus, Pluto, Aquarius, and Scorpio.

I should also like to point out why the Moon is said to fall in Scorpio. Fall, in the Soul-centered approach, does not mean so much that the Moon is weak in this sign, as much as it indicates the Moon's particular association with the personality. In this respect, the Moon is esoterically considered a "dead body"—one having no real potency in terms of the dynamic expression of the Soul. The Moon is the storehouse for all that is in the past experience of the lower vehicles, especially the astral body. In Scorpio's final triumph, the power of desire, centered in the lower self and indicated by the Moon, ceases to exert any control on the Soul-centered individual. Thus the power of the Moon falls. The reader might wish to compare what has just been said to the traditional view of the Moon when in this sign.

Scorpio is the way out of the personality life. It is called the sign of the "reversing impulse," for it is through Scorpio that the Way of the Disciple is revealed. Aries and Scorpio are very closely related in terms of this transitional reorientation. Aries, sign of the "initiating impulse," begins a cycle of incarnation in which the seeds of life anchor into manifestation on the mental plane and await their focus into form through Taurus. Scorpio, the eighth sign from Aries, begins a new octave of the expression of the life energies begat and birthed through the Ram. In this respect, Scorpio could be said to be a higher octave of Aries, just as in traditional astrology, Pluto (exoteric ruler of the Scorpion) is said to be a higher octave of Mars (exoteric ruler of Aries). When we examine Scorpio from the Soul-centered approach, we find that Mars is its ruler on both levels of expression, and thus closely links it to its "brother sign" of the Ram.

This association has several major implications in terms of the planets and the Rays. The function of Scorpio on the personality level is to attract those circumstances—especially on the emotional plane of desire—which engage the personality in battle. First there is a battle with and within oneself to annihilate those thought-forms which keep the personality connected to the emotional, collective karma of the mass consciousness. The personality must individualize and refine itself. This is very much the work of Pluto and the First Ray of Shiva, Lord of Destruction. Pluto is also closely connected to the function of the Dweller, as the latter embodies the tremendous forces of the personal and collective subconscious, or the "underworld" of Hades/Pluto. These subconscious elements of the three lower vehicles (and their attachments to the collective physical, emotional, and mental planes) have to be brought into conscious awareness so that the battle may be fought, and through Mars, the Disciple may emerge victoriously.

The final test of Hercules symbolizes this ordeal. Hercules battles his Dweller, in the form of Cerberus, the three-headed dog who abides in Hades. He subdues this "monster" (of his own making) and carries the creature out of hell and into the daylight of waking consciousness. Hercules takes Cerberus to the mountaintop as proof of his strength over his lower self. The mountaintop is, of course, symbolic of the place of initiation, and hence the sign Capricorn.

Aries, the aspirant-warrior, sets forth into the form life, learns his lessons, and does battle in Scorpio to emerge as the One-Pointed Disciple in Sagittarius, and as we shall soon see, the Initiate in the sign of the Mountain Goat.

The tremendous Will-to-Be of the First Ray energy of Aries does battle in the Fourth Ray conflict of Scorpio so that this initiating fire of life may emerge with greater harmony of purpose and conscious devotion to the Plan. Mars, planet of the Sixth Ray, is the force behind this evolutionary emergence. In its lower octave, Mars is the god of war, fighting to occupy the "territory of the incarnating Lord." Mars/Aries clears the way for each Spiritual Warrior—each Son and Daughter of the Divine Flame—to tread the Path. Mars/Scorpio engages in the battle for self-sacrifice, the absorption of the lower self into the Higher, so that the EnLightened Soul may enter into conscious service to Humanity and the Plan, thus furthering the union of Fourth and First Ray energies. This connection can also be seen from yet another planet and Ray perspective. Mars is the exoteric ruler of Aries, and rules Scorpio from the Soul-centered level. Scorpio is a Fourth Ray sign, while Mercury is an emanating vehicle for Fourth Ray energy in the solar system. It must also be mentioned in passing, in order to present a more complete picture of these complex relationships, that on the Hierarchical level, Mercury rules Scorpio. This means that after all the various battles have been won, and the Soul-centered Disciple has triumphed, the Power of the Word may use the cleared battleground in order to implant into the collective consciousness of Humanity those Ideas (that is, birth those Sons and Daughters of Mind) which are created to express the Plan on yet a further turn of the evolutionary wheel.

Finally, we should mention Scorpio's polarity, Taurus, and the function of Pluto and Vulcan. Both of these planets are the expressors of the First Ray. It is the task of the Lord of Destruction to break the personality's hold on those desires associated with personality life. Yet such conflicts have to be created so that the battle may ensue and the triumphant Disciple may earn the right to be one with his developed consciousness. This battle takes place through the Fourth Ray of Humanity and the signs of this Ray: Taurus, Scorpio, and Sagittarius. It is through the gateway of the Archer that the arrow of truth, having pierced the illusions and maya of material and emotional desires, readies the candidate for initiation into the Halls of the Ancient Wisdom Teachings.

SCORPIO *on the Mutable Cross (totally personality-centered individual).* This is the evolutionary stage of the completely unredeemed lower self. The symbol is the Scorpion, and the focus of the life urge is total selfishness. In the love dance of scorpions, one partner seeks the destruction of the other, so that sexuality and death merge. This is not the death of the lower self, but the mortal death of the partner/adversary through the total supremacy of one ego over another. Scorpio at this level is constantly engaged in such a dance of death with everyone. Another symbol that characterizes this type of individual is the spider. The spider weaves her web in order to attract her victims. Once caught, the trapped insect struggles until exhausted, and then the spider extracts the vital fluids of its victim. The Scorpion is so far removed, so much into the darkness of the underworld, that it does not experience its own life, light, and vitality. Its focus is in the magnetic energies of the web of the astral plane, which it employs to bring people into its environment. It may then use the other person's resources completely for its own advantage. After a while, these "fluids" turn to poison, and if the Scorpion stays unredeemed, this toxicity kills her and sends her further into the underworld. The destiny of such an individual usually involves a series of self-annihilating experiences, the purpose of which is to create enough pain that he awakens to the latent element of redemption which is ever-present. In this respect, Pluto's rulership of Pisces reveals itself—a relationship we shall discuss more fully in its proper sequence.

SCORPIO *on the Fixed Cross (awakening to the Soul-personality relationship)*. The Eagle, symbol of this level of Scorpio's expression, flies high and occasionally perches on the mountaintop. Then this bird of prey must swoop downward into the running waters of rivers and streams in order to capture a fish to feed itself and its young. It is thus that the Eagle Scorpio moves between heaven and earth, air and water, opening itself to duality, and battles with the pairs of opposites.

The Eagle has a very sharp eye—one that is not centered so much in instinctive vision and response, as is the eye of the Scorpion. The Eagle has a certain degree of objectivity and patience, as well as an inner brilliance that lets it know just how fast and how far it has to swoop from its lofty position to capture the trout swimming in midstream. The Eagle is loyal to its mate and its offspring, feeding the latter before itself.

The Eagle is supportive, helping others to make their transition from life in the nest to freedom in flight. It is brave and easily enters into battle for what it believes, for Mars on this level works as the defender of the faith and enforcer of just ideals (Sixth Ray). Yet the Eagle's desire nature is very strong. It seeks the heights of ambition and the passion of sexual and social conquest. It seeks to exalt the personality more than it seeks to destroy it. It is ruthless (as are all Scorpios) in achieving its ends and relentless in the pursuit of its desires, even if such desires are for the well-being of others and not just for personal gain. The Eagle is still attached to its aims, lusts, and goals, but there is also a growing awareness of the futility of many of these personality-centered battles. It is now that the Eagle's eye sharpens to the light of the sun radiating through its own noble heart.

The Fixed Cross Scorpio in later stages is the battleground in which the aspiring walker on the Path finally anchors him- or herself on the Way. It is a stage of test and trial, as we have already mentioned, but it also the place of ultimate triumph!

SCORPIO on the Cardinal Cross (the Soul-centered individual). The Disciple emerges and the Eagle is transformed into the Phoenix who, rising out of the ashes of the desires of the personality, bursts forth aflame with inner radiance and abundant healing and magnetic powers. The essential unity of the lower and Higher selves has been achieved. He is now ready to do battle for the Plan and fight for humanity as a whole. The Phoenix is the embodiment of love winning out over adversity, harmony arising out of unavoidable conflict, and the resurrection of the life force through a totally dedicated and Self-conscious human being. The Warrior is now ready for further tests that await him, and after a proper sojourn with the Teachers and Teachings of Sagittarius, will approach the Gates of Capricorn's Initiations.

SCORPIO KEYWORDS

Mutable	Fixed	Cardinal
Scorpion	Eagle	Phoenix
Selfish desires	Dualistic desires	Selfless desires
Degeneration	Regeneration	Resurrection
Urge for death	Battle with life	Immortality
Hides in darkness	Soars in air	Abides in Light
Enslaves	Ensouls	Enlightens
Hurts	Heals	Transforms
Kills	Sustains	Revitalizes

Scorpio Keyword Phrases

Let maya flourish and let deception rule. This and the key phrase that follows need little interpretation. Maya is illusion on the plane of desires. It represents the mirage of personality-centered emotions. Maya is clouded water that distorts and obscures the eye of the Eagle and the Heart of the Phoenix from penetrating into the darkness of matter so that the lower self may be irradiated with love and resurrected into Light.

Warrior I am and from the battle I emerge triumphant. This phrase is written on the banner of the Disciple as he marches out of the battlefield and into his field of service to humanity.

SAGITTARIUS
A beam of directed, focused Light.

In this the point of light becomes the beam, revealing a greater light ahead and illumining the way to the center of the light.

Rays of manifestation:

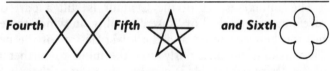

Fourth   Fifth   and Sixth

Planetary rulers and their Rays:

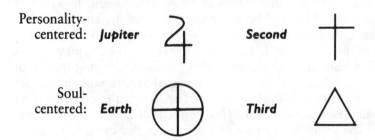

Personality-
centered: *Jupiter*   *Second*

Soul-
centered: *Earth*   *Third*

Sagittarius is very much a human sign. It exemplifies the struggle each person undergoes to free himself from the fetters of the personality, and thus move into a more expansive, spiritual reality. One of the fundamental purposes of an incarnation with the Sun or rising sign in Sagittarius is for the individual to orient himself to some lofty objective—one which will unfold a higher goal and a conscious direction in life. It is this Sagittarian quest which promotes the question often heard by astrologers, both from within themselves as well as from their clients: "What is my purpose in life?" Although such a purpose may be ascertained by looking at the natal chart from the Soul-centered perspective, one has to *earn* the right to connect with this higher aim. Only then does the struggle to achieve the goal really begin. On the reversed wheel, Sagittarius represents that stage of preparation through which the new vision of oneself emerges out of the conflicts of Scorpio. The mountain peak of Capricorn, now sighted upon the horizon, is yet to be climbed. These three signs—Scorpio, Sagittarius, and Capricorn—are said to represent symbolically the "valleys, plains, and mountaintop" of the initiatic process at work in humanity's spiritual quest.

There are some very enlightening factors standing behind the various glyphs and symbols used to represent Sagittarius. The Centaur, half horse and half man, is the most ancient of these. It is rooted, as are all the basic symbols of the zodiac, in Atlantean times. The Archer on his white horse, the Knight in Shining Armor, are more recent developments of the Sagittarian principle. Yet the juxtaposition of these two representations shows a clear demarcation between the personality-centered Sagittarian and the Soul-centered one.

The animal aspect of the Centaur is still a part of the human, revealing an attached or "fused" duality, in which there is no objectification between mind and the lower desires of the personality self. The Centaur unconsciously uses the mind to further the expansion of the desire nature. He is capable of seeing neither the difference nor the relationship between the two. This is Sagittarius totally given over to the attachment and acquisition of form. The Knight, however, is riding the horse: Man and his personality vehicles are connected, but the Rider can dismount whenever he chooses to do so. He has dominated the animal and can use the lower self for the purposes of Mind. This state of "unattached duality" is the underlying quality of the "equipment" needed by the Soul-centered Sagittarian who wishes to serve humanity to his fullest. It is this unattached freedom to serve which qualifies a person as a "One-Pointed Disciple," and is represented by the arrow in the bow of a spiritually dedicated Knight.

The symbolism of the arrow should be expanded, for the arrow is, in actuality, a clear shaft of light released by the Higher Mind of a developed human being in order to bring expanded awareness into the lives of the people of the world. Sometimes the immature or overly good-natured Sagittarian releases his arrows at the wrong time. This misfiring can result in the loss of the objective, and misunderstanding ensues. Refinement of aim and the intuitive grasp of timing in order to reveal the innate truth which Sagittarius guards is part of the training ground that the young Knight must experience in his journey to the mountaintop.

Sagittarius is devoted to his aims and to his inner truth. He undertakes his adventures so that, through the fulfillment of his outer urges for experience, his subjective realities can be made more conscious. This is the quality of the Sixth Ray, one of the three through which Sagittarius unfolds the full range of its orientation to life. It is the Sixth Ray, focused through Mars, that characterizes the one-pointed, sometimes zealous, approach of one who treads the Path. The Knight holds to his quest and purpose; nothing and no one can deter him from achieving it. This is indeed the quest for the Holy Grail.

In order for such a vision to succeed, there has to be a fusion of all opposites and extraneous energies into a greater harmony. This blending and synthesizing takes place through the actions of the Fourth Ray, another of the lines of manifestation upon which Sagittarius finds itself. The Sagittarian is guided on his Path by the intuitive perception gleaned from the previous accumulation of knowledge. In this respect, we see the influence of both the mutable quality of the sign and the Fifth Ray of Concrete Knowledge. All four of the mutable signs are gatherers of experience in the outer world:

Gemini amasses the understanding of how ideas, people, and objects relate and interrelate.

Virgo learns about the practical uses of tools, processes, and methodologies in order to further the focus of form as an extension of the creative life principle.

Sagittarius gains the "Wisdom of the Ages"—the philosophy of life—in order to comprehend and teach the common links between all people, thus serving as a vehicle for planetary love and unification (Jupiter and the Earth are its rulers). Yet, and this is a most important point, the Sagittarian must prove himself worthy of the power of the Wisdom of which he is at first merely the container. This requires one-pointed devotion to his vision of the Plan, and consistency of effort in reaching the foot of the mountain.

Pisces holds the secrets of that alchemy which joins the visible and the invisible, redeeming the lower self and thus becoming a channel for the release and distribution of that Universal, Loving Substance of which we are all a part.

Sagittarius is also the sign of the boomerang, or as the Tibetan Master states, "the returning arrow of intuition." The undeveloped Centaur is most likely to state in this respect, "I shot an arrow into the air, it fell to earth, I know not where (nor do I much care!)." The more developed Archer on his or her "vision quest" is more likely to find out: "I shot an arrow into the air, it fell to earth and hit me!" This is the arrow of aspiration which returns to the sender as a ray of intensive fire of enlightenment, gleaned from the experiences of an Earth-based incarnation. The Earth as a planet is very important to the Soul-centered Sagittarian, as it rules this sign esoterically. In order to serve the purposes of the Plan for the evolution of humanity, the idealistic, expansive, and altruistic Sixth Ray orientation of the Archer has to be grounded in an Earthly pragmatism. The tarot card representing Sagittarius is highly significant of the Earth as the esoteric ruler of this sign.

Here we see the Angel of the Presence ready to bestow all of the Questing Knight's (Disciple's) rewards, symbolized by the golden cups full of the waters of life. These waters are not the same as those in which the Angel has placed one of his feet, as these are the waters of the collective unconscious. The water flowing between the cups has been irradiated by the Light of Understanding, coming through the experience of many incarnations. Yet this understanding has to be utilized and distributed wisely. The Sagittarian must use his words and knowledge carefully, constantly tempering the fires of his eagerness to teach, share, and uplift, with the Wisdom of the Silence. The Angel stands poised, the upwardly pointed triangle of the Soul at His heart chakra, the Hebrew letters for the Name of God, Yahweh, inscribed above the highest point of the Triad. The Angel balances the flow of the waters of wisdom (gained by human experience) as He stands with one foot in the diffused collective pool and the other upon the earth. "Temperance in all things," He states. "It is only when right judgment is used, and the Knight is fully anchored in the Higher Mind (the revealer of the Wisdom of the Ray of Love/Wisdom), that he may move along to the Mountaintop of Initiation." Out of the deep waters emerges the Path which leads to the Place of Initiation. Beyond the Angel is the Crown of the Anointed One, waiting for the one who has passed this significant test of the right use of mental energy and has totally balanced all of the lower forces into a harmonious working unit.

In Sagittarius, the intellect is developed to a higher level of expression, due to the influence of the Fifth Ray. Yet it is through the Third Ray influence of the Earth, and by Ray affiliation, Saturn, as well, that the mind becomes sensitive to the intuitive perceptions of truth. It is through Saturn and the Third Ray that Sagittarius is intimately related to Capricorn. Sagittarius climbs out of the deep valleys of doing battle in the underworld of the lower self in Scorpio and, using his new mental equipment, moves upward onto the plains of the Earth. It is there that the mountain is seen, fostering the type of spiritual attunement and aspiration that will take the questing Knight to its summit.

The encompassing vision of the Second Ray (Jupiter) is strongly at

**"Temperance," the Tarot Card
Symbolizing Sagittarius**

(Tarot card designed by Pamela Coleman Smith and Arthur Edward Waite, © U.S. Games Systems, Inc., Stamford, CT.)

work in the outer life of the Archer. On a lower level, this can give rise to a certain tendency toward excessive and indiscriminate behavior. Yet Jupiter is balanced by its polarity—Mercury and the Fourth Ray—which, through Gemini and Virgo, teach discrimination in form and ensure those lessons which allow the mind to be the proper instrument for the Soul's purposes. Sagittarius and Aquarius are both on the Fifth Ray, thus linking these two signs, through the influence of Venus, to the Law of Right Human Relations.

SAGITTARIUS on the Mutable Cross (totally personality-centered individual). When a person is expressing this sign completely on the ordinary wheel, the influence of the "kama-manas," or the desire mind, will be at its highest. Mental energy will be totally under the direction of emotional desire, without the individual being aware that such a situation exists. This would tend to keep a person very busy indeed, as the mutable, fiery activity of the mind constantly creates more desires to be satisfied. An unconscious process of elements and energies uses the individual. No integration of these forces has been attempted—the horses run wild.

The adventurous nature of the sign expresses itself very indiscriminately at this stage. The unconscious and impulsive need for fire to blaze forth into life has neither the direction of cardinality nor the focus of fixity when manifesting mutably. The fires burn wherever desires take them. The Sagittarian at this level uses the mind to create purposes and ideals to rationalize and justify his or her egocentricity. The positive Third Ray influences of the Earth and Saturn are completely absent. The lower expression of Jupiter predominates, and there is thus a tremendous impracticality about one's activities, as well as a totally irresponsible attitude toward any aspect of self-discipline. The urge to increase experience without having a structure or inner truth to guide such expansion leads one into a great diffusion of energy. This means that a Mutable Cross Sagittarian is apt to travel from New York City to Washington, D.C. by way of Los Angeles (especially if some "damsel in distress" is waiting in Chicago!). Sagittarius at this level is totally identified with the horse and not with the rider, with the car and not with the driver.

SAGITTARIUS on the Fixed Cross (awakening to the Soul-personality relationship). Directed life energy is the keynote for the Fixed Cross Sagittarian. The Archer is in the process of acquiring and holding a firm eye, hand, and stance prior to firing those arrows that, when correctly aimed, will lead him or her to the Gates of Capricorn. This means that the process of refining his purpose and goal orientation is a conscious one. Fire now takes on the steadiness of fixity, tempering and adding strength to the expansive quality of Sagittarius's natural mutability.

At this stage, Sagittarius must acquire the necessary self-discipline to accomplish in the practical world what he envisions. The use of one-pointed will is absolutely required if Sagittarius is to move on and mount the Cardinal Cross. The Knight not only has to know how to dominate his horse, he also must know how to love it, treat it properly, and co-create with it so that it may guide him toward his successful mission. In no other sign is *the urgency to achieve the creation of a vision of purpose* more clearly noted than in Sagittarius. The achievement of its creation as a guidepost is often more important than the feeling of success at its culmination. This is the Sagittarian's "raison d'etre," so that as soon as the quest has been accomplished, the fires must once again move forward in the establishment of still another goal. The Path, though sometimes curved and filled with obstacles, is an unbroken and consistent one, and it is in the Fixed Cross of Sagittarian experience that the nature of that Path becomes an unfolding reality.

In the latter stages of the personality life, when the Presence of the Soul is becoming an increasing point of awareness, the control of desire by the mind (as the latter subtly but surely becomes the vehicle for intuition) becomes a very fixed perspective. This should be contrasted with the Mutable Sagittarian's use of mind to increase and expand desire! When on the Fixed Cross, Sagittarius uses all of his intelligence to bring about the transformative processes of the Fourth Ray and integrate the previous experiences of Scorpio, thus finally resolving duality.

SAGITTARIUS on the Cardinal Cross (the Soul-centered individual). Human nature and its inherent dualities cease to attract even the most altruistic facets of Sagittarian character. Instead, Sagittarius begins to identify with the Fifth Kingdom of nature—the Kingdom of Souls or Hierarchy. He then begins to merge completely with the Higher Mind, and through its exigencies, *to serve humanity.* This means disassociating himself from the pleasures and frustrations of human dualism (and the innate conflict of the "broken arrow") as it focuses on the astral plane. Mental polarization and the mastery of mind become the keynotes to life. This is not the same as intellectual expertise. As a result of the strong Fifth Ray influence, the Sagittarian may indeed be a storehouse of knowledge and have developed a substantial intellect. Yet all of this knowledge, and the entirety of the intellectual faculties, are synthesized by the Higher Mind. It is there that knowledge merges with Earthly experiences to become Wisdom.

Life is now led from the place of consciousness of the Teacher/ Healer/Lover of Humankind. Sagittarius has become the true visionary and prophet, leading humanity from one goal to the next, constantly expanding and uplifting so that increased opportunities for the externalization of the Soul are made possible. The true Sagittarian Teacher will not and cannot take the test of initiation for another. But he will bring the student to the Gate, give him the fiery impulse to move on and achieve, while inspiring the gift of one-pointed devotion to the Plan.

SAGITTARIUS KEYWORDS

Mutable	Fixed	Cardinal
Indiscriminate	Purposeful	One-pointed
Self-centered experiences	Integrating experiences	The Goal of experiences
Desire dominates mind	Mind and desire relate	Higher Mind emerges
Horserider	Rider and horse	Riderhorse
Centaur	Knight	Bow and Arrow
The jungle	The clearing	The Path

Sagittarius Keyword Phrases

Let food be sought. This phrase symbolizes the urge to gain experience, something that Sagittarius on the ordinary wheel of life does quite indiscriminately. Any food will do—the idea is just to gather the basic substances of life in order to bring about those situations that stop the Horse "in his tracks." When he is thus satiated and bursting, he may then realize that he had better take control of the reins, since he is the rider as well as the steed.

I see the goal. I reach that goal and then I see another. This sentence clearly depicts the frame of reference of a Sagittarian on the reversed wheel of discipleship and initiatic promise.

 CAPRICORN
The Light of Initiation.

This is the light which clears the way to the mountaintop, and produces transfiguration, thus revealing the rising sun.

Rays of manifestation:

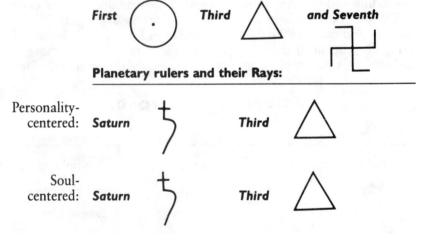

The Ram, the Scapegoat, and the sacred Goat are Three in One and One in Three. The Ram becomes the second and the second is the Third. The Ram that breeds and fertilizes all; the Scapegoat, in the wilderness, redeems that all; the sacred Goat that merges in the Unicorn and lifts impaled upon his golden horn the vanquished form—in these the mystery lies hid.[14]

---

[14]This is taken from an ancient and unpublished astrological text. The quote is found on pp. 155–6 of Bailey's *Esoteric Astrology*.

Within the symbolism and experience of Capricorn are some of the most profound and mysterious aspects of Soul-centered astrology. As Capricorn is found on the First, Third, and Seventh Ray lines of manifestation, it is the connecting link between the Divine Creative Will as it operates through Mind in order to produce the myriad forms of physical plane life. Thus Capricorn connects the most subtle to the most dense—the Power of Life Itself to the Mineral Kingdom. Through its relationship to its planetary ruler, Saturn, Capricorn provides the structure and order by which the Laws of Manifestation work themselves out, thus propelling the Plan of evolution into objective existence.

Capricorn is the sign of initiation—the gateway through which the Accepted Disciple, having walked the Path of life through nine tests and phases, is now ready to culminate her journey and ascend to the Mountaintop. Once at the peak of her evolutionary progress, the trained Disciple receives the necessary contact with the consuming and regenerating Fire of the Will-to-Good. She must now descend from the Mountain, return to the valleys of human existence, and relate to humanity, either through the pathway of Aquarius and World Service, or through the goals of the World Savior radiating Love/Wisdom in Pisces.

The primary initiations are three in number. The first is closely related to the understanding that all of humanity is a single, living organism within a larger unit of being—the Planet. The actions of a person who has passed this stage are reflective of this initial anchoring of the Soul's Presence in the life of the personality. One looks at and treats life and all people wholistically, as one Earth Family with billions of Soul brothers and Soul sisters.

The second initiation is a place of tremendous testing for so many of us, as it involves the dominance by Love over the desires of the astral body. This does not necessarily entail total chastity, but it does require that sexuality be *conscious* in its expression and that it, plus any other desires, be placed under the aegis of the inner demands of the Soul life. The experiences outlined in our discussions of Scorpio and Sagittarius are very much the testing ground for the second initiation.

Capricorn is most closely connected to the third of these major phases of personal evolution. It is through the gates of the third initiation that the individual becomes totally mentally polarized, and a conscious linkage takes place whereby the individual's talents, abilities, and particular Ray makeup are linked to the collective purpose of the Plan. Surefootedness, emotional balance, and the ability to function wisely in the physical world have been tested and retested. The Pathwalker is now ready to assume a major responsibility for the benefit of all, taking his or her earned place among the serving brothers and sisters.

There are three horned animals in the zodiac: Aries, Taurus, and Capricorn. The horns of the Ram are turned downward and represent the involutionary arc of the creative Will. This is the urge to enter incarnation and manifest form. The horns of the Bull are turned upward, indicating the evolutionary arc, pushing toward heaven and the goal of illumination, and the release of consciousness and light from matter. The First Ray energy of Vulcan is the vehicle for this liberating force. The two horns of the Mountain Goat symbolize the duality of Spirit and matter, but there is another symbolic horned animal representative of Capricorn and the resolution of this eternal duality. This is the Unicorn, whose single horn reveals the one-pointed resolve of the Initiate, in whose consciousness matter and Spirit are One. In effect, the charging Ram eventually is transmuted into the Scapegoat who, through his conscious self-sacrifice, allows the manifesting creative Spirit entrance into incarnation. Once the illusions of the material plane are clearly evinced, then the Eye of the Bull shines forth with the Light of Life Itself. And when the materially-oriented Mountain Goat perceives the hidden spiritual essence contained within every ambition and every form of such ambitions, he then becomes the Unicorn.[15]

The "Mountaintop" has traditionally symbolized a peak initiatic experience, and a place of intimate connection with the "Mysteries of the Spirit." Martin Luther King, Jr., himself born under Capricorn, said in his most famous and eloquent speech, "I've been to the mountaintop, and I've seen the future." He went on to say that like Moses, he saw the Promised Land but would not necessarily be able to go there. Martin Luther King, Jr., was a Capricorn of Initiatic standing who possessed the courage, joy, vision, insight, and steadfast devotion of the Disciple. He exemplified through his life the highest attributes of the three horned animals of the zodiac: the Scapegoat and Sacrificial Lamb of God, the "Illuminato" who possessed the Third Eye of the awakened Bull, and the one-pointed, disciplined, and devoted focus of the Unicorn. Saturn had its exaltation through this man, balancing Will/Power and Active Intelligence with the Love and Wisdom which stood behind his actions and deeds.

There are two outstanding Mountaintop experiences in the Bible.

---

[15]There are two other symbolic representations of Capricorn, which are related to each other. In the Egyptian zodiac, Capricorn is depicted as the crocodile who lives half on land and half in the water. This is symbolic of the potential spiritual resources contained within the crystallized forms of the earth. The Mer-Goat or Sea-Goat, like the crocodile, is half related to the water and half to the earth, and has a meaning similar to the crocodile. In essence, both represent the stage of unfoldment of Capricorn on the Fixed Cross.

From the Old Testament, we have the archetypical symbol of Saturn in Capricorn: Moses on Mount Sinai. After Moses heard the Will of God, he took the Tablets of the Law (Saturn in Libra) and gave them out to his people—in effect, as an Initiate, to all people. Saturn is the Lord of Karma, and the "thou shalt nots" of the Ten Commandments clearly outlined the rules and regulations for what was to become a major foundation for Western civilization. As the people of the Ten Commandments, the Jews were chosen as the "karmic clearinghouse" for the peoples of the world, thus giving to this ancient race (ruled by Saturn, Capricorn, and the Third Ray) an especially creative but historically difficult position.[16]

The presence of the Initiate, Lord Jesus, on the Mount of Transfiguration occurred when He received the vision of the Father and His Mission was revealed. The Christ was incarnated into human form in the sign of Capricorn at the winter solstice. He placed His Disciples in touch with the energies of Aquarius when He directed them to go to Jerusalem, where they were to meet a man "bearing a pitcher of water" on his shoulder. The latter would take them to an "upper room" (the Higher Mind), where they could commune in peace with each other, though they were from many different backgrounds. These twelve Disciples represent the twelve signs of the zodiac, with the Christ symbolizing the unifying principle of the Soul, emanation of the Second Ray. Thus the Initiate born in Capricorn becomes the World Server through His Disciples in the sign Aquarius and the World Savior through the self-sacrifice represented by Pisces and the crucifixion. It is as a Great Initiate that, while on the Cross, Jesus says, "It is finished." This does not refer only to the end of His physical life. It points to the end of the Age of Aries and of a particular cycle, and the birthing of a new cycle of twelve World Ages. This new Great Year began some two thousand years ago when the precession of the equinoxes entered Pisces for the first time in 25,960 years. (For a more detailed explanation of the precession of the equinoxes, as well as a discussion on the movement from the Age of Aries to the Age of Pisces, please consult *Alan Oken's Complete Astrology*.)

The work accomplished through Capricorn has to crystallize and be grounded on the Earth. This is shown to us through several affinities. In the first place, Saturn is intimately connected to our mother planet, as they are both vehicles for the expression of the Third Ray. These two planets are thus co-workers in the function of Active Intelligence, organizing and relating the energies of Will and Love to their eventual manifestations in the various forms of life. This

---

[16]Bailey, *Esoteric Astrology*, p. 167.

relationship links the Third to the Seventh Ray, upon which we also find Capricorn.

Saturn teaches its lessons of materialization, crystallization, limitation, and right choice through the Earth and the things of the Earth. Capricorn is one of the earthy signs and governs, more than any other, the active, creative potential available through the correct harnessing of the Earth's resources. To accomplish this properly so that all people may benefit requires a great deal of objective, mental energy, unfettered by the urge for personal gain and self-aggrandizement. Saturn is the planetary ruler of the Third Ray, and its lessons create that transpersonal mental alignment absolutely essential to the working Disciple. I might also add at this point that the Third is the Ray of money, and the lessons concerning the right use of financial resources come through this planet-sign-Ray combination.

Saturn and Capricorn teach us how to break free of our attachment to the material forms of life, so that we are left free to be the co-creators of those forms. Time and time again we place our hopes, dreams, and ambitions on the material forms of life to which, at earlier stages of our evolution, we are unconsciously and instinctively attached. And then what happens? Either we become totally stuck in the forms of those physical objectives (and their accompanying *thought-forms* and *desire-forms*), or the earth quakes and the objects, persons, places, or things are lost! These are the "karmic blows" of Earthly limitation that put us in touch with our own mortality and "the way of all things." If such events happen frequently enough—if we are fortunate enough to learn the essential factors of the limitations of egocentric ambitions, desires, and thoughts—then Saturn ceases functioning as the exoteric ruler of these aspects of our lives and becomes instead the Soul-centered Teacher. What may be interpreted as stoppages and limitations to the grieving personality are experienced by the aware, Soul-infused individual as guidelines and parameters for the expression of the Higher Life. We thus progress on our Path and make those conscious choices which lead us from self-discipline to Discipleship.

Saturn is therefore not only the Lord of Karma, but also the Dweller on the Threshold! It is Saturn that we confront when we wish to start a new cycle of becoming on yet a higher turn of the evolutionary spiral. What is the Dweller, if not the sum total of those habit patterns that have ceased being (or maybe never, ever were) vehicles for the proper expression of our creative life urges. The Dweller will reflect our attachment to these now useless illusions of mind, feeling, and body. It will block our passage to the Mountaintop until we release our hold upon them with the one-pointed focus of Devotion and Will required for the next step on our Path. Let us keep in mind that it is at the winter solstice in the northern hemisphere that the Sun begins to stay ever longer in the heavens. Daylight lengthens, and as the "dark night of the Soul" recedes, we are spiritually regenerated. It is also in Capricorn that we celebrate the New Year, and thereby renew ourselves also in the temporal sense. From a geocentric perspective, both our spiritual and physical beginnings and endings have their roots in the sign of the Unicorn.

Finally, we should mention that, just as Cancer is the Gate into incarnation, and most specifically functions as a means for the creation of the foundation of personality, Capricorn is the Gate out of incarnation and into the immortal life of the true Initiate. The Initiate moves in and out of incarnation unattached to form, but returns in cyclic fashion to serve and save humanity, advancing His or Her "younger brothers and sisters" a bit farther along the Way.

CAPRICORN *on the Mutable Cross (totally personality-centered individual).* Capricorn on the Mutable Cross represents a culmination of the crystallization of the personality, and thus a total attachment to the physical plane. As such, it is often indicative of an incarnation with certain very difficult lessons. The attachment to form is so complete that one is totally earthbound in orientation. The effects of one's biological heritage and current familial circumstances create adherence to deep psychological patterns which allow little freedom of individual choice. One is conditioned by the physical environment and there is little, if any, objective awareness of anything "living" within the forms of life. The expression, "what you see is what you get," is a very apt description of this phase of evolution.

Saturn acts in its most limiting fashion at this point, creating in Capricorn a most worrisome disposition. The apprehensions of lack and loss, of not getting what one wants or losing what one has attained, are paramount in the mind of such an individual. Life seems like a constant uphill battle, and it is. This Mountain Goat is dragging behind it all of the excess karmic baggage from many other lifetimes. One uses the force of the entire ego's nature to keep such habits, thoughts, and feelings "strapped to one's back," like so many bricks. These bricks are glued into place through nonregenerative, emotional habit patterns which are centered squarely in fear.

Capricorn on any level cannot be complacent. This is a cardinal sign—motivation is at the core of its being, and ambition is at the heart of its drives. This ambition pulls Capricorn forward, and when expressing itself through the Mutable Cross, such self-seeking leads to further karmic accumulations, until the bricks turn into boulders and one collapses under the weight. Once this occurs, and the ego is "rent," some glimmer of light penetrates the condensed, hard-packed earth, and a ray of the birthing Christ awakens the unconscious heart.

CAPRICORN *on the Fixed Cross (awakening to the Soul-personality relationship).* At this stage, Capricorn is creating a growing awareness of the hidden, potential spiritual value within the forms of life. The desire for worldly status and recognition is transforming itself into the aspiration to take on those responsibilities that may be of some benefit to others. The urge to create form out of purpose is paramount, and the will factor, in this respect, is usually very strong. Thus the Fixed Cross Capricorn has far-reaching goals toward which she works assiduously, with great determination for success. It is when the Sea-Goat acts ambitiously, without attachment to either that ambition or to the ultimate success of her endeavors, that a major evolutionary step in consciousness has been achieved. Capricorn has begun to plant those seeds of self-sacrifice that will lead to the mounting of the Cardinal Cross, in which the Path becomes the Goal, and the culmination of every moment is in the moment itself.

The Mutable Cross Capricorn needs to amass property and objects in order to create a world of appearances which mask the great inner insecurity to which she is subjectively attached. As the nature of the Fixed Cross emerges, material forms become vehicles for the externalization of consciousness and the world of ideas which is so much the province of Saturn. This is why a Capricorn on this level gives much less importance to money for money's sake, and is very happy to have the opportunity to "sacrifice a pawn" in order to "capture a castle." She will even sacrifice the castle in order to win the game. In the earlier stages of development, no such release is possible, and the obsessive collecting of objects, so characteristic of the personality-centered Cancerian, manifests through the Capricornian polarity with even greater ferocity.

To the Fixed Cross Sea-Goat, money and objects are increasingly viewed as representations of energy and power. Capricorn, at this level, is far more capable of relating concept to form (Third Ray to Seventh) than is the Mutable Mountain Goat. It is the objectification of the Third Ray facet of Capricorn into waking consciousness that greatly separates the Goats on the first two Crosses. Mutable Capricorn is working instinctively with mind in order to formulate those objectives in the physical realm that will safeguard her shaky "Cancerian" underbelly. The contact to the foundation of personality may be strong, but the anchor of the concept of Self in any higher orientation is completely lacking. As a result, she is far removed from her creative source center. On the Fixed, which is primarily the Cross of the realization of relationship, and the merging of the Soul and personality to reveal the Love aspect of Life, the Mer-Goat is unfolding her awareness to the fluid actions of the creative rhythms (that is, Soul force) within the forms of life.

CAPRICORN on the Cardinal Cross (the Soul-centered individual). The magnetic and synthesizing qualities of the Cardinal Cross Capricorn are very highly developed. In addition, the energies of the three Rays upon which the Unicorn manifests all feed into a unit of wholeness allowing for a tremendous outpouring of creativity. The Unicorn is always sensitive to the Plan, and to the Will aspect of Divinity. When she is focusing through her highly evolved Active Intelligence, she is able to externalize the objective of the Plan through the faculties of the Higher Mind. The Unicorn is then able to harness subjective forces and resources, and bring about the necessary Organization and Order, thus allowing the original creative impulse to be carried forth into the outer world. The combination of the First, Third, and Seventh Ray influences endows Capricorn with the ability and strength to eliminate anything that has been previously created, and bring about a new form for the externalization of the Plan. Capricorn may thus appear to be cold, aloof, and at times absolutely unrelenting in her need to bring about transformation and change. All of the Unicorn's actions are very one-pointed. That point is directed at the Heart of Humanity so that it may open ever wider, allowing for the unfoldment of the Human Soul—the Light of the Christ. Simultaneously, the earthy element inherent in Capricorn, and the structural focus of Saturn and the Third and Seventh Rays, create the needed channels and forms through which this Light may externalize as the Way-shower for Humanity.

CAPRICORN KEYWORDS

Mutable	Fixed	Cardinal
Mountain Goat	Sea-Goat	Unicorn
Ambitious	Objectifying purpose	Culminating purpose
Prisoner of form	Relating energy to form	Perceiving the energy within the form
Encased by structure	Relating to structure	Creating structure
Earthbound	Anchoring ideas in Earth	Server to the Earth
Abuser of resources	User of resources	Creator of resources

Mutable	Fixed	Cardinal
Attached to form	Relating through form	Free to transform
Coal	Crystal	Diamond

Capricorn Keyword Phrases

Let ambition rule and let the door stand wide. On the ordinary wheel, ambition drives Capricorn toward achievement. The door to initiation and the freedom to serve humanity from a focus of loving awareness are always there. Yet fear and instinct blind Capricorn into believing that freedom is gained through attachment to form. The opened Gate remains unseen until such time as material illusion ceases and spiritual reality is revealed.

Lost am I in light supernal, yet on that light I turn my back. The totally Soul-centered Capricorn Initiate may remain in the consciousness of Divine Love. She has culminated a long journey and may now pause, rest, and be rewarded. Yet the call to service is so strong that by "turning her back" on this supernal state, she takes the Gate In through Cancer and returns into incarnation for further service to humanity.

AQUARIUS
The Light that shines on Earth, across the sea.

This is the light which ever shines within the dark and cleansing with its healing rays that which must be purified until the dark has gone.

Ray of manifestation:

Fifth

Planetary rulers and their Rays:

Personality-centered: *Saturn*   *Third*

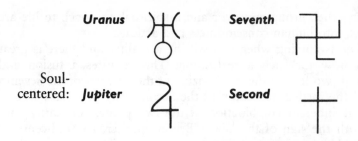

	Uranus	Seventh	
Soul-centered:	Jupiter	Second	

Soul-centered, esoteric astrology is primarily concerned with the study of the unfoldment and externalization of consciousness. As we shall discuss in part 3, we can use the rules and methods of traditional exoteric astrology in order to predict events. But it is through our use and understanding of the esoteric planetary rulers and the Ray energies that we may determine the level of consciousness which will be manifesting through these events. The rising sign greatly determines the force field through which the Soul expresses itself into the outer world. At this point in our history, the rising sign of the planet Earth has just moved into the sign of Aquarius. This means that the Water Bearer can be said to be the primary field of expression for the Soul of Humanity.

It is through the characteristics and nature of Aquarius, therefore, that the collective human purpose during the next two thousand years will be revealed. This is a transcendental frame of reference, insofar as it affects the entire overview of human effort and is the supreme astrological influence, coloring and impulsing all activities and evolutionary permutations. This also means that no matter what sign our individual Sun, Ascendant, Moon, or other planet is in, we can all be said to have Aquarius rising, if not in our actual natal charts, then certainly transcendentally in the expression of our consciousness. It is therefore of tremendous importance for us to understand the nature of this sign and all of its implications. Many of the latter are outlined in chapter 4. It is especially important that these pages be carefully studied and reviewed. The underlying themes contained therein will not only help us to understand the inner urgings of the developed Aquarian individual, but will also aid us in unfolding the urges of "Aquarius rising" in our own charts.

Just as the Pisces-Virgo polarity has been the underlying influence of humanity during the past two thousand years, the implications of Aquarius-Leo must concern us at this time.[17] As these two signs are on the Fifth Ray, science, technology, and the products of the Concrete Mind will be the vehicles through which the unanimity of humanity is demonstrated. This will occur with the greatest of possi-

---

[17] See *Alan Oken's Complete Astrology* for further information.

ble results when group endeavor and a spiritual approach to life are objectified into human consciousness and actions.

The time is coming when this will be a reality, and there is great potential now for such a realization. This requires a fusion and blending of two forces: the synthesizing of the energies of the Seventh Ray, and the further activation of the Second Ray of Love/Wisdom. This is the inherent combination of the two planets primarily concerned with the sign of the Water Bearer: Jupiter, its Soul-centered ruler, and Uranus, its personality-centered one. The action of these two bodies, plus the additional energies of the other two signs on the Fifth Ray, Leo and Sagittarius, and their respective esoteric rulers, the Sun and the Earth, make for a potent combination.

Let us examine this set of signs, planets, and Rays in terms of the life of the individual Aquarian. This microcosmic view will be reflected in the macrocosmic, collective experience we are all sharing through the current Aquarian influence. The evolutionary process begins through the ever-changing experiences encountered on the Mutable Cross of the personality. The crises of the Fixed Cross of aspiration (a particularly Aquarian keyword) work to create the proper focus of transmutation for the Soul's expression. Finally, attachment to the personality and form life is released through the transcending qualities and tests of the Cardinal Cross.

The urge to serve and to be all things to all people is a very Aquarian one. But in the earlier stages of evolution in Aquarius, the urge is for service to the personality. The superficial, egocentric, disseminating actions of the Aquarian lower self are eventually transmuted into a profoundly capable orientation toward World Service. The awakening to the Soul's reality in this sign brings in the expansive and magnanimous energies of Love/Wisdom inherent in Jupiter. This planet is also the exoteric ruler of Sagittarius, another Fifth Ray sign, and gives the Aquarian the gifts of the Higher Mind and worldly experiences gleaned through the Knight's quests.

Yet the kind of love Jupiter expresses on the Soul level is not the personal, romantic kind. It is quite impersonal, indeed, but its strength and cohesiveness of expression is neither blocked nor inhibited by the exclusivity which often marks love on the personal level. This quality of loving detachment and loving impersonality marks the advanced Aquarian individual. Accustomed as we are in the West to the heat of passion as our expression (and acceptance) of love in so many cases, it is actually the Soul-centered Aquarian who exhibits the purest form of love in terms of humanity. It is pure and potent because it emanates from Jupiter and manifests through the forms of the Fifth Ray. This means that universal love will be demonstrated through science, technology, education, the mass dissemination of information, and most of all, through group orientation and group consciousness. The promise of our Age has the blessings of the Greater Benefic, Jupiter, behind it. The astrologer might wish to note that, should a person have the Sun or rising sign in Aquarius with Jupiter trine, conjunct, or sextile (especially a trine from Gemini, the Second Ray sign), the potential to be a vehicle for such loving abundance is greatly enhanced.

Aquarius is the preeminent human sign, leading to a developed humanitarian consciousness, and hence, to the externalization of the heart center. This is due to several reasons:

1. The nature of Jupiter and the Sun as Second Ray influences which act through the heart center.

2. The heart is the fourth chakra, and corresponds very closely to the Fourth Kingdom in nature—the Human.

3. Aquarius is a Fifth Ray sign, and as such, is a vehicle for the exteriorization of the First Ray of Will and Primary Cause (the Will-to-Good) through Concrete Knowledge. Our present humanity is also evolving along the line of the Fifth Ray (see tabulation 2, p. 140), and has as its focus the increased development of science and technology for the purpose of externalizing a more humanitarian consciousness. This is our part in the One Work of the Plan in the collective evolution of the human race.

4. Uranus, the exoteric ruler of Aquarius, is the planetary vehicle for the Seventh Ray. Yet Uranus has several other correlations of great esoteric importance which link its effects to humanity. Uranus is the higher octave of Mercury, which is the ruler of the Fourth Ray, the principal Ray of the Human Race, and the planet which corresponds to the Fourth Plane of Manifestation, the Buddhic. Through Mercury, Uranus is the bestower of intuition. This is the ability to "think in categories," and as such, allows the Aquarian (or anyone with a developed intuitive sense) to encompass a great many facts in one sweeping and instantaneous vision, and then put these factors in their proper order. This ordering of data is very much an expression of the Seventh Ray of Uranian rulership. This is why it is so important for the Disciple to forge a conscious link between Mercury and Uranus, thus fusing the intellect with the intuition.

I'd like to expand a bit here on the nature of Uranus, Aquarius, the Fourth Ray, and humanity. The other vehicle for the expression of Harmony through Conflict is the Moon, Mother of All Forms. The Tibetan Master refers to the Moon as the veil for the action of Uranus. Most students of esoteric astrology find this reference to the veiling qualities of a planet to be very obscure indeed. Perhaps the following thoughts might help to "unveil" this particularly esoteric reference, as well as shed some further light on the relationship of Uranus and Aquarius to human consciousness.

We know that this sign and planet combination are very much the "revolutionaries"—through their energies and force fields, new archetypes reach human consciousness. In fact, Uranus is exalted in Scorpio, the sign of the death of the form (of desire), and the release of the life energy contained within it for the processes of regeneration. In effect, the actions of Uranus on more subtle levels of manifestation are "birthed" by the Moon into the outer world. The advanced Disciple and the Initiate often do Their part in the Work from behind the illusion of form. Such individuals work in group concert from the levels of the Higher Mind and Intuition, impregnating the lunar matrix with those Ideas born in the Mind of God. In this respect, the esoteric astrologer should recall that Uranus is the Hierarchical ruler of Aries, thus revealing itself as the higher octave of Mercury, the Soul-centered ruler of the Ram. Although the above paragraphs may contain only a little meaning at this point for many, it is hoped that they may at least open the door to the understanding of this important factor in our study.

Leo, as the polarity to Aquarius, is a most important counterpoint to the expression of the energies of this sign. Leo is a Fifth Ray sign, but is found on the First Ray as well, bringing a direct contact to Aquarius from the "place where the Will of God is known." This contact is reinforced planetarily as Jupiter, the ruler of the Water Bearer, and the Sun, ruler of Leo, are both vehicles for the Second Ray. Leo and the Heart of the Lion (the Sun) bestow courage and strength, plus, in the life of the advanced Aquarian, a steadfast and solid foundation in the personality which may be utilized by the Soul for Its collective purposes.

The status of the personality is quite different for an Aquarian who is moving along on the ordinary wheel (from Aquarius to Leo through Capricorn), from one on the reversed wheel, taking the same journey but through Pisces. On the ordinary wheel, the sense of self is very superficial. There is the constant need for attention, which is usually solicited through outrageous and unpredictable actions, unconventional modes of dress, etc. One involves society in what one does, but it is a very egocentric orientation at best, and sociopathological at its other extreme. The personality needs direction and self-discipline, and gets all of this and more when incarnating through Capricorn. Successful and integrated self-consciousness finally occurs a bit down the Path when the integrating and consolidating energies of Leo are experienced, and the personality has been trained as a healthy anchor in the outer world.

The more advanced Aquarian, having learned the lessons of the personality, and having had the necessary tests of reorientation in Scorpio, is now prepared for the group work which service to humanity entails. The "waters" of the Man with the Urn may now be successfully poured into the collective life stream of Pisces and be distributed through the Grace of the World Savior. It is understood, of course, that both of these processes are taking place simultaneously— that Grace is always available, as is superficial egocentricity.

Probably the greatest gift of the Water Bearer is his vision of equality and essential unity. Aquarius also possesses the Fifth and Seventh Ray qualities that blend and synthesize a myriad ideas, then categorize and distribute them through an overall, ordered structure. If we observe a highly developed Aquarian at work, we will find him taking a little from this place, adding a bit from that, and finally, shaping all of these varied "ingredients" into a fine "recipe" for his creative project. The results are almost always original in their presentation, and please a great cross section of people. This is the practical application of the relationship between Uranus and the Moon, as outlined above.

What is important to notice is that the unevolved Aquarian has to project himself into society, but often in a diffused and rather confused manner. There appears no logical explanation for the things he may do; and there is a complete absence of the positive qualities of the rational mind and the Fifth Ray of Concrete Knowledge. The advanced Aquarian, on the other hand, is very anchored in his individual center, thanks to the security of the personality achieved and polarized by Leo.

From this center, Aquarius moves outward through his conscious awareness of the various interplays and dynamics of human energy. He will thus express himself through one or another field of creative endeavor, yet all the while remain conscious of the whole relative to his own level of participation. He can then reverse the process and, taking from all the various streams of human life, bring these expressions of creativity back into himself, thus furthering his own inner awareness and synthesis. Once such understandings are gathered from this "circulatory system" and resettled in his "heart," he can then add to and redistribute this newly assimilated information. He is aided in this respect by his own "pulse of life," centered in the Second Ray Heart of the Sun and expanded magnanimously by Jupiter through the networking of Uranus in the outer world.

Aquarius—along with Taurus, Leo, and Scorpio—is a fixed sign. The primary purpose of the four signs of this quality is for the transmutation of desires and values for the greater expression of the Higher Self. It is important for us to follow this process from its inception in Taurus through its culmination in Aquarius, as this particular passage along the Path is very definitely the "Passion of the Disciple."

Desires are developed, experienced, and expressed in an instinctual and unconscious way when a person is evolving on the Mutable Cross in the sign of Taurus. The individual who has "mounted the Bull" on the Fixed Cross is learning to make such desires conscious and reorient them for higher purposes. The transcending nature of the Cardinal Cross allows for the dissolution of these desires when the consciousness of Taurus reaches this level. The process of Leo on the Crosses involves the anchoring, reorienting, and relinquishing of attachment to the personality, and the awareness of the meaninglessness of a life led purely for selfish ambitions. In Scorpio, the battle between the lower and the Higher selves ensues and the Disciple eventually emerges victorious, ready now to seek out the purpose for all efforts undertaken in Sagittarius. When the traveler reaches Aquarius, the meaning, beauty, and function of the group becomes increasingly apparent. Life is then led as a conscious service to humanity and to Those Who also Serve. This is the New Group of World Servers and their numbers, inspired by the Water Bearer, continue to swell from a blending of all peoples and all signs.

AQUARIUS on the Mutable Cross (totally personality-centered individual). The sense of the personal self is not particularly anchored in the undeveloped Aquarian. This leads to a great diffusion in which the magnetic center of the personality, being very weak and lacking in self-consciousness and coherence, attracts to itself a myriad life experiences. The personality is unable to prioritize and differentiate the importance of such encounters and is thus likely to be very indiscriminate in its choice of associates and life objectives.

This superficial self-awareness can sometimes be perceived as an attitude of detachment. In actuality, there is no profound personality center. Such an individual really suffers much more from a case of airy empty-headedness than from an aloof preoccupation with life. The lessons of Capricorn are next in line on the ordinary wheel, and consequently, this stage of Aquarius is among the least practical of all the thirty-six divisions (that is, the twelve signs multiplied by the three Crosses). There is the tendency to "throw oneself away"—to diffuse what little vitality there is into a maze of interwoven confusion. This also gives the mutable Aquarian the consistent opportunity to make something out of nothing, and thus to invent unnecessary complications in human relations. Right Human Relations, so much the lesson of this sign, have yet to be learned. Before Aquarians can consciously seek true equanimity in relationships, they first have to pass through the painful stage whereby relationships are made and lost indiscriminately. Aquarius at this level tries to be all things to all people, usually exhausting himself in the process.

All Aquarians have a strong awareness of others and a sensitivity to group orientation. Those Water Bearers without a firm grasp of the lower self may seek to join those cults and sects where group identification takes the place of individualization. The Aquarian likes to represent something; to stand for a set of collective values. Yet if personally developed discrimination is lacking, the Aquarian will be attracted to the order and ceremony of the group collective, and seek to merge into an unconscious mass, headed by equally blind Leo-type personalities. It is interesting to note that, while Mutable Cross Leo tries to firmly establish the lower self as the pivotal point around which the rest of the universe revolves, Aquarius tries to rid himself of any vestige of an individualized personal self. At this rather unconscious level, such a mutable orientation can lead one into some very difficult circumstances, which are further crystallized in Capricorn.

AQUARIUS on the Fixed Cross (awakening to the Soul-personality relationship). The purpose of developing on the Fixed Cross is for the egocentric Aquarian, who uses society for his personal benefit, to re-orient into the humanitarian who gears his life for the benefit of others. It is here that personal opinions are transformed into wider social concepts, and egocentric values become the urge to unite disparate points of view. It is in this process of reorientation that we see the effects of Jupiter beginning to infuse themselves through the outer expression of Uranus. Aquarius at this level can then use his natural means of networking with others in order to bring into consciousness some greater, unifying principle. The lower and the Higher selves are in communication, as Aquarius's urge to make an individual mark on society through his creative efforts is modified by the need to benefit society by so doing.

This outpouring of creative self-expression helps to synthesize the lower self into a cohesive unit. We should note that each of the four fixed signs represents one of the facets of the lower self: Taurus is the physical body; Leo is the mental; Scorpio is the emotional body; while Aquarius is the synthesizer, uniting these three lower vehicles into a unit of externalization for the Soul. This process is underscored by the blending actions of Uranus and the Seventh Ray, and by the urge for cohesiveness so much a part of Jupiter and the Second. Once the lower self is psychologically self-confident, it may then creatively self-actualize, bringing the innovative qualities of Aquarius to the forefront of life.

Social progressives and revolutionaries are very much an expression of the Water Bearer's character at this level. There is a tremendous need to see freedom and equality in human life. Abraham Lincoln in politics, and Charles Dickens in literature, are two such examples, although I would place the former on the Cardinal Cross of self-sacrifice. The scientific Fifth Ray is exemplified in the lives of such Water Bearers as Thomas Edison, whose inventions in electricity and communications certainly have succeeded in global networking; Charles

Darwin, whose ability to categorize the life forms of our world revolutionized (and spiritualized) the natural sciences; and Galileo, whose telescopes and astronomical insights helped to blend and join our planet to the rest of the universe in the minds of humanity.

AQUARIUS on the Cardinal Cross (the Soul-centered individual). The more individualized our consciousness, the more universal. The greater our connection with our Self, the greater is our vision of the One that is the Self. This movement of expanded awareness leads one inevitably into Service to Humanity and (in our Age) to the furtherance, in some individualized though group-oriented fashion, of the outer manifestation of the six Laws and Principles of the New Age.

From the Mutable Cross Aquarian, who bears the weight of his own unfocused ego upon his shoulders, to the more advanced Fixed Cross human being, who in his awareness of world suffering attempts to create artistic and social projects to aid humanity, we come at last to the World Server on the Cardinal Cross. The vision of such a person is planetary in scope and involves an alignment and attunement on intuitive levels to the Plan. Working with his or her group (both on subjective and objective levels), the World Server in the New Age moves forward to anchor those seeds that will be incorporated into the consciousness of all men and women in the present, as well as in the future. The interested astrologer might like to take note that Cancer's exoteric ruler, the Moon, is the Hierarchical ruler of Aquarius. The great Servers and Teachers of humanity, the Planetary Hierarchy of Souls, have their connection, through this sign and its Cardinal Cross mediators, to the mass consciousness of a waiting humanity.

AQUARIUS KEYWORDS

Mutable	Fixed	Cardinal
Dispersed	Cause-oriented	Service-oriented
Indiscriminate	Directed	Activating vision
Egocentric	Humanitarian	Planetary
Personal	Impersonal	Transpersonal
Reflective	Inventive	Birther of new archetypes
Superficial	Expansive	Universal

Mutable	Fixed	Cardinal
Anarchist	Revolutionary	Knower of the Plan
Chaotic movement	Purposeful movement	Cyclic movement
Disassociative	Organizing	Uniting

Aquarius Keyword Phrases

Let desire in form be the ruler. The need to give shape and form to the dispersed and airy quality of the Aquarian lower self is achieved to some degree in the earthy sign of the Mountain Goat. It is here that the ego may try to incorporate the ideas and ideals so important to the Water Bearer into their practical and physical forms. The experiences in Capricorn will train the lower self to understand the relationship between the real and the ideal as the lessons of physical limitations and responsibilities reveal themselves.

Water of life am I, poured forth for thirsty men. True esoteric knowledge forms the basis for white magic—that Seventh Ray quality which teaches the Laws of Manifestation behind the alchemy of the Soul. Aquarius on the higher levels is a training ground for the transformers of humanity, as these enlightened and dedicated people serve to distribute the Love and Wisdom that saves the world.

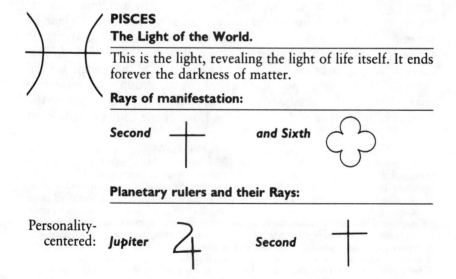

PISCES
The Light of the World.

This is the light, revealing the light of life itself. It ends forever the darkness of matter.

Rays of manifestation:

Second ——— *and Sixth*

Planetary rulers and their Rays:

Personality-centered: *Jupiter*   *Second*

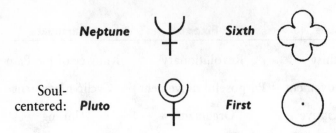

Neptune ♆ Sixth

Soul-
centered: *Pluto* ♇ *First*

The principal duality of Pisces is reflected in its symbol and glyph: two semicircles and a line drawn between them, and two Fish connected by a silvery cord. Both of these representations speak about the essential passion, suffering, and redemption of Man caused by the simultaneous attraction and separation of the Soul and the personality. It is in this archetypical setting that we find the evolutionary frame of reference, not only for the humanity of the Piscean Age, but for that of the Age of Aquarius, as well. The difference, and a quintessential difference it is indeed, is in the *form* through which the resolution of this cosmic duality is achieved.

In the Piscean Age, such liberation came from the crucifixion. It was in this most painful way that the lower ego sacrificed itself for the Higher Self. This act led to a mystical union with the Universal Source, and a consequent resurrection, resurgence, and rebirth of the potency of that essential Love for the betterment of all humanity.[18] In the New Age, individual evolutionary progress occurs as a result of the conscious merging of a fully individualized self within a transcendental group collective. This "initiation" leads to a tremendous increase in the availability of the powers latent on the Fourth Plane of Intuition. The results are a channeling of the positive currents of Uranus, Buddhi, and the energies of the planetary heart chakra. This "downpouring" stimulates service to Humanity as the vehicle for the expression of a great potency for individual, group, and collective enLightenment. In the Aquarian Age, the Mosaic Law given out at the inception of the Age of Aries, and the Love of the Christ externalized

---

[18]The exclusivistic type of Sixth Ray traditional Christian churches would say that this Love (universal and catholic by its very nature) is *only* available to one who can accept it through a dogmatic path of approach. This, of course, limits something which, by its very beingness, is unlimited in scope. Such Love is there for the asking. To me, all one has to do is ask and it is given. Part of the pain and duality of the Piscean Age, and a continued cause for suffering, is the insistence on the part of Sixth Ray churches and their followers, upon the preferentiality and "ultimate truth" of one or another of the many "noble" approaches to this freely offered Grace. This was a far more difficult set of circumstances for humanity in general, and nontraditional believers and thinkers in particular, when historically, the churches and the states in Europe were one. Sixth Ray fanatic exclusivity of belief continues to be a problem in today's despotic theocracies. As we shall see in chapter 10, this is one reason why Mercury is in detriment in Sagittarius and falls in Pisces.

at the time of the birth of Lord Jesus, are to be synthesized into various forms of distinctly *human expression* during this Seventh Ray world period.

Pisces expresses the fact that no matter what the Age, the struggle to fuse the lower and the Higher selves is always at work. The nature of this duality, as it expresses particularly through the Fish, is taught by the Tibetan Master through three pairs of keynotes:

1. *Bondage or captivity:* The Soul is imprisoned, due to its connection to form. It is not left free to experience totally the nature contained within its own dimension of experience. This is the act of its *sacrifice,* a theme which underscores a great deal of Piscean characteristics. This urge to sacrifice, to "make holy and whole," is part of the dynamic drive of the Fish, and contributes to a sense of personal martyrdom and exclusivity of belief in the personality life; that is, "It is whole and holy because everyone now believes as I do."

The bondage of the Soul to the lower self occurs in the early Mutable Cross stages of evolution. At a further "turning" on the reversed wheel, the personality is brought under the magnetic control of the Soul, yet "bondage" of a sort still exists. In traditional as well as Soul-centered astrology, Venus is exalted in Pisces. A clue to the reason for this placement lies in the ability for Venus to merge this fundamental and often painful duality into a joy-filled harmony.

2. *Renunciation or detachment:* In the Piscean Age, the life of a monk or a cloistered nun was the personification of the renunciation of the outer life of form, in order to move closer to the mystical qualities inherent in the life of the Soul. One aspired to become a vehicle or channel for its healing love currents, and there is no doubt that among a great deal of bombastic zealotry, much good was done in the world through the self-sacrifice and dedication of such workers. Yet the outer forms for the necessary self-discipline of this Way required the mortification of the flesh and a great deal of self-inflicted pain.

People who are born with either the Sun or rising sign in Pisces are often victims of self-induced acts of personal sabotage. They frequently create those sets of circumstances which give rise to the need for detachment, renunciation, and a turning away from the past. Many seek to annihilate the "burden" of the lower self through drugs and other addictive substances or personal habits, only to find that they have disintegrated the personality instead. As we shall soon discuss, once Pisces has incorporated the more mentally polarized energies of Mercury and Virgo, discrimination and objective ideation are added to this urge for the transfiguration of the lower self.

The Soul stands between two great centers: Spirit and matter. From a profoundly esoteric reality, the Soul is in the constant act of self-sacrifice. It has "moved down" out of love from "the Father's House" (which, as we know, is the Dwelling Place for the Second Ray of Love/Wisdom) so that it may be a "Way station" as well as a Way-shower. It may then act as a bridge for the ultimate descent of the Stream of Life into matter, and for matter to go Home once again. The Soul serves a double function: It endows Spirit with a focus for the externalization of Itself and the expression of Divine Purpose. It also allows matter, and all things of matter (including you and me) to know themselves as Divine in origin and intent. Such is the blessing of Love.

Thus the involutionary stream, passing through the Gates of the Soul (be it a planetary, group, or individual Soul), finally ceases its descent and, through the evolutionary current, reverses its direction. This is yet another renunciation—one this time to form. The great struggle for Pisceans is that they are usually caught somewhere in midstream!

The Saviors of the World are examples of great sacrifice, as they are conscious manifestations of released Beings who "die" to their state of Paradise, though an aspect of Themselves (just as a fragment of each one of us) is always rooted in Eden. Such Enlightened Ones appear periodically to help humankind in its struggle. In effect, the man Jesus sacrificed Himself to the Lord Christ while the Anointed One sacrificed Himself to Man, and hence, to the world of men and women. Can we take this sacrificial movement yet another step and probe even a greater Source for sacrifice? The Father/Spirit/Monad sacrificed His Son (a fiery fragment of His Own Being) and gave Him to humanity. Is this not the sacrifice of that aspect of Divine Intelligence that incarnates in human form—a loving intelligence of the Second Ray seeking to unite and make whole all human Souls within the One Consciousness? Are we not all the products of this same Father's Sacrifice?

Humanity (matter) often has to reach its lowest point—its "bottom"— in order to begin its climb back to the unity of the Father's House (symbolized by Neptune in Cancer). The feeling of separation and alienation which characterizes this state, whether we are Piscean or have just trodden the Via Dolorosa (Way of Suffering) at one time or another in our lives, leads each of us to ask the same question at our "dark night of the Soul": "Father, Father, why hast thou abandoned me?"

Yet abandonment is often the goal of Pisces or the Piscean Era person. It is a goal to which the collective archetype of the Age (and the Age is still with us at this cuspal time in human history) demands conformity. Drugs and alcohol, sexual abuse, wars based on religious intolerance, are still with us, and many will still walk down one or more of these sad roads. Yet in the darkest cavern, there is the

Soul/Savior/Love/Consciousness uniting the human Path to both the cave and the Mountaintop.

The presence of the Soul as the "light which ends forever the darkness of matter" is also reflected in Greek mythology. The hero Theseus, on his quest for illumination, has to enter the cavernous labyrinth of the Minotaur. This monster must be slain in order for Theseus to proceed along his Path. His lady friend, Ariadne, offers him a ball of string with which he may find his way out of the cave once he has accomplished his mission. Theseus attaches one end of the cord to the world outside the cavern, makes his descent, kills the beast of the lower nature, and as a result of the Lady's Gift, is able to make his way out of the dark labyrinth and emerge victoriously into the light of day. The string is the symbol of the Antahkarana—the silvery cord linking the personality and the Soul, the darkness and the Light. It is formulated out of the substance of the mental plane, thus requiring the discriminating focus of Virgo and Mercury in its construction. Once the Antahkarana/Rainbow Bridge is forged, one can then traverse the various planes and fields of consciousness and not lose one's way. This is the Thread of the Warrior/Disciple, who goes forth in the act of self-sacrifice, in order to do battle for the unfolding purpose of the Plan.

3. *Self-sacrifice and death:* The Ancient Wisdom Teachings tell us that there is no such thing as death; that is, utter and absolute annihilation. There is only the mutation and transformation of matter, and the subsequent release of consciousness and spiritual essence for the purposes of Creation. Pisces teaches the lesson that when the lower self is sacrificed, even when given up through physical death, there is a continuum of life by which loving redemption—that is, the recognition and identification with the Soul—carries us into the transcendental life stream of immortality. This "stream of life" is always there. It is through those tests and trials of reorientation that we are brought to that level of consciousness which allows us to *know and experience* this immortal, universal linkage. It is this understanding that is the inherent, mystical awareness of the more advanced Pisceans (and older Brothers and Sisters) among us. It is this factor which constitutes the Grace and the Joy of knowing ourselves as Divinity incarnating in human form. This knowledge and its dissemination is a very important part of service in the New Age.

Pisces is closely related to three other "signs of death": Aries, Cancer, and—from an especially potent Soul-centered perspective—Scorpio. Aries is the vehicle for death by fire. It is the focus of the Will of God, and possesses both the fostering and nourishing nature of heat, as well as the fire which burns and destroys. The Tibetan, quoting an ancient and unpublished text called the *Old Commentary,* says: "[In Aries] the jungles of experience are set on fire and dissolve in flames, and then the Path stands clear and unobstructed vision is achieved." This means that the attachments to the past cycle of incarnations, culminating in the diffused residues of Pisces, are dissolved and purified in the fire of the Ram, so that Life may express Itself anew. The Work of the World Saviors allows the waters of the Fish to take on their healing and cleansing properties. One of the functions of Pluto, as the Soul-centered ruler of Pisces, is to provide the necessary destruction of the old forms of past incarnations, so that such renewal may take place. This gives us yet another indication why Pluto is considered by many astrologers as the co-ruler of Aries, as well as the higher octave of Mars. There is another poetic, yet nonetheless authentic, esoteric significance for the "death" in Aries. The Ancient Wisdom Teachings tell us that once we are birthed into incarnation, we "die to life and are born into death." It might be quite revealing and uplifting to "ponder on this."

Another death is the one in Cancer, in which the personality anchors for a cycle of incarnations. It is through the waters of Neptune that the Crab relates very strongly to the Fish, as this planet is the Soul-centered ruler of Cancer and the personality-centered ruler of Pisces. The Soul, sacrificing an aspect of itself for the purposes of a given incarnation, descends into the often obscure and dark waters of the physical realm. It is through the process of transmutation and transformation (Pluto and Pisces) that the waters are clarified, irradiated by sunlight, and become purer reflections of the focused intent (Aries) of the Plan. Neptune links the watery matrix of one person, family, and tribe of Cancer, to the entirety of the ocean of humanity in Pisces.

The connection between the Fish and the Scorpion is quite profound, as Pluto's rulership links them in a deep bond. The Death of the personality occurs in Scorpio, allowing the Soul to come forward and achieve its "victory" of self-fulfillment on Capricorn's Mountaintop. The individual, triumphant Soul then goes forth to join "the army" of the World Savior, consciously sacrificing and linking itself to the One Soul, so that the Plan of Love/Wisdom may continue to evolve and externalize. The cycle is thus renewed in the universal waters of the Fish. This "diving into the pool of the Christ/Soul/Self" results in the reemergence of the "fiery spark" of incarnation in Aries, now newly bathed in Love and ready for physical life.

The above process leads to the death in the purifying waters of Pisces. It is here that one dies to all the desires and other influences that keep a person on the wheel of rebirth. The promise in the sign of the Fish is salvation from the never-ending turnings of the Mutable Cross. The breaking of these bonds of Neptunian illusion are part of the workings of Pluto and the First Ray, and are achieved through the battleground of Mars and Scorpio.

It is in Pisces that the Victory of Love is achieved. It is through the Sixth Ray of both Pisces and Neptune that Mars is also brought into this arena. This is why the nature of the Christian faiths took on such a militaristic quality during the Piscean Age: the Crusades, the Inquisition, the Conquest of Mexico and Peru, the Knights Templar, the Jesuit Order of the Soldiers of Christ, etc. Surely it wasn't the Second Ray energies of Lord Jesus which encouraged humankind to do battle and murder one another in His name. The message of the Christ is an inclusive one, yet, when expressing itself on the Sixth Ray of Religion, several other influences alter and militarize this perspective.

As the rulers of the Sixth Ray, Mars and Neptune relate very strongly to the solar plexus and the astral body (see tabulation 2, p. 140). This quickens the urge for the expression of temporal power through the personality. But the personality is not only an individual manifestation. Nations, tribes, and religions also have personalities. We could say in this respect that Christianity is, in its essence, in its Soul force, a Second Ray religion, but has exhibited a decidedly Sixth Ray personality in the Piscean Age. Instead of Neptune acting as an illuminator of spiritual truth and Mars being utilized as a vehicle for the death of the personality, just the reverse has happened. The emphasis on the personality, the solar plexus, and the astral plane makes Neptune a vehicle for spiritual illusion and glamour, and focuses Mars as an instrument for religious wars, asserting and defending attitudes of self-righteous exclusivity of belief. And yet through all of this maya, the loving Message and Presence of the Christ can still be heard.

Under the Seventh Ray domination of the Aquarian Age, the functions of Pisces, the Sixth Ray, Mars, Neptune, and the established churches will all become modified. This is an Age of equalitarianism, humanism, of the blended synthesis of many traditions, and past social streams and currents. It is an Age in which the energies of Venus and the Fifth Ray (the Ray line of Aquarius), Jupiter and the Second Ray (the Soul-centered ruler of the Age), plus Uranus and the Seventh Ray (the exoteric ruler of the Era) predominate. This great and benefic potency makes an Age of peaceful and global cooperation and co-creativity possible, as the emotionally polarized energies of the previous World Era harmonize into the more mentally polarized energies of the present period. As the World Savior enters and *becomes* humanity and all of humankind's creations, the sensed, subjective unity of the One Soul will become the apparent, objective truth. This requires devotion to the Plan and the recognition and support by men and women of Goodwill of the reality and beauty of our unity in diversity. I believe that we are equal to the opportunity before us, and I hold this as my vision and personal commitment.

PISCES on the Mutable Cross (totally personality-centered individual). This individual is sensitive to everything and everyone, but unable to discriminate the sources, levels, and movements of that sensitivity. The astral plane and the solar plexus are usually quite open and undisciplined, so that sensation is often mistaken for consciousness, empathy for compassion, psychic impressionablity for spiritual understanding.

The urge for experience is instinctual, and is usually carried out through the emotions. The energies of Neptune and Jupiter are working out through the personality, giving a need to expand the contact with the world of the senses, but not necessarily with any form of structured or logical approach. The strong Sixth and Second Ray influences of these planets often indicate a wide range of acceptance and tolerance as part of the nature of a person at this level of evolution. Yet the extent and breadth of this attitude is not often grounded through any focus of practicality. These frequently altruistic sentiments usually give rise to the tendency to "throw oneself away" on someone, or to blend so completely into the energies of the environment, group, or society, that one almost disappears. This is an aspect of martyrdom and self-sacrifice that is unhealthy, for it is a totally unconscious one.

There is an opposite extreme to the influence of Jupiter and Neptune when manifesting through the personality and focused in the lower centers. The expansive nature of Piscean waters extends without any shoreline or dams and floods the surrounding area. This means that Pisceans can often completely dominate their environment, family, and friends, as they tend to ooze out indiscriminately. Water merges with everything, blending and obscuring sharp lines of focus, clouding all separations and structural patterns. Thus in her effort to extend herself, Pisces on the personality level has the tendency to take over and, through subtle "seepage," sometimes manages to control her surroundings to an amazing degree.

The idealism and dreamy quality of Jupiter, Neptune, and the watery signs in general (though to a lesser degree with Scorpio), are in full manifestation in the Piscean personality. The urge for other worlds and other existences often leads such individuals to abuse alcohol, drugs, and other substances, and to indulge in escapist practices. They are attracted to those religious groups that demand total obedience and which place a very strong emphasis on emotionalism in their ceremonies, liturgies, and social ethics. Pisceans on this level are very attracted to spiritual glamour as well. They would rather attend a session in which someone is acting as a medium for Channel Seventy-six from Planet Redeye III than to sit eye to eye with an older sister or brother, or establish the necessary mental discipline to un-cover the thread of their own wisdom.

PISCES on the Fixed Cross (awakening to the Soul-personality relationship). The Mutable Fish flows upstream, downstream, in any stream at all. The Fixed Fish has begun to orient herself along specific currents so that there is a sense of direction within the framework of universal potential. The fluidity which is at the very core of the Piscean nature remains, but it is a much more conscious rhythm—one which begins to seek a balance between its high and low tides. At high tide, Pisces is able to bring an enormous amount of cohesive understanding into any plan or project. She has the full backing of the collective experiences of the past upon which to draw, and a seemingly unlimited supply of inner and outer resources. No barrier can withstand the tremendous force of the oncoming rush of the ocean. Yet Pisces needs the direction of Aries and the structures of Capricorn to give a practical and focused expression to this enormous potential. Should an individual born with the Sun or rising sign in Pisces also have some strong placements of planets or points in either Aries or Capricorn, a much better balance of self-expression is made possible when the high tide comes in.

At low tide, Pisces needs to withdraw, to gather herself together, to "wring out the sponge" of all the unconsciously absorbed energies from the environment. Pisces is one of the most magnetic of the signs. It seeks to attract everything within its auric force field, as there is a need to gather and unify all currents and streams. On a personal level, this can create a great deal of havoc in relationships, as not everyone wants to be blended into the Piscean waters, no matter how comforting and universal.

At this level of development, Pisces is much more the "mediator" than the "medium." Although the world of color, smell, and sensa-tion in general still pulls very strongly at Piscean sensuality, the "other foot" is planted in an attunement to higher values and, de-pending on the level of "fixity," to a growing spiritual reality. There is thus the need to interweave and blend the "real and the ideal," the instinctive and the intuitive—even the sacred and the profane. Sensi-tivity to others takes on a much more solid grounding, as this Piscean has developed the necessary discrimination to be able to decipher the "tints and hues" of emotional coloration.

At this stage, a relationship has been established between Pisces and Virgo; between the emotional and the mental. A process of linkage is now taking place, so that the resultant synthesis will lead eventually to the unfolding of true intuition, conscious self-sacrifice, and an attitude of universal service.

PISCES on the Cardinal Cross (the Soul-centered individual). The awakening of Pisces to the task of the World Savior and to his or her

particular part within the universality of this One Work is the function
of the Cardinal Cross. Pluto and the other First Ray planet, Vulcan, as
well as their associated signs of Scorpio and Taurus, come into full
play within the consciousness of such an individual. The task at hand
is for the smashing of all crystallized forms of life that inhibit the flow
of spiritual reality and loving inclusivity. It is thus that the true
"Soldiers of God" are born, carrying with them the strongest weapons
of all—Love and Wisdom. To me, Mother Teresa exemplifies this
First, Second, and Sixth Ray blending of energies in the combination
of Pluto, Vulcan, and Pisces. Nothing and no one stands in the way of
the total spiritual strength embodied by this small, old, and frail woman.
Yet her Will, Love, Wisdom, and Devotion to the Work of the One
Soul carry her forth as a power-filled representative of the Group of
the World Savior. It is within this context that a Catholic woman has
spent her life primarily serving Hindus and Moslems, healing, helping,
and self-sacrificing. The lessons are very obvious: the lesser is *always*
sacrificed for the Greater; the Way of the Soul is *always* inclusive.

The waters drowned the man. The fish was made to disappear. It
then appeared again only to die or else to die and bring salvation.

—Alice A. Bailey[19]

PISCES KEYWORDS

Mutable	Fixed	Cardinal
Opaque water	Translucent water	Waters of Life
Medium	Mediator	Savior
Unconscious responsiveness	Directed sensitivity	Universal inclusivity
Sensation	Compassion	Identification
Undisciplined life	Crucified life	Resurrected Life
Bondage	Reorientation	Liberation
Addictive	Preferential	Detached
Slave	Servant	Server

[19]*Esoteric Astrology*, p. 97.

Pisces Keyword Phrases

Go forth into matter. This is the call into manifestation, to refine and create a proper set of vehicles out of the personality for the purposes of the Soul. It is a call to sacrifice: "Go forth, descend, and make yourself a willing instrument." This is the Grace of Love which shines forth for all. If the ego (matter) is to be a self-conscious entity, it must be irradiated with consciousness, and as a result, also come to know itself as divine.

I leave the Father's House and, turning back, I save. This is the message from the Soul who knows that It has made a supreme sacrifice by leaving "the place where the Will of God is known"—the Father's House. It has left this bliss-filled Oneness in order to serve the Plan and Humanity.

The Soul occupies the Middle Way.

10

The Esoteric

Significance of the

Planets in the Signs

We may define Esoteric Astrology as that side of the subject which views all stellar phenomena from the standpoint of unity; whilst Exoteric Astrology begins its study from the side of diversity and separateness. The Esoteric Astrologer looks upon the whole expression of life as proceeding from one central and primal source, and therefore seeks to understand the subject from the point of view of the One flowing forth into the many. In the solar system the Sun is the center of all and the starting point of his philosophy, for to him all things come forth from the Sun; and it is the solar life in which all things live and move and have their being.

—Alan Leo
Esoteric Astrology

In the future, instead of speaking of the orthodox (traditional) planets when dealing with the planetary influences, we will speak of the exoteric and the esoteric planets, and so bring our vocabulary and definitive words more into line with the inner teachings.

—Alice A. Bailey[1]
Esoteric Astrology

In order to understand the functions of the planets in the Soul-centered chart, we have to consider the interplay of the Ray factors as being of primary importance. In addition, the nature of the expression

[1]These words were written by the Tibetan Master shortly after World War II. It would appear that the "future" is now!

of the planetary energies from the Soul level is quite different from when these same planetary energies are being used by the personality in the outer, daily life. The following paragraphs are to serve as a guide to the *astrologer's intuition*. It is, after all: ". . . intuitional astrology which must eventually supersede what is today called astrology, thus bringing about a return to the knowledge of that ancient science which . . . informed humanity as to the basic interrelations which govern and control the phenomenal and subjective worlds."[2]

In this chapter I will briefly synthesize the meanings of the planets. Some of this information comes from traditional sources, as certain planetary effects maintain their validity in a Soul-centered approach. In addition, certain esoteric elements will be included, especially that information about the Ray qualities of the planets and signs which deeply influences a Soul-centered delineation of the natal chart.[3] The nature of the planetary forces for the average, personality-centered individual do indicate the direction of the unfolding karma and fate. The more conscious we become, the more we can work within the larger wholeness of the Plan, and thus come to co-create the direction of our destiny and the levels of our evolutionary unfoldment. This will come about for each of us as our purpose for being is directly revealed to us through our efforts at growth and World Service. In the New Age, and at the present time, this process is and will be intimately connected with our group work and affiliations.

As Soul contact grows, the direct effects of the planets and signs as elements of character and personality delineation weaken and the influences of the Rays strengthen. The esoteric indications are that the nature of the force fields flowing through the planets, that is, their signs and the Ray energies of those signs, take on increasing potency as the individual becomes more collective and Soul-focused in his or her orientation to life.

I am attempting to present in this book a means of approach by which the astrologer can attune his intuition to the developing consciousness of a growing number of brothers and sisters, as well as to his own evolutionary progress. In this manner we will be creating an astrology for the New Age which is able to serve the needs of our time. As astrologers and students of this incredibly beautiful symbolic system, we have already ascertained the efficacy of the houses, planets, signs, and aspects. Practical esoteric astrology is the newest developing branch of our ancient science, and is currently in a very

---

[2]Bailey, *Esoteric Astrology*, pp. 3–4.
[3]To compare the esoteric meanings of the planets with their exoteric counterparts, consult *Alan Oken's Complete Astrology*.

experimental phase of development.[4] What follows is the result of personal study, meditation, intense "Love/Wisdom" sessions with other students, and trust in my own intuition and guidance in this matter. What is offered to the reader at this time is far from the final word about the subject. It is not absolute, nor does it claim to be an infallible interpretation or system. But as an Aries with Mercury in that sign, I hope that it is a beginning for many, and an "impulsing" addition to the work of others in the exploration of the astrological significance of Love in Manifestation. I encourage you to share your researches with me and with each other.

THE SUN

Soul-Centered Ruler of Leo
Planet of the Second Ray

The Sun is matter and the Sun is spirit.

—H. P. Blavatsky
The Secret Doctrine

Function: The Sun is the source of physical consciousness—the self-conscious "I"—and serves to sensitize and activate the self in relation to its environment. The Heart of the Sun stimulates and enlivens Soul awareness. In essence, the Sun's purpose is to act as a vehicle for the Second Ray. This takes place physically, on the Soul level, and spiritually.

Sun sign: In Soul-centered astrology, the primary purposes of the Sun sign are as follows:

1. It reveals the energies, temperament, and characteristics of the present incarnation.

2. It speaks about the nature of the personality life and the "equipment" brought in from previous lifetimes in order to live out the current lifetime.

3. It is the force field through which the personality activates itself so that it comes to a realization of its own consciousness.

4. It reveals those indications which point to the Ray makeup of the personality.

---

[4]In the late 1940s, when Bailey's *Esoteric Astrology* was actually written (though not published until 1951), the author said: "By the end of this century, it (esoteric astrology) will have won its rightful place in human thought."

SUN IN ARIES: Soul-centered e_____ Aries' expression on the First and Seventh R_____ stance of the Sun has the opportunity to move_____ Spirit/Will/Power down through all the lowe_____lizing its consciousness on the physical plane. _____ s of the "return journey"—from matter back t_____ od of the Father manifests through Aries as th_____

  Soul-Level Purpose: To be a fertile fiel_____vi-ronment in order to initiate a new phase of _____

SUN IN TAURUS: Self-consciousness takes _____ture, which must be irradiated with Love/Wisdo_____ fecund expression for the Will. The Second Ray is _____ Fourth-Ray force field. It seeks to express itself as b_____ as harmony through those conflicts which arise when _____ in matter. This is a clue as to why fire and earth are ot_____ ble on the personality level.

  Soul-Level Purpose: To add magnetic attraction to an in_____ so that matter will form around it, giving it the necessary _____ for life on Earth.

SUN IN GEMINI: Harmonizing Will and Form through i_____ gently applied Love is very much the orientation of this combina_____ of energies. This is pure Second Ray, and thus produces the activity _____ self-awareness through the blending of any opposing forces.

  Soul-Level Purpose: To serve as a vehicle for communicating the Law of Right Human Relations.

SUN IN CANCER: With this placement, one's activity centers around creating an environment for the nurturing of form. The Second-Ray energy of the Sun expresses itself through the Third and the Seventh Rays. Love combines with Intelligence to produce a fertile matrix for the birthing into the environment of whatever may be needed by the individual. This may then be distributed wherever and however it is required to fulfill the Soul's purpose.

  Soul-Level Purpose: To anchor a continuous foundation of re-sources and establish a network by which to distribute them.

SUN IN LEO: Soul-centered and personality-centered ruler. The Ray of Love/Wisdom becomes expressed as the dynamic fixity of purpose through the First-Ray orientation of Leo. This is carried forth into the minds of men through Venus, Lord of the Fifth Ray, upon which Leo also manifests. The planet/sign combination of the Sun and Leo is the only one which maintains itself on personality, Soul, and Spirit levels. This allows *the Purpose of the evolution of the solar system*—that is, the unfoldment of consciousness—to proceed in a direct fashion from the Will of God to the "little wills of men."

Soul-Level Purpose: To create opportunities for the expression of consciousness, both individually and for humanity. The latter is achieved through group purpose via Leo's polar opposite, Aquarius.

SUN IN VIRGO: A very Love-filled state, in which the Second Ray energy of the Sun expresses itself through the Second and Sixth Ray orientation of this sign. The Sixth brings about the one-pointed devotion and the necessary strife (through the energies of Mars and Neptune) so that the Work of consciousness may proceed.

Soul-Level Purpose: To provide the necessary forms through which consciousness may do the work of the Healer and bring a greater sense of wholeness into manifestation.

SUN IN LIBRA: *Soul-centered fall.* An interlude in the expression of consciousness in which one is neither totally linked to personality nor totally to Soul. A place to balance, consider, and choose. The Sun falls, as Libra modifies the outgoing urge of Aries to manifest, as well as the fixed focus for the creative use of the Will found in Leo.

Soul-Level Purpose: To hold opposing forces in check so that greater awareness may be achieved equally by all. This is usually accomplished through the expression of ideas (Third Ray) and their distribution in society (Uranus).

SUN IN SCORPIO: The incarnation is always involved with some form of conflict, which gives the individual the opportunity to observe and express his or her own inner battle for personality dominance. The interlude of Libra is over; the Dweller on the Threshold appears. The reorientation of the desire nature will instigate a process by which attachment to the lower selves will have to be released. The Soul excises and regenerates the empty space provided by the "death" of the personality.

Soul-Level Purpose: To be a catalyst for the transformation of others, and by so doing, to transform the ego; an opportunity for Grace.

SUN IN SAGITTARIUS: Many influences are at work at once: the twofold purposes of the Higher and lower selves need to be resolved. A battle ensues, highlighting this duality through the Fourth Ray. One has the urge to cultivate the mind through the Fifth Ray, and the profound need to have a mission in life through the devotional aspects of the Sixth.

Soul-Level Purpose: To gain control of the personality so that it may become the perfect "steed" for the Soul's Goal. To teach the ways of walking the Path.

SUN IN CAPRICORN: Love/Wisdom expresses itself through the creation of those mental structures needed to carry forth and distribute the Will of the Plan into the world of form. This is very much the result of the interplay between the Second Ray of the Sun and the First, Third, and Seventh Ray lines of manifestation of Capricorn.

Soul-Level Purpose: To culminate self-consciousness in the awareness of collective purpose. To shoulder this responsibility so that others may be supported in their efforts to serve.

SUN IN AQUARIUS: Soul-centered detriment. Potent self-consciousness is strongly diminished in this sign, thus the individualizing aspect of the Will is in detriment. Yet from the center of Leo's Light, Aquarius awakens into the consciousness of a transcending whole. It can thus be said that group consciousness is *exalted* in the Water Bearer's sign.

Soul-Level Purpose: To create those human links and contacts that allow the Love/Wisdom of the solar system to be expressed very specifically through the human mind. In a sense, this is an example of the pure human spirit in manifestation. (The Fifth Ray acts very potently here, as it is a vehicle for both Leo and Aquarius.)

SUN IN PISCES: In this incarnation, one seeks to dissolve all separatist thoughts, feelings, and actions into a universal matrix so that through human aspiration and effort, the Soul may emerge to carry more Light. The quality of this Light is Love/Wisdom, and the pathway of its expression is through devotion. Self-sacrifice allows the greater to replace the lesser, and the seed is sown for tomorrow.

Soul-Level Purpose: To undergo those tests of awakening which allow one to identify with the diversity of human experience while serving the Wholeness of the One Soul.

THE MOON

Soul-Centered Ruler of Virgo
Planet of the Fourth Ray

The Moon is a dead planet from which all the (life) principles are gone. It is a substitute for a planet which seems to have disappeared from view (Vulcan?).

—H. P. Blavatsky[5]
The Secret Doctrine

The Veiling of the Moon: The vast majority of humanity is still quite fully focused on the life of the personality. Attachment to one's biological karma, instinctual emotional responsiveness, patterns of early family conditioning, and conformistic sociological behavior, all lunar influenced, are still very strongly integrated into the mass consciousness (Cancer). This adherence further extends itself so that the collective sensitivity and identification of humanity is with the form life, the lunar life, and thus, life on the Mutable Cross.

As we individualize our consciousness and begin to mount the Fixed Cross, an objective relationship occurs to this formative world. A gradual perceptive objectification of our awareness begins to unfold, revealing to us the essence "alive" within the form. Once we have mounted the Cardinal Cross, yet another shift takes place. We evolve our consciousness to identify ourselves completely with the Life which enlivens the form. At that stage of development, we are no longer magnetized by the personality, or by any of its three vehicles or bodies.

This book is primarily dedicated to the nature and expression of human consciousness when one has reached the level of the Fixed Cross. In this respect, the Moon will still have a great deal of significance. Although our attunement with the essential wholeness of life is steadily growing, a great number among us are still struggling with the relationship between our Soul awareness and our involvement with our physical, mental—and especially—our emotional lives. This is the "Cross" that we bear, is it not? And it is this "Cross," and the sacrifices and reorientations that it requires, which lead us most assuredly to a place of greater consciousness.

From the Soul-centered perspective, the Moon has no essential life value. It is a storehouse for the past—especially that past which is

---

[5](The words in parentheses are the author's.)

characterized by outworn and discarded astral images and desires. It is a place no longer "visited" by the advanced Disciple, although it is utilized to present pictures of understanding to others still "living" in the "Moon's domicile." This means that an advanced Soul can frame a life lesson in and through certain emotional patterns so that another may be able to accept this understanding. But the solidly Soul-centered person is not attached to this use of emotional, lunar energy. Let us say that a young man has detached himself from the "psychic umbilical cord" and now perceives his mother from an emotionally detached place. He sees her lovingly as a "sister," although she sees him still as an aspect of her physical self and perpetuates all of the patterns associated with that relationship. In order to approach his mother, to communicate his "lesson," the Soul-centered son consciously assumes the energy patterns of the mother-son relationship. In this way he can reach his mother through a door of great familiarity and offer his "gift." He is not attached to their relationship, but utilizes its thought-forms and astral particulars to reach his mother in a way that she can accept. He is practicing loving detachment, but he is also utilizing the energies of the Moon. These energies are still part of his mother and the past relationship between the two. But such energies and their attachment are no longer part of the son's personality. He has synthesized them into a greater sense of loving detachment and his focus on the impersonal life. He has not lost anything, nor has his mother. The son still loves his mother, but can serve her (and himself) much better through his objective perception of (1) the essential love between them, and (2) the need for that love to be placed into a specific form.

When an individual has learned how to detach himself from the magnetism of this lunar past, one of three planets can be substituted for the Moon's placement and traditional function in the natal chart: Vulcan, Uranus, or Neptune. The Moon is then said to "veil" that planet's effects.

When a person is leaving the Mutable Cross and is about to mount the Fixed, the effects of Vulcan are very noticeable. Vulcan rules that process which "breaks the chains" to form. As the "Blacksmith of the Gods," Vulcan forges new tools for the expression of consciousness. Past patterns of behavior and instinctual biological karma are dissolved in favor of a growing awareness which leads ultimately to detachment from the desires and compulsions of form.

When the Moon veils Uranus, the individual becomes a vehicle for the birthing of new archetypes of human consciousness. One is freed from the past—Uranus the "revolutionary" has seen to that. A new focus for form—one more appropriate to the current evolutionary stage of life—appears. When the energies of Uranus are substituted for the position of the Moon in the natal chart, the individual consciously

acts as part of a group effort, working to bring in these new archetypes for the betterment of humanity. This is a predominant theme at
the present time, as the majority of people on the Fixed Cross are
becoming increasingly responsive to the incoming Aquarian Age, its
association with Uranus, and the unfolding of intuition and group
consciousness. As we pointed out earlier, one of the greatest transitions
in the evolution of human consciousness at the present time is the
shift from intellectual awareness to an intuitive perception of reality.

Yet this shift does not deny the presence of intellectual talents and
sensibilities. *The evolution of consciousness proceeds from a focus of
synthesis.* The intellect forms the vehicle and the foundation point for
the externalization of intuition. In a similar way, the basis for the
emotional attachments within the personality (the Moon) serves as the
foundation point for the proper externalization of new social archetypes (Uranus). This is due to the natural affinity which exists between the astral body of the lower self and the intuitive body (vehicle
for the creation of new archetypes) of the Soul. (A further examination
of diagram 4 and chapter 2 might help to clarify this statement.)

The nature of the Soul-centered, esoteric energies of the planets
does not negate their personality-centered, exoteric indicatives. A
blending is taking place—one which gives rise to an ever-increasing
inclusivity. The nature of the interrelationship between the energies,
forces, and Ray qualities of the planets and signs reveals to us these
patterns of unfoldment and their directions. The Soul-centered individual has neither forgotten nor abandoned the past. *That aspect of
himself that deals in the world of form is still under those Laws of
Manifestation and Karma that govern the world of form life.* The
effects of the Moon and its sign placement, as we understand them to
be from the angle of personality-centered and psychologically oriented
astrology, are still valid in this respect. But there are other, more
refined or highly evolved influences which the Moon *veils*. These
esoteric inferences and effects dominate and supersede the earlier,
lunar-based ones in the consciousness of the Soul-centered individual.
It is in the determination of this aspect of Soul-centered astrology that
a great deal of intuition is required on the part of the astrologer.

Yet such intuitive development is a natural part of one's growth
and evolutionary unfoldment. As we study these deeper, more esoteric
aspects of astrology, we will find that our own intuition expands
accordingly. This is one of the gifts of astrological studies—they
expand our consciousness. The methods work if we do!

We can explore our intuition in this area by first examining ourselves. Where is the Moon placed in our horoscope? Where are we
still attached to its influence as a storage place of past karmic imprint-
ings? Where does the focus of our own attachment reside, and where

is our resistance to its release? All of these questions can be answered by carefully examining the lunar position by sign, house, and inter-planetary aspects. Now, let us substitute the energies of Vulcan for the Moon, in terms of influence. Where are the chains of the past being severed? What is the current focus of emotional upheaval? Where is the "unredeemed" area of one's attachment to form still alive in the present and not as yet relegated to the Moon and the past? It is the energy of Vulcan acting through the Moon, at the lunar position in the natal horoscope, that reveals the answer to these questions.

Let us say that an individual has the Moon in Gemini in the seventh house, and it is natally square Venus in Pisces in the fourth. The nature of this position from the personality-centered perspective would show an individual who has a very difficult time finding the right form or place in which to anchor his feelings. He constantly finds himself in the wrong type of relationship for the kind of emotions that he is seeking to communicate. This square gives no lack of opportunity for relationships or social interchange, but such rapports are often very inappropriate to the assumed needs of the personal life.

If we substitute Vulcan for the Moon here, we find another, more energized and complex picture unfolding. If this were the horoscope of someone who was just stepping onto the Fixed Cross of experi-ence, he would just be learning how to objectify his feelings through the pain engendered by such awkward situations. He would not only be trying to find the right person in the right place at the right time so that his intimate feelings could be expressed, but would be maintain-ing an attachment to the personal emotions, as the Moon is still operating in the chart in its Mutable Cross way in the personality life. In addition, this individual might also be perceiving the need to break out of such patterns in order to express his Soul-centered purpose and evolution. This would thus bring Vulcan into play.

Now, what if we substituted Uranus for the Moon? This would be in the horoscope of an Accepted Disciple—an individual who is far along on the way of the Fixed Cross, who is dedicated to serving humanity, and who is very much focused in group consciousness. The esoteric rulerships of the signs are at work. Since the Moon (Uranus) is in Gemini, it is square its own dispositor (esoteric sign ruler), Venus. One of the most important rules in astrology in general is that if the dispositor of a planet is in aspect to that planet, it strengthens the nature of the aspect. This means that one of this Soul-centered individual's most important karmic lessons would be to break down attachments to past patterns of relationships.

In the personality-centered chart, the Moon square Venus shows that this has to be done first in the personal life. At the crisis of the reorientation of consciousness and the mounting of the Fixed Cross, the energies of Vulcan may be said to be squaring Venus, acting as the "conditioning" factor of awareness. This is then brought into the impersonal life through the energies of Uranus squaring Venus. At this point, the individual is working on a collective level. This means that through his particular talents, abilities, and creative contributions within the focus of a group dynamic, he is working to bring in some new social patterns relative to the Law of Right Human Relations, in order to bring about some greater harmony for humanity. This would be accomplished at some great cost (the square aspect) in terms of the personality life.

The third, and probably the most esoteric lunar veil, is that which concerns Neptune. I will treat this factor rather briefly, as it is very impersonal in nature, completely collective in operation, and individualized through the consciousness of very few people at the present time.[6] The functions and details of Neptune's effects in the horoscope will be discussed in their appropriate place in this chapter. When the Moon veils this planet's effects, it may be said that Neptune rules all life on the astral plane—the entire feeling-sensitive nature. The average person is unaware of the vast majority of impressions which bombard his consciousness and to which he responds unconsciously (yet, nevertheless storing many of these impressions).

This is very much like walking through midtown Manhattan in the afternoon, when the air is filled with the "silent" buzz of hundreds of radio and television emissions. We do not hear a thing, as our physical ears are not attuned to these subtle electrical impulses. But they are there, and they do bombard the nervous system. The same is true for the impinging waves of astral energy from the collective unconscious. This energy is not consciously registered, but affects the astral body in most definite ways. The Moon—that is, the form nature—blocks and veils these impressions from revealing themselves, and a good thing it is, too, as it would be extremely disturbing to have total access to the collective astral plane without the properly structured tools of perception. The construction of the "tools" for the channeling of awareness is within the province of Vulcan.

The various levels of the permeating energies of Vulcan, Uranus, and Neptune through the Moon, as representative of the past and the formative nature, are quite important. This is especially so to those of us working upon the Fixed Cross. We are moving through the illusions of the Moon, trying to perceive beyond the maya of preconditioned forms of body, mind, and emotions, and into the reality that is Love/Wisdom.

Neptune is operative when the Disciple is switching from the Fixed

---

[6]As always, the reader is encouraged to pursue any further interest in this subject through an examination of the suggested works in the Bibliography.

Cross to the Cardinal Cross. Its function is to dissolve the sense of separateness, while maintaining the sense of individualized Self-hood. Neptune, in this respect, is connected to that process which we might call "the redemption of form" and the bathing of matter in "the waters of the Life" which is Love. This connects the Moon, the Fourth Ray, and the Fourth Kingdom (Humanity), to the nurturing substance of the Mother, and reveals yet another facet of Neptune's esoteric rulership of Cancer.

Moon signs: The writing of the following twelve paragraphs was very challenging. I have had to synthesize many factors in order to arrive at an explanation which has some practical application in determining the value of the lunar position in the natal chart from the Soul-centered perspective. Please keep in mind that what follows is meant specifically for those individuals—the majority of the readers of this material—who still relate to the emotional vehicle of the personality, but who are influenced by the energies of Vulcan and/or Uranus in their relationship to the form life. The Fourth Ray quality of the Moon will remain very important in this respect, as it is Harmony through Conflict which conditions one's approach to the impersonal life and to the life of one dedicated to serving humanity.

MOON IN ARIES: Mercury, the esoteric ruler of Aries, is on the same Ray of manifestation as the Moon—the Fourth—thus bringing it into great activity.

Soul-Level Purpose: To reorient the emotions so that they come under the dominance of the mental body. The subsequent creation of form will then be the proper vehicle for "the birthplace of ideas." Naturally, the crisis of the reorientation of the emotional/form nature is under Vulcan, while the expression of these new ideas comes through Uranus. Please consider the relationship between Mercury and Uranus in light of the above.

MOON IN TAURUS: Soul-centered exaltation. When the Moon is in this sign, the individual has a powerful ability to create any form of manifestation required for the fulfillment of personal desire and self-interest. Such needs may be altruistic and magnanimous, but they are based on the motivations of personal emotions.

Soul-Level Purpose: When Vulcan, the esoteric ruler of this sign, is seen to be in operation, the form nature, as a vehicle for the fulfillment of desire, is transmuted by the Will-to-Good and becomes a vessel for the expression of the power of the First Ray. Thus the Moon (form life) becomes exalted as it serves the purpose of the Plan. Uranus serves as the vehicle for the birth and release of new human and social archetypes. Thus, when the Moon veils Uranus in this position, the individual would stive to serve humanity through the creation and nurturing sustainment of these new archetypical patterns.

MOON IN GEMINI: This combination provides a tremendous potential for the communication of harmony and for the use of form by the mind in order to help foster the Law of Right Human Relations. This can be seen by the interplay of the Fourth Ray quality of the Moon and the Second Ray energies of Gemini. Venus—esoteric ruler of this sign, as well as the vehicle for the Fifth Ray of the Concrete Mind—is also very active.

Soul-Level Purpose: To create patterns of relationships and communications which either break down outworn models of social interchange (Vulcan) or instigate new ones in most original ways (Uranus).

MOON IN CANCER: Personality-centered ruler. On the personality level, this provides the strongest link to the past, allowing the individual to create an environment that may nurture but does not necessarily provide an opportunity for evolutionary growth.

Soul-Level Purpose: Neptune emerges as the planet most often veiled by the Moon in this position, as it is Cancer's ruler on the Soul level. The Sixth Ray devotional aspect predominates so that through the combination of Cancer's Rays—Three and Seven—the mind is used to create those ideas that sustain a potent quality of loving nourishment. Such an individual would be quite willing to foster those social circumstances that would support any and all humanitarian efforts. The effects of Vulcan in this sign would serve to release the individual from personal needs and concerns so that universal purposes could be better served.

MOON IN LEO: On the personality level, the Moon in Leo represents the epitome of emotional egocentricity. Self-consciousness is centered through the formative nature of instinctual response to environmental circumstances. When the moon is in the sign, even more advanced personalities still center their deeply passionate feelings (in a most personal manner) on those whom they love.

Soul-Level Purpose: To transform the form life as an expression of self-consciousness into the proper vehicle for group consciousness through individualized efforts and talents. Leo and Aquarius are both signs of the Fifth Ray, making for a natural ease of movement of the energies which pass between them. The Second Ray quality of the Sun, on both the personality and Soul levels, makes a most potent focus for the creative use of form with this position of the Moon. The effects of Vulcan are utilized to reorient personal needs to those of the group. Uranus and its affinity to Aquarius would aid in the expression of individual efforts for the purposes of the collective.

MOON IN VIRGO: *Soul-centered ruler.* As the Moon is the esoteric ruler of this sign, its placement herein gives a person a great potential toward world service. The Moon in Virgo masks or veils the presence of the Christ within, the Child of Heaven.

Soul-Level Purpose: To reveal the indwelling purpose and function of Love within the forms of life. The work the individual undertakes would involve a very strong, loving devotion to service, thus bringing forth the characteristics of the Second and Sixth Rays, through which Virgo manifests. Such endeavors might entail caring for the lower kingdoms in nature, such as the vegetable and the animal, as they too are representatives of the Light which is Love. Vulcan would serve to help break down patterns of selfish service and the manipulation of matter for one's own ends. The actions of the energies of Uranus when in this position easily lend themselves to the creation of those innovations and inventions which serve to unite humankind, making the awareness of our essential wholeness that much easier to perceive by the mass consciousness.

MOON IN LIBRA: On the Soul-level, the most natural affinity that this combination holds is with the planet Uranus, esoteric ruler of Libra.

Soul-Level Purpose: To expand human relations into the impersonal networking required to unite humanity into a consciously working whole. On the personality level, personal emotional security is anchored in partnerships and relationships. But on the Soul level, the Seventh Ray qualities of Libra and Uranus become very potent. Thus the focus for the creation of form is to be a vehicle for the synthetic blending of humanity, and for the harmonious externalization of the principle of unity in diversity. The function of Vulcan in this position would be to instigate those crises of reorientation that would transform the individual's attachment to relationships from the personal/emotional level to the impersonal/collective level, and eventually to the transpersonal/universal level.

MOON IN SCORPIO: *Soul-centered fall.* In traditional astrology, the Moon is said to fall in Scorpio for several reasons: (1) It is difficult to get in touch with the feeling nature when the Moon is in this sign; (2) A person can be quite unloving and unnourishing when the Moon is manifesting through the Scorpion; (3) There is a tendency to "cut people off," and abandon them from any kind of personal sustenance at the least provocation. But from the Soul-centered perspective, the Moon falls in Scorpio because the personality is "killed" in this sign! The function of form loses all potency and power, as the final victory in Scorpio is the emergence of the "triumphant Disciple," and the externalization of the Soul.

Soul-Level Purpose: To use the form life as a *total expression* for the healing properties of the Higher Self. The power of Vulcan to create the crises of transition required to bring about this reorientation of one's attachment to the desire/form life would be very marked. Look to the house position of the Moon to see where in the life such upsets would come about.

As Scorpio is the sign through which the transformation of energies from the personality to the level of the Soul is tested, the placement of the Moon in this sign when veiling Uranus is quite important. The dynamic force of the Fourth Ray—Harmony through Conflict—is at its strongest, as both the Moon and Scorpio are of this Ray energy. Through the forceful breaking down of old, instinctive, nonregenerative emotional habit-patterns in the life of the lower self, the potent release of the new archetypes (Uranus) for service to humanity comes forth. Uranus, as a vehicle of the Seventh Ray, stimulates the interplay between Spirit and matter for further creative manifestation.

MOON IN SAGITTARIUS: The personality-centered indications of this position express the dual expansion of the form/desire nature; that is, the need for emotional fulfillment through the physical senses, and through the formation and achievement of one's ideological goals.

Soul-Level Purpose: The Earth and the Third Ray become the rulers, giving rise to the awareness of humanity's practical needs. In addition, there is the ability to structure people, events, and ideas so that the most good may be distributed where it is most needed. Altruism takes on a pragmatic modality; idealism merges with practical considerations in order to sustain humanity's well-being. This is a very encompassing position for the Moon. It involves a very strong, initial Fourth Ray (Human) orientation insofar as the Moon and Sagittarius both manifest on this line of energy. The Fifth Ray, and thus Aquarius and Uranus come into play. One should keep in mind that Jupiter, the exoteric ruler of Sagittarius, is also the esoteric ruler of Aquarius. Finally, the Sixth Ray and Neptune (another of the Moon's veiled planets) also add the dimension of nurturing self-sacrifice to this complex pattern of influences.

If the Moon veils Vulcan in this position, it requires detachment from one's personal beliefs as universal truth, so that humanity's needs can be met with true wisdom. The Moon veiling Uranus in this position would inspire a universal philosophy which would be used to anchor the new archetypes for the betterment of humanity.

MOON IN CAPRICORN: Soul-centered detriment. As one evolves, the power of the form to control one's motivations in life lessens, until all material attachment ceases, and one moves on to the various initiatic states of the Cardinal Cross. The Fixed Cross is that state which establishes the relationship between the two extremes of total attachment and total detachment.

Soul-Level Purpose: (For one on the Fixed Cross with the Moon in Capricorn.) To awaken awareness of this dualistic frame of reference. This is accomplished through the structuring of those personal and collective resources for which one is responsible, so that they may be used for group purposes. Vulcan, when veiled by the Moon in this position, gives rise to the tensions which the first steps toward this detachment necessitate. The combination of Capricorn and Uranus allows for the structuring of the form life for greater use by the Will-to-Good, as the Seventh Ray of this sign and planet is in direct contact with Ray One and the Purpose for manifestation.

MOON IN AQUARIUS: On the personality level, this position is not the warmest or most nourishing, due to the rather impersonal qualities of the emotions when working through the Water Bearer. But it is precisely this impersonality which makes the Moon in Aquarius very potent for Soul-level work.

Soul-Level Purpose: To arm oneself with the tools (shaped and sharpened by Vulcan) for world service. This is an excellent position for the Moon, as it lends itself so easily to the transitional orientation of the unveiling of Uranus and the Soul-centered rulership of Jupiter. The rulership of Jupiter activates the Second Ray and adds that most important ingredient of all, Love, to the nature of impersonality and detachment.

MOON IN PISCES: On the personality level, the undisciplined emotional responsiveness of the Moon in Pisces can lead one into unending mutations of desire, thus perpetuating life on the Mutable Cross. Yet when the individual begins to orient himself to the Fixed Cross, several very potent forces come into play. This can be one of the most valuable positions in a horoscope for Soul-focused activity. The Moon unveils Vulcan and Pisces reveals its Soul-centered ruler, Pluto, thus bringing about a tremendous emphasis of the First Ray quality of Will/Power. In addition, the Sixth Ray energy of Pisces evokes Mars, and the Moon then unveils the other planet of this Ray, Neptune (now expressing itself as illumination, rather than illusion). Jupiter, the Sun, and the Second Ray also contribute their loving potentialities to this combination.

Soul-Level Purpose: To harness the Will in order to activate the Plan of Love/Wisdom, through never-ending compassion and devotion. The work of a person with this position would, first of all, be to break his or her attachment to the thralldom of emotional sensation and stimulation (Vulcan). After this process has occurred, the form nature can then be used to integrate and distribute a new orientation (Uranus) toward universal compassion and understanding (Neptune).

VULCAN

Soul-Centered Ruler of Taurus
Planet of the First Ray

*Such is the test of Vulcan, ruling Taurus, of the Soul,
ruling desire, of the Son of God, fashioning His instrument
of expression in the depths, grasping the divine purpose,
and so bending the will of the little self to that of the
greater Self.*

–Alice A. Bailey
Esoteric Astrology

Position in the natal chart: Until more astronomical data is available,
the consensus among esoteric astrologers is that Vulcan, this most
esoteric—that is, hidden—of planets is to be found within 8 degrees,
20 minutes of the position of the Sun. The intuition of the astrologer,
plus his or her understanding of the meaning of this planet relative to
the signs, will be necessary to ascertain Vulcan's position, should the
Sun be cuspal.

Function: Much concerning the meaning and energies of this planet
has been said in our previous discussions of Taurus and the Moon.
We can summarize the effects of this physically small but esoterically
powerful planet by linking its effects to the earthy element and to the
First Ray of Will/Power. It is the stimulating energy of Vulcan which
creates the need to penetrate through our material existence—indeed,
through the use of matter and form—in order to detach ourselves
from identification with the form life. The Soul-centered individual
can then utilize matter in order to shape those tools necessary for the
externalization of the Soul force. When there is a war, matter is all
too often used against humankind, and the power of this planet is
inverted through the improper use of will (Mars, as the personality
ruler of Aries, externalizing itself through the First, Sixth, and Seventh
Rays). On a higher level of manifestation, Vulcan establishes the link
between humanity and the Plan. This is due to Vulcan's First Ray
energy, manifesting through its Fourth Ray ruler, Taurus, and the
relationship that the latter has to the Fourth Kingdom of nature.

Vulcan and the Crosses: Although Vulcan has an effect on the mass
consciousness, through its function as a tool to unfetter humanity
from its attachment to material forms, its purpose in terms of the
evolutionary process is more specific. My current thoughts on the

subject seem to point to Vulcan's primary use as a vehicle of transfer from the Mutable to the Fixed Cross. When on the Mutable Cross, the totally personality-centered individual is not aware of the unconscious influence of Vulcan working to create detachment through the loss of physical objects and relationships. But when the objectification of the relationship existing between essence and form begins to crystallize in the consciousness of an actively evolving person, the perception of Vulcan's effects changes accordingly. At this point, one is actively cultivating the first stages of conscious detachment from the form life. In this respect, Vulcan now serves as the agent which assists us in this transition of values, and our subsequent release from the Mutable Cross.

Once Vulcan has done its work and the individual is firmly anchored on the Fixed Cross of Discipleship, we can then say that for all intents and purposes, Vulcan becomes a "dead planet." Its primary function in the reorientation of consciousness has been completed. One would then tend to move much more into the domain and influence of Uranus, as discussed in our previous section on the Moon. The Soul-centered individual can now utilize the energies of the crisis-producing presence of Vulcan in order to effect this necessary transformation. This, of course, would be carried out within the greater context of the part in the One Work undertaken by such a Soul-centered person.

Vulcan in the signs: The following twelve paragraphs will point out Vulcan's nature when operating at the point of transition from the Mutable to the Fixed Cross, and its effects when operating through the life of the Soul-centered individual who has securely mounted the Fixed Cross.

VULCAN IN ARIES: This is a very potent position leading to the right use of will as the First Ray energies of sign and planet unite. When in the transitional state, this position of Vulcan often indicates a person with a very strong but highly self-righteous mind. The "tools" which Vulcan serves to fashion in this sign allow for the mind (Mercury's rulership of Aries) to align itself with the Will of the Plan. This requires a detachment of the mind from its service to the ego. Once the transition to the Fixed Cross is accomplished, the mind of the individual is then focused on service to humanity, as Mercury connects with Taurus (and hence with Vulcan) through the Fourth Ray. A person who can consciously utilize Vulcan in Aries can help to break down other people's resistance to higher consciousness, through the decrystallization of nonregenerative thought forms.

VULCAN IN TAURUS: Soul-centered ruler. In the transitional phase, the individual is presented with many, often painful tests of detachment. This may manifest as loss of either objects or people. The purpose is to aid the individual in breaking his or her thralldom with the desire nature as it centers in form. Once the Fixed Cross is mounted, the natural magnetism and power of Vulcan in Taurus allows the person to create a vital channel for the expression of the Will and Power of the First Ray. The Soul-centered individual then becomes a vehicle for the "redemption" of matter, so that it (as well as the individual) may serve some larger, impersonal function. The area in the life in which this higher purpose may be found can be ascertained through Vulcan's house placement in the natal horoscope.

VULCAN IN GEMINI: In its initial phase, Vulcan in this position gives rise to a very critical mind, ever seeking to destroy those opinions that contest one's own. Yet once a person secures herself on the Fixed Cross, a very intimate relationship is created for the positive use of Vulcan's energies. Venus, esoteric ruler of Gemini, is also the personality-centered ruler of Taurus. A person with this position can thus utilize Vulcan's function to forge a link between the First and the Fifth Rays. This could lead her to create those inventions and scientific discoveries that evoke the hidden Light contained within matter. The externalization of this inner design could then be used for the benefit of humanity.

VULCAN IN CANCER: This is a very important position on the collective level, as it is here that Vulcan is confronted with the energies of the mass consciousness. Its primary function—to instill detachment from form—presents itself quite distinctly. When on the transitional stage of the Crosses, Vulcan's placement in this sign points to those tests of release from past patterns of attachment, especially relative to the expression of the emotions and the astral body. The Will/Power of the First Ray must be free to create, without being hampered by the nurturing energies of Cancer. Nurturing, in this respect, means the matrix which forms itself around the impulse of the Will, aiding its descent into the lower planes and kingdoms. Yet if this matrix becomes too solidified, through patterns of repeated desire, the movement of the Will becomes impeded. When on the Fixed Cross, this position would tend to stimulate the creation of those mental and physical channels and structures (Cancer's relationship to the Third and Seventh Rays) that would be most appropriate to the unfolding of the Plan.

VULCAN IN LEO: When moving off the Mutable Cross, Vulcan in Leo indicates those tests which serve to free the individual from a self-centered attachment to the creative potentials of the lower self. Ego-centricity now must yield to a focus of group consciousness. Once this repolarization takes place and Vulcan is externalizing through the Fixed

Cross, all the potency of the Will and the Concrete Mind (Leo's association with the First and Fifth Rays) can be utilized as expressions of group consciousness and channels for the Second Ray energy of the Sun.

VULCAN IN VIRGO: Soul-centered fall. I'm going to postulate that Vulcan is in its fall in this sign. The detachment from form seems to be particularly difficult when one is making the transition to the Fixed Cross with Vulcan in this sign. As the Moon, Mother of All Form, is the ruler, this placement of Vulcan creates a great conflict, because the attachment to the nurturing process is quite intense. The individual would have to allow the healing and cohesive life force of the Universal Mother to sustain the objects of her caring. This means releasing herself from the strong personal emotional expressions of the Second, Fourth, and Sixth Ray energies in this position (Virgo and the Moon), so that the focus of Will can externalize, unimpeded by the lower self. When the Fixed Cross has been mounted, the individual with Vulcan in Virgo is aligned with the Mother, and can then be a conscious vehicle, co-creating the focus for any necessary healing.

VULCAN IN LIBRA: A most interesting position, with some important possibilities! The relationship of the First and Seventh Rays is particularly strong, and there is also a powerful influence coming from Rays Three and Five. The stress on the One-Three-Five-Seven line of manifestation points to this position of Vulcan as being very Will-focused. Let us outline the Ray elements: Vulcan—First Ray; Libra—Third and Seventh; Uranus—Seventh; and Venus as Libra's ruler on the Mutable Cross brings in the Fifth Ray. There is a very close affinity with the First and Seventh Rays as they relate to the inherent relationship between Spirit/Will and Matter/Manifestation. The esoteric focus of Libra, with its connection to Aquarius through Uranus, is of course the Law of Right Human Relations and the Law of Group Endeavor. During the transition from the Mutable to the Fixed Cross, a person with Vulcan in Libra is apt to experience a deep change in the scope of his personal relationships. Even if he is on the Path of World Service at the time, the nature of his social aspirations and his integration within a group context in order to externalize some collective purpose is bound to undergo a major shift. Will cannot be sustained by the lesser self for the purpose of structuring collective human energies according to his personal, mental image of same, no matter how idealistic. A merger must be made with the Higher Self/Mind (Third Ray) so that he is acting in concert with an unfolding group process. The latter is firmly placed in motion once the individual has made the necessary transformation to life on the Fixed Cross. Uranus then overshadows Vulcan, and group will and purpose emerge.

VULCAN IN SCORPIO: Soul-centered detriment. I am postulating that Vulcan is in its detriment when found in this sign, but there is no negative inference in this placement. The primary function of Vulcan is to break attachment to outmoded forms so that new tools of consciousness may be forged for the liberation of the Soul's presence in the outer life. The energies of Mars, Scorpio, and Pluto work so effectively at this task that the need for Vulcan's effects in this position is diminished. One could say that in Scorpio, those situations necessary to bring forth the required results for mounting the Fixed Cross are intensified. The First and the Fourth Rays are brought into play through Scorpio, Pluto, Vulcan, and Taurus, while Mars and the Sixth Ray lead to the cultivation of the one-pointedness required for maintaining one's focus of Soul orientation (Discipleship) on the Fixed Cross.

VULCAN IN SAGITTARIUS: As the teacher, Sagittarius has to be "armed" with those concepts which serve to widen humanity's horizons, so that a greater universality of thought is achieved. The individual leaving the Mutable Cross (and his attachments to the personality) must undergo those transmutations which serve to harmonize and blend the degree of understanding he has achieved through the experiences of the personality life with the collective wisdom stored by the Soul. Vulcan in this position breaks those attachments to the personal mental body, allowing the Third Ray influence of Sagittarius's ruler, the Earth (and hence also the influence of the other Third Ray planet, Saturn), to function from the level of the Higher Self. This position may indicate that in the present incarnation, the individual may encounter some crisis of disillusionment with his previous belief systems. This leads to the acceptance of those higher concepts and broader ideas that can be communicated to others for the benefit of all.

VULCAN IN CAPRICORN: This is a very strong and powerful placement for Vulcan. It definitely strengthens the influence of the First and Third Rays, as it calls forth an interplay between this planet and Saturn. Nonregenerative thought processes are challenged and broken down as the lesser self finds that it can no longer maintain its place or status in the outer world. The individual begins to lose her attachment to whatever influence has been achieved over others, and a direct movement is made toward mounting the Fixed Cross. Initially, this may be perceived as a loss of power or strength. Such a transition requires a person to restructure her will and broaden her awareness so that new mental patterns are created. These structures are aligned to the needs of the collective, and serve to anchor the evolutionary Plan for humanity that much more concretely in the material world (Seventh Ray influence of Capricorn and Uranus).

VULCAN IN AQUARIUS: In traditional astrology, Neptune is the higher octave of Venus, Pluto of Mars, and Uranus of Mercury. I believe that in Soul-centered astrology, we can look at Uranus as the higher octave of Vulcan (as well as Mercury). Once Vulcan has helped to destroy the attachments and adherence to the forms created by the lower self, Uranus can then work as the channel for the birthing of new archetypes for the evolution of the individual and humanity. The connection between Vulcan and Uranus is therefore very strong when the former is placed in Aquarius. As Jupiter is the esoteric ruler of the Water Bearer, there is a blending of Rays One (Vulcan), Five (Aquarius), Seven (Uranus), and Two (Jupiter). The Fourth Ray of Vulcan's sign, Taurus, influences all placements of this planet, and its connection with the Fourth Kingdom of Humanity should be kept in mind when studying Vulcan's effects. Indeed, we can say that all "vulcanic" crises are particularly human in their effects, especially in relation to a person's transition from the Mutable to the Fixed Cross. The function of Vulcan in Aquarius is to shatter all human attachments that do not serve the purpose of the Higher Self, and hence the needs of the collective. In initial phases, the individual with this placement may find that there is a crisis in the life brought about by gradual detachment from friends and associations. He begins to look for "brothers and sisters of like minds" with whom he can interact with loving impersonality. This differs widely from associations that fulfill personal emotional needs or are maintained due to purely social obligations or status. When the Fixed Cross has been mounted, the motivation for relationships becomes increasingly centered in the urge for World Service.

VULCAN IN PISCES: Soul-centered exaltation. Once again, I am inclined to postulate about Vulcan's placement by sign, and feel that it is in exaltation when in this position. The First Ray energies of this planet combine with those of Pluto and express themselves through the Second and Sixth Rays. The universal, loving focus and the ultimate death of anything that is not useful to the Soul are very much at the heart of the function of Pisces. This is the sign of baptism, of the cleansing waters that remove all traces of previous attachments to the emotional aspect of the personality life. It is the sign of preparation for the resurrection of Life as it manifests anew through Aries. Vulcan's purpose in this evolutionary rhythm is thus made very clear, and aligns the Cosmic Blacksmith to the Work of the World Savior. An individual with this placement in her natal chart would experience a crisis of releasing any blocks to the power of Love as it seeks to express in the outer world. Personal prejudices would thus "go the way of all things" and be replaced by a gradual expansion of loving devotion to the Plan and—once a person is mounted on the Fixed Cross—by the urge to be of service to the expansion of Love/Wisdom in the world of humanity.

Please note: The position of Vulcan in the natal chart is always conjunct the Sun, and very often conjunct Mercury, as well. The effects of Vulcan are *only* experienced by one who has mounted the Fixed Cross or is very close to doing so. The conscious application of Vulcan's energy can only be said to be utilized by one firmly anchored on the Path, and who is spiritually active in the service of humanity. It can be seen that, due to Vulcan's proximity to the Sun and/or Mercury, the unfolding, evolutionary process of a Son or Daughter of Mind is very much associated with the positive destructive force of this tiny planet. Once Vulcan has done its work, the energies of Uranus (in the creation of new archetypes for the expression of the Loving Will/Power of Creation) will supersede in the life.

MERCURY

Soul-Centered Ruler of Aries
Planet of the Fourth Ray

Mercury is called the first of the celestial Gods, the God Hermes . . . to which God is attributed the invention of and the first initiation of men into Magic. . . . Mercury is Budh, Wisdom, Enlightenment, or "reawakening" in the divine science.

—H. P. Blavatsky
The Secret Doctrine

Function: Mercury occupies a most important position in our lives and in Soul-centered astrology. It is Mercury, representing the Mind, which acts as the "illuminating principle" of human life. Mercury is a planet emanating the energies of the Fourth Ray and as such, it is intimately connected with that function of human intelligence which separates mankind from the animal kingdom. It is Mind which allows humanity to be a conscious conduit for the downpouring of energies coming from higher realms (notably from the source of intuition). This faculty of awareness is not available to the animal kingdom.

In this sense, Mercury is truly the "Messenger of the Gods." Its association with the fourth level of manifestation—the Buddhic Plane—

brings it into contact with the intuitive nature, and thus with the process of the birthing of new archetypes into the consciousness of humanity (Uranus).[7]

On the personality level, Mercury is associated with duality, as well as with all facets of communication between people. On the Soul level, it is exclusively a planet of relatedness and a harbinger of harmony. As we shall see in the following twelve paragraphs, this relatedness expresses itself in Aries as the bringing together of Spirit and matter; in Gemini as the interrelatedness of Soul and body; in Virgo, connecting Mother and Child; and in Scorpio, as the "Word made Flesh." Mercury also plays a vital role in two other important areas of relatedness: it focuses the synthesis of the mind (cognition) to wisdom, and hence functions to aid in the distribution of the Second Ray of Love/Wisdom; and it helps in the rhythmic exchange of energies through the Rainbow Bridge/Antahkarana. It thus facilitates the interplay of the evolutionary and involutionary currents conditioning the relationship between the Soul and the personality.

MERCURY IN ARIES: Soul-centered ruler. Mercury's function as the illuminating principle mentioned above is at its strongest when found in the sign of the Ram in the natal chart. This is the Mercury of the "Illuminati"—the seers of any Age. Mercury (and the individual who has this position) serves to "lead humanity into the light" of Buddhic consciousness when placed here. Its actions center upon the diffusion of illusion and the expansion of the Higher Mind into the outer life. As the vehicle for a great deal of Soul activity, Mercury functions as an intermediary, helping to relate the creative urgings of Spirit to the form life of matter. One of the primary characteristics of a person who finds Mercury in Aries in his natal chart is a powerful use of the will (First Ray quality of Aries) to pierce through the darkness of consolidated thought-forms, thus freeing the life force for the birthing of new Ideas. Mercury's action, in this respect, brings it into close association with Vulcan, which often conjoins Mercury and/or the Sun, and further implements the presence of the First Ray.

MERCURY IN TAURUS: This is a very strong Fourth Ray position, as both this planet and sign are highly active through this Ray. The Idea in the Mind of God must be anchored in the physical realm, even if previous forms have to be destroyed in order to create a greater beauty and harmony. Nowhere are Vulcan and Mercury more closely associated than in this combination, and the task of bringing

---

[7]This connection is expressed through esoteric astrology by Mercury's rulership of Aries on the Soul level and Uranus's rulership of Aries on the Hierarchical, or most collective, originating level.

forth the illumined "Eye of the Bull" is uppermost in the mind of one with this position in the natal chart. Form *will* be made into a correct expression for ideas, while art and the professions will be the channels. In Taurus, Mercury joins with Venus, the esoteric ruler, creating the Divine Hermaphrodite. This is the perfect unity of male and female in one, and thus is illustrative of the perfect wedding of the idea to its form.

MERCURY IN GEMINI: Personality-centered ruler. Such a lively position, and so full of possibilities! On the Soul-centered level, we have the joining of Mercury and Venus once again, this time not in the earthy element of the Bull but in the airy matrix of the mind. This position endows a person with the potential to harmonize and relate many streams of diverse thought into a vision and expression of harmonious unity. The combination is of Rays Two (Gemini), Five (Venus, as esoteric ruler of the sign), and Four (Mercury). The "pure reason" of the Mind expresses Love unquestionably through the vehicle of science and technology, in order to advance the evolution of humanity and our planet. Individuals active on Soul levels who have this position of Mercury in the natal chart will seek to use the inventiveness of the mind for the benefit of all. On a more personal level (but still anchored in the Soul), there is usually grace of speech and manners, and an ability to agree with everyone without compromising the perception and expression of truth. The urge is to harmonize and relate all the thinking processes of any group of people into a focus of active unanimity.

MERCURY IN CANCER: This is an interesting position, as it links the two Fourth Ray planets when operating on the personality level. Here Mercury and the Moon combine to create those forms of communication in the environment that allow the individual a sense of emotional security and control. But on the Soul level, Neptune joins with Mercury, bringing a strong Sixth Ray influence into this position. The Mind merges with Devotion to the Plan for the sustained nourishment of humanity and the planet. Great resourcefulness is part of the gift of this position, giving the individual the ability to bring people and ideas together. Neptune impressing itself upon the Moon helps to shape the form of the astral-desire body so that it can be the proper "mother"—the producer of the necessary forms for the expression of Divine Ideas. The mental focus of this position should not be underestimated, as Cancer externalizes through the Third and Seventh Rays.

MERCURY IN LEO: As Mercury is the ruler of Aries, its position in Leo also harnesses the Lion's affinity with Will/Power. Yet the ruler of the Lion is the Sun, planet of the Second Ray, clearly indicating Mercury's function in this position as the link between Rays One and Two. Mercury represents the Son, the Son of Mind, the Son of the Divine Idea of Manifestation. Thus in a very esoteric sense (but one which is analogous to human progeneration), Mercury and the Sun (Father/Spirit) are one! When Mercury is found in this position in the horoscope of a Soul-centered individual, the creative powers are very strong. There is an immediate and totally intimate connection with the process of thought, and the manifestation of that thought process into an externalized expression. This is often channeled through Leo's other Ray, the Fifth, and thus presents itself through the Concrete Mind. It is interesting to contemplate the physical proximity of Venus to Mercury and the Sun in this respect, as the combination of these three planets is very vital to today's humanity. The Sun is representative of the Second Ray of the Lord of the Solar System, while Mercury is of the Fourth Ray of the Human Kingdom. Venus is of the Fifth, relating both to the dominant Ray of our present humanity, as well as to the Ray of the sign of the incoming Aquarian Age (see tabulation 2, p. 140).

MERCURY IN VIRGO: Personality-centered ruler; Soul-centered exaltation. This position is related very closely to Mercury in Cancer, as the affinity to the Moon in both cases is strong. Here the Mother is ruled by the Son, as the Idea in the Mind of God takes root in the nurturing formativeness of the Moon and the earthy element of the Virgin. Thus, when Mercury is found in this position in the natal chart, the Soul-centered individual has the ability to hold an Idea in gestation. This Idea gains in strength as it connects to the magnetic quality of the Earth, the Mother, and the Second and Sixth Rays, until the time is right and the Idea can be born into the "world of men." The fruit of this Idea may then be shared so that all may be nourished by it and by the human being who birthed it.

MERCURY IN LIBRA: A Soul-centered individual with this placement of Mercury is very active on the Path of World Service, as he or she communicates the Law of Right Human Relations. This combination brings Uranus and the Seventh Ray very strongly into play, thus fostering a very humanitarian vision, expressed by this person through his activities in the world. The Third Ray of Active Intelligence is also involved through Libra, as is its planet of exaltation and Third Ray ruler, Saturn. The combination of the Third and Seventh in this position helps to generate an individual who would be very partial to the construction of communication networks to disseminate evolutionary Ideas. Another facet of his work would be to function as a liaison or link between individuals and groups in order to expand these networks and further the externalization of these Ideas.

MERCURY IN SCORPIO: Another very potent position for Mercury, as the link with the Fourth Ray is strengthened by Scorpio. This placement gives rise to a mental power which can not only be transformative in one's personal reorientation, but which can also do a great deal to break down and reorient the thought-forms of others. Thus the mind of the mass consciousness is freed to be impregnated with the unfolding evolutionary concepts of the Plan. Mercury in Scorpio is a placement of great tests (as with all planets that tenant this sign), and a strong sense of adherence to the Path has to be demonstrated before Mercury in Scorpio can serve as a vehicle for the potential of its great power. This is where the function of Mars and the Sixth Ray enter, and the trials which lead to the one-pointedness of the Path are undertaken. Mars is the exoteric ruler of Aries and the ruler of Scorpio on both the personality and Soul levels. Mercury is the esoteric ruler of Aries, and rules Scorpio from its highest focus of collective manifestation, the Hierarchical.[8] A person with Mercury in Scorpio is thus very active in transforming people's mental energy from its use in communicating the desires of the lower self to its use as a vehicle to communicate the Will/Power of Higher Mind.

MERCURY IN SAGITTARIUS: Soul-centered detriment. When Mercury is acting on the personality level, it functions as the vehicle for the rational mind. But when the Soul-centered level is achieved, intuition replaces reason. Thus, reason falls under the domination of intuition, and becomes an extension of the communicative ability of this higher faculty. Sagittarius is the sign of the Higher Mind, and hence Mercury is in its detriment when placed herein. This should not be interpreted as a weakness, but more as the Higher Mind overshadowing the lower. A person with Mercury in Sagittarius is a natural teacher who comprehends the larger issues in life. His goal is to impart this vision of truth to everyone he may meet along the Path of his travels. There is another, more esoteric reason for the weakening of Mercury's energy in the sign of the Archer. As the Pathwalker seeks the goal of initiation, he finds that a gradual but eventual disassociation with the human personality must take place. He then turns his attention devotedly to the Fifth Kingdom of Souls, and toward the Fourth Kingdom of Humanity as a focus for loving service. The impersonal life supersedes the desires, thoughts, and physicality of the personal life. Mercury is a planet of the Fourth Ray,

---

[8]I have mentioned this term several times previously relative to the planetary rulerships. Let me just reiterate that this category of planet-sign relationship is pertinent only to the most collective (and hence abstract, in ordinary human terms) levels of manifestation in the solar system. I bring up Mercury as Scorpio's Hierarchical ruler at this point so that the reader may know about the deep connection this planet has to this sign. Its overall effect is to bring about the collective transformation of consciousness for all of humanity so that everyone may transfer from the Mutable Cross to the Fixed and the whole of Humanity may walk the Path of World Service. That is a primary focus of our collective destiny (eons though it may take for it to come about), and an essential element of Mercury's astrological significance.

and Sagittarius the sign prior to Capricorn, the Initiate. Thus the human son must "die" and resurrect as a conscious Son (or Daughter) of Mind.

MERCURY IN CAPRICORN: As Capricorn is found on the First, Third, and Seventh Rays, Mercury's function in this sign is to relate intelligently—that is, consciously—the Spiritual Man with the individual living his or her human life in the outer world. Not only does Mercury relate these two poles of the human constitution, he facilitates that initiatic process which helps the lower self to realize its reality as the Soul! Thus the Plan of the Creator is brought down to Earth through the spiritualized mind of humanity, and is expressed through those forms of civilization and society which constitute the outer collectivization of humankind. The Soul-centered individual with Mercury in this position is usually very creatively intelligent. He is aware of the use of the human mind as an extension of the Mind of God. Active Intelligence is very strong in the life of such an individual, who serves as a tool for the focus of the Third Ray in the creation of the outer forms of life.

MERCURY IN AQUARIUS: This position relates very strongly to Mercury in Libra, as Uranus, the esoteric ruler of the Scales, is the exoteric ruler of the Water Bearer. The Laws and Principles of the New Age are very much the major archetypes of thought in the mind of a contemporary, Soul-centered individual with this placement in the natal chart. The Second Ray energy of Jupiter stands behind Aquarius and urges Mercury to communicate the unifying ideas and philosophies that further the loving integration of humanity. A person with Mercury in Aquarius will thus seek to unite others into a group focus of shared ideas and principles. Active work in service to humanity will be very much at the heart of his life. The intuition is very strong and he can easily perceive the patterns of energy as they interplay within any given life situation. As one would expect from Mercury acting through a sign of the Fifth Ray, there is a tendency for a person with this placement to be very interested in those inventions of science and technology which implement the expression of his humanitarian efforts.

MERCURY IN PISCES: Soul-centered fall. When in the sign of the Fish, Mercury relates mind and love. The Mind is always the vehicle for the expression of the Love/Wisdom which is the essence of Life. Yet, after a certain stage of evolution is reached, there is no longer a need for the mind to act as a mediator between the Soul and the personality. The Rainbow Bridge/Antahkarana has been created, and the Soul and the personality are indeed one. Then Mercury and the Sun unite, and the Son returns to the Father. Pisces is the sign which, when experienced in its fullness, reveals the totality of Soul conscious-

ness. Is not Pisces the sign of the Christ in all? There is thus no need
for mind to relate this Presence to the personality. *The Presence has
incarnated as the personality.* "It is finished," and a new cycle is
ready to begin in Aries. The Soul-centered individual with Mercury in
Pisces does not allow the limitations of mind to inhibit the perception
of the indwelling Love/Wisdom principle in the outer life. She is able
to awaken an awareness of this factor in others by communicating
Love as the energy which transcends mind. Such individuals do well
working in areas that are not intellectually focused (such as the
sciences). As a rule, they serve far more effectively in those fields
where empathy and compassion are needed to communicate the Plan.

VENUS

Soul-Centered Ruler of Gemini
Planet of the Fifth Ray

*That which is on its way comes as a cloud which veils the
Sun. But hid behind this cloud of immanence is love, and
on the Earth is love and in the heaven is love, and this—
the love which maketh all things new—must stand revealed.
This is the purpose back of all the acts of this great Lord
of Knowledge.*

—Alice A. Bailey
Esoteric Psychology

*Venus is the Earth's alter ego. . . . Venus is to the Earth
what the Higher Self is to man.*

—Alice A. Bailey
A Treatise on Cosmic Fire

Function: The predominant concept which we hold as love—especially
that aspect of love which is romanticized, exalted in song and poetry,
searched for to the ends of the earth, and generally thought of as the
quintessential sharing between human beings—would hardly be thought
of as being logical in nature! Yet the essential quality of consciousness—
the primary emanation of Divinity on the plane of casuality, and Its
incarnation in humankind—is a pure expression of Universal Mind.
On the Soul level, Venus is the vehicle for the emergence of this Love
Principle of Life, through the focused will of the Mind of God. It is
this spiritual aspect of Venus which reveals the Son of God (Venus

exalted in Pisces) as the Son of Mind perfected (the Initiate). It is this consecrated human being Who is the instrument of God's Love.

Venus functions to turn knowledge into wisdom. It harmoniously links the lower and the higher mental faculties through the rhythm of relatedness embodied in its sign, Gemini. Its focus in the human organism is through the Ajna Center—the Third Eye, the Eye of the Bull, The Horn of the Unicorn, etc. This is the seat of wisdom and the lens through which the more highly developed human being perceives the world. Venus is thus the focus of synthesis, the resolution of polarity (that is, the right and left eyes), and the blending quality which aids in the resolution of duality. It is the energy of Venus which promotes diplomacy and establishes Right Human Relations between all people, and between nations. Venus's great potency lies in its ability to bring about harmonious relationships within pairs of opposites, thus furthering creative manifestation on all levels. This may be compared to the function of Mercury, which awakens consciousness by relating opposites, but does not harmonize or blend them.

One of the most beautiful aspects of this function of Venus is also one of the most esoteric. In the Ancient Wisdom Teachings, we find that the work of Venus helped to give humanity its special quality of being. Venus, through Gemini, brought about the attraction of the Third Kingdom of Nature (the Animal Kingdom) and the Fifth (the Kingdom of the Souls). The result of this "marriage" was the birth of the Fourth Kingdom (the Human)—beings whose Souls are attached to animal forms and whose great lesson is to redeem the animal self through those initiatic phases leading to total Soul infusion of the lower self.

When Venus is working through the consciousness of a Soul-centered individual, the concept and function of love takes on a very different connotation. This new concept of love gives one the objective of coordinating one's Active Intelligence so that it produces cohesive acts of goodwill and furthers Right Human Relations. This often requires a sacrifice of the lower, personality-centered love nature so that the more transpersonal qualities of love may bring about an increasingly impersonal orientation to life.

Life then becomes more mentally polarized; that is, more perceptive into cause rather than effect, essence rather than form. This should not be confused with a life which is intellectually centered, as this indicates an emphasis on the lower mental faculties. The latter serve to store knowledge, formulate opinions, and structure logic. Once a person is thus mentally polarized, his perception of reality is freed from the thralldom of the astral-desire nature, and true service may be externalized into the world. It must be mentioned that as love has a strongly synthetic quality about it, one doesn't "lose" anything by having a lovingly detached, impersonal attitude. Venus can still bring the partner, but such a one will be a Soul mate—a co-working brother or sister and a companion along the Way.

VENUS IN ARIES: Soul-centered detriment. The Sun is so strong in this sign that the immanence of the Spiritual Presence creates a great sense of immediacy in Venus's "urge to merge." Thus, reason gives way to automatic fusion, as relationships become quickened by direct perception of Light. One could say that the energy of Venus speeds up when in Aries, and thus loses some of the grace of its more natural rhythm. The creation of a balanced relationship becomes less important than the immediate fusing of opposites. This occurs through a direct use of the Will. The power of this combination is such that one often has a tendency to lose sight of the differences between people, in the effort to effectuate a more direct bonding of human energies for some greater goal.

VENUS IN TAURUS: Personality-centered ruler. At the Soul-centered level, this potent placement of Venus reveals the urge or desire for increased knowledge. This understanding may then be transmuted into wisdom for the benefit of all. In the personality-centered chart, Venus in Taurus gives the need (and the ability) to attract form—money, possessions, etc. The esoteric perspective is naturally quite different. Here, the individual is seeking out an understanding or attunement with *the idea which embodies a particular form.* Venus in Taurus is thus quite perceptive of the quality of energy represented by a specific physical manifestation, whether this is a person or a particular object.

VENUS IN GEMINI: Soul-centered ruler. In the life of a fully Soul-centered being, Venus in this position gives one the understanding of the spiritual purpose behind any relationship. On the personality level, Venus in Gemini frequently indicates two diametrically opposed relationships simultaneously occurring in a person's life. He is often caught in a difficulty duality: "How can I have both? Which one do I choose?" The Higher Mind will always choose *both*, and then blend them into a harmonious *third*, capable of increased creative activity and love. This is the secret of synthesis, and synthesis is the Soul's process of growth.

VENUS IN CANCER: This placement blends the activities of three Rays: the Third and Seventh (Cancer) and the Fifth (Venus), and is thus a very mental position, quite dissimilar from the sentimental and emotional qualities of this combination when expressed through the personality. On the Soul-centered level, one perceives the reasons for the sustaining nourishment of the various forms of love in one's life, and is able to make the necessary connections that allow such giving and sharing to continue. It is through such activities that Venus joins with Cancer's esoteric ruler, Neptune, bringing forth a greater consciousness for the universal application and source of love.

VENUS IN LEO: On the personality level, the intense self-consciousness of Leo creates a very prejudicial kind of relationship, as favorites are constantly being played in the choice of one's companions. Yet on the Soul level, all people are the children and love objects of the Spirit/ Father, and Venus in Leo is able to increase opportunities for the dynamics of that Creative Spirit in action. The Fifth Ray energies of both Venus and Leo strengthen the nature of that Ray quality in one's life so that the mind may unveil the hidden, spiritual potential in every aspect of human relations.

VENUS IN VIRGO: Soul-centered fall. On the level of the lower self, Venus in Virgo is in its fall, due to the critical nature which often accompanies this position. But this placement, when considered esoterically, expresses the deepest commitment Love may unfold. The Son of Mind, the indwelling Christ Principle inherent in Virgo, descends into matter. It is thus that pure Love/Wisdom incarnates in the earth element and the Loving Spirit "descends" into the womb of mother/matter. This "fall" is for the purpose of "raising up" humanity and is one of the sacrifices Love makes for mankind. A life is chosen by a Soul-centered person with Venus in this position so that she can perform those healing tasks which allow the Light of Love to re-emerge from its protected but heretofore obscure dwelling place.

VENUS IN LIBRA: Personality-centered ruler. The primary function of Venus in this position is to awaken in the consciousness of the Soul-centered individual a point of balance by which material, personal desire is able to fuse with intelligent, spiritual love. The results of this union invoke the energies of Libra's other ruler, Uranus, and thus allow one to be a vehicle for the dissemination of the higher nature of love into the practical world. Two astrological relationships prepare and augment this higher purpose: Venus's rulership over Taurus (physical desire) and Saturn's exaltation in Libra (the rule of Spiritual Law in the expression of Love).

VENUS IN SCORPIO: Soul-centered detriment. As the love nature expresses through Scorpio, it prepares itself for that great fusion with Spirit in the sign of Capricorn. Intelligence and the mental faculties must "die" in order to birth the pure, intuitive cognizance of the Initiate. The mind battles to retain its strength and dominance, but must eventually yield to the greater power of the Spiritual Presence. On the personality level, a person with this position often manipulates her relationships so that the dominance of the lower self may prevail, often through the magnetism of sexuality. A person on the

Soul level is aware of the struggles of the mind to maintain its equilibrium between the desire nature and the Spiritual Presence (that is, the lesson just learned from Libra), yet it has no choice but to yield to Spiritual Will. This is a true test (as are all experiences in Scorpio) of loving sacrifice—a sacrifice which a person with Venus in this position has to make herself, and one which she helps to facilitate in others.

VENUS IN SAGITTARIUS: This position joins Venus and the Earth, Sagittarius's esoteric ruler. A very special relationship exists between these two planets—one which symbolizes the overshadowing of the lower self (Earth) by the Higher (Venus). Those individuals who have Venus in this sign may find that they are especially gifted in the application of abstract, technical, or metaphysical information to the practical needs of the Earth and humanity. From the personality level, this position is often much more ideal than real, about one's personal relationships. On the Soul-centered level, the Fifth Ray of Venus and Sagittarius joins with the Third Ray influence of the Earth to produce a lively intelligence that easily communicates its messages of unity to the world.

VENUS IN CAPRICORN: A very potent and deeply significant position. This is very much a combination of the First, Third, and Seventh Rays, and reveals a direct mental line for the externalization of Love from "the Place where the Will of God is known" to the outer world. The Soul-centered individual with this placement is always at work creating structures and interconnections between people, nations, and world resources, so that the sustaining and cohesive qualities of loving intelligence may manifest for the collective benefit of all. This is the sign in which Mind is irradiated by Divinity—a process which is very much a part of initiatic fusion. Personality-centered people with Venus in Capricorn in their horoscopes wish to know people at the apex of the social ladder. On the Soul-centered level, a person with Venus in Capricorn is aware of his or her relationship with the One on the Mountaintop.

VENUS IN AQUARIUS: As Venus joins with Jupiter in this position, it is a placement which embodies a tremendous blessing and a most powerful potential for the distribution of the Second Ray of Love/ Wisdom in human relations. The mind is inspired to work toward the creation of those technical advances which serve to provide a pathway for Jupiter's Love to enter the life stream of humanity. Soul-centered individuals with this position are drawn into the forefront of service to humanity. As a rule, one is especially developed in the ability to view people in categories. This permits an immediate attunement to the interconnectedness of diverse peoples and groups. On the personality level, Venus in Aquarius may indicate a diffused and superficial quality in the way one relates to friends and associates. On the Soul-centered level, however, a person radiates Love in all directions while maintaining an anchored center as a stable focus for networking.

VENUS IN PISCES: Soul-centered exaltation. With this position, Love must conquer all opposition and differences. Pluto, esoteric ruler of Pisces, serves to dissolve the cord which binds and separates the two Fish, so that they may join and fuse. In this respect, the struggle of duality between the lower and the Higher selves is finally brought to a harmonious conclusion, liberating the loving consciousness of the Soul so that it may penetrate deeply into the hearts of all people everywhere. Those individuals with Venus in this sign learn how to blend the discrimination of reason with the urge to love all people universally. This allows them to be "Teachers of Love" through the communication faculties inherent in Venus and its ruling sign, Gemini.

EARTH

Soul-Centered Ruler of Sagittarius
Planet of the Third Ray

> There is one aspect of energy for which the modern as-
> trologer makes very little allowance, and yet it is of para-
> mount importance. This is the energy which emanates
> from or radiates from the Earth itself. . . . Astrologers
> have always emphasized the incoming influences and en-
> ergies as they beat upon and play through our little planet,
> but they have omitted to take into adequate consideration
> the emanating qualities and forces which are the contribu-
> tion of our Earth . . . to the larger whole.
>
> —Alice A. Bailey
> *Esoteric Astrology*

Position in the Natal Chart: The Earth in the horoscope is always 180 degrees from the natal position of the Sun. Thus, if the Sun is at 1 degree Scorpio, the Earth will be found at 1 degree of Taurus.

Function: Very little attention has been paid to the astrological implications of the Earth in the natal horoscope. One of the most important fields of research for the Soul-centered astrologer involves delineating the indications of our planet, especially as it interfaces with other bodies through mutual planetary aspects and as a pointer to the terrestrial Path. I am offering here, and in chapter 12, some speculations and postulates that I hope will prove to be helpful and, in my own Aries fashion, at least initiate an opening into further research about this vital area concerning the Earth's astrological influence.

As the Earth is the esoteric ruler of Sagittarius, and the latter points the way to the Mountaintop of initiation with his bow and arrow, the Earth in the natal chart represents the physical location of a person's Path. The house position in the natal chart will reveal this location. The meaning of that house position, by traditional definitions, will show where the Pathwalker must "tread the ways of men." For one who is walking upon the Fixed Cross, the Earth's position indicates where service to humanity takes place. The Soul-centered meaning of the houses (see the next chapter) will point to the inner journey that is taken simultaneously.

This balance between the inner and the outer journeys—between the envisioned goal and the actual field of service that we have to create in our physical reality—is very much in the nature of the "Temperance" tarot card indicated in our discussion of Sagittarius. The Sons and Daughters of Mind must be able to function with equal ability through both the inner, mental life and the outer, physical one. This is inherent in the Fourth Ray quality of Sagittarius (and Mercury), and is part of the basic constitution of the Fourth Kingdom. The polarization and the eventual synthesis of the animal nature and the Presence of the Soul, the battle and the fusion, takes place on the Earth. The postion of our planet in the natal chart thus reveals two things: the area of one's life where Active Intelligence anchors into the form of our daily existence; and the place where the work of the present incarnation has to be expressed, via our physical presence and influence on others.

I have previously mentioned (and will discuss in greater detail in chapter 14) that the Sun in the Soul-centered chart is indicative of the "creative equipment" a person brings into the present lifetime. The Earth, 180 degrees opposite, reveals where that equipment "lands" for its proper use. This indicates the nature of an individual's personal life experience as a Soul contributing to the whole of Humankind. As Saturn is the other planet of the Third Ray, its influence is always present, wherever the Earth may be. The Lord of Karma accompanies the Earth's placement and motivates the outworking of one's personal responsibility to the planet. *Could we therefore infer that Saturn represents one's karma, while the Earth represents one's dharma?* —that is, what one has to accomplish, and the way one goes about accomplishing it.

The goal of life on Earth is to become an Initiate, and unfold that aspect of the Christ Consciousness which dwells within each of us. The form of that expression differs from person to person, relative to the nature of individual dharma and karma, but the *essential* Love/Wisdom of that unfolding consciousness is the same for us all. This is our unifying link. Sagittarius and Capricorn, sign of the Initiate, are linked through the Third Ray association of the Earth and Saturn, and provide us with yet another insight into the importance of the experience gained through life on this planet. These two signs also point to the relationship of the Path to the Goal. In all the combinations which follow, the reader is advised to include the influences of Saturn and Sagittarius, for wherever the Earth is placed, so too is the karma of the Path and vision of the Goal.

EARTH IN ARIES: This position points to a life that serves to release or birth Active Intelligence into the environment. This is done through awakening oneself, and then others, to the latent possibilities for the creative expression of the Earth's resources, and of matter in general. This is balanced by the Sun in Libra, indicating that such resources have to be distributed (through Uranus and the Seventh Ray) according the Law of Right Human Relations. This combination blends the energies of Rays One and Seven (Aries) with Ray Three (the Earth) and is thus very much related to the relationship of Spirit and matter through the focus of Active Intelligence.

EARTH IN TAURUS: A most potent position for the dispelling of material glamours and illusions! This placement reveals that one of the most essential tasks the individual has to accomplish in this incarnation is the creation of those forms which will be the proper instruments for the expression of the Will-to-Be. The Third and the Fourth Ray combine in this position, providing a potent and challenging life. This Soul-centered person would be constantly involved in the process of breaking down those forms and structures which are no longer able to transmit Light. The keyword for this position could be "I break down and unblock," as this function characterizes one who is born with the Earth in Taurus and the Sun in Scorpio. It should be remembered that Venus, exoteric ruler of the Bull, is considered the Higher Self of the Earth. The Earth in Taurus helps to reveal the inner truth of the spiritual reality hidden all too often within the context of terrestrial life and material forms.

EARTH IN GEMINI: Soul-centered detriment. This is a very challenging combination to interpret, as its esoteric significance is most profound. Since the Earth rules Sagittarius, it would be natural to assume that this planet would have its detriment in the sign of the Twins. Yet Venus rules Gemini, and the connection between the Earth and Venus is a highly positive and beautiful one. I can only speculate here, and so ask the reader to consider the following conclusions in this light. It is a fact that Gemini, through its association with Venus, creates in the minds of humanity an increased awareness of the essential duality which exists between material, sensual desires and the urge to align oneself with the Will-to-Good of the Spirit. In effect, the basic duality of one on the Fixed Cross is this conflict between the will of the lesser self and the Will of the Creator. This is a collective, planetary, and particularly human dilemma. It appears to me that this duality is increased when the Earth is in Gemini and the Sun is in Sagittarius, thus giving a heightened spiritual opportunity to one with this placement.

On the personality level, this may indicate that the energies of the lower self tend to scatter and become dissipated in the unconscious attempt to integrate egocentric motivations. A Soul-centered individual with this placement in the natal horoscope would tend to be quite aware of the disparity existing between the values and goals of the personality and those of the Higher Self. The house position of the Earth would reveal that area of the life in which this duality is most pronounced. In the symbology of the Twins, the Ancient Wisdom Teachings tell us that the Earth is related to the Brother "whose light is waning"—that is, the material plane and its desires. Venus is more closely connected to the Brother "whose light grows stronger, cycle by cycle." This, of course, refers to the increasing expression of Soul-focused love. *It should also be clearly stated that one of the most important facets and goals of human evolution at this time is the creation of the conscious link, the collective Rainbow Bridge, which is joining humanity (the Fourth Kingdom) to the Fifth Kingdom of Souls—the Planetary Hierarchy, and the unfolding Christ Consciousness. This exalted, loving Place is very much related to Venus, the Fifth Ray, Aquarius, Jupiter, and to the Third Eye, in the centers in the human organism. Please take some time to consider this statement.* The detriment of the Earth in Gemini is thus, in my estimation, conditioned by its planetary association with the "material Twin." And yet—and this is perhaps the greatest duality of this position—such a polarized state allows the Earth to be utilized as a base of operations for the very same Hierarchy that lovingly seeks to join itself with incarnating (literally, "becoming in flesh") humanity. I marvel and am filled with Joy at the thought and experience of it!

EARTH IN CANCER: Soul-centered fall. I think that the fall of the Earth in Cancer (and here again, I am postulating) is much easier to grasp than the position of its detriment. Cancer is the "Gate In," and anchors the incarnating Soul onto the planet in terms of the personality and the mass consciousness. It is a beginning of the evolutionary arc which first seeks to develop self-consciousness in Leo, and then group consciousness (and subsequent world service) in Aquarius. From the Soul-centered perspective of one who is born with this position, and thus with the Sun in Capricorn, the emphasis on the Third Ray is paramount. Cancer is the primary sign of the expression of this Ray, and Capricorn is found here as well. Saturn, ruler of the latter on both Soul and personality levels, is the primary planetary expression of Active Intelligence, and is partnered in this respect by the Earth. This is thus the purest Third Ray expression possible (although Earth in Capricorn, as we shall see, also has a potent Third Ray expression). The dharma of the life is clear: to create those physical structures and thought-forms that allow Light to be utilized as a source of strength for others. The house position will reveal this "well of spiritual waters sunk deeply into the Earth," so that all may come to drink of the Father (in this case, the Father of the Waters, Neptune).

EARTH IN LEO: The mental quality of this combination is very strong, as we have a blending in Rays One and Five (Leo) and Three (Earth). Yet the Sun is of the Second Ray, so the potential for creating those forms of expression of Love/Wisdom is very great. The Sun in Aquarius brings in the polarized energies of yet another Fifth Ray sign, and its Second Ray ruler, Jupiter. The Aquarian will be able to find an Earth-based focus (that is, the Earth's house position) for the urge to network and unite groups of various individuals. The self-conscious quality of the Earth's Leo placement will point to exactly where the Water Bearer has to distribute his "burden" of consciousness.

EARTH IN VIRGO: This is the position wherein the "Mother of All Forms" can do an incredible amount of good to release the potency of the hidden Christ Child in the Soul. This combination points to an incarnation in which the individual works hard at healing and making the life on Earth more whole. Spiritually, it is a very strong position, given the fact that the Sun is in Pisces, and the energies of Pluto are also manifesting. The Earth-based focus gives Pluto a chance to "unearth the underworld," evoking from the depths of materiality the essential quality of love which lies in dark obscurity for the majority of humanity.

EARTH IN LIBRA: There are three sets of connections which should be mentioned in regard to this position: It is highly mental in nature, as it is composed of Rays Three (Earth and Libra), Five (Venus), and Seven (Libra and Uranus). It involves the impulsing of the Sun in Aries and its focus in the "Place where the Will of God is known," with the linkage of the Higher and lower minds (Third and Fifth Rays, and Venus). This position also indicates the externalization of the Divine Ideas for the unfoldment of the Plan of Creation into the "minds of men." This is accomplished through the relationship of

Rays One-Three-Five and their synthesized expression through Uranus and Ray Seven. The Mind of the Soul-centered person with the Earth in Libra and the Sun in Aries will act as a tool for the birthing on Earth of those essential Ideas "whose time has come."

EARTH IN SCORPIO: This position continues to reveal the incredible opportunity for individuals on the Scorpio-Taurus polarity in their quest for the Path. It also reveals the very particular type of service one may render while discovering and co-creating the Way. The Earth and Mars enter into an intimate relationship through this combination, breaking down all resistance to the reorientation of material values and the release of Spiritual Will. The house position of the Earth in Scorpio is a clear indication of where a tremendous focus of detachment and sacrifice has to be made in order that a greater realization of wholeness and healing can be created. The potential for healing is very powerful, as this combination is incredibly magnetic, drawing to itself matter of a much finer and Soul-centered nature to replace the destruction of the forms of desire so associated with its signs and planets.

EARTH IN SAGITTARIUS: Soul-centered ruler. The potential of the Second Ray is at its highest in this combination. The Path on the Earth will be conditioned in the daily life by Jupiter, the exoteric planetary ruler of the sign. Its polarity is the Sun in Gemini, both influenced exclusively by Love/Wisdom. Through the tremendous duality of Gemini-Sagittarius, the Soul-centered individual finally comes to know the Path he is to take on the Earth. The dharma of the life *is* to anchor oneself on the Path, and through such efforts, to communicate and share with others the focus of this struggle. I find it very interesting to note that the astronomical center of the universe is located in the sign of the Archer. When the Earth also finds itself in this sign, it would appear that a very special link is formed. Perhaps some further insight about this combination of energies may be revealed through the following passage from *The Old Commentary:*

> When the dual forces of the cosmic brothers (Gemini) become the energy of the one who rides toward the light (Sagittarius) then the fourth becomes the fifth. Humanity, the link, becomes the Hierarchy, the bestower of all good. Then all the Sons of God rejoice.[9]

When the Soul-centered individual anchors his feet firmly on the Path of the Earth in Sagittarius, he opens the Way for many others to follow.

[9]Quoted in Bailey's *Esoteric Astrology*, p. 356.

EARTH IN CAPRICORN: Soul-centered exaltation. My feelings are that this is the proper place for the exaltation of our planet. As we know, Capricorn is the "Gate Out" of ordinary incarnation, and onto the wheel of initiation and the birthing of the Christ Consciousness hidden in the womb of the Virgin. The position the Earth occupies in the natal chart when the Sun is in Cancer reveals the place and function by which the Soul-centered individual can most positively release his or her portion of the One Life into manifestation. Both the dharma and the karma of the life conjoin through Saturn's association with Capricorn, the Earth, and the Third Ray. Should Saturn also be found in Capricorn, conjunct the Earth, and in actual opposition to the Sun in Cancer, this incarnation points to a great culmination of previous efforts in former lifetimes and a great challenge is revealed in the current one. The challenge involves the proper structuring of the life forces so that they are put under the total Will of the Father. There is no room for duality in this position, and the light of the one-pointed Disciple must shine through the illusions of the material life. No one said it would be easy!

EARTH IN AQUARIUS: The developed sense of self-consciousness found in the life of the Soul-centered Leo individual finds ample opportunity for world service when the Earth is in the sign of the Water Bearer. This combination shows an emphasis on the mental plane, as this is a Third Ray planet acting through a Fifth Ray sign. The effects of Saturn, as co-ruler of Aquarius on the personality level, as well as its Third Ray connection to the Earth, are also significant. This position points to the need to create those structures of mind which channel and distribute innovative concepts into the collective consciousness. The work to be undertaken in this capacity involves the loving use (Jupiter) of the Concrete Mind for the advancement of those Ideas and Principles that will bring a sense of unified wholeness to human existence.

EARTH IN PISCES: A most potent placement, as there is a strong blending of the three Rays of Aspect through Pluto (First), Earth (Third), and Pisces (Second). The synthesis occurs through the Sixth Ray quality of the Fish and the devotion of the Soul-centered individual to humanity, the Christ Consciousness, and the Plan. The dharma involves selfless work to release people from those facets of the astral/desire nature which inhibit the flow of the universal, loving matrix (Second Ray). For the individual with the Sun in Virgo, the outer field of service will be indicated by the house position of the Earth in the natal chart. Jupiter and Neptune, the exoteric rulers of this sign, add even more loving idealism to this effort, but the fundamental nature of the Earth itself serves to balance such aspirations within the context of practicality.

MARS

Soul-Centered Ruler of Scorpio
Planet of the Sixth Ray

(Mars requires) the entire life of man . . . to be swung into the conflict, leaving no side of human nature uninvolved; hence again the need for the disciple to carry his physical nature, his emotional or desire nature, and his mental processes up into heaven. This takes place as a consequence of overcoming the . . . form nature . . . by means of the "serpent of wisdom," which is the esoteric name oft given to the soul.

—Alice A. Bailey
Esoteric Astrology

Function: As both the exoteric and esoteric ruler of Scorpio, Mars has a dual expression. It is very definitely the ruler of the desire nature. On the Soul Level, this is the desire for physical incarnation, and hence the rulership of Mars over Aries on the personality/physical level. It is here that Mars reveals itself as a vehicle for sacrifice, as it is through physical incarnation that the Soul is seen as descending into matter and thus "sacrificing" an aspect of itself for life in the denser physical world. It is that process which evokes the "death" of an aspect of one's Higher Self so that manifestation in the three worlds of the lower self is made possible. This is the true "mortification of the Soul" and the willing sacrifice of the "Light which is Love" so that It may be born into the world of Man, and thus be of benefit to humanity. This descent into matter is part of each of our Paths. Our "rebirth into Light" always requires the redemption of the lower self by the Higher. It is the "journey home," as we progress through the Path of Discipleship to the Door of Initiation in Capricorn. It is also the testing ground of the "Doorkeeper"—the Lord of Karma, Saturn.

The desire for the release from manifestation is also a function of Mars, as the personality seeks its death—the "mortification of the flesh"—so that its inner, spiritual Essence may join with the Parent-Soul after the experiences in an Earthly incarnation. Mars is thus the ruler of the death of the Higher Self as it seeks to birth itself in the personality. It is also the ruler of the death of the personality (including physical death) so that reunification with the Soul may take place.

Mars stimulates physical vitality through its association with the bloodstream. It can be said to have rulership over the entire physical body while consciousness is polarized exclusively in the lower self. This facet of its rulership has a great deal to do with the relationship Mars has to sexuality and the urge to reproduce oneself—and thus, in the biological sense, at least, conquer death. In a very specific way, Mars is associated with the solar plexus center, the source of the astral-desire body of the personality, and is thus thoroughly linked with the passions of the five senses.

For the person who is mounting the Fixed Cross, Mars brings about those tests and trials which are so much a part of the life of the Disciple and reveals the connection the Path has with Scorpio. Mars is thus the agent of the "war of dualities"—primary among which is the battle between the Soul and the personality. This particular duality has been interpreted by the major (Mars- and Neptune-dominated) Sixth Ray religion, Christianity, as the "battle between good and evil." Christianity embodies many of the Sixth Ray, martial qualities so closely associated with this planet. It is a religion of intense devotion, idealism, and courage. When examining it at its height during the Crusades and its Inquisitional period (which did not officially end until the nineteenth century), a certain degree of fanaticism and consistent preoccupation with the "blood of Christ" is also a fixed quality of its expression, especially in its Catholic forms. The "war of opposites," characterized by Mars, also applies to the war which traditional Christianity has had with sexuality: its obsession with sinfulness, antifeminism, and clerical male dominance.

The higher Sixth Ray quality of this religion would be embodied in Mars's higher octave, as viewed from the Soul level, Neptune. The Lord Jesus was a Master of the Sixth Ray of devotion to Love and its inclusive, catholic nature. It is through Neptune and Cancer, and by extension, Virgo and the Moon, that the loving nature of the Holy Mother is brought into the archetypes of Christianity. It is Neptune's modification and overshadowing of Mars that brings forth such Christian leaders as Pope John XXIII, Mother Teresa, and Martin Luther King, Jr. It is when Mars and the Sixth Ray are expressed through the religion of the personality and the collective expression of the solar plexus that the so-called and self-proclaimed "armies of God" are created, which slaughter and maim others. This facet of Mars and its effect on religion is not limited to the Christian sects, but applies equally to any one of a number of religions which may claim superiority over any other way to the One Divinity. In the Aquarian Age, we can look for a calming of such warlike religious expressions, as the Sixth Ray dominance gives way to the unfolding Seventh Ray influence of the times.

In the Soul-centered natal horoscope, the position of Mars by sign and house will indicate several matters:

1. Where and how the desires of the flesh have to be transmuted into the desires of the Soul;

2. Where the battle between the Higher Self and the lower is most likely to occur;

3. Where the primary magnetic attachment of the personality, and especially that which relates to the emotional perspective of "me-my-mine," is located;

4. Where the Soul-personality fusion is likely to occur once the Fixed Cross has been mounted.

As to the timing of these events, transiting aspects of Pluto and Neptune to Mars are likely indications that the battle lines are being drawn and the objectification of the inherent tensions of duality are about to take place. (For a fuller discussion of the nature of the aspects in a Soul-centered chart, see chapter 12.)

MARS IN ARIES: Personality-centered ruler. The "Lamb's" sacrifice has a great deal to do with those tests in life which require the Soul-centered individual to transform the urge to manifest personal desires. It is the task of such a person to do battle wherever it is necessary in order to clear an avenue for the unfolding of the Path. A reorientation of the will takes place in which the individual chooses to be a vehicle for the externalization of "Divine Mind and Order." The individual with Mars in Aries is likely to insist upon initiating some new phase of the group work in which he is involved, as the urge to channel the "Fire of Life" into objective manifestation is very strong. Look to the house position of Mars in order to determine where in the life this battle for Light will take place.

MARS IN TAURUS: Soul-centered detriment. The great battle over the attachment to the desires of the form life, which is so much at the center of Taurus's struggle, falls under the dominion of Vulcan. Thus, from an esoteric perspective, the energy of Mars is overtaken by the Blacksmith, who wields the hammer shaping the weapons for the death of the personality. An individual with this placement in the natal chart may discover that she is often at war with the physical life, fighting to remain free of those magnetic attachments to materiality that so overwhelm the majority of people. This battle with the form life often manifests as a denial of sexuality and/or in the incorrect use of sexual or financial energies. The cultivation of a proper rapport with Venus, and the creation of right relationships with love and money on the personality level, may serve to assist her in dealing with Mars in this position.

MARS IN GEMINI: During the first stages of personal unfoldment on the Fixed Cross, this position increases the tensions of duality normally associated with this sign. Gemini seeks to relate (and then through Venus, blend and join) the Soul and the forms it takes. When Mars tenants Gemini, the "space" between the relationship of these two poles seems to intensify. This tension serves a very positive purpose, however, as it gives rise to a clear distinction in the mind of the individual between the nature of the energies and associated desires of the Higher and the lower selves. Yet the victory of the Soul is assured as Venus, ruler of Gemini, promises the eventual "marriage" of this pair of opposites.

MARS IN CANCER: Soul-centered fall. The significance of the term "fall" can be seen in a most poetic sense when Mars is in this position. It is here that the Sixth Ray influence is so strong (due to Neptune's presence, as well as Mars's), that the devotion to the Soul is at its greatest. This creates an overwhelming urge for birth in incarnation and the capture of the Soul in the form of the Mother's womb. The desire to manifest that was initiated with Mars in Aries will definitely "see the light" of a physical incarnation when Mars is in Cancer, the "Gate In," as we have been told. The battle to detach from emotional adhesion to the desires of the physical life is also at its height, making the path to "return Home" that much more difficult. Release can come through the Third Ray influence of Cancer—the right use of mental energy and the repolarization of the emotional body to the intuitive.

MARS IN LEO: The potential battle of transformation in this position is quite beautiful. It indicates the passage from the energies of the physical Sun (animal vitality) to the service of the Heart of the Sun (Love as the Creative Source for manifestation). This is a most fiery combination. Fire is the "great liberator," and with Mars in Leo, it indicates the liberation from a focus of self-consciousness to one in which the will of the individual is eventually given over to the service of the group. Self-consciousness and the desires of the lower self are very strong when Mars and the Lion join on the personal level. The battle that has to be fought is often a very difficult one, as the dynamic vitality and creative urges of the ego have to come under the direction of the Soul. This often takes place through the Fifth Ray mental qualities of Leo, as fiery passions give way to enlightening ideas.

MARS IN VIRGO: As we have previously discussed, Virgo is the sign symbolic of gestation, but it is specifically that portion of pregnancy known as the "quickening," when the fetus is first felt stirring in its mother's womb. It is at this point that the Soul makes its initial contact with the physical form preparing itself for birth. Mars in

Virgo is therefore known as the "quickening of the spiritual life." Mars here makes a way for the birthing into objective consciousness of the presence of the indwelling Soul/Christ. Mars is always indicative of the creating of a "space" (the birth canal) for the revelation of Light, and in this sense, should not be considered a malefic influence, as it is in traditional astrology.

MARS IN LIBRA: Soul-centered detriment. The strength and function of Mars is lessened in the sign of Balance as the battle between the form and the Soul reaches a resting place. When Mars is placed in the signs Aries through Virgo, the initial urge to manifest goes through its various consolidating phases, until it reaches culmination in the incarnating Christ Child.[10]

The "space" which Mars creates in Libra serves to bring about a distinct demarcation between the Soul and the personality of the individual. Eventually, the "two selves" come to full awareness of each other. Later on, in Sagittarius, they will join, become the "one-pointed Disciple," and come to meet an even higher expression of self at initiation in Capricorn.

When Mars is placed in any of the signs between Scorpio and Pisces, it is significant of the "Path of Return." In this case, the lower self (especially the desires of the physical nature) has been redeemed through the battle in Scorpio, and has cleared a space for the expression of the Higher nature. A Soul-centered individual with Mars in Libra is often led to act as an arbitrator between warring factions. Libra, Venus, Saturn (exalted in this sign and connected to Libra through the Third Ray), and Rays Three and Seven are the major contributing factors to this function of Mars. Thus, when placed in the Scales, Mars acts as a standard-bearer for the Laws of Manifestation.

MARS IN SCORPIO: Soul-centered ruler. At this point, the tremendous importance of this position should be quite obvious. Mars is strongest in Scorpio, for several reasons:

1. It brings the essential battle of the Pathwalker directly to the "door of the Soul," insofar as Mars is both the personality ruler and Soul-centered ruler of this sign. There is no avoiding the issue when Mars is in Scorpio—the battle leading to the Soul's ultimate victory is on!

2. As Mars is the controlling factor of the desire nature (and for the personality, of the entire physical, animal response nature), its place

---

[10]Each of us takes this same journey. Each of us is the Christ Child. Each of us is birthed into incarnation to realize our true nature, make a loving and conscious sacrifice, and continue to walk our Path. The Passion of Lord Jesus was symbolic of the forms of the Path of the Disciple in the Age of Pisces. At the present time, humanity as a whole is acting as the vehicle for the Christ, and is externalizing the forms of the Path for the Aquarian Age Disciple.

in Scorpio is highly critical. It is here that the entire lower aspect of the sexual nature will burst forth in its fullness. The lower self will make its "last stand" as it squares off to do battle with the Higher Self. If the lower self is "victorious" and loses (and hence merges with the Soul), this battle will never have to be repeated.

3. Finally, Mars in Aries indicates the birth of the personality into manifestation, while its placement in Scorpio is indicative of the death of the personality and the release of the indwelling Christ Presence (anchored in Virgo) onto the objective Path of Sagittarius.

MARS IN SAGITTARIUS: In the Soul-centered individual, Mars in Sagittarius brings out a very strong Sixth Ray element, and is indicative of one who is absolutely devoted to the Path. The purpose for Soul control over the lower self is revealed through his life and actions in this position. The Mars in Sagittarius person will not let anything stop him as he marches on toward the accomplishments of his spiritual goals. While he moves forward, he opens the Path for others to follow, displaying courage and wisdom, love and determination. The goal has been sighted and the Pathway toward its achievement is often indicated by the house placement of Mars in this sign. We can say that Mars is actually the arrow in the bow of the Archer.

MARS IN CAPRICORN: Soul-centered exaltation. We can look at the exaltation of Mars in this sign from two perspectives (naturally!):

1. From the personality level, it is indicative of the victory of personal ambitions and drives over the limitations of the material world. The ego has become successful in dominating its environment. Mars in Capricorn can be said to be the "Aristotle Onassis" of astrological positions.

2. From the Soul level, desires have been placed under the total dominance of the Soul. The victory over the lower self has involved their merger and the expression of an even greater field for the externalization of the Will-to-Love (First Ray, expressing through our Second Ray solar system).

A Soul-centered individual with this strong placement of Mars would most likely find herself in some form of executive position, having earned this responsibility through demonstrating the right use of will and an understanding of the Laws behind the structuring of energy.

MARS IN AQUARIUS: The Soul-centered individual with Mars in this position tends to utilize this energy as a vehicle for encouraging group identity and its consequent collective service. At an earlier stage in development, the battle is one in which the person tries to make any group of people bend to his personal will. After mounting the Fixed Cross, the will of the individual is placed under the service of the group. Idealism is often quite strong, as the Second Ray energies of Jupiter blend with the Sixth Ray focus of Mars. This often creates those situations in which a person is ready to do battle in order to defend the ideals and principles of the group to which he belongs.

MARS IN PISCES: The Sixth and Second Rays are very strong in this placement, and tend to work out in a personality-centered horoscope by a certain blind devotion to romantic or political ideals. The focus of the will is replaced by devotion to emotion, and the individual may easily be swept away by the movements of the mass consciousness. When Mars in Pisces comes under the direction of a Soul-centered individual, the First Ray quality of Pluto strengthens the presence of the will and brings about a different orientation. The individual is then able to infuse consciously directed purpose into any set of circumstances, while transforming and reorienting the energies of the lower self in the process.

JUPITER

Soul-Centered Ruler of Aquarius
Planet of the Second Ray

Every separate entity, or individual Soul, has been derived from a great over-Soul, and although divine in the beginning of its Soul-birth, it was destined to descend into denser planes of matter in order to win, through personal effort and merit, its conscious immortality.[11]

—Alan Leo
Jupiter

Function. Jupiter's primary purpose is one of fusion. It is instrumental in blending the lesser dualities of head and heart, mind and love, in order to produce *wisdom.* It is a primary focus for the energies of the Ray of Love/Wisdom, and acts as a vehicle through which the Ray of Consciousness may externalize the Divine Plan in our solar system. It therefore works to create the ultimate synthesis in order to exteriorize universal harmony and abundance. This message is carried forth even in terms of Jupiter's personality-centered sign rulerships, as Jupiter is the Lord of Wisdom in Sagittarius, while in Pisces he is the Lord of Love.

[11]Alan Leo, *Jupiter*, p. 6.

We are most blessed to be living in the current cycle of the World Ages. As the esoteric, Soul-centered ruler of Aquarius, many of Jupiter's limitless blessings are being externalized through humanity. This will work out in the material world of forms through the human networking, group relations, and new sociological patternings of Uranus and the Seventh Ray. Such externalizations will allow for the more transcendental aspects of Love to permeate the collective humanity, and will evoke the Law of Right Human Relations into the fabric of each of our lives.

Jupiter, along with Mercury, governs the four signs of the Mutable Cross from the personality level—Gemini, Virgo, Sagittarius, and Pisces. The function of these two planets on inner levels, however, is to fuse and blend the enormously vast dualities inherent in mankind. The combination of these two planets brings the nature of the Second Ray and the Fourth together, evoking the latent energy of Love/Wisdom that reveals itself through the unfolding process of Harmony through Conflict. This mutual and combined influence leads humanity out of attachment to material desire and into the awareness of divine love. The resolution of duality through the systematic synthesis inherent in the evolutionary processes of life brings the restless mind of the personality into a state of stability. This allows the mind to integrate the various aspects of the personality so that eventual Soul infusion is made possible. It is Jupiter's specific function within this alchemy to awaken one to the presence of Love as the essence which abides within any given form. Jupiter is thus the tool for the expansion of love/consciousness.

In the natal horoscope of the Soul-centered individual, Jupiter points to several functions:

1. It is a key to spiritual purpose, as it reveals the use of the Second Ray in the present incarnation. What one does in an individual way to accomplish this purpose will be revealed by the nature of the Ascendant and its esoteric ruler (see chapters 12 and 13).

2. The house placement of Jupiter will indicate where there is the greatest tendency toward fusion, and the possibility for the greatest achievement regarding this facet of the Higher Self. Thus, Jupiter in the ninth house reveals a developed ability to fuse and blend various doctrines, philosophies, religions, etc., in order to teach others about the universality and inclusivity of beliefs and creeds. Jupiter in the second house can fuse resources, both of the material and spiritual kind, in order to demonstrate the boundless abundance available to humanity once we deposit our consciousness in the "Soul's bank."

3. Its position in the natal chart also points to that area where the individual can evoke the most love and wisdom out of the environ-

ment, and hence, where a great deal of his spiritual contribution to and from life may be found.

JUPITER IN ARIES: This is a very potent position from the Soul level, as it blends the influences of Mercury, Jupiter, and the element of fire. The net result of this combination is the ability to instill and inspire a wider awareness of Love/Wisdom in people's lives. Jupiter in Aries gives a consistent sense of inner, personal revelation of the underlying concepts behind objective manifestation. There is a great urge to teach and share, to stimulate perception, and to link up extraneous and divergent thoughts, while revealing their unified Source. The main theme here is that Aries is on the First and Seventh Ray line, while Jupiter acts to emanate the energies of Ray Two. This allows Love/Wisdom to flow from the Idea in the Mind of God directly out into the world. The individual is particularly interested in sharing his or her line of teaching with others, as Aries is ruled esoterically by Mercury and is strongly connected to the Fourth Kingdom of Humanity.

JUPITER IN TAURUS: On the personality-centered level, this place-ment gives an inordinate need for expanded material possessions, ease, and luxury. Yet on the Soul-centered level, it reveals the pres-ence of Love/Wisdom within all the forms of nature. Thus, an individ-ual who is firmly anchored on the Fixed Cross would tend to teach the spiritual aspects of material abundance to others and, if other features in the chart support it (such as strong and positive connec-tions to Venus, Pluto, and/or Saturn), would easily be able to manifest whatever material resources may be required in life. Vulcan's influ-ence has a great deal to do with breaking down the concept that the material and the spiritual are two different spheres, and brings the understanding that they represent different vibrational densities of the One Life.

JUPITER IN GEMINI: Soul-centered detriment. From the personal-ity level, it is quite easy to understand why Jupiter's influence is lessened in the sign of the Twins: wider philosophical issues are usually reduced to personal opinions by one with this placement in his natal horoscope. In addition, there tends to be a diffusion of intellectual interests, and the individual often confuses this mental superficiality with the opinion that he has arrived at some profound, universal understanding of life. From the Soul level, I find it very difficult to arrive at a reason why this planet of the Second Ray, manifesting through a sign of the Second Ray, would lose power. It appears to me that Jupiter in Gemini, functioning from the Higher Self, tends to facilitate the harmonizing and blending of mental energy for the purpose of clarifying the expression of Love in life. The Tibetan Master states that the reason Jupiter in Gemini is in detriment is "one of the secrets of initiation." If such is the case, some of the implications regarding the status of Jupiter when in this sign still remain a mystery to the author.

JUPITER IN CANCER: Soul-centered exaltation. In this sign, the desire for incarnation, first projected through Aries, find its anchor in form. This is accomplished for the physical vehicle through the "Mother of All Forms"—the Moon. Yet the process of the linkage and fusion of the Soul and its physical manifestation are greatly facilitated through the energies of Jupiter and the Soul-centered ruler of Cancer, Neptune. A Soul-centered individual with Jupiter in Cancer will have a highly developed spiritual awareness; that is, the presence of the Second Ray and the energy of Neptune will be strong. The individual would be well aware of the dynamic relationship existing between the Higher and the lower selves. The presence of the Mother would be strongly activated in the daily life, and one would therefore be very quick to nurture the correct forms for the purposes of the Higher Self in the most mundane of life situations.

JUPITER IN LEO: The Second Ray is very strongly emphasized in this position, as the Sun's influence is naturally quite potent. In the life of the Soul-centered individual, this would be through the Heart of the Sun, thus stressing the influence of Ray Two through its expression in the Human Kingdom. This placement serves to fuse the will and the mind for the intelligent and creative expression of Love/Wisdom, and indicates a person who will be most active in his particular life endeavors. Kindness, courage, intuitive perception into the "heart of the matter," plus the urge to expand the awareness of the Spiritual Presence in the environment, are all characteristics of Jupiter when found in the Lion's sign. This position also brings a strong sense of Joy into the life—Joy which is often reflected in the lower self, as Jupiter in Leo gives abundant vitality to the physical body.

JUPITER IN VIRGO: Soul-centered detriment. It is most important to take an esoteric view of Jupiter's detriment in Virgo. Jupiter is intimately linked with the Second Ray, which is also the second aspect of Divinity, and thus relates to the Soul or the Christ Principle. When in Virgo, the Christ descends into matter and lies hidden in the womb of the Mother. Thus, on the level of the personality, an individual with this placement would tend to be very materialistic in nature and view her self-expansion purely in material terms. But the Soul-centered person with Jupiter in Virgo (ruled, as we recall, by the

Moon), is incredibly sensitive to the living Soul Presence within every form of manifestation. The service such a person would tend to perform in life would be to "quicken" the identification of the Christ Consciousness in the world of forms. Certainly, the Second and Sixth Ray qualities of Virgo would be a most suitable expression for Jupiter, especially where some devotional activity would be undertaken to reveal the hidden spiritual potential in any act of true service.

JUPITER IN LIBRA: This is a most important position at the present time, as it indicates a combination of the energies of Uranus and Jupiter. Since these are the exoteric and esoteric rulers of Aquarius, respectively, a Soul-centered individual born with this placement gears himself to a life which represents the Law of Right Human Relations. The Seventh Ray qualities of Libra and Uranus are the perfect expressions for the contemporary externalizations of the Second Ray. Thus, from the Soul-centered level, a person with this position in the natal chart would be directed toward linking those ideas that tend to foster human well-being. This would be done very specifically in the realm of communications and the creation of those ideological bonds between individuals and groups of people which facilitate the networking of ideas.

JUPITER IN SCORPIO: The Second-Fourth-Sixth Ray line is very prominent with Jupiter in this sign. This position gives a courageous and determined nature—one which will do battle in order to create the necessary transformations in human consciousness. Idealism is quite strong, as the energies of Mars blend with Jupiter. The individual is usually quite religion-oriented, but when operating on the Soul level, is able to see the validity of all Paths to the One Goal. The important issue is not so much the choice of a particular Way (although on the personality level, Jupiter in Scorpio can give a very rigid and fanatical adherence to one's particular beliefs), but the nature of the Path itself. Thus, Jupiter in Scorpio is a teacher of the Way of Transformation and would, on the Fixed Cross, go through many reorientations of personal belief systems. A Soul-centered Jupiter-in-Scorpio person is highly motivated to assist other people in their struggles to transform their own inner values and concepts in order that they too may walk the Wider Road.

JUPITER IN SAGITTARIUS: Personality-centered ruler. One of the primary goals of Jupiter in this sign is for the fusion of the lower and the Higher Mind. It is an extremely positive position, indicating a person who is earning and solidifying the necessary equipment to be a Disciple of the Path. Through Sagittarius, the individual learns how to direct thought power in order to achieve the goal of an expanded consciousness of Love/Wisdom. This achievement helps to create the one-pointed Disciple who is a living representative of the Ancient Wisdom Teachings in any of its many forms. The practical and mental exteriorization of Wisdom is emphasized with Jupiter in Sagittarius, as the latter is ruled by the Earth. An individual with this placement encourages spiritual aspiration in others.

JUPITER IN CAPRICORN: Soul-centered fall. As a highly focused expression of the Second Ray, Jupiter's energy is dualistic. It is very magnetic in its fusing power, and extremely expressive in its ability to expand the presence of Love/Wisdom as a result of the resolution of duality. Its fall in Capricorn is also twofold in nature. On the personality level, Jupiter in the sign of the Mountain Goat represents the crystallization of the material desires of the lower self. But on the Soul level, it is this crystallized, material nature which "falls" away, leaving the Soul-centered individual as victor over the lower self. The Tibetan says: "Love is fallen and blinded when desire is rampant; desire vanishes when love triumphs."[12] The function of Jupiter in Capricorn on the Soul level is to create those structures in thought and on the physical plane (Third and Seventh Rays) for the expansion of the Will-to-Love. This individual may demonstrate the Love/Wisdom of the Christ Consciousness through the fusion and blending of material resources.

JUPITER IN AQUARIUS: Soul-centered ruler. A person with this position epitomizes the ability to fuse heart and mind for the purpose of service to humanity. The individual with this placement has the potential to be a very active vehicle for the expression of Love/Wisdom. This is accomplished through a positive mental expression, placing what is discovered and initiated at the disposal of humanity. Jupiter joins with Uranus in this sign and bestows many of the same urges, aspirations, and talents as it does in Libra. All of the above deals with the creation of avenues of communication for the distribution of those ideas and projects that serve to create a greater sense of unity and purpose. This is a highly idealistic placement, but one which finds a practical outlet through the function of Aquarius on the Fifth Ray of the Concrete Mind.

JUPITER IN PISCES: Personality-centered ruler. If Jupiter in Sagittarius provides the equipment to harness the Wisdom of the Second Ray, Jupiter in Pisces emphasizes the Love. In the life of the Soul-centered individual, the fusion of love and mind is completed in the sign of the Fish, producing the compassionate consciousness of the presence of

---

[12]Quoted in Bailey's *Esoteric Astrology*, p. 171.

the World Savior. The call to service is very strong, and the strength of Will/Power found in Pluto is available to break down any barriers to Love. It is through Jupiter in Pisces that the universal application of Love for the salvation of humanity is demonstrated. Those who find this combination in their natal charts would always tend to make themselves available for the Work of Grace in the lives of others.

SATURN

Soul-Centered Ruler of Capricorn
Planet of the Third Ray

Initiation—characterized by self-initiation—is the demand of man today. The stars declare it and decree it. The Hierarchy therefore intentionally collaborates. The crying demand and aspirations of man indicate appreciation of the opportunity and recognized understanding of the proved necessity. The Spirit of Life enforces this.

—Alice A. Bailey
Esoteric Astrology

Saturn, Shiva, and Jehovah are One.

—H. P. Blavatsky
The Secret Doctrine

Saturn is the focal point for the transmission of cosmic mind.

—Alice A. Bailey
A Treatise on Cosmic Fire

Function: Saturn is representative of the Law of Economy on all levels of the personality. It is not an agent of deprivation, as much as it is a testing ground to prove a person's level of maturity and responsibility in dealing with what he has learned or achieved. We can say that the relationship between Saturn and the Sun has a great deal to do with physical vitality, and thus we see the application of the Law of Economy to the physical level. When we examine Saturn in relationship to the Moon, this Law extends itself into the emotional area of the personality life. The relationship of Saturn to Mercury conditions the extent of the lower mental aspect of the lower self.

Saturn is the Lord of Karma. He stands at the Gates of Initiation, ready to put all who approach it to the test. This position in Christian symbology is occupied by St. Peter, who acts as the Guardian at the Doors of Heaven. As one approaches Paradise, one's deeds are weighed on the Scales of Ultimate Justice. This is represented by the position of Saturn in Libra, where it is in its exaltation.

From an astronomical perspective, Saturn is the farthest planet visible from the Earth with the naked eye, and its planetary rings are certainly its most impressive feature. The rings are, of course, symbolic of limitation and the parameters of the Law of Karma. The position Saturn holds in space is indicative of the fact that a person cannot incorporate the energies of the farthest planets—Uranus, Neptune and Pluto—into his individualized consciousness without first passing the various tests of personal responsibility so that he proves himself capable of handling the energies of a more evolved state. We can note this particular "guardianship of consciousness" in Saturn's rulership over the throat chakra. In order to awaken the potentials of the two highest vital centers, located at the brow and the crown, an individual first has to stimulate personal awareness from the level of the throat. (See tabulation 3, p. 155).

Another term for "guardian" which we have discussed in relation to karma is "Dweller on the Threshold," and indeed, that is exactly who Saturn is. The Dweller is another of his many titles, duties, and responsibilities in the unfolding of the Path. As such, Saturn represents the crystallization of the past, so that debts may be paid and one may undertake present opportunities for the future. "Opportunity" is one of the most descriptive words that can be applied to Saturn, as he offers those crises and life situations that bestow conscious freedom of choice. It is through our restrictions, and the pain which often accompanies thwarted desires or aspirations, that we come to a greater comprehension of the Laws of Manifestation. The structure and administration of these Laws are also under the rulership of Saturn.

Eventually, through the opportunities Saturn gives us, we have balanced a great deal of past karma and have reached a place where conscious choice becomes an actual possibility. At this point, the choices we have to make for our evolutionary advancement become clear to our awakening eyes. We know that if we accept the work and service in front of us, we shall be tested. Yet our vision encourages us to shoulder some of the collective burden for advancing humanity and the expression of Love/Wisdom in the world. Saturn's house position will reveal where our dharma/duty lies in this respect, and where we may expect such tests of restriction and self-discipline to arise. Once these tests are taken and passed—once the Path of Discipleship has been achieved—the very advanced individual passes on to the Cardinal Cross where, it is said, "Saturn cannot follow men." Once human consciousness has reached this initiatic state, the Laws of human Karma have been learned and incorporated into oneself and the "gate which Saturn guards and protects has swung open."

Saturn and the Earth are very closely related, due to their dual connection with the Third Ray. Saturn controls the creation of structural patterns for mental energy. It is the "form" side of the term "thought-forms"—that is, the crystallization of mental energy so that the Active Intelligence of Divinity may manifest in the outer world and on the Earth. *It is on our planet, therefore, that the karma of our solar system consolidates into physical form.* So does the opportunity for the purification of karma and the eventual upliftment and "greater sacredness" of both humanity and the planet upon which we live. As the planet of the "Law of Cause and Effect," Saturn also bestows positive rewards. He is definitely the "Grim Reaper," but he is also the benevolent Father. The rewards and punishments we receive are especially true, relative to the way we handle the Earth's resources and the energies of the lesser kingdoms: mineral, vegetable, and animal. The synthesis of these three other kingdoms is the Human, so that our ultimate testing ground has once more to do with our administration of the Law of Right Human Relations.

Saturn, as ruler of Capricorn, is directly related to the process of Initiation. But Saturn on the exoteric level is also the co-ruler of Aquarius. It will be through the correct application of the Laws and Principles of the New Age, so very much influenced by this planetary "Gatekeeper," that we shall be able to co-create and fulfill our individual karma relative to humanity's collective life in the Aquarian Era.

The position of Saturn in the signs is particularly indicative of several major characteristics:

1. The sign will point to which Ray qualities may be inhibited on the personality level, so that such energies are brought into much more objective manifestation by the individual.

2. Such tests and crises will be reflected by the forms of such restrictions in the personal life; that is, some will be affected financially, others romantically, others physically, etc.

3. The sign position also reveals what the Soul is seeking to perfect in the present incarnation, in order to foster its own growth and aid in the externalization of the Plan for humanity.

4. The combination of sign and house placement will point to the urge for the fulfillment of a specific type of karma, and the kinds of circumstances which will bring about the necessary testing in one's life.

5. It must be clearly understood that these tests and trials are invoked through the Soul-centered individual's conscious choice. This

is part of living on the Fixed Cross, and indicative of one who is assuming the responsibility for co-creating the structure of his spiritual life and material destiny. The right use of the mind, and the tests of polarization of the emotions and the personal life to the mental plane and the impersonal life, will definitely be encountered along the Way.

SATURN IN ARIES: Personality-centered fall. From the Soul-centered perspective, I believe this to be an excellent place for Saturn, but certainly not so from the level of the personality, where Saturn "falls" the farthest. Once again, we have to take the term "fall" from a rather occult point of view. The meaning is very collective in its orientation, and refers to the fact that when the Sons of Mind (Humanity) "fell" into incarnation, the Lord of Karma "fell" right along with us. We all certainly know that this is the case, and no matter how hard we may try, it is impossible to escape the Law of Cause and Effect.

Mercury, as esoteric ruler of Aries, blends its energies with Saturn, allowing the Third Ray energy full access to the Messenger's entire range of communication. The Soul-centered purpose for this position would seem to be involved with the ability to properly discipline and structure the mind for the constant birthing of new ideas. If this does not occur, problems could arise from a lack of responsibility in the proper use of mental energy. Once the right use of will accompanies the right use of mind, Saturn in Aries can be an excellent position.

SATURN IN TAURUS: There is a very strong connection between this most earthy sign and the Earth itself. From a practical perspective, Saturn in Taurus can be extremely helpful in the structuring of those ideas that can precipitate material abundance into one's life. Yet, if one is polarized in the desire nature (which is so much a part of personality-centered Taurus energy), such manifestation of resources can be greatly inhibited. The Soul-centered purpose has a great deal to do with harnessing material possessions and the treasures of the Earth for the service of the Soul and the needs of humanity. Once the reorientation of values is accomplished on the Fixed Cross, this position of Saturn is a very positive and powerful one. Look to Saturn in Vulcan's sign to break through and destroy anything in the formative world that inhibits the movement of Active Intelligence from the place of the Soul.

SATURN IN GEMINI: The earlier part of the life can indicate certain difficulties in personal relationships, as Venus rules this Second Ray sign. In order to achieve right loving, one may have to go through many tests, disappointments, and restrictions. The individual may not be well understood or may choose partners with whom communication is very difficult. Yet this is a very potent position from the standpoint of the conscious and intelligent use of mind. The Soul-centered purpose is for the individual to become an agent for the Law of Right Human Relations. The dualities and crises in his own relationships are the training ground for a deeper understanding of the dynamics that exist between the personal and transpersonal facets of his life. Once these lessons are learned, Venus's rulership of Gemini and Saturn's exaltation in Libra become the vehicles of great Joy.

SATURN IN CANCER: Soul-centered detriment. The Lord of the Gate Out of incarnation finds himself in the sign of the Gate Into incarnation, and is thus in quite a restricted set of circumstances. The individual with this placement may find that as a Soul, she is in conflict with the physical, emotional, and/or mental environment of the personality. She struggles against the restraints and restrictions that seem to limit her higher expression and deepest sensitivity. In order to bring about a transformation of his attachment to the earlier difficulties of her family life and surroundings (characteristics which often accompany this position), she has to undertake certain personal responsibilities. These require the offering up and detachment from her pains and emotional suffering. Thus pain is viewed objectively, and the associated suffering on the personal level is used as a vehicle for greater compassion and worldly understanding. What is required to bring about this transformation is the construction of a stronger mental body. The potent Third Ray contact which Saturn and Cancer hold is the key to success in this respect. "Give up the personal pain and grow mentally" is the message.

SATURN IN LEO: On the personality level, a person with this position often has difficulty with the administration of personal power. Louis XIV of France's famous remark, "L'Etat, c'est moi—I am the state," is very indicative of Saturn in Leo working out through the lesser self. The lesson here has to do with the alignment of the will in order that the mind may create the proper structures for the Will-to-Love. The boundless urge for power and the incredible frustrations of lost opportunities, so much a part of this combination when working through the Mutable Cross, work out quite differently from the perspective of the Fixed Cross Path. Here, the structures of personal power are directed toward the service of the group. From the point of view of the Ray energies, this transition is quite a natural one to make, as Leo and Aquarius are both on the Fifth Ray. Libra, ruled exoterically by Venus (also on the Fifth Ray), and the sign of Saturn's exaltation, helps to bring about proper judgment in the administration of the Will (Leo and Capricorn's contact with the First Ray).

SATURN IN VIRGO: The Soul-centered purpose of this position is to build the correct structures in life (as always with Saturn, they are centered on the mental plane) for the unfolding of the Christ Consciousness. The urge is to create those patterns of interchange that foster the process of synthesis, and thus serve a healing capacity. From the Soul level, this position gives an intuitive perception of what "works" in a given life situation. Its focus of practicality comes from knowing what will create an inclusive wholeness in life. Saturn joins with the Moon when it is placed in Virgo, and therefore, the form nature becomes a very important tool in the exteriorization of those conceived patterns of Active Intelligence. Virgo (the Moon, the Fourth Ray) births these patterns into form where they may be put at the service of humanity (Second and Sixth Ray characteristics of Virgo).

SATURN IN LIBRA: Soul-centered exaltation. The true strength of this exalted position can be seen in its fullness if we examine all the Ray relationships inherent to it. We then find that through Saturn and Capricorn we have the energies of the First, Third, and Seventh Rays, while Venus, exoteric ruler of Libra, brings in the Fifth Ray, and Uranus, Soul-centered ruler of the Scales, further emphasizes the Seventh. The latter is the Ray for the externalization of the Laws of Manifestation (symbolized by Saturn in Libra) into the world of form. Thus, a Soul-centered individual with this position will function to administer right judgment in the economic use of energy, whether this be in terms of money, sex, or human justice. In effect, Saturn in Libra bestows the "Mind of Solomon" with an impartiality and attunement to what is right and fair in any given life situation. On the personality level, the individual will always be seeking out the answers to life's apparent imbalances, especially in his interchanges in relationships.

SATURN IN SCORPIO: This is often not the easiest position to handle, as it combines the influences of Saturn and Mars, and thus the Third and the Sixth Rays. Mental energy often clashes with the emotionally polarized focus of Mars. It is through the Fourth Ray of Scorpio that harmony will have to be established out of this very basic conflict. On the personality level, this position may give some very distinct difficulties in dealing with one's sexual nature. The latter can either be used as a device for controlling others, or can be a great source of personal frustration because of restraints in its expression. Once one has mounted the Fixed Cross, Saturn in Scorpio helps in the transformation of personal desires. It works to break down the compulsive nature of nonregenerative emotional habit patterns, so that more refined mental structures may be built for the externalization of the Soul. These last sentences should be carefully considered by the reader.

SATURN IN SAGITTARIUS: Both the planets of the Third Ray—Saturn (mental structure and patterns) and the Earth (the practical application of such patterns)—blend their energies in this position. While the Archer gives access to the Purpose for walking the Path, the two planets involved in this combination reveal those pragmatic steps along the Way. On the personality level, Saturn in Sagittarius may produce a person who is so attached to his personal philosophy that he is restricted in developing a wider and more inclusive comprehension of the world, its creeds, and its religions. From the Soul level, the individual can take from all the "noble pathways," and develop those methods for sharing and teaching the Wisdom which transcends (and includes) all differences.

SATURN IN CAPRICORN: Soul-centered and personality-centered ruler. As Saturn is the ruler of Capricorn on both the personality and Soul levels, this position is especially powerful. It allows the individual the opportunity to build the "Spiritual Mountain," which is the goal for human evolution on the Earth. When accompanied by love and wisdom, the Saturn-in-Capricorn person can serve to create those structures and steps that may lead her and others to this Mountaintop. Saturn in Capricorn is thus a ladder up from the material to the spiritual (the Seventh to the First Rays and planes of consciousness), as well as down from the heavens to the Earth, as the inner Will-to-Be unfolds and anchors Itself and the outer Plan. The Third Ray is at its most potent and active when expressing itself through Saturn in Capricorn, endowing the Soul-centered person with astute mental abilities and a very strong, dynamic magnetism. One of the biggest pitfalls along the Way for the personality-centered individual with this placement is the tendency to take the Law into her own hands. This is often expressed by the lesser self thinking that it is the Law and thus abusing power.

SATURN IN AQUARIUS: From the Soul level, this is one of the most benevolent positions for the Gatekeeper. It combines the influence of Jupiter (exoteric ruler of Aquarius) and the Second Ray, plus Venus, ruler of the Fifth Ray, upon which we find the Water Bearer. Venus is also brought into play through Uranus's rulership over Libra esoterically, and Aquarius exoterically. We thus find a Soul-centered individual who can be hard at work creating those social structures and networks that will anchor the new archetypical ideas of the Age into human consciousness. This position gives an inherent ability to blend those ideas from the past that have proven their usefulness with those unfolding concepts for the future. This differs markedly from Saturn in Aquarius on the personality level. Here, a person is totally circumscribed by his own ideologies and concepts which, for the most part, have been socially conditioned and inherited from the past. It is to these ideas that one tenaciously adheres, no matter what their more collective value in the wider field of human need or experience.

SATURN IN PISCES: I do not know of any Saturn/sign position that differs more in its effects when activated on the personality or the Soul level. On the personality level, Saturn in Pisces is indicative of the creation of walls and barriers without logical reference to actual circumstances. It is a combination that, unless otherwise mitigated in the natal chart, is fraught with fears and foreboding. One feels continuously on the verge of being trapped or restricted, and yet doesn't necessarily know by what or whom. Unless one displays a certain mental brilliance (in which case, this position is excellent for the laboratory scientist, engineer, military specialist, or even the metaphysical philosopher), Saturn in Pisces on the personality level usually brings a great deal of confusion into the life. But on the Soul level, another perspective presents itself. Pluto joins with Saturn in a most powerful combination to pierce the veils of glamour and illusion which block and restrict the passage of Active Intelligence into the world. Thus the individual with this placement is able to uncover many of the hidden, subconscious problems and fears that plague humanity and, once uncovered, destroy, transmute, and restructure them.

URANUS

Soul-Centered Ruler of Libra
Planet of the Seventh Ray

The goal of externalization (of the Plan) is not so much to enable individuals to reach a heavenly state of conscious-ness as it is to bring it to Earth. It is not enough to think and meditate about this transformation. It is up to the aspirants and Disciples of the world to make practical application of what they know . . . and to apply the prin-ciples of the Aquarian Age.

—Two Disciples
Rainbow Bridge II

Ancient astrology was obviously incomplete, but until man became patently responsive to the influences which come to him from Uranus or Pluto, for instance, which affect the Soul life far more than they do the personality life, they remained undiscovered, except by trained esotericists. Today, humanity is rapidly responding to the higher spiri-tual influences. . . .

—Alice A. Bailey
Esoteric Astrology

Function: In order for the energies of Uranus to express themselves in a conscious way in a person's life, he must pass through Saturn's "Door." This means that he has created an integrated personality, linked with the Soul force, and is thus a spiritually responsible indi-vidual. More likely than not, such a person is linked to a sense of group purpose and is very service-oriented. There is quite a difference between the way Uranus functions in the personality chart and the way its energies externalize once Soul contact has become established.

Briefly, Uranus on the personality level is always indicative of creating difference through the use of the will. A strongly personality-centered Uranian (that is, Uranus rising, the Sun or Moon in Aquarius, or conjunct, opposing, or square Uranus, or Uranus at the midheaven of the natal chart) will strive to be different just for difference' sake. In this respect, one may dress very unconventionally, seek out avant-garde or bohemian friends, and in extreme cases, engage in pointedly antisocial behavior patterns. These are not at all negative traits in themselves, for such people strike at the core of the established order (that is, Saturn) and create a perspective whereby society must question its values. Yet when such characteristics are not consciously linked to the Soul and to group intent from the level of the Higher Self, personal whims and egocentric motives are often at the center of such activities and practices.

Uranus functioning through the Soul level has quite a different purpose. As the ruler of Libra, the unfolding of Uranus in the consciousness of one on the Fixed Cross leads to the reversal of the wheel of destiny. Libra represents a pause, a moment of Soul-focused reflection, a place wherein the values and energies of the personality and the Soul meet and are balanced against each other. The individual can thus make the choice of his or her direction, and either move on to a greater sense of material expression in Virgo, or take the test of one who willingly battles to walk the Path in Scorpio. Uranus lies beyond the rings of Saturn and is thus a major step in evoking that state of transformation whereby the self-conscious individual merges into a greater group orientation. This step toward greater inclusivity, and the subsequent refinement of individual self-expression, is a vital "rite of passage" in one's evolutionary progress.

Once the "crossover" has been made, the energy of Uranus begins to flood the consciousness and affect the conditions of one's outer life. Some of the effects of this Uranian transmutation may be outlined as follows:

1. *Heightens the intuition.* One is now able *to perceive the quality of energy* which inhabits a form, whether this form is physical, emotional or mental. Thus a "Uranus-awakened" individual can see the person who lives *inside* of his body, can perceive the consciousness of an artist by looking at his paintings, may understand the need of the Soul expressing itself through a personal emotion, etc.

2. *Quickens the urge to change the established order.* Uranus is the planet of the Seventh Ray—Ceremonial Order and Magic. When its energies are stimulated, it allows one to be in tune with the relationship between the external order of life and the unfolding Will-to-Create. Both *Cause and Effect* are cyclical in expression. Cause (First Ray, Will and Power) is constantly stimulating matter to be the proper response to its initiating impulse. The Seventh Ray is very much involved with the process of this fusion. Uranus functions in this respect as a vehicle which breaks down those forms that are no longer consistent with the involutionary and evolutionary movements of the Life Force. Yet this is not the anarchistic, egotistical, destructive power of Uranus that expresses on the personality level. The urge to change social structures and the prevailing collective ordering of life come from an attunement to Cause and are effected through group function. The First Ray has a very direct and intimate relationship

with the Seventh, as can be seen from the fact that Aries and Capricorn appear on both these lines of manifestation. Aries is the primary sign of the Will-to-Be, while Capricorn, and its relationship to Saturn and the Third Ray, is very much connected to the forms and structures for that Beingness.

3. *Stimulates the aspiration to better the human condition.* The awareness of the relationship of the Higher and the lower selves having been established through Libra's influence, Uranus works to blend more completely the energies of humanity's essential duality. This process of synthesized fusion has as its purpose the creation of improved social systems for humanity's physical well-being, as well as the stimulation of the spiritual climate for inner growth and development. These two facets of human life work out through networking, an especially Uranian and Aquarian activity.

4. *Fosters individual activity within the group context.* When intuition, Soul-focused social aspiration (that is, a true perception of collective need) group consciousness, and direct contact with Spiritual Will are fused and blended through Seventh Ray activity, one steps forward to do one's individual part in the One Work. In effect, Uranus leads the individual to the Occult Way and is known by the name of the "Hierophant of the Mysteries of Initiation." The Occult Way can be characterized as the Path of Divine Knowledge, of Ordered Magic, and is the practical application of the Ancient Wisdom Teachings to the daily life. It is thus the Way of the Mind (as opposed to the Path of the Mystic, which is the Way of Union through the feelings), and utilizes knowledge as the vehicle which reveals Wisdom and Light.

URANUS IN ARIES (1927–1934):[13] Aries is always the vehicle for the birthing into the collective consciousness of new, archetypical ideas from the Mind of God. But there is a very special connection in terms of this function which intimately links the Ram to Uranus and to Aquarius. Uranus rules three signs: Aquarius from the personality level, Libra from the Soul level, and Aries from the level of Hierarchy. This means that the fiery pulses of this sign of the First Ray are the emana-

---

[13]I am indicating the years of Uranus, Neptune, and Pluto transits through each of the signs for two primary reasons: (1) Those individuals born in the year indicated by a planet/sign combination personify the energies of that placement. We are affected by them individually, as well as by the collective input of that particular Uranus, Neptune, or Pluto generation; and (2) When these planets transit a particular sign, they bring forth a new Ray influence, which also has its effects on us individually (depending upon where the planet falls in our natal chart) and collectively. I am limiting these periodic indications to the twentieth century. As Uranus frequently retrogrades, it may overlap the years indicated by its sign placement. Thus it was in Cancer until August 1955, then went into Leo from August 1955 to January 1956. It went back into Cancer at that time, and stayed in that sign until June of 1956, when it entered Leo until 1962. Please consult your ephemeris for the exact dates of entrance and departure of the planets in each of the signs.

tions through which innovations in the collective consciousness of humanity are birthed. These "pulses of Life" are then focused in Aries, distributed through Libra at the Soul level, and enter the physical realm of our daily life through Aquarius. If we examine the Ray picture of this relationship, a very exact ordering appears: Aries—Rays One and Seven; Libra—Ray Three; Aquarius—Ray Five; Uranus—Ray Seven. Thus these three signs and Uranus, their ruler on their respective levels, carefully and precisely reveal the passageway of Divine Ideas from their Source in Will to their eventual externalization in matter.

The Soul-centered individual with Uranus in Aries in the natal chart is inclined to be an innovator in whatever field he or she may serve. There is a very strong urge to create those relationships and interchanges between people which focus the Will-to-Good for all.

URANUS IN TAURUS (1934–1942): Soul-centered fall. The crystallization of the form life and its associated desires is very strong in Taurus. This is, after all, the placement for the exaltation of the Moon, the "Mother of All Forms." As we have discussed, the Moon veils Uranus, so that when the latter is found in the sign of the Mother's exaltation, its effects are even more obscured. Yet the occulted presence of Uranus does not mean that the planet loses its ability to produce an awareness of inner Light. It just indicates that it will be through Taurus's Fourth Ray of Harmony through Conflict that the realization of this Light will be accomplished. A person who has this combination in her natal chart may often suffer certain sudden financial reversals. This teaches her to penetrate beneath the physical form in order to uncover the true meaning of these problematical situations. When manifesting on the Fixed Cross, this position endows the individual with the ability (and the aspiration) to lead others out of the darkness of form into Uranus's awakened perception of Light.

URANUS IN GEMINI (1942–1949): This is a very good position for Uranus, as it brings this planet into contact with Venus on the Soul level. This combination of energies evokes the Law of Right Human Relations. It helps to make the individual with this placement an effective communicator for collective goodwill. Gemini works to relate the lower and the Higher minds so that Love/Wisdom may be externalized. The effective use of the Seventh Ray, embodied by Uranus, extends the Second Ray out into the physical plane, allowing it to underscore the networking and interpersonal interchanges so important to our Age. Since a natural affinity exists between Uranus and Mercury, Gemini's exoteric ruler, this position heightens the relationship between intellect and intuition.

URANUS IN CANCER (1949–1956): Until anchoring on the Soul level is firm, this is not a particularly easy combination. Even on the

Soul level, it presents a definite set of challenging circumstances. The Seventh Ray energies of Uranus combine with the Sixth Ray energy of Neptune and the Fourth Ray quality of the Moon. The urge to create new forms in the outer life is challenged by the traditional orientation and urge to establish foundation so apparent in the lunar influence representing the past. The devotion and emotionally focused characteristics of the Sixth Ray and Neptune are totally juxtaposed to the energies of Uranus. It is only when the individual is able to joyfully accept that some degree of sacrifice on the personal level is required, to effectuate collective purpose and New Age transformation, that the inherent conflict of this position may be resolved. As a large percentage of individuals have Uranus in Cancer square to Neptune in Libra, many people of this generation will be personifying the Sixth-Seventh Ray conflict in their own lives.

URANUS IN LEO (1956–1962): Personality-centered detriment. On the Soul level, this is an excellent position, as it enhances a person's ability to contribute to the collective well-being from an individual expression of creativity. The Sun combined with Uranus brings the energy of the Second Ray into contact with the Seventh, thus energizing the externalization of the Will (Leo's First Ray affiliation) into the world of physical forms. Prior to this more positive expression of Uranus in Leo, there is that facet of this combination which leads to it being called Uranus's detriment. The intense, self-conscious focus of Leo on the personality level has to become transformed into group consciousness in order for Uranus to be able to effectuate the kind of contribution mentioned above. The love of the lower self (Second Ray energy through the ego) has to be transformed into the Self who loves, which expresses itself through group purpose. This is the test of many people who have this position, especially those born from August 1955 to January 1956, and from June 1956 to May 1959, when Neptune squared Uranus (most of this time from Scorpio).

URANUS IN VIRGO (1962–1969): The urge to create improved standards for humanity is very much at the forefront of this combination. There is a definite inventiveness and a consistent pull toward creating a "better mousetrap." This is very true on the personality level, as well, as Uranus in Virgo stimulates a curiosity about the form nature and the urge to investigate how things work. It is especially positive in the realm of physics and science in general. On the Soul level, these tendencies are taken a bit further, as one also perceives the hidden truth lying within the form. Thus, investigative and scientific pursuits may be undertaken with the conscious awareness of society's needs for the fruits of one's labors. From the level of personality, such inner meanings and purposes behind one's work may remain obscure.

To the Soul-centered individual, the energy of Uranus in this sign is experienced as a furtherance of Love and the urge toward wholism (Virgo's connection with the Second and Sixth Rays). Form (the Moon, ruler of this sign) becomes the conscious vehicle for the expansion of Wisdom.

URANUS IN LIBRA (1968–1975): Soul-centered ruler. The years of Uranus's passage in this sign were remarkable, in terms of social change and upheaval. It was a period of greatly increased activity on the part of women, gays, and blacks to liberate themselves from the restrictions of the past. Patriotic idealism gave way to humanistic realism during the antiwar movement of that time. The urge for "peace and love," so much the characteristics of Venus in Libra, were the outer expression of the call for the birthing of new, collective, Uranian social archetypes. Soul-centered individuals born in these years will personify and carry forth this vision of world unity and freedom. They are very much the harbingers of the Laws and Principles of the New Age, as this planet/sign combination is the embodiment of the Aquarian Age on the Soul level.

URANUS IN SCORPIO (1975–1981): Soul-centered exaltation. The transformative nature of the planet behind the Ray of Ceremonial Magic (itself the science of the transmutation of matter), is very much at home in the sign of Death and Rebirth. The struggles of the Fourth Ray are very much the struggles of Uranus as it works to stimulate the interplay between Spirit and matter. The birth of the new archetypes, both for the individual and for the collective, can only come about through the death of outdated thought-forms. Attachment to form (Taurus) provides the necessary polarity for those lessons of detachment and reorientation which come about when Uranus is in this sign. The function of Uranus in Scorpio on the personality level is connected to the sexual processes, as Uranus rules the gonads, and its Seventh Ray energy is directly linked to the physical plane. The correct use of sexual energy is thus very much a testing ground for this generation.

URANUS IN SAGITTARIUS (1981–1988): This combination is found in the horoscopes of a generation of people who are to teach the Laws and Principles of the New Age. The philosophical orientation is very strong, and the urge to build a better world on the Earth is certainly indicated by the rulership of our planet over this sign. These individuals can utilize their collective understanding about life, inherent in the sign of the Pathwalker, and work to blend and fuse the new human archetypes within their sense of history. On the personality level, it combines the influence of Jupiter, exoteric ruler of Sagittarius, with Uranus, exoteric ruler of Aquarius. This is a highly idealistic combination that may lead to a great deal of overemphasis on the ultimate wisdom of personal knowledge. One may believe oneself to be far wiser than truth can substantiate. On a collective level, this combination of Jupiter and Uranus is very suitable for the creation of global educational techniques, leading to greater universal tolerance and unanimity of world purpose.

URANUS IN CAPRICORN (1905–1912; 1988–1995): From the personality level, this powerful position leads to a basic tension; the urge for Uranian freedom and idealism, expressed through a framework of Saturnian restriction. This is certainly being illustrated in the current Soviet efforts at "glasnost." Other "Saturnian" nations, such as Red China and the Eastern European community of nations, will also experiment with reorienting their economic and social systems. The Western countries too will experiment with modifying their economic structures and policies during the years when Uranus is in Capricorn— they will have little choice. Yet Saturn and Uranus are both the exoteric rulers of Aquarius, so we could say that this combination is symbolic of the "perestroika" (restructuring) of the New Age.

Individuals born with this placement in their natal horoscopes will be very form-conscious. They will seek to restructure society at its roots and foundations. The Soul-centered individuals among them will be doing this from their vision of a new world order of social improvement. The strong egos among those born during these years will have an unbridled urge for personal power, and perhaps a certain ruthlessness in their urge to achieve their envisioned positions of leadership. The Third and Seventh Ray qualities of this position are very potent, as Saturn stands behind Capricorn and joins with Uranus. In 1988, Saturn and Uranus conjoined three times in our physical heavens, so the political and social movements of that year will very much condition the seven-year period in which Uranus is in Saturn's sign and, to some extent, the seven-year period following, when these two planets act through the influence of Aquarius.

URANUS IN AQUARIUS (1912–1919; 1996–2003): Personality-centered ruler. When Uranus appeared in this sign the first time in this century, it signified the beginning of a war that would last over thirty years (the period between World War I and World War II was just long enough to breed another generation to continue the fight). By 1945, the political and social structure of the world was totally and irrevocably altered. Even the physical nature of our world concept changed with the use in 1945 of the atomic bomb. We could say that science and technology (Aquarius and the Fifth Ray) were used by humanity against itself in order to destroy much of its form life (collective expression of the Seventh Ray). We should keep in mind that Pluto rules atomic energy on the physical level, and is one of the planets of the Ray of the Destroyer.

Thus, the people who were born during this first period when Uranus was in Aquarius grew up in an era of world turmoil unprecedented in recorded history. Uranus returns in 1996 to take us into the twenty-first century while in the sign of the New Age. And yes, once again, there should be a period of tremendous world change. The twentieth century saw the end of the Piscean Age—an Era of world suffering, a time of the domination of the Sixth Ray. The twenty-first century is the beginning of the Aquarian Age—an Era of world enlightenment, a time of the domination of the Seventh Ray. I believe that those Soul-centered individuals born with Uranus in Aquarius will be the innovators of those social systems and beliefs that will firmly anchor humanity beyond the cusp of the Age and into the Age itself. They will know how to apply Jupiter's Second Ray influence through the field of human endeavor characterized by Uranus's networking and linkages.

URANUS IN PISCES (1920–1927): These are the years that coincide with the rise of fascism in Europe and Japan. It was a time in which the collective energies of Pluto would be used by those underground forces to bring about the greatest period of human destruction the world has ever witnessed. This was a time for the gathering of the Dark Forces so that the Lord of Destruction could, for whatever reason, clear away certain sociological and physical forms for the current restructuring of the world. When Uranus was last in Pisces, it was a preparation for that great ocean of human suffering birthed when Uranus transited Aries, and anchored fully in form when Uranus passed through Vulcan's sign, Taurus.

Yet Pluto, the esoteric ruler of the Fish, is not representative of annihilation but of regeneration. Uranus takes this regenerative quality (remember, it is exalted in Scorpio) and births the new forms for individual and collective evolution. Those Soul-centered people born with Uranus in Pisces have a special talent for perceiving into the forms of life in order to reveal their hidden mystery. They can thus work to release inner power and strength in any set of circumstances. Very often, such a transition occurs through the sudden washing away of the status quo, but this is to be replaced by a greater sense of inclusivity and unity of purpose.

NEPTUNE

Soul-Centered Ruler of Cancer
Planet of the Sixth Ray

The fish goddesses who have leapt from Earth (Virgo) to water (Pisces) unitedly give birth to the Fish God (Christ) who introduces the water of life into the ocean of substance and thus brings light to the world. Thus does Neptune work.

—Alice A. Bailey
Esoteric Astrology

Function. Neptune is a most mystical and, from the level of the Soul, a most benefic influence in one's life. Neptune is the expression in the solar system of the "heart of the spiritual Sun." It is the planet most closely linked with the work of the Soul in manifestation, and is thus the vehicle for the Christ Consciousness, which is indeed at the Heart of Divinity. Through Cancer, Neptune may be thought of as the higher octave of the Moon. The latter is the Mother of All Forms, but form is always used in our solar system to express Love/Wisdom, the Second Ray, the Soul aspect of Spirit. We know this to be, when manifesting in the Human Kingdom, "Love Incarnate"—the indwelling Christ Principle.

This Principle is most important, as it functions on two levels: personal and collective. On the personal level, the indwelling Christ Principle is actually our Soul—more particularly, that aspect of the Soul which is Love. It is this facet of ourself that we pray to and evoke for healing, nurturing, and spiritual sustenance. Collectively, it is the indwelling Christ Principle in humanity which, when invoked, brings forth these healing properties from mankind. We can see this in action when huge sums of money are collected on charity telethons, or through such recent events in the 1980s as Hands Across America, and the Live Aid, Band Aid, and Farm Aid concerts.

The Moon veils Neptune just as, in the mass consciousness (Cancer), form veils the subjective love alive within the form. Yet in traditional astrology, the veil is taken *to be* Neptune, and the illusion, or mask of form, is seen to be the influence of this planet. This is not the true essence or function of the "God of the Waters," for Neptune comes to us from the Soul level as the Initiator, planet of the Christ. Its trident is symbolic of the Trinity (Shiva-Vishnu-Brahma; Father-Mother-Son; Will-Love-Intelligence); its recent purpose, to serve as the stimulator of the Piscean Age.

Neptune also holds a very important place in the Aquarian Age. The goal of human evolution is to produce the Messiah, the Initiate, the Mahdi, the Coming One. This is a cyclic event which resulted two thousand years ago in the birth, passion, and eternal contribution of Lord Jesus during the last World Era. *In the Aquarian Age, the World Disciple is to be Humanity, and the Coming One comes through each of us, the collective impact of which is World Goodwill, realized by group endeavor and spiritual intent.* Neptune, through Cancer, births the Christ Consciousness in every man and woman, connecting each of us to the passion of our own initiatic process, crucifying us on the Fixed Cross of Discipleship, and resurrecting us in the loving and wise consciousness of our Soul.

In light of the above, we can see that Neptune is closely related to three signs and their rulers: Cancer and the Moon; Pisces and Pluto; Scorpio and Mars. Cancer is the sign of birth, of generation, and the urge to manifest in form. This urge is so strong that it magnetizes the Soul into a form (Moon) of expression and gives rise to physical incarnation. This "sacrifice" of the Soul into the "death which is material life" is under the impulse of the planet Neptune. It is devotion to the Plan and to the Christlike principle of self-sacrifice which brings the Soul to Earth. There is much to contemplate here which is analogous to the "Father giving of His only Son" and reveals most clearly that each of us is a Son or Daughter of our Cosmic Parent. It is when we remove our identification with the form that the veil masking our own essential divinity is lifted and we come face to face with the Soul which is our Self.

The process of this realization is closely connected to Mars and Scorpio. As Mars is also a planet of the Sixth Ray, it has a very close affinity to Neptune. The latter can be viewed as a higher octave of Mars, although I think the term "the redeemer of Mars" might be more appropriate. As we know, Neptune is connected to the waters of the astral plane, but it is also a strong influence on the expression of the heart, as it represents the Heart of the Sun, or Divine Love in manifestation. Mars is also connected to the astral plane, as it is the planet of desire-in-action, and thus the vehicle for the creation of karma on the emotional/desire level. On the level of the personality, Mars is the ruler of the solar plexus center, which is very closely aligned to the use or abuse of the personal will as it manifests through the realm of personal desires.

Once the individual has mounted the Fixed Cross, the wheel of life enters into a phase of tension, signified by the need to reorient one's life values and tread the Path of Return. Mars then becomes the formidable vehicle for the one-pointed Disciple, who undertakes all the necessary tests and trials in order to become first the observer and then the server. Neptune is the energy of devotion and self-sacrifice, which this time manifests as the personality giving itself up to the Soul.

This is the Path of the passion and the crucifixion. In the stages of initiation, this combination of Neptune and Mars (and the influence of the Sixth Ray) is connected to the Second Initiation. This great step in our growth involves the detachment from the solar plexus (and the influence of Mars on this level) and the reorientation of the influences of the astral plane and the solar plexus to the desires of the Soul and the needs of the Heart. This produces an intensification of transpersonal love and increases the desire for the generation of the Christ Self. Once this overshadowing of Mars by Neptune takes place, a major change occurs in our lives. We find that our previous, compulsive attachments and addictive desire patterns no longer keep us enthralled. We rapidly begin to develop new trends toward higher, subtler, and more spiritual goals and aspirations. We identify more with the hidden, spiritual essence of life than with the material, physical forms which that life takes. The latter are used as tools of convenience in order to express spiritual goals and principles.

This expression of one's devotion to Love/Wisdom (Neptune and the Sixth Ray) has a direct "passageway" into the physical world through Cancer's expression of the Seventh Ray. We should note that Capricorn/Saturn is also on the Seventh and gives the necessary structure to these forms as they align themselves with the Will of the Plan, Aries (the third Seventh Ray sign).

Neptune is the personality-centered ruler of Pisces, while Pluto is the Soul-centered ruler of this sign, as well as the exoteric co-ruler of Scorpio. When Neptune is functioning from the level of the lower self, the energies of Mars, the lower astral plane, and the desire nature of Scorpio are brought into full play. This combination produces that blinding glamour and illusion (maya) so closely associated with the Fish and its exoteric ruler.

The combination of Neptune and Pluto on the Soul level gives tremendous potency to the fusion of Will and Love. From 1943 until 1993, these two planets are in sextile to each other. The generations born with this 60-degree angle of relationship have the potential to produce a harmonious link between these two planets and their respective Rays. A study of the angular relationship from Uranus to these bodies can also prove to be very revealing about the collective purpose of our peers, children, and (for those born in the 1960s, 1970s, or 1980s) parents—the three generations of "First-Born Children of the New Age."

NEPTUNE IN ARIES:[14] On the personality level, this combination brings in the strong Sixth Ray potential of Mars, which, when joined with Neptune, can lead to a great deal of false spiritual egotism. The devotional aspect can point to an individual who lives under the glamour of martyrdom. Such an individual could go to any lengths to promote the object of his or her beliefs, utilizing the fire of personal will in the process. From the Soul level, this position brings in Mercury, and indicates a person with the potential to be a communicator of spiritual truths and a true voice of the Soul.

NEPTUNE IN TAURUS: On the personality level, this brings in the influence of Venus, and is thus a contributing factor in a person who can easily fall prey to the illusion of material desires. Neptune in Taurus indicates one who may be a skilled designer or artist, as the Fifth and Sixth Rays combine when Venus joins Neptune. The great test of this placement, however, would be one of creating a clarity of spiritual purpose, as the sensual expression of these energies is so strong. Once the Fixed Cross has been mounted and the influence of Vulcan and the First Ray present themselves, this individual can be instrumental in revealing the spiritual purpose contained within the artistic forms of life. From the mental level, Neptune in Taurus can give adherence to belief systems and religious sects that stimulate the lower self, while from the Soul level, it gives the ability to break through these illusions into a more inclusive frame of reference.

NEPTUNE IN GEMINI: This placement occurred only briefly in our century, having left this sign by 1902. Thus, its main influence will not occur again until well into the twenty-first century. From the personality level, the combination of Neptune and Mercury (Sixth and Fourth Rays) can lead to a very fertile and creative mind. The real and the ideal may come into some focus of conflict as one tries to unite one's inner visions with their needed forms of expression. One would have to be very careful about holding on to false ideas that can easily be made to fit any self-created pattern of reason. From the Soul level, this is a very potent and most beautiful position, as it combines the highest facets of Venus with Neptune. Such a placement can produce an individual who is very spiritually aware and who can easily communicate this attunement to the need of the environment. This is also a position that can give rise to the resolution of medical problems and diseases, as the combination of Venus and Neptune (the Fifth and the Sixth Rays) is a very healing and wholistic one.

---

[14]Although this combination (along with Neptune in Taurus and Pisces) does not appear again until the twenty-first century, it might be of interest to explore its potential effects in light of what we know about the influence of the planets, the signs, and the Seven Rays.

NEPTUNE IN CANCER (1902–1916): Soul-centered ruler and personality-centered exaltation. We have already discussed the primary relationship between Neptune and Cancer from the Soul level. It involves the creation and nurturing of the indwelling Soul presence within the forms of life, especially in the Human Kingdom. An individual with this placement is able to foster the awareness of this Presence of Love through his or her contacts with others. Neptune in Cancer is the Mother Principle at work in her most spiritual state. The Moon is the esoteric ruler of the Virgin, and the interchange of these two planets from the Soul level invokes only cohesion and wholeness.

NEPTUNE IN LEO (1915–1929): From the personality level, this placement produced a very romantic generation, as the cohesive and loving energies of Ray Two combined with the devotional and self-sacrificing impulses of Ray Six. It is a generation of great emotional stress, as tens of millions of these men and women were separated as young couples or suffered otherwise during World War II. From the Soul level, this is a very powerful position. Neptune in Leo represents the Heart of the Sun, and points to the ability to be creative from deeply spiritual impulses. This combination is the embodiment of Love in Action. Those individuals born with this placement are capable of instilling an awareness of the Presence of Love around them as they work in their own creative fields of self-expression. On the highest level, this position serves to transmute the desires and romanticism of the lower self into True Love, so that evolutionary advancement is made possible for others.

NEPTUNE IN VIRGO (1929–1943): Soul-centered detriment. It is interesting to note that on the personality level, people who have this placement in their natal charts seem to take small details out of proportion to their true worth. Thus, there is a tendency to make something out of practically nothing, and to exaggerate the importance of relative minutia. Yet this particular characteristic makes a great deal of sense when examined from the Soul-centered perspective. Neptune manifests the indwelling Presence of Divinity (Love) as devotion. In Virgo, it expresses itself through the sign related to the development of all the forms of creation, down to the smallest dot of crystallized matter. Perhaps the reason for the traditional assignment of "detriment" to Neptune when in this sign is the fact that that great Center (which is the Source of the Love of God for humanity and for all manifested life) has to "come down" in order to vivify all the multitudinous forms of Its expression. Therefore, Neptune in Virgo can be seen to symbolize a great sacrifice as it moves through the involutionary arc into matter.

NEPTUNE IN LIBRA (1943–1957): This is the author's generation, and as he has Venus in Pisces in his natal chart, he is quite (some would say "too") familiar with this placement! On the personality level, this position is characteristic of the search for the ideal balance in relationship. It signifies the projection of self-sacrifice and devotion into the interpersonal dynamics of life. It is also significant of an entire generation of "relationship counselors" who work at trying to create a science of relationship (through Venus's Fifth Ray connection) that will serve humanity in this cuspal period. From the collective, Soul-level perspective, this generation personifies the consciousness of the cuspal phase between the Piscean and Aquarian Ages, as the vast majority of people born during this time have either the trine or the square between Neptune and Uranus.

NEPTUNE IN SCORPIO (1956–1970): This generation is to develop an expression of the right use of sexual energy, leading to the collective transformation of the lower self. They mature at a time (the 1980s and 1990s) when the incorrect/unconscious/veiled expression of sexual desire can lead to serious diseases and even physical death. In terms of the nature of the astral plane and the centering of emotions through the solar plexus, this generation is truly working out an important facet of collective karma. This contribution has a great deal to do with the need for a more conscious participation in the process of progeneration. From the personality level, this combination definitely gives rise to a blindness where sexual pleasure and self-indulgence are concerned. Yet from the Soul level, Neptune in Scorpio is incredibly beautiful and powerful, in that it fosters the rebirth of the indwelling Christ Self over the ashes of the lower self as the Pathwalker begins the return journey Home.

NEPTUNE IN SAGITTARIUS (1970–1984): The Sixth Ray is strongly emphasized in this position, and it gives rise to a generation that will have some very profound religious and philosophical beliefs. The inner need to practicalize these understandings will bring these attunements to Love/Wisdom down to Earth, so that they may be integrated into the forms of daily life. On the personality level, there can be great confusion and impractical behavior (even to the point of fanaticism) relative to such urgings. The strong devotional sense, indicated by Neptune and the Sixth Ray facet of Sagittarius, is exaggerated by Jupiter and the expression of the Second Ray through the lower self. Such individuals are easily swayed by emotionally charged zealotry. This generation is filled with the urge for self-sacrifice and personal devotion but, when expressed through the Mutable Cross, these ostensibly altruistic impulses can be easily manipulated by glamour-ridden demagogues and unscrupulous "spiritual" leaders. On the Soul level, this combination will help to produce a large number of wonderful teachers and inspired world workers whose vision of spiritual purpose will be backed by practical actions. A lot of young "old Souls" will make themselves known to us in the coming years!

NEPTUNE IN CAPRICORN (1984–1998): Personality-centered fall. The personality-centered expressions of this combination and its Soul-centered ones could not be more different. On the level of the lower self, Neptune in Capricorn indicates a generation of people who are totally fooled by matter, intoxicated by form, swept away by the urge for personal power, etc. As a result, Love is restricted and veiled by the desire for personal power and the amassing of individual resources. But from the level of the Soul, a generation is born which embodies Christ Incarnated—the goal of human evolution has become established. These highly evolved workers are attuned to Law and Order and will harness the Will and the Mind, to create those expressions for Love and Wisdom that the times will require. These few (relative to the numbers of those who will be expressing Neptune in Capricorn from the lower self), are the self-realized Workers in the Heart of the Sun (Son). The personality-level meaning of Neptune finding itself in "fall" in this position couldn't be clearer: Love is trapped in the crystallization of matter and old thought-forms. The Soul-centered reason for this "fall" is quite poetic, but nonetheless true: the birth of the indwelling Love Presence is completed in Capricorn. The Highest element has "fallen" into its lowest expression—matter. After the work of the Soul is completed, this lowest expression will also "fall" to reveal its hidden, spiritual reality.

NEPTUNE IN AQUARIUS (1998–2012): This position takes us into the twenty-first century. The years 1998–2003 should be ones of great scientific achievement, as during this period both Uranus and Neptune will tenant Aquarius, sign of the New Age, as well as a major expression of the Fifth Ray. We could say that from the level of the New Group of World Servers, the Aquarian Age will begin in earnest during these five years. This position is a joining of Neptune and Uranus, as well as the Sixth Ray of the Piscean Age and the Seventh Ray of the Aquarian. Those individuals born in the Neptune-in-Libra generation now come into their mature years and will be "inheriting the Earth." Perhaps this will be a time when the Neptune-in-Libra, Uranus-in-Gemini ideals of "love and peace" will find their anchor in the social and political forms of the times. Those Soul-centered individuals born with Neptune in Aquarius will embody a great, spiritually impersonal love for humanity, one which will allow them to further the urge to be of service to all brothers and sisters on this planet. These are the spiritual scientists who will work together in teams and groups in order to resolve the problems which world climatic and population factors will engender.

NEPTUNE IN PISCES (2012–2026): Personality-centered ruler. As this combination occurs in the second and third decades of the twenty-first century, I can only speculate here about the potentialities of this position. The last time it occurred was toward the end of the Piscean Age (1849–1862), and it coincided in its last degrees with the end of American slavery (ruled by Pisces) during the Civil War. It is quite obvious that, from the Soul level, this combination will produce a great many lovers and saviors of humanity. Could this be the "army of the Christ" that comes resurrected without having to burn anyone in the fires of self-righteous fundamentalism, or impale anyone on the swords of martial Christianity? Is it possible that a generation could be born which will embody a living devotion to the indwelling Love Principle, and see it externalized through their right actions? Will the inclusivity and wholeness of the Soul find a collective and true outlet for Love/Wisdom in the twenty-first century? Will such children birth a New World Religion and lead humanity to a stage of unanimity (although not uniformity) of belief in the One Loving Will-to-Be in which we all have our breath and life? It is possible. Yet the duality of Neptune's effects in Pisces also lead to another simultaneous vision of possibility. There is the likelihood that several false prophets and messiahs will be born during this time. These will be men and women of great magnetic potency, capable of doing much harm and destruction as they channel the energies of Pluto through the collective solar plexus center. Their ultimate contribution will be that the glamour and illusion of their work will be revealed as the maya it is, furthering humanity's quest for the spiritual truth inherent in Love and Wisdom.

PLUTO

Soul-Centered Ruler of Pisces
Planet of the First Ray

By understanding the evolutionary intent of the Soul, we will be able to identify the evolutionary lessons that are represented in this life for any individual. . . . By understanding the collective evolutionary past (humanity) we will be able to understand the collective present, and the choices that humanity faces that will create the future.

—Jeff Green
Pluto—The Evolutionary Journey of the Soul

Functions: Pluto is extremely important in the lives of those of us who are undergoing the process of fusion of the Soul and the personality. Pluto is the agent of death, whether this is the death of desire, the death of our attachment to form, or the total death and surrender of the lower self as it merges and gives its life to the Soul. This is the death of liberation; the death of the resurrection. Pluto serves as the vehicle for the First Ray energy of destruction. It represents that process which breaks down the sense of selfishness and separateness of the lesser ego/personality, so that our little, personal will becomes the Will-to-Good of the realized Soul-self. It is a purifying energy which, in its external mode of expression, leads to the disintegration of form so that the Spirit of man may triumph. This Human Spirit is the indwelling Christ, the Loving Presence of the Soul. This is why, from the esoteric level, Pluto is the ruler of Pisces, sign of the World Savior. Yet it has to be clearly understood that the passion of the death and resurrection of the Anointed One is the same Path and Passion for each of us. The form of this Way in the Aquarian Era is outlined in the Laws and Principles of the New Age. Yet the energetics—the transcendental dynamics of the Path—remain constant throughout the Ages.

The Earth, the material realm, and the physical body represent the polarity to Pluto. It is in the physical world that our attachment to our desires is the greatest, and our illusions the strongest. Pluto and the other First Ray planet, Vulcan, teach the lessons that relate to the process of detachment from matter. Pluto may bring change, (temporary) darkness, and death, *but it can never destroy consciousness.* On the contrary, the work of the First Ray and its planets frees the individual to become more closely in touch with the consciousness aspect of Life.

The breaking down and detachment from forms, especially on the emotional level, is most painful. Indeed, this is the sacrifice the personality renders out of Love to the Soul. It is this undertaking, which becomes increasingly more conscious as spiritual evolution unfolds, that leads the individual from the experiences in Scorpio to the emergence of the indwelling Christ in Pisces. This relationship and transference of energy also helps us to understand how Pluto is the co-ruler of Scorpio from the level of personality and the ruler of Pisces from the level of the Soul.

Birth and rebirth are painful processes. The physical and emotional pain a woman endures in the process of giving birth to an infant is highly symbolic of the esoteric process of generation. The mother (form) is pulled apart and broken as the child moves out of her womb and onto the Earth. What was once existing within one and thus creating a whole has now become two, and all duality is painful in nature. The birthing of the individual out of the womb of his previous forms of containment (no matter how secure and comfortable) is absolutely essential for evolutionary development. The undying Spirit of Life is always creating new Ideas, and humanity consists of the Sons and Daughters of Mind. The above says something to us of the relationship of Neptune as the Soul-centered ruler of Cancer and the personality-centered ruler of Pisces. The relationship of these two water signs (and hence, an extension of meaning to Pluto and Scorpio) might well be worth contemplating at this point.

Pluto is the instrument for the development of the Spiritual Will. This comes about through the trials and tests on the Path of Discipleship. For this reason, Pluto is the personality-centered co-ruler of Scorpio, as it serves to facilitate the many deaths and transformations associated with this sign and its Path. The combination of the First Ray (Pluto) and the Sixth (Mars) leads to those battlegrounds that are so rightly associated with the Scorpion.

There are two brief quotes from the archives of the Ancient Wisdom Teachings that I would like to share. They speak about death. The first is the death in Scorpio, and the second passage describes the death in Pisces:

> ... (the) Ancient One (the personality, the Dweller) dies by drowning.... The waters envelop him and there is no escape.... The fires of passion are then quenched. The life of desire ceases its appeal and to the bottom of the lake he now descends. Later, he reascends to Earth where the white horse (Sagittarius) waits his coming. And this he mounts, proceeding toward the second death (Pisces).

> ... (the) Ancient One (the personality, the Dweller) is no longer seen. He sinks to the depth of the ocean of life; he descends into hell, but the gates of hell hold him not. He, the new and living One (Initiate) leaves below that which has held him down throughout the ages and rises from the depths unto the heights, close to the throne of God.[15]

Pluto transited Aries and Taurus from the middle to the end of the nineteenth century. This passage will not occur again until the latter third of the twenty-first century. Pluto's transit through Capricorn, Aquarius, and Pisces will happen during the first two-thirds of the next century, but I will comment upon these five positions for four reasons:

1. For those who might wish to research the past and equate Pluto in these five signs with the cultural events and the nature of human consciousness of those times;

2. For visionaries who might like to speculate on the events and consciousness of the future, and for those of us who will witness (or grandparent or great-grandparent) the Pluto in Capricorn and Aquarius generations;

[15]Quoted in Bailey's *Esoteric Astrology*, p. 214. (The words in parentheses are mine.)

3. For the student of Soul-centered astrology, so that a wider understanding of the blending of planets and Rays is possible;

4. For the pleasure of esoteric speculation.

PLUTO IN ARIES: This combination is a tremendous focus of Will, as a planet of the First Ray expresses itself in the primary sign of that Ray. This will be a generation of powerful mental pioneers, destroying old ideas and social patterns so that new ideas may take their place, as the energies of Mercury combine with those of Pluto. On the personality level, this can give rise to people who are very willful, seeking to take power into their own hands for their own purposes, and who destroy themselves (at least, their lower selves) in the process. From the level of group consciousness, these individuals will be a very dynamic force for the expression of the Will-to-Love.

PLUTO IN TAURUS: Personality-centered detriment. From the personality level, the energy of the Will is deeply masked in the earthy form of the Bull. Will is then used to anchor the form life, and thus create a deeper point of polarity for the reorientation to the life of the Soul. Yet from the Soul level, this is a most powerful position, as the energies of Vulcan combine with those of Pluto in order to produce a highly potent expression for the First Ray. Thus the dominance of the form life is challenged, producing the intense battle characterized by the Ray of the Bull—the Fourth, Harmony through Conflict. The Soul-centered generation which finds Pluto in Taurus in its natal horoscope will be very much in the forefront of a confrontation with the forces of materialism. This generation's dharma will be to help release consciousness from its imprisonment in form. Some very important contributions in showing how matter may be used by the Will of the Spirit can also be made. The last time Pluto was in Taurus was in the latter part of the nineteenth century—a time of intense Victorian materialism, but also a period in which a great surge of experimentation and inventiveness appeared. It was also a time of great spiritual movement, including the form establishment of the Theosophical Society.

PLUTO IN GEMINI: The energies of the First and Second Rays combine in this placement, producing a potent source for human advancement. This combination will not occur again until the early part of the twenty-second century. I would think that as Venus (Fifth) combines with Pluto (First) in a sign of the Second Ray, great advances will be made scientifically. Perhaps during that period, humankind will come to know that "God is Love in Action." In this century, Pluto occupied the sign of the Twins until 1913. Pluto in Gemini brings about the death of the awareness of separateness, giving to those who are born with this placement an instinctual sense of wholism. Soul-centered individuals born with this placement should be listened to very carefully, as they will be able to communicate an understanding of the Love which sets us free.

PLUTO IN CANCER (1912–1939): On the personality level, this may not be the easiest position, as it points to lessons which deal directly with the death of the form life. This is the generation which fought in and experienced World War II, in which a tremendous uprooting took place. The family as a central psychological unit, and the tribe as a central cultural unit, would forever be transformed, as that terrible war destroyed so many of humanity's previous foundations. The waters of Neptune would wash away the past, allowing a new incarnation for humanity to take its place. This sense of the destruction of foundations can be seen from the Ray energies that are involved. Pluto, Lord of Destruction and planet of the First Ray, combines here with Cancer, found on the Seventh Ray (the outer, material world). Yet Pluto is a regenerative source, for it does not destroy or bring death to consciousness. The First Ray will work out through Cancer on the Third and Seventh to structure a new world in the external life of forms. This same generation had to begin this new building process, as well, once the war was over. The Fourth Ray energy of the Moon's exoteric rulership of Cancer would also be a strong influence on the function of this placement.

PLUTO IN LEO (late 1937–1958): Personality-centered fall. The primary function of this position on the Soul level is to facilitate the death of self-consciousness so that the birth of group consciousness is made possible. The individualized ego falls in this sign and is rebirthed in Aquarius, as one's personal expression of the urge to serve humanity. The intense focusing on the lesser self, so characteristic of this "me generation," serves the purpose of leading one to the door of the Higher Self and the resulting awareness of humanity as a collective whole. The force of the Will-to-Create is very potent in this combination, as Pluto's First Ray energy manifests through the First and Fifth Ray expression of the Lion. This strongly stimulates the mind, helping to flood it with the Second Ray energy coming from the Heart of the Sun. At this level, the Sun is veiling Neptune, so that Pluto in Leo is very much involved with the rebuilding of a new foundation for humanity's expression of group consciousness.[16]

---

[16]The Sun is the ruler of Leo on both the personality and Soul levels. In this respect, on the level of the lower self, the Sun is the physical Sun. From the Soul's perspective, the Sun in Leo represents the Heart of the Sun. In this case, we say that the Sun is often used as the vehicle of expression for Neptune. This is a highly esoteric principle which aligns the Second and Sixth Rays. But what may be inferred for our purposes is the fact that the creative force in the universe (Sun) sacrifices itself through devotion to humanity (Neptune), in order to birth (Cancer, Neptune's sign) the Sons and Daughters of Mind. The ultimate expression of this birthing process leads to the externalization of humanity as the World Savior (Neptune and Pluto's relationship to Pisces).

PLUTO IN VIRGO (1958–1972): This combination, on the personality level, produces a very materialistic generation, much concerned with those things of Virgo: health and fitness, work and career, as well as the acquisition of possessions. The urge to transform (Pluto), and those lessons which this process entails, come through the sign of the Horn of Plenty and the Harvest. Yet this is an unconscious urge on the level of the lower self. When such an awareness occurs on the Soul level, then the highest aspect of the Moon joins with Pluto, and Virgo's Second and Sixth Ray energies are also a part of this Soul-focused blending of influences. At this level, Pluto in Virgo nurtures and sustains the intense modifications of life direction which lead to the detachment from the form life. It is an incredibly potent force for healing and wholism, as it leads one to the very door of the Mother and Her limitless spiritual resources. Many people with this position in their natal charts who have heard the call to service from the Soul will most likely find themselves drawn to one form or another of the healing arts.

PLUTO IN LIBRA (1971–1984): In the years between 1971 and 1975, both Pluto and Uranus, the Soul-centered ruler of Libra, were in this sign. These years are highly significant in the birthing of a group of individuals who, if Soul-centered, will work to personify and invoke the Laws and Principles of the New Age—especially the Law of Right Human Relations and the Law of Group Endeavor. In general, Pluto in Libra creates the death of attachment to relationships on the personality level, and provides the opportunity to enter into service to humanity. The process of Soul orientation is one of synthesis. Thus, those relationships which may have been created when an individual was working through the Mutable Cross can be resurrected to another level of rapport once he has mounted the Fixed Cross. In Love nothing is lost, as Pluto does not destroy the consciousness aspect of Divinity. What is added to the life when Pluto tenants this sign is the quality of loving detachment.

PLUTO IN SCORPIO (1982–1995): Personality-centered ruler. One of the major lessons of Pluto in the sign of its exoteric rulership is the right use of sexual energy. This is the period of the AIDS epidemic, which should have its cure by the time Pluto enters Sagittarius. The Soul-centered purpose of this passage is to teach the death of desire so that Love may be released in greater fullness through the sexual processes. Personality-centered people born with Pluto in Scorpio in their natal horoscopes will find that they must do battle with will-power so that it may eventually come under the loving direction of the Soul. Those who mount the Fixed Cross from this generation will be the vehicles for a great transformation in human consciousness.

They will prove through their actions, both in their personal lives and in their participation in the collective life, the victory of Love over desire, the reorientation of human natures, and that fusion of Will and Love which produces healing.

PLUTO IN SAGITTARIUS: This placement of Pluto takes us into the first decade of the next century. The delineation of the birthchart of the twenty-first century (and the Third Millennium, C.E., January 1, 2001, midnight GMT) deserves a chapter of its own. The indications are very favorable. The Sun is in Capricorn in harmonious affinity with Saturn in Taurus, while Neptune and Uranus are in Aquarius, and Pluto is in the sign of the Pathwalker. To me, it is the millennium of the Earthly Disciple, as the field for service to humanity is so beautifully supported by these planetary influences. Those Soul-centered individuals born with Pluto in Sagittarius will personify the death of the separatist paths toward the One Truth. These are the Teachers of the Ancient Wisdom, and the world should be in a much more receptive place to hear them speak. From the personality level, many strong, egocentric individuals will stand forward, each having his or her own group of followers, and each proclaiming that he or she is the embodiment of that Truth. Thus, dualism in the outer life will continue as the little religions remain opposed to one another. Yet the promise of true ecumenicalism will also come forward, through the teachings and group activities of those whose Sagittarian visons are empowered by the Will-to-Good.

PLUTO IN CAPRICORN: This position challenges the status quo of those who hold unequal power; that is, power unequal to their Soul development. From the personality level, this can produce some incredibly will-filled people (especially those born with the Sun also in the sign of the Mountain Goat), who may strive with incredible force to obtain terrestrial power and dominance over others. The Soul-centered born with this placement will know that they are the vehicles for the Will/Power of the right use of Mind, and will strive to birth those structures on the planet that will make the Earth's bounty available for all. This combination blends the First, Third, and Seventh Rays, so that the right use of the Will has to be externalized through Active Intelligence into the outer world of form.

PLUTO IN AQUARIUS: Soul-centered exaltation. This position embodies the death of the ego's attachment to the concrete mind so that the latter may be used as a vehicle for the direct expression of the collective Will-to-Good. The resurrection of the lower mind occurs through its conscious fusion to the Soul, as consciousness proceeds outward into the form life. This contact is quite direct, as the exoteric ruler of Aquarius is Uranus, ruler of the Seventh Ray. From the Soul level, this is an exalted position indeed, as Pluto joins with the esoteric ruler of the Water Bearer, Jupiter, planetary vehicle for the Second Ray of Love/Wisdom. The potential is for a generation to be birthed whose Soul-centered members will be very instrumental in using the technological and scientific facets of their mental capacities for dedicated service to humanity. Certain individuals among this group (perhaps those with Aquarius rising or the Sun in that sign) will stand out as very powerful contributors to human betterment.

PLUTO IN PISCES: Soul-centered ruler. This position occurs in the middle of the twenty-first century, and will be experienced as a trine by the natal Pluto-in-Scorpio generation. Could this mean that the potential Love that is released by the former group will now reach its culmination of experience through the lives of the Pluto-in-Pisces generation? We have seen earlier in this section that death in the Scorpion leads to the resurrection of the indwelling Christ in the Fish. The promise here is for the actualization of the Soul itself (the Spirit of Man) in the outer life. On the group consciousness or Soul level, this placement of Pluto can certainly point to the birthing of a number of individuals who will be eager to continue, within the Aquarian Age context, the Work of the One Who inaugurated the Age of the Fish.

I I

The Mansions of the

Soul–The Houses of

the Natal Chart

Light is undiminishable, eternal and omni-present. In every religion that existed these qualities have been recognized as divine. So that we are forced to the conclusion that light—actual sensible light—is indeed the direct vehicle of divinity: it is the consciousness of God.

—Rodney Collin
The Theory of Celestial Influence

The houses of the horoscope have to be considered as places of crystallization or limitation, whether this is from the perspective of the Soul or the personality. It is through the fields of activity signified by the houses that the energies of both the lower and the Higher selves meet, blend, and express themselves in the present incarnation. I am assuming that the reader has studied traditional astrology and is already familiar with the interpretations which have been developed by exoteric, humanistic, and psychologically oriented astrologers, both past and present.[1]

The application of the meanings of the houses is a very fluid area in Soul-centered astrology. The traditional significance of each house will remain accurate, for the most part, as the vast majority of us still lead a very active personality life. The additional Soul-centered factors which follow have to be integrated into the delineation of the

---

[1] Those who wish to review the implications of these house meanings may refer to this section in my earlier work on the subject—*Alan Oken's Complete Astrology*—and/or read the books recommended in the Bibliography.

chart through the application of the astrologer's intuition, as the latter is the tool by which one assesses another's level of Soul growth.

Most of us are working out our present lives either through an anchoring of consciousness on the Fixed Cross or in one or another of the stages of preparation to mount it. This will be true for the reader, as well as for the people who come to have their horoscopes cast and interpreted by those of us who are professional astrologers. The blending and integration of these two facets of house meanings is the most important method of approach to the esoteric inferences of the house positions. There will be considerably more to say about horoscope delineations from the Soul-centered perspective in chapters 13 and 14. For the present, please keep in mind that you would do well to first examine the horoscope thoroughly from the personality-centered, exoteric view. Then, observe the chart as follows:

1. Notice the sign on the cusp of each of the houses and apply the Ray characteristics of that sign to the activities of the house esoterically considered.

2. Find the Soul-centered planetary ruler of that house, and notice its position by house and sign. The Ray quality of this ruler will play a significant part in your interpretation of the effects of the energies involved with the house placement.

3. Juxtapose the personality-centered ruler of the house in question with its esoteric counterpart. Note if there are any aspects between the two and the type of aspect; that is, harmonious, inharmonious, or variable. This will reveal much about the nature of the interfacing between the Soul and the personality, relative to the activities of that house.

4. The Ray characteristics of the exoteric, personality-centered ruling planet of a house will pertain to the life of the lesser self. The Ray characteristics of the Soul-centered planetary ruler will pertain to the life of the Higher Self.

For the sake of convenience, I am going to list the major house factors from both esoteric and exoteric perspectives. As mentioned above, the reader may wish to consult other sources for a more complete survey of the meanings of the house positions relative to traditional astrology. Additional information concerning the esoteric implications of the zodiacal mansions will come about in the course of time through further research, the application of this method of approach, and the Tibetan's guidance. The results of the work of other esoteric astrologers will amplify and continue to clarify these initial efforts.

The material in this chapter, and in the three chapters which follow, represents the development of my work and studies concerning the Soul-centered delineation of the horoscope. It comes as a response to my own inner questing, as well as from those students, clients, and colleagues who have also been seeking answers in their charts for questions concerning their evolving realities—answers which traditional astrological interpretations do not completely satisfy. Esoteric astrology is unfolding at an equal pace with the externalizing consciousness of the Soul in human awareness. It is a developing branch of an ancient science. In the Soul-centered approach to the natal horoscope, esoteric astrology should also be viewed as:

1. an adjunct to the science of the Soul and the building of the Rainbow Bridge;
2. a guide to the Path of Discipleship;
3. an exposition as to the nature of the Seven Rays;
4. an underlying conditioning factor of esoteric psychology;
5. a method of charting the rhythms of those energies passing between the Soul and the personality.

The evolution of human consciousness, and the astrology which seeks to define it, have not and can never cease. The evolution of the Soul is a process that has no temporal finality in terms that we may discern or describe at this point. The crises of reorientation in our approach to our own indwelling Divinity (and the accompanying victories and joys) continue into greater and greater unity of purpose and awareness for each of us. Human destiny is infinite.

THE TWELVE HOUSES OF THE HOROSCOPE—A COMPARISON

THE FIRST HOUSE

Traditional	Soul-Centered
1. The physical body and its form	The Soul Body (Causal Lotus)
2. The physical appearance	The aura
3. Activities of the personality	Emergence of the Soul purpose
4. Characteristics of the ego	Qualities of the Ray type
5. Brain and head	Head centers/chakras
6. Urge for personal space or dominance of the environment	Expression of manifested will
7. The ego in action	Activities of the Soul

The importance of the Ascendant in Soul-centered astrology cannot be emphasized enough. The understanding of the Ray energies of the sign on this cusp, plus the position of its *Soul-centered, esoteric ruler,* will help to answer the question: "What is my Soul's purpose in this incarnation?" These positions should be viewed and balanced with the nature of the sign and its ruler from the traditional point of view. The following twelve-part delineation of horoscope 1 focuses primarily on the house cusp signs and the positions of the house rulers.

As Aries rises, the ruler of the Ascendant from the personality perspective is Mars, which is in Libra in the seventh house. The search for the "perfect partner," in order to fulfill both emotional (square to Moon in Capricorn) and spiritual (trine Jupiter in Aquarius) needs, occupied the entire adult life up until two years ago. All creative efforts were channeled into the need to "marry the anima,"

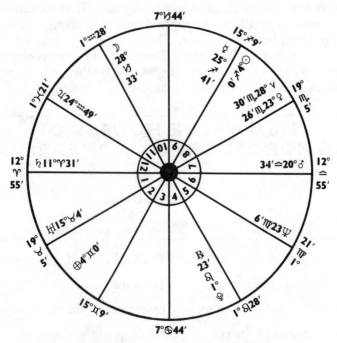

Horoscope 1: T. I., born in Los Angeles, California
November 26, 1938 at 2:06 P.M. PST

or the objectification of his female self. This resulted in many difficult and idealized relationships (Venus in Scorpio square Jupiter and ruling the seventh house), as well as several divorces, and the loss of finances (Venus ruling the second house). The ego sacrifices itself to the form of the female, polarizing itself, and denying its own completion by not integrating with its own anima. It thus consistently loses creative power (Mars's position, its square to the tenth house Moon, and its connection to Venus). This tendency is in constant conflict with the individual's sincere "search for the Holy Grail" (Sagittarius Sun with Jupiter trine the ruler of the Ascendant). The form life and the magnetism of the solar plexus (Mars square the Moon) inhibit and do battle with his true urge for the spiritual expansion of the ego (Jupiter trine Mars).

The lessons of Mars having been learned and the integration of the anima having been accomplished, this individual mounted the Fixed Cross, and his horoscope can now be read and applied from the Soul-centered perspective. Just in terms of the Soul purpose, we can note the following:

1. The sign on the Ascendant is Aries, indicating that the Soul is being activated through the First Ray, and that there will also be some strong Seventh Ray tendencies.

2. The esoteric ruler of the chart is Mercury in Sagittarius in the ninth house. Mercury is a Fourth Ray planet, and is in a sign of the Fourth Ray as well. Thus, the Soul purpose will be conditioned by Harmony through Conflict, expressing through lessons of the First and Seventh Rays.

3. The dispositor of Mercury, the Earth, is in Gemini in the second house. This brings in the strong Second Ray quality of the Twins.

4. Mercury's primary aspects are the square to Neptune in Virgo and the trine to Jupiter in Aquarius. Neptune's position is very strongly Sixth Ray, while Jupiter's Second Ray energy is manifesting through the Ray of Concrete Knowledge, the Fifth.

5. There is a basic conflict between the energies of Rays Four and Six. This is shown on the personality level, as Mars (Ray Six) is in square to the Moon (Ray Four). On the Soul level, Mercury (Ray Four) is square to Neptune (Ray Six). In our discussion of the fourth house, we shall see how this conflict resolves itself.

Some conclusions: The Soul urge (Mercury) has always been present in the life, as this individual has always sought higher knowledge, consciously recognizing it as a vehicle for the expression of his love (Mercury in Sagittarius in the ninth house, with the Earth in Gemini). Jupiter's sextile to Mercury also reinforces this condition, as its Second Ray quality adds to Gemini's in this respect.

The square to Neptune shows that the Sixth Ray urge for devotion took this man to various countries in the search for those gurus and teachers who would stimulate his inner unfoldment. He always encountered the grace and the information he was seeking, but was inhibited from integrating this understanding into the right use of his personal will (Saturn in Aries on the Ascendant). (Planets within 3 degrees of the Ascendant in the twelfth house are considered to have first house influence.)

The great spiritual conflict—one typical of Saturn in this position—has always been involved with the giving up of the Will/Power and the avoidance of personal, spiritual, and creative responsibility. This is one of Saturn's effects on the personality level. On the Soul level, just the reverse occurs. In fact, the correct assumption of Will/Power in the training of the mental vehicle is very definitely a major Soul purpose in the life of this man.

The interplay of Rays Four and Six between the ruling planets of the chart reveals a major core issue in the present incarnation. The devotional urge comes into direct opposition with the need to create form out of the indwelling spiritual life. This man's desire to give himself up to his spiritual aspirations and ideals has always been juxtaposed with his tremendous impulse to achieve some material goal in the physical world through the professions. In this case, the outer work chosen has been the writing of screenplays with New Age, spiritual themes. Such topics traditionally have not been well received by Hollywood! Yet this creative choice, as the astrologer will note, is very much an expression of his Mercury/Neptune connection. His urge to communicate profound spiritual truths and to have them disseminated to as many people as possible speaks to us of the Mercury/Neptune/Jupiter relationship from the Soul level. The square of the Soul-centered and the personality-centered rulers by Neptune and the Moon, respectively, has made the synthesis of these tendencies a very difficult one. The dominant tone of the Fourth Ray of Harmony through Conflict (Mercury in Sagittarius) sounds out very clearly in this horoscope.

The individual is currently undergoing training in the shamanistic, healing traditions. This is a very Seventh Ray/Ceremonial Magic path, and reveals this facet of that Ray's quality in Aries. Saturn's influence, both through its natural rulership of Capricorn, as well as its placement in Aries on the Ascendant, also seems to increase the Seventh Ray influence in this chart. The shamanistic path involves devotion to the teacher, but it also requires the individual student to stand firm and take on personal responsibility for the right use of will. The healing facets of shamanism require the abundant use of Fourth Ray energy, as one has to blend and balance many of the forces associated with the Animal Kingdom, while invoking the healing power of the

Kingdom of the Soul. The use of Mind as the healer and the refinement of the Will/Power is revealed through Saturn's position. The importance of Mercury, both as the Soul-centered ruler of the Ascendant, and as Saturn's dispositor, is also a major factor in this respect.

THE SECOND HOUSE

Traditional	Soul-Centered
1. Finances, personal resources	Storehouse of life energy or prana; spiritual resources and values
2. Use of material resources	Use of life energies
3. Attitude about money	The control of forms; the shaping of matter as the expression of spiritual values
4. Losses resulting from wrong material values	The withdrawal of the life energy from its forms so that energy is left free to reformulate
5. Gains resulting from right use of matter	The acquisition of spiritual values

In terms of the acquisition of spiritual values, look to the house placement of the esoteric ruler of the cusp and this will tell you where this process will be found. In the case of horoscope 1, the esoteric ruler of the second house, Vulcan, is located in Scorpio and conjunct Venus in the eighth house. (The position of Vulcan in this and in the horoscope of Mahatma Gandhi are approximate.) This is a very significant placement, as it clearly shows that the reorientation of personal values would occur through the destruction of this individual's nonregenerative relationships (Venus, dispositor of Mars and ruler of the seventh house, in Scorpio). The conflicts resulting from the frustration of the desire nature (Fourth Ray influence of Scorpio) would lead eventually to the greater harmony of the Path once the individual mounted the Fixed Cross. The likelihood of finding the "perfect partner," or the Soul mate, is greatly enhanced for this individual as a result of Vulcan's work in the breaking down of these forms of material attachment!

THE THIRD HOUSE

Traditional	Soul-Centered
1. The rational mind; mental processes	Manas; mind substance/energy
2. Communication; the spoken and written word	Mental telepathy; mental transference of energy
3. Search for knowledge	The unfoldment of the knowledge necessary to complete the journey on the Mutable Cross
4. The process of relating with others	The way of developing the Rainbow Bridge and the relating of the Higher and lower selves
5. Short journeys	Steps along the Path
6. Brothers and sisters	Soul brothers and sisters or companions along the Way; members of one's Group, but not the Group collective

The ruler of the third house in our sample horoscope is Venus, as Gemini is on the cusp. It is interesting to point out the relationship which Venus has to the seventh and third houses, linking them through her exoteric and esoteric rulerships, respectively. Her placement in Scorpio, conjunct Vulcan, is a further example that this individual will find his partner among his Soul sisters along the Way. This will occur as a result of the transformation of values outlined in the second house.

THE FOURTH HOUSE

Traditional	Soul-Centered
1. Biological inheritance	Biological karma, inherited from family and genes
2. Mother and immediate family	The Mother (relationship to the Mother Principle), the Group Soul from Whom come our Soul brothers and sisters

Traditional	Soul-Centered
3. Psychological foundation	The foundation of the Soul, its anchoring in the present incarnation; the foundation for the building of self-consciousness
4. Endings	Karmic conclusions to life circumstances
5. Home	The Ashram of the Master; the spiritual home of the Disciple

It is very easy to see the difficulties that T. I. had with his own mother, and the consequent sense of lack of emotional nourishment from women. The Moon is the ruler of the fourth house from the personality level, and is in its detriment sign, Capricorn. In addition, the Moon—the forms that nourish the personality—is further debilitated by the square to Mars (also in detriment) and by a strong opposition from Pluto in the fourth house. The biological mother is not only not a source of sustenance, but is in direct conflict with the personality's integration and development (the square to Mars).

When we examine the fourth house from the Soul level, we find that Neptune is the ruler and is trine the Moon. This signifies that devotion to the Mother Principle will provide the necessary healing to the earlier psychological injuries suffered through his biological mother. It should also be noted that the trine between the Moon (Fourth Ray) and Neptune (Sixth Ray) resolves the basic conflict outlined in our discussion of the first house implications of this chart. The foregoing reveals the karmic conclusions to this life crisis. The healing and synthesizing qualities of the Moon, Neptune, and Virgo, when seen from the Soul, bring this about. The individual becomes an active agent for healing, and is thus healed by the Mother/Soul.

THE FIFTH HOUSE

Traditional	Soul-Centered
1. Personal will	Expression of Spiritual Will
2. Active, creative self-expression	Actualization of the Higher Self

Traditional	Soul-Centered
3. Romance, love affairs	Love manifesting as the Will to merge with the Plan through one's creative expression
4. Children	Creativity stimulated by the Soul's Love
5. Hobbies, favorite activities	Expression of the Will to serve
6. Games and sports	Activities which stimulate the Will

The natural rulership of the Sun (Second Ray) and Leo (First and Fifth Rays) over this house leads to the blending of Love and Will, as well as to the activities of the Concrete Mind. In our sample horoscope, Leo is on the cusp of the fifth house with the Sun in Sagittarius in the eighth, trine Saturn and Pluto. The Sun in the Soul-centered chart is our indication of *the equipment one brings into the present incarnation.* The trine from Pluto to the eighth house Sun tells us that the Will/Power will have to undergo a major focus of transformation for the release of the higher knowledge expressed through Sagittarius. The mental body (Saturn at the Ascendant) has the great potential to be vivified by Love (Sun trine) and given direction and purpose as an extension of the Soul's activities (Sun in Sagittarius; Saturn conjunct the Ascendant) once the transformation of will is undertaken. The position of Vulcan and its relationship to Venus, and the latter's contact to Mars, speaks to us very clearly about the reorientation of desires in relationship that will quicken this necessary transformation.

THE SIXTH HOUSE

Traditional	Soul-Centered
1. Servants	Servers
2. Health	Synthesis of the lower vehicles; integration of the Soul qualities
3. Employees	Students, patients, those who are served
4. Pets and small animals	Service to the Animal Kingdom

Traditional	Soul-Centered
5. Work	Service to humanity through healing and nurturing
6. Techniques and skills	The required knowledge to build the Antahkarana

From the Soul-centered perspective, we find that the ruler of the sixth house is the Moon in the tenth, trine to Neptune in the Sixth. As the ruler of the fourth, Neptune shows us the ending of the karmic situation involving the realization of the Soul's purpose in the life. Thus this individual's choice of the healing path, of the building of the proper forms which nurture others through service, is clear. The square from Mars and the opposition from Pluto in the fourth house tell us that many psychological barriers and injuries from the relationship with the biological roots (and specifically the mother) will have to be encountered and overcome. The correct nurturing and healing of others requires the healing and synthesis of the lower vehicles first.

THE SEVENTH HOUSE

Traditional	Soul-Centered
1. Open enemies	The Dweller on the Threshold
2. Partners	Soul mate and/or special co-workers
3. Marriage	The Path of Union between the Soul and the personality

The position of Mars in Libra as the ruler of the personality-centered chart reveals how this man created an "open enemy" of himself in his consistently enforced polarization of his anima and animus. Venus in Scorpio extends this dynamic. Uranus is the ruler of the seventh house from the Soul-centered perspective, and its trine to Neptune shows that the Soul mate will be found along the spiritual Path of his chosen field of healing. The opposition of the Soul-centered ruler and the personality-centered ruler (Uranus/Venus) is an outstanding indication of the intense struggle of reorientation that he would have had to undergo in order to develop a clear attitude about the direction of marriage and partnership in his life.

THE EIGHTH HOUSE

Traditional	Soul-Centered
1. Transformation and regeneration	The Path of Discipleship
2. Sexuality	The vehicle of rebirth into the consciousness of the Soul
3. Transmutation of values	Transmutation of personal desires into the wishes and requirements of the Group
4. Other people's resources	Transformation of personal and material resources into group and spiritual resources
5. Death	Transformation of dense expressions of energy into more subtle ones
6. Desires of the personality	Liberation into world service and the victory of the Soul

We have amply discussed the presence of the Sun, Vulcan, and Venus in this house. Mars in Libra in the seventh house, and its square to the Moon, shows the conflicts of the personality in relation to the circumstances governed by the eighth house. Uranus, the Soul-centered dispositor of Mars, is trine to Neptune. This indicates that from the Soul level, right relationships and the proper balancing of eighth house energies will be available to this man along his Way, because Neptune (the Heart of the Sun) comes to dominate the solar plexus, previously ruled by Mars, once a person is full anchored on the Fixed Cross. One should also consider Uranus's opposition to Venus once again, as this is one of the core issues of the life. (See chapter 12, p. 373.)

THE NINTH HOUSE

Traditional	Soul-Centered
1. Long journeys	The Path
2. Religion and philosophy	The repository of the Truths contained in the Ancient Wisdom Teachings
3. Differing orthodoxies	Unification of all belief systems; synthesis of all religions/philosophies
4. Higher education	Mental permanent atom; Higher Mind
5. Legal activities	The knowledge of Cosmic Law
6. Publishing	The Akashic Records

The fact that the Soul-centered ruler of the horoscope is in this house (in Sagittarius with this sign on its cusp) tells us in no uncertain terms that this individual has the potential to attune himself to the Path and to all of the other factors listed above. Jupiter's sextile from Aquarius in the eleventh house is a further indication that he can communicate the Teachings to others through the world of the personality. So much depends on his ability to communicate and relate the right use of Will/Power (Mercury in the ninth house and the dispositor of Saturn) in order to bring about this beautiful possibility in the outer world.

THE TENTH HOUSE

Traditional	Soul-Centered
1. The father	Divine Will revealed as the culmination of spiritual purpose
2. Authority figures	The Masters; Hierarchy; your particular teachers
3. Honor and status	Opportunity for spiritual advancement and responsibility

Traditional	Soul-Centered
4. Social responsibility	Enforcing the Plan of the Masters
5. Career and profession	Externalized field of service

The tenth house is definitely the one which concerns our goals, be they material or spiritual. A goal for the Soul does not have to be in material form. Some people have very specific tasks to accomplish in the present incarnation. These can be seen in both the Soul-centered and personality-centered charts. Yet the goal for the Soul can also be the establishment of a form or the creation of a channel for the exteriorization of an energy or Ray. This is achieved through one's activities while in the physical body, and is no less an accomplishment than some more tangible factor, from the standpoint of world acclamation. *The goal for each of us is the Path, and the Path represents the unfolding Love/Wisdom consciousness of the Soul.*

Saturn is both the exoteric and esoteric ruler of the tenth house in our sample chart. Its placement on the Ascendant, trine the Sun, shows us that this man came into incarnation at this time to fulfill a definite purpose. The requirement of his Soul is that he work to create a highly structured and refined mental body (Saturn in Aries, ruler of the tenth and conjunct the Ascendant—he is his own teacher, ultimately). He may then proceed to take on any of a great range of spiritual responsibilities, as he has thus anchored the right use of Will/Power through the mental vehicle.

THE ELEVENTH HOUSE

Traditional	Soul-Centered
1. Friends	Members of your group
2. Hopes and wishes	Spiritual visions and aspirations
3. Organizations and clubs	Your Group; the New Group of World Servers
4. Political activities	Service to humanity through communication

The second house from any other is the container of its resources. The eleventh house is the second from the tenth. From the Soul-

centered perspective, the tenth is the house of the Masters. Its resources (the eleventh house) are strongly connected to the New Group
of World Servers, and to the expression of the Law of Group Endeavor and the Principle of Unanimity.

This is the most "honored" of the houses in our example. Jupiter,
Soul-centered ruler of Aquarius, is in this sign, and in the house which
it rules from the level of the Higher Self. When this individual consciously took to the Path, he encountered his Group co-workers, and
found ample opportunities to heal the wounds of the personality
(Jupiter trine Mars). This Second Ray planet is in sextile to the Soul
ruler, thus adding Love/Wisdom to the great potential seen through
Mercury's position. The opportunity for tremendous spiritual growth
is very much heightened when Jupiter is in aspect (even difficult
aspect) to the esoteric ruler of the horoscope.

THE TWELFTH HOUSE

Traditional	Soul-Centered
1. Hidden enemies	Unredeemed past karma; the dark forces of ignorance
2. Self-undoing	Inversion of the Soul force
3. Prisons and institutions	Bondage to the personality
4. Secret activities	Selfless service to humanity
5. Hidden resources	Access to the collective experiences of one's past lives
6. Crucifixion of the personality	Resurrection in service to the World Savior (the Soul)

Pluto, the esoteric ruler of the twelfth house in the sample horoscope, opposes the Moon and trines the Sun. The release of the
personality (the Sun) to do the work of the present incarnation (its
trine to Saturn and the Ascendant) has a great deal to do with the
detachment from the forms of the past (opposition to the Moon).
This points once again to the biological karma connected to this
man's family, and especially to his mother and her background. The
Moon in Capricorn is especially indicative of family history and
tradition. In other words, the biological karma of this man's family is
a very deep and ancient one. This is reinforced by the position of the

Capricorn Moon in the tenth house. Once Pluto has destroyed this ancient connection, Neptune's rulership over the fourth house (and its connection in this chart to the twelfth house, as well) allows the individual the opportunity to heal these wounds through the creation of his "spiritual family." His experience now is that the Mother will provide the necessary forms for the work of his Creative Spirit through his Soul. He comes to *trust* the female aspect, both in women and in himself. His healing is complete, and he is ready to serve.

12

Soul-Centered Planetary

Relationships, the Rays,

and the Aspects

It is impossible to attain our Divinity or to reach perfection without passing through the Soul and becoming a Soul. When we come in contact with our Soul, fuse with Its Light and grow as a Soul, then the mysteries will be revealed to our opening eyes, and the past, present and future will be ours. We shall become free Souls, free from time and matter, and we will enjoy the presence of the ever-existent Light.

—Torkom Saraydarian
The Hidden Glory of the Inner Man

One of the most important elements in correctly delineating a horoscope, whether from the Soul or personality level, is an understanding of the nature of interplanetary relationships. In traditional astrology, such connections are conditioned by three primary factors:

1. *Dispositorship.* A planet is always vibrationally connected to the planet which rules the sign in which it finds itself in the natal chart. Thus, Saturn in Taurus would automatically have an affinity with Venus. Likewise, Mars in Aquarius would be in contact with Uranus, and the Sun in Pisces would be directly modified in its expression by the position of Neptune, etc.

A more complex form of dispositorship is *mutual reception.* This is when two planets find themselves in each other's sign. Mars in Libra and Venus in Scorpio; Venus in Pisces and Neptune in Libra, are two examples of this condition. Mutual reception brings the two planets into a very close bond of association. This is made even stronger if there is an actual geometric aspect connecting them.

2. *Aspect.* All students of astrology are familiar with the geometric

angles which planets make to one another. These aspects condition and modify the blending of planetary energies. The major aspects are the conjunction (0–10 degrees), sextile (60 degrees), square (90 degrees), trine (120 degrees), inconjunction (150 degrees), and opposition (180 degrees), while the so-called minor aspects are too numerous to list in their entirety. The most important of these are: semi-square (45 degrees), quintile (72 degrees), and the sesqui-square (135 degrees).

Should a planet be in actual geometric aspect with its dispositor, the nature of that contact is accentuated, relative to the harmony or disharmony of the aspect itself. The 60-degree, 120-degree, and 72-degree aspects tend toward ease of circumstances, while the 90-degree, 150-degree, 180-degree, 45-degree, and 135-degree angles tend to produce stress. The conjunction is a variable aspect, its effects totally modified by the affinity or lack of affinity between the planets in question.

3. *Octave.* Traditional astrology holds that Mercury, Venus, and Mars are the lesser expressions for Uranus, Neptune, and Pluto, respectively. Indeed, this is the truth, for in the horoscope of the personality, these relationships are most significant.

In Soul-centered astrology, there are very specialized modifications to the three categories listed above, as well as several additional factors. These may be outlined as follows:

1. *Dispositorship.* This is based on *esoteric rulerships.* Thus, Saturn in Taurus is disposited by Vulcan; Mars in Aquarius is connected to Jupiter; the Sun in Pisces has its affiliation with Pluto, etc.

Should a planet be in aspect with both its esoteric and exoteric dispositor, the implications are that there is a very strong link between the Soul and the personality, relative to this planet's energy and Ray. Thus, if Saturn were in Taurus and in trine to a conjunction of Venus and Vulcan, or if Mars in Aquarius were sextile to Jupiter and square to Uranus, such a condition would then be said to exist. An extension of this pattern would be seen if the two dispositors were in mutual aspect. If the Sun were in Pisces, and Neptune were sextile to Pluto, we would draw the conclusion that a harmonious relationship exists, allowing the Sun's energy to pour through and link both the personality-centered and the Soul-centered charts.

The above is especially important for the rulers of the Ascendant. A very crucial point to note is the relationship between the Soul-centered ruler of the chart and its personality-centered equivalent. Thus, in a horoscope with Cancer rising, it is vitally important to consider the relationship of Neptune and the Moon. Six categories of this relationship should be noted:

a. *Link by sextile or trine.* An incarnation in which the fusion of the soul's purpose with the activities of the lower self is potentially advanced with ease and naturalness.

b. *Link by square, opposition, or inconjunction.* An incarnation in which this fusion is accomplished with greater difficulty. One reason for such circumstances, especially in the case of the opposition of the two rulers, is for the individual to gain a greater awareness of the relationship existing between the lower and Higher selves.

c. *Link by conjunction.* An intense urge toward fusion and the possible birth of a very potent expression of the Soul's purpose in the present incarnation.

d. *No link by aspect.* A life in which the Path of Fusion has to be undertaken with great effort. This leads to the gaining of personal, spiritual responsibility and a very active focus in the co-creation of one's destiny.

e. *The personality ruler and the Soul-centered ruler are the same.* In the case of Scorpio, Leo, and Capricorn, both rulers are the same. The relationship of dispositors to this planet becomes most important. If Mars rules and is in Virgo, note the relationship between Mercury and Mars and the Moon and Mars. The placement by house and sign of the personality-level dispositor (Mercury, in this case) will tell us much about the use of Martial energy by the lower self. The Soul's focus will be revealed by the examination of the Moon's placement by house and sign (Soul-centered ruler of Virgo).

If neither of the two dispositors aspects Mars, then one would focus on the relationship between the Moon and Mercury to amplify the significance of Mars on the personality and Soul levels.

f. *Soul-centered ruler is in dignity.* Should the Moon be in Virgo with Virgo rising (or Jupiter in Aquarius with Aquarius rising, or the Sun in Leo with Leo rising, etc.), an incarnation has been taken in which the potential for the Soul's expression is very strong. Look to the planets closest to the ruler by major aspect for guidance relative to the Ray factors which will condition this unfolding.

2. *Aspect.* The aspects between the planets remain a very important factor. As mentioned above, look to see which level of dispositorship is being activated, and determine the relationship to the houses of the Soul-centered and/or personality-centered chart. This transcendental perspective is very important to the entire system of Soul-centered astrology. The astrologer has to be able to move back and forth between the personality and the Soul levels in order to present a comprehensive picture of the horoscope in question. This is why a thorough grounding in traditional astrology is absolutely mandatory before Soul-centered astrology can be successfully practiced.

The majority of people for whom a Soul-centered chart will be read are individuals whose lives vacillate either on the Fixed Cross or between the Fixed and the Mutable. A few people that we meet "along the Way" are fully anchored upon the Fixed. These will either act as our teachers or our "older" brothers and sisters. In some cases, we are these teachers and older ones, and our horoscopes can be read almost, if not entirely, from the Soul-centered perspective. Our personality charts would then reveal our karmic past, the places where we started in our transformational growth in the present incarnation, and what we leave behind us as we walk the Path. Occasionally, we are blessed by the Presence of a true Initiate whose life energies are being expressed on the Cardinal Cross. Ask Him or Her for a reading!

3. *Octaves.* The nature of what can be considered "octaves of relationship" in Soul-centered astrology differs from the traditional perspective quite considerably. There are three categories of such relationships:

a. *Sacred and non-sacred planets.* Seven planets in our solar system are considered sacred. These are: Vulcan, Mercury, Venus, Jupiter, Saturn, Uranus, and Neptune. The sacred planets serve to fuse the Soul and the personality, and to externalize the Soul force in the daily life. Sacred planets are also involved with the fusion of consciousness and form, and serve to quicken the development of intuition.

Five planets are considered non-sacred; the Earth, Mars, Pluto, the Moon (when not veiling Vulcan, Uranus, or Neptune) and the Sun (when not veiling Neptune). It should be remembered that in the Soul-centered horoscope, the Sun stands for the *physical Sun,* and represents the energy equipment of the personality (what the personality brings into the present incarnation). Once the personality has been fused in consciousness with the Soul, the sacred, Love/Wisdom-centered energy of the Sun emerges into the life.

The effects of the non-sacred planets have much more to do with the life of the personality and with those crises of reorientation which bring about the transformation of consciousness to the indwelling Soul principle. However, it should be mentioned that very few people can respond in an individualized way to the energies of Pluto. Pluto's process of transmutation will work out rather unconsciously in the vast majority of lives. Those who have been awakened to the right use of Will/Power, from the level of the Soul, do have conscious contact with this First Ray planet. Vulcan never expresses through the personality, and should always be considered from the Soul-centered perspective.

b. *Ray relationships.* In the case of five of the Rays, two planets emanate the Ray energy. One of the planets is sacred and one is a non-sacred body. Only the Fifth and the Seventh Rays are associated with a single (sacred) planet. The Ray/planet relationships are as follows:

Ray One: Vulcan and Pluto
Ray Two: Jupiter and the Sun
Ray Three: Saturn and the Earth
Ray Four: Mercury and the Moon
Ray Five: Venus
Ray Six: Neptune and Mars
Ray Seven: Uranus

c. *The Soul and personality rulers of the signs.* Although the Soul-centered rulers cannot be properly classified as "higher octaves" of the personality-level rulers of the signs, they both have to be studied and related, especially pertaining to the houses. As mentioned above, whenever the two rulers of the same sign are in actual aspect, it aligns the personality and the Soul in a very strong bond relative to the houses, Ray energies, and path of fusion concerned.

THE GEOMETRIC ANGLES OF THE SOUL-CENTERED CHART

There are just under four hundred major aspects possible between the twelve planets used in Soul-centered astrology—more, if we take the Ascendant and Midheaven into consideration. It would require a book at least half the size of the current work to outline each of these interconnections in substantial detail. Perhaps one day the author or some other esoteric astrologer will publish such a work. What follows is a table of aspects which, though brief in individual conclusions, will hopefully serve to give the reader an initial understanding. At the very least, each of these passages can amplify the comprehension that has already been established through the reader's foundation in traditional astrology and his or her own study and perusal of this and other esoteric texts. Before presenting this list, it might serve us to review some essential ideas about the major aspects, the Rays, and the planets as they function in Soul-centered astrology, as a summary and an easy reference guide.

The Major Astrological Aspects[1]

1. The *conjunction* (0–10 degrees separating two or more planets) is the most intense interaction of energies between the spheres. It points to the direct fusion of the forces represented by the planets, and has a most dynamic impact on the house in which it is found. It carries a First Ray energy, as it is always indicative of the end of one cycle of relationship and the beginning of another. Thus, the conjunction is a simultaneous vehicle for the Destroyer and the Creator. At its highest expression, it serves to synthesize the energies and Ray qualities of the planets concerned, in order to birth some new expression of Soul potential. In this respect, the conjunction also implies some of the qualities of the Seventh Ray.

2. The *opposition* (180 degrees separating the planets with an orb of +/− 8 degrees) functions to bring about a greater awareness of the relationship between the planets concerned. In order to produce a greater harmony between these two energies, the relationship between them has to be made more conscious and refined, as does the energy of each of the planets and their Ray qualities taken individually. Thus, the opposition can be clearly seen as a Fourth Ray (Harmony through Conflict) aspect. It is an aspect of duality, and epitomizes the struggle between opposing forces. Perhaps the Sixth Ray is also involved with the opposition, as well. After all, it is a Ray of doing battle for principles, ideals, and the affairs to which one is devoted. The opposition does delimit a focus for such battles, as the planetary and Ray forces stand in "counterparallel" to each other.

The battle signified by the opposition will always be played out objectively: an internal force will trigger an external manifestation (in opposition to it); an external manifestation will always trigger an internal conflict. Should the Soul-centered ruler of the Ascendant be in opposition to its personality-level ruler, the "line of battle" between the Higher and lower selves would be very clearly drawn. This makes identification of the major life crises a simple matter to ascertain, although not necessarily simple to resolve. *Look to see if there is a third planet sextile to one end of the opposition and trine to the other. This planet, and its Ray qualities, will be very instrumental in the resolution of the particular Soul-personality conflict.*

[1]To my knowledge, no work has been done up to this time on the relationship of the geometric angles to the Rays. What follows is based on the author's intuition and practical experimentation. The reader is advised to take what is said as the author's conjecture—a conjecture open to revision, additional suggestions, and research.

3. The *square* (90 degrees separating the planets with an orb +/– 8 degrees) is indicative of the crystallization of energy into a tightly anchored thought-form, or pattern of expression. It shows that in the present incarnation there will have to be a release of the energies so contained. It is another aspect of the Fourth Ray, as it reveals a very definite conflict, but without the benefit of the immediacy of relationship inherent in the opposition. There are some Sixth Ray energies involved in this aspect, as usually one is very compulsive and one-pointed about the continuance of the pattern indicated by the square. One is *devoted to past karma* in this respect, and a definite crisis of transformation (Fourth Ray process) has to ensue in order to allow for the freer expression of the energies concerned.

Should the square involve the two rulers of the chart, a very intense battle between the Soul and the personality is quite likely. *Look for a major transit of a slow-moving planet to trigger this conflict. Such a transit will be square to one of the planets and either in opposition or conjunction with the other. This indicates a true time of opportunity for Soul growth and personal evolution.* If two planets of the same Ray are in square (one will be sacred and the other non-sacred), the energies of the non-sacred body will eventually have to yield to those of the sacred. Thus, if Mars is square Neptune in the natal chart, a very potent Sixth Ray conflict is a constant source of pain to the individual in question. It also means that once this struggle has been resolved, the energies of the solar plexus center (Mars) will have fused with those of the heart (Neptune). That would be an incredible struggle and an equally incredible victory!

4. The *trine* (120 degrees separating the planets with an orb +/– 8 degrees) is an aspect of the Third Ray. It shows that there is a great deal of creative activity and movement between the planetary energies and their Ray qualities. It reveals the potential for the continuance of such creative expression in most harmonious ways. An ease of interchange is indicated between the Soul and personality when the rulers of the Ascendant are found to be in this aspect. This same ease of movement between the centers/chakras of the planets so interconnected should also be noted by the astrologer.

5. The *sextile* (60 degrees separating the planets with an orb +/– 4 degrees) carries the energies of the Fifth Ray. The sextile links energies in a very positive way. It is very much connected to Active Intelligence (much as the sextile is a lesser dynamic of the trine), and distributes the energies of the planets and their Ray qualities in a much more detailed radius than the trine. The sextile is concerned with rhythm and movement, and works like Venus, to harmonize and blend opposites and differences.

6. The *inconjunction* (150 degrees separating the planets with an

orb +/– 4 degrees) is an aspect of adjustment and reorientation. It serves to create the need to rebalance the energies of the planets in this condition so that they express themselves in some new and more harmonious manner. In its stressful quality, it brings in some of the energies of the Fourth Ray. In its urge to birth a new expression for an existing pattern, it speaks of the Seventh Ray and the function of Uranus (and the carrying forth of the First Ray through the Seventh). Like Uranus, the effects of an inconjunction are the least predictable of all the aspects. Yet we must consider it as a major geometric link, as it very strongly activates the urge for reorientation and recreation.

The influence of the Second Ray is a part of all the aspects as it, like the geometric angles themselves, serves to fuse and blend. The Second Ray can be called "the cosmic urge to merge," and the astrological aspects embody this magnetic quality.

Application of the Aspects to Delineation

A good rule to follow is that in the Soul-centered chart, planets in square, opposition, and inconjunction are indicative of karmic patterns and energy interchanges in need of reorientation and/or balance. When these aspects connect Soul-centered rulers of houses to personality-level rulers, a clear conflict between the energies of the two selves is manifesting. When planets are in trine or sextile, the energies of the planets and their particular facets of the Ray qualities are harmoniously linked. A fluid and creative stream of energy has been established. As with the more crisis-producing indications above, look especially to the interchange between levels of manifestation to see the Soul and personality pattern emerge.

An understanding of the planets and their signs will reveal the degree of harmony or disharmony inferred by the variable nature of the conjunction. In general, the conjunction gives an opportunity to fuse, blend, and consequently birth some new pattern of relationship between the planets in question. Use your understanding of traditional planetary significances as a guide, but make sure to integrate your understanding of the Rays within this context in order to complete your synthesis of planetary meaning.

Planets and Rays in Aspect
in the Soul-Centered Chart

The Sun should always be looked upon as a vehicle for the energy and Ray of the personality. The Sun always brings in the energy of the Second Ray, adding cohesion and creative potential to one's life. Yet a close examination of the Sun's sign, and that sign's exoteric and esoteric rulers, is very important. Should the Sun be in Aquarius, for example, one would know that the personality is operating through the Fifth Ray as an important field for its expression. Should the Sun be in Capricorn, three Rays are important to the personality (First, Third, and Seventh). In this case, look to the sign Saturn tenants and the Ray of that sign. If Saturn is in Libra, for instance, you know that the Third Ray will be emphasized, as Libra is only found acting through this energy field. If Saturn were in a sign that was not found on any of Capricorn's Rays, look to see what the predominant Ray makeup of the entire chart would be. This will provide a clue as to which of the three Rays may be seen to dominate.

The sign Sagittarius is a special case, as its esoteric ruler, the Earth, is always opposite the Sun, and in this instance, would always be in the sign of Gemini. Thus, we have a very complex combination of Ray forces. The Sun, which is Second Ray, is expressing through a sign of the Fourth, Fifth, and Sixth Rays. We get no clue as to the predominance of any of these three by an examination of the dispositor, since the Earth is a Third Ray planet and Gemini is a Second Ray sign. If we look to the exoteric ruler, Jupiter, we find another source for the Second Ray. It would thus appear that the energy of Jupiter and the Second Ray have a very important, overriding influence on the sign of Sagittarius. After all, the Second Ray is the Ray of Love/Wisdom, and the Archer is very much the embodiment of the Wisdom facet of this Ray. Jupiter and the Sun carry the Love facet, while Gemini is always relating Love to Wisdom and Wisdom to Love.

The dharma of a personality incarnating in Sagittarius—especially a personality that has been or is in the process of being irradiated by the Soul—is the sharing of Love-Wisdom through teaching, and other forms of the distribution of Higher-Mind energy, and is absolutely at the core of that individual's personality purpose. The function of Jupiter and the Second Ray is to blend and fuse. In a sign as complex as Sagittarius—one in which the Second, Third, Fourth, Fifth, and Sixth Rays so strongly predominate—this fusion and blending is seen to be at its most potent in its field of operation. The astrologer's intuition is always going to be the ultimate revealer. This intuition is based on the fusion of his comprehension of exoteric and esoteric astrology and his affinity and compassion for the person in question. This is the Ray of Love/Wisdom in action.

The Moon connects the individual to the past. It brings in the energy of the Fourth Ray and the struggle between form and essence. It represents those patterns and forms of self-expression that have been created and anchored in previous incarnations. It is also the source of the form life, and must come under the direction of the Soul. This control will usually be from several major areas:

1. Vulcan and Uranus—the planets which break down old patterns and provide for the birthing of new archetypes (see passages on the veiling of the Moon).

2. Neptune—the Moon's higher octave, and source for the sacrificial Love which lends itself to be utilized in the world of physical manifestation.

3. The Soul-centered ruler of the chart—the directing impulse for the Soul's purpose in the present incarnation, and thus the controlling, creating focus for the proper forms of expression of that purpose.

Vulcan, planet of the First Ray, is always involved in the process of destruction of outworn "tools" of the personality. It breaks down patterns and thought-forms, desires and attachment to desires, so that the Soul may further externalize its purpose and work.

Mercury, when in aspect with another planet, brings in the energy of the Fourth Ray, but as a harmonizing influence. The energy and function of Mercury seeks to relate pairs of opposites so that a greater creative harmony may eventuate. It is very definitely a vehicle of refinement, as it ever seeks to birth those Divine Ideas for the Plan of human evolution.

Earth's position tells us where, in the practical reality of our daily lives, we may find our dharma/duty/Earth-based responsibility. When in aspect to other planets, it adds the energy of the Third Ray. This serves to give a cohesive focus to Active Intelligence, in order to externalize those concepts and ideas so that dharma may be fulfilled.

Venus is the harmonizing influence of the Fifth Ray, which serves to blend and fuse opposites into greater creative wholes. Venus always gives the potential for greater evolution, development, and abundance of spiritual potential to any planet that she touches. Naturally, when such contact is by a difficult aspect, these benefits may be a bit harder to achieve, but the potential for victory is there.

Mars adds a note of dissonance, so that a greater purity and sense of one-pointed purpose is gleaned from the battles it provokes. It is a planet of great blessing, in this respect, as its ultimate goal is to reorient desire to serve the Plan. That is the function of devotion, as Mars expresses the Sixth Ray on the Soul level.

Jupiter is pure Second Ray, and adds cohesiveness and heart qualities to whatever planet it touches. It works to blend and fuse love and wisdom, heart and mind, into its interactions with other planets and points in the horoscope.

Saturn works primarily on the mental plane, as it serves to structure thought-forms into cohesive patterns for the externalization of the Will/Power. Thus it is the embodiment of the Third Ray of Active

Intelligence. Saturn is also the vehicle for the Dweller on the Threshold, and stands for the Lord of Karma—a barrier to greater conscious expansion, unless Love/Wisdom supersedes all other influences.

Uranus, as planetary significator of the Seventh Ray, is very much involved in the production of new archetypes of manifestation in the outer world. Yet, before such externalizations take place, Uranus helps to condition the intuition so that proper perception of need in the physical reality is attained. It is then that the production of right forms may take place, giving a proper anchor to the One-Three-Five-Seven Ray line of manifestation.

Neptune, when functioning in its purest sense, is a highly spiritual influence on the life. It brings the illumination of the indwelling Love Presence, and serves as a vehicle of sacrifice so that impurities (desire-ridden personality expressions) are reborn into more wholesome expressions of the Love that is the Light. Its Sixth Ray effect on the planets it touches has a great deal to do with the process of dissolving barriers to Love/Wisdom.

Pluto is a powerful First Ray planet that not only destroys nonregenerative patterns of personality expression, but also brings up new sources of creative energy that may be utilized by the Soul. It is thus a limitless pool of resources whose method of expression always requires the destruction of that which is useless for the furtherance of the evolutionary Plan.

Aspects of the *Ascendant* help to define, direct, and modify the expression of the Soul's purpose in the present incarnation. The Rays of the sign on the Ascendant show the force field through which the Soul will be externalizing in order to express its work and orientation to the physical life. *The Ray of the Soul-centered ruler must be blended and understood in order to have a deeper sense of contact with the Soul's purpose.*

Aspects to the *Midheaven* help to define, direct, and modify the culmination of the Soul's purpose in the present incarnation. The Soul-level chart is very instrumental in revealing that culmination of energy (the Goal of the Path). The personality-level chart might be more likely to reveal that Goal as a form of materialized expression in the daily life. The aspects between the two rulers of the Midheaven will be very instrumental in showing the relationship of energy to form in the manifestation of personal destiny. This connection should be studied with particular care, as the results of such an effort are very definitely rewarding.

THE PLANETARY ASPECTS

Please Note: The symbol (+) indicates the results of a trine or sextile between the planets. It is also indicative of a quintile (72 degrees + /– 2 degrees) but to a somewhat lesser extent. The quintile is an aspect that releases energy from the Soul level, and is only effective in the life of one who has developed a certain degree of Soul awareness. The symbol (–) indicates the results of a square, opposition, inconjunction, and to a lesser extent, the semi-square and the sesqui-square. The conjunction (c) should be viewed in light of what was said about its nature on p. 354. In all cases, it indicates a powerful and focused expression between the planets and the Ray energies they represent. The more the unification of the Soul and the personality progresses, the less important are the qualifications of the (+) and (–) aspects. *In essence, the aspects will eventually indicate the Path of achievement and struggle an individual has had to undergo in order to realize the goal of Soul alignment.* It should be carefully noted that the influences of the houses and the aspects (and even the signs, to some extent) gradually give way to the dominance of the Ray energies, as the Soul's influence externalizes.

Aspects of the Sun

Sun/Moon—indicates the creative potential of the personality as it links with the forms of its expression in the past. When in (+) or (c), those proper forms for the expression of the personality are created which nurture the lower self and help it to refine and develop its receptivity to Soul impressions. When the aspects between the two are (–), all creative potential becomes crystallized as a result of unregenerated forms of past activities. The crises of release and reorientation of the lower self would occur throughout the incarnation, until the form life comes under the direction of the Soul.

Sun/Vulcan—is always conjunct in the natural chart. In this combination, the First Ray conjuncts the Second, revealing the constant interplay between Will/Power and Love/Wisdom. The duality and conflict of this position (and the ultimate increase of harmony) is worked out through situations involving the Fourth Ray, as the latter is the fusion and blending of Rays One and Two. Mercury, planet of the Fourth Ray, is never too far from either Vulcan or the Sun.

Sun/Mercury—is always either conjunct or out of orb of a conjunction, as these two bodies can never be more than 28 degrees from one another. Mercury is very much the Son of the Sun in the Human Kingdom. It is the expression of the Son of Mind which is man (Mind being the creative impulse of Divine Manifestation). The expression of Will/Power externalizes through the cohesive power of Love/Wisdom in the world of the conflicts and victories of the Human Kingdom (Fourth Ray). It is Mercury as the Messenger of Mind who relates the First and Second Rays through the activities of the Fourth.

Sun/Venus—can only be conjoined or semi-square, as Venus is never more than 48 degrees away from the Sun. This combination evokes the spiritualization of the Concrete Mind and the application of Love/Wisdom to the functions of science and technology. It is the cohesive expression of the Will-to-Good as realized through the Law of Right Human Relations. The Second Ray blends with the Fifth, producing in the (+) and (c) aspects the qualities mentioned above. When the Sun is semi-square Venus, there is a need to cultivate a balance in one's assessment of the proper application of Love/Wisdom to the world of the Concrete Mind. Difficulties arise in the life when the individual's urge for greater harmony is impeded through the joining and blending of wrong ingredients and/or people.

Sun/Earth—are always in opposition. Their relationship indicates the awakening of the personality to its dharma/Earthly task. The Second and Third Rays blend, resulting in the need to create a loving and wise application of one's mental energies through the establishment of an Earth-based expression of Soul purpose.

Sun/Mars—functions to unite Love/Wisdom with a one-pointed focus for its expression. Mars and the Sun tend to activate the struggles of the Pathwalker along the Way and serve to purify the personality. The Second Ray blends with the Sixth in the (+) aspects to give courage and compassion. The solar plexus is in harmony with the heart, and the power of the lower self comes under the direction of Love/Wisdom. When Mars and the Sun are in (c) or (−) aspect, a battle between the use of personal power and the struggle for Soul control ensues, especially involving the emotional body.

Sun/Jupiter—results in the dynamic expression of the Second Ray. This fusion of energies—especially the (c)—is indicative of a person who serves as a teacher or counselor, with a deep love of knowledge and of humankind. The (+) and (c) aspects usually bestow abundant physical vitality, and a magnanimous and compassionate disposition. Jupiter and the Sun work to blend and fuse differences in beliefs into a single expression of inclusive Love/Wisdom. When in the (−) aspects, one may become blind to the differences one is seeking to blend. There can be an overabundance of optimism and a sense of self-righteousness and self-importance that is out of balance with the circumstances in which one finds oneself. The heart must be brought

into harmony with one's ideals for the proper application of Love/
Wisdom.

Sun/Saturn—combines the Second and Third Rays to bring in the
right use of the Will/Power, as the rulers of Capricorn and Leo pull in
First-Ray energy, giving it focus. This planetary interchange is also an
incredibly potent combination for applied intelligence. When in the
(+) aspects, compassion and Active Intelligence combine to produce
a very masterful individual, quite capable of using the Mind to manifest
his or her function in the Plan. When in (–) or (c) aspect, the manifestation of goals is blocked until the right use of the personal will comes
under the direction of the Soul. The more difficult contacts often
indicate a certain lack of courage and a fear of the creative powers of
authority and responsibility, both from within and outside of oneself.

Sun/Uranus—combines the energies of the Second and Seventh
Rays to produce new forms for the Soul's expression through the
personality. This combination serves to awaken one to the interplay
of the individual and the collective for the purposes of the Higher Self
and the Plan for humanity. The Soul may acquire additional
opportunities to utilize the lower self for its spiritual purposes. With
the (+) aspects, and in certain cases the (c), the personality quickens
to the awareness of archetypes, helping the individual to be able to
perceive and think in categories. The personality easily links with
others in order to demonstrate inclusivity and unanimity as a way of
life. In the (–) aspects, and sometimes in the (c), as well, the personality experiments with ways of self-expression that are contrary to the
Soul purpose. Will goes astray, and the urge to individualize becomes
erratic and completely out of line with the inner Plan for the individual.

Sun/Neptune—leads to a very high degree of spiritual potential,
since Love/Wisdom and devotion are very strong in this combination.
Neptune represents the energy of the Heart of the Sun when it
demonstrates its focus of illumination, unveiling the true nature of the
Soul: inclusive, creative, sustaining Love. The personality in the present incarnation is given the opportunity to sacrifice itself (literally,
"make itself holy/whole") for the Soul purpose. The house position(s)
of Sun/Neptune will reveal where such healing is to take place. In the
(+) aspects, the personality awakens to the spiritual potential of the
life as it becomes a conscious mediator for the externalization of
the Soul consciousness. The individual is able to perceive the inclusive
quality of Love in all interchanges with the outer life. One is most
comfortable when living from the inner self, and may thus prefer
regular periods of solitude. With the (–) and (c) aspects, one may
confuse Soul purpose with desires of the personality, and can give or
devote oneself to causes or people that drain one's vital energy. Fanatic

devotion to causes (addictions) occurs as a result of misapplied Second/ Sixth Ray energies.

Sun/Pluto—is a very powerful combination of First- and Second-Ray energy, as the destructive aspect of Pluto provides a constant opportunity for the renewal and regeneration of Love in the outer life. Constant crises of transformation and reorientation lead to the potent right use of Will/Power by the lower self. With the (+) and (c) aspects, the personality recognizes such crises as part of the Path of its alignment to Soul purpose, and more easily lets go of those nonregenerative habit patterns in its use of creative energy. The individual may serve as a vehicle for catalytic changes in his or her environment. This is a potentially strong contact for healing, but regardless of geometric angle, this combination will bring in the need to transform or release certain nonregenerative facets of the personality life. The (−) aspects are much the same as the above, except that alignment of the personality with the right use of the will may be much more difficult to achieve, even if one sees the crises of the life as part of one's Path. Areas of the personality life in need of transformation are often much more entrenched, and thus harder to uproot and regenerate.

Aspects of the Moon

Moon/Vulcan—always represents a challenge to the past and to the forms of expression through which the Soul must manifest itself in the outer world. The consistent test is one of detachment from the crystallization of matter in order to release new creative potential. The (+) aspects give a consciousness of Soul purpose which makes the needed transformation easier. The (−) and (c) aspects indicate a greater difficulty in the release of these patterns of attachment, which have been a constant issue in one's karma—especially relative to one's biological inheritance.

Moon/Mercury—is an opportunity for the refinement of forms, as Mercury will function to relate those expressions of the past use of energy to new opportunities for the Soul's purpose. The influence of the Fourth Ray is paramount in this combination, and the sign of Virgo and its significance in the horoscope will also be quite important. The (+) aspects, and in some cases, the (c), give the required attunement to the Soul in order to produce the correct forms for the greater expression of harmony in the outer life. The more evolved individual would be aware of the need to produce beauty, as well as a nourishing environment, for the physical sustainment of one's (and others') work on the Path. The (−) aspects, and sometimes the (c), indicate mood swings and constant shifting of activity as the process of detachment from the past is encountered with some degree of difficulty. Inner conflicts resulting from loyalties to previous patterns of behavior, and the urge to continue communicating through these outworn modalities, are also encountered.

Moon/Venus—can bring great spiritual insight into the world of matter. The Fifth and Fourth Rays combine, allowing the Concrete Mind (when focused through the Soul) to be the vehicle for releasing those forms of expression that will be of benefit to humanity. This interplay of planets and Rays also brings about a potential for increased beauty and refinement in the life. The (+) aspects and the (c) add an ease of expression to the above, and can indicate a healing path, as one is able to blend and fuse opposing forces with naturalness and fluidity. The (–) aspects indicate one whose search for perfection in the expression of form leads to an overly mental, critical, or sensuous nature, and an inability to sustain wholeness. There is a conflict between "taste" and nourishment.

Moon/Earth—reveals the interfacing of the past with the dharma of the present incarnation. The relationship between these two bodies is therefore a very important one. Some hints about the significance of this planetary contact to the present incarnation can be gleaned from a study of the positions of the Moon and the Earth relative to the location of the Sun in the natal chart. The (+) aspects lead to the unfolding of the proper forms for the expression of one's Earth-based responsibilities. The Mind serves the purposes of the Soul in relation to our planetary dharma. The (–) aspects and the (c) indicate difficulty in aligning the past and the present; the above is achieved through some very definite crises of detachment, and a consequent reorientation from the past. Some previous, incompleted task has to be fulfilled by the individual in the present incarnation. The house positions of the Earth and the Moon will indicate where such a task has to be completed.

Moon/Mars—is not the easiest of combinations, as there can be a very strong, emotionally-based attachment to the past which inhibits future growth. Fourth and Sixth Ray energies combine, but as Mars is associated with the solar plexus, a distinct crisis in detachment is required in order to bring about the entrance of Neptune, the higher octave of the Moon, and its more evolved, heart-focused Sixth Ray energy. In the (+) aspects, the battle to be fought in order to release past attachments is in alignment with Soul purpose. An individual with the (+) aspects of Mars and the Moon is also able to support and heal others as they go through this battle themselves. The (–) aspects and the (c) show the need for release described above, as the square and opposition embody the "battle of detachment" from previous emotional responses conditioned by personal and biological karma.

Moon/Jupiter—is a combination of Second and Fourth Ray energies which help support the fusion and blending of heart and mind. It is a positive influence, in most cases, especially as it serves to create those forms of human interchange very much geared to the Aquarian Age. This is due to the relationship of Jupiter and the Moon, and their associations with Aquarius and Virgo. The (+) aspects and the (c) stimulate the awakening of the presence of Love in all forms of life. The Moon and Jupiter are a very positive combination for the blending of all seemingly different influences into cohesive wholes for the expression of one's Soul purpose. The (–) aspects can indicate great restlessness and frustration in the expression of one's ideals. There is a tendency to excess and dissatisfaction in the creation of those forms which anchor one's sense of higher purpose.

Moon/Saturn—produces a strong mental focus in the creation of those structures required for the Soul's purpose. There is also the need to establish channels of externalization for the Mind and the expression of Active Intelligence in the outer world. This combination of Third and Fourth Ray energies also gives an awareness and appreciation for process and orderliness. With the (+) aspects, the above is accomplished with ease, and one is also receptive to taking on responsibilities in the physical world. With the (–) aspects and the (c), one is often very manipulative in making sure that one's structures and ideas dominate the environment. One's biological inheritance usually passes on doubt and fear of abandonment, or lack of material sustenance. Often there is too much reliance for personal support on the form side of life. The past thus interferes with the spontaneous mental processes leading to the production of new thought-forms.

Moon/Uranus—indicates a blending of the Fourth and Seventh Rays, and gives a keen perception into the nature of the archetypes and categories in which most human interchanges take place. The intuition is usually quite strong, and there is generally a certain developed skill in handling group situations, as the relationship between the one and the many is part of one's outlook. With the (+) aspects, strong organizing abilities come from the integration of the qualities mentioned above. One can bring great harmony into group dynamics, and is also able to birth new forms of expression for the Soul's purposes, especially when the latter center on organizational and collective goals. With the (–) aspects and the (c), the past is in conflict with the future, and a rebelliousness against the established social order is usually part of the circumstances of one's life. The conjunction gives an especially strong need to express one's rebelliousness against past patterns. This may sometimes be in conflict with the Soul's purpose.

Moon/Neptune—indicates the potential expression of some very strong qualities of love and devotion. An element of sacrifice is always present as, regardless of the individual's personal history or karma, the past has to give way to the needs of the present and to the inclusive quality of the Soul. Part of the purpose for the present incarnation has much to do with the birthing of forms for the in-dwelling Christ Principle. With the (+) aspect, and sometimes the (c), as well, personal needs and desires can easily give way to the needs and desires of the Soul. Reverence for life and a mystical attunement to the unity of all beings are part of the spiritual qualities of the Moon/Neptune. With the (–) aspect, and sometimes the (c), the urge for self-sacrifice may be anchored in the personality, evoking a sense of personal hurt and martyrdom when true giving of oneself is re-quired. There is confusion as to the form and process of releasing the needs and desires of the lower self. One may also possess an exclusive and strongly dedicated focus of one's own spiritual vision.

Moon/Pluto—can give wonderful opportunities to regenerate the past, destroying what is unneeded and making better use of what remains. Will/Power combines with a vision of greater harmony, even though the process definitely involves conflicts in the learning and administration of the right use of will. The future of the Soul's purpose rises up over the ashes of nonregenerative habits, thoughts, and feelings. Detachment must be complete, so that the lesser may be made into a fully conscious vehicle for the Will/Power and Purpose of the Greater. One with the (+) aspects is unafraid of disrupting the past for the benefit of the Soul's purpose. There is a break with the biological karma which can be painful even with the (+) aspects, but the realization of this crisis is a conscious one. With the (–) aspects and the (c), fear enters each time a break with the past is required, so that when it becomes necessary to detach from people and/or the environment, one can do so quite ruthlessly.

Aspects of Vulcan

Vulcan/Mercury—is always either in conjunction with the Messen-ger or out of orb of this aspect. The relationship of Mercury, Vulcan, and the Sun is a very intimate one. The Mind is constantly required to convey new Ideas as an expression of the Creator's Purpose. Vulcan aids in this Work by breaking down the individual's attachment to previous forms of ideation (Fourth Ray) so that new patterns may be utilized as tools for the birth and rebirth of such Ideas (First Ray). It is then that the Soul-centered individual may stand as a mediator for the externalization of the Plan for humanity, and act as a link between the Mind of God and humanity itself. The (c) intensifies this function.

Vulcan/Venus—can only be conjunct or semi-square. Will/Power is added to the Concrete Mind in a sense that renews and vivifies. Human relations are given direction and purpose in order to facilitate the development of new skills. Mercury (which can never be too far away from this contact, either by actual celestial longitude, or by the fact that Venus is the ruler of Gemini) then "delivers the message" to mankind. Old patterns of disharmony, based on the war between opposites, are dissolved through this contact, although the process with the semi-square (and sometimes with the conjunction, as well) can be somewhat painful. Yet we have to realize that Vulcan's effects are only experienced through someone who has achieved a certain amount of Soul contact, and is thus, to some degree, conscious of the reasons for the process which is taking place. The sign of Taurus and the house that it rules in the natal chart will be very important relative to the Venus/Vulcan combination.

Vulcan/Earth—shows that new tools have to be developed or old ones refined in order to fulfill the individual's dharma and sense of responsibility to the planet. Vulcan is always in opposition to the Earth, since it cannot be farther than 8 degrees, 20 minutes from the Sun. When the energies of the First Ray are in opposition to those of the Third, there is a necessity to harmonize Will/Power with Active Intelligence, in order to produce the necessary mental structures and channels for the expression of the Plan. The individual experiences this conflict in his urge for greater alignment of the inner life with his outer activities.

Vulcan/Mars—functions to break any attachment to the personal desire nature, thus allowing the Will/Power to be used for the collective good inherent in the Soul's purpose. Thus, any aspect between Vulcan and Mars will be one of some conflict. If the aspect is (+), this is more likely than not to come under the conscious direction of the Soul as it serves to channel the Will/Power. The (–) aspects and the (c) will add to the intensity of this battle of reorientation.

Vulcan/Jupiter—breaks down inhibitions to the development of new concepts which increase the individual's spiritual awareness. This combination is instrumental in what may be termed the "crises in consciousness" brought about through the periodic doubting of one's belief systems. The result of the blending of Rays One and Two, in this respect, leads to an increase of the focus of Will/Power through Love/Wisdom, thus helping Jupiter to further his function of fusing the heart and mind. Although most aspects between these two planets can produce stress (in fact, all contacts with Vulcan produce tension), the net result is the widening of the inclusive factor in one's way of loving. Naturally, the (+) aspects and the (c) will facilitate the unfolding of these factors, while the (–) aspects bring a more consistent focus of crisis into the life in this area.

Vulcan/Saturn—are difficult to harmonize. Mental patterns are challenged and destroyed so that new structures for the externalization of the Ideas in the Mind of God may work out through the Mind of Man. On a personal level, this produces challenges relating to believing in oneself; that is, in the rectitude of one's mental approach to life. As one can imagine, such a crisis would be very difficult (and suitably required) for a person who is very connected to the One-Three-Five-Seven line of Ray manifestation. The (c) is the most intense indicator of this crisis, while (+) aspects can indicate that this breakdown has already been accomplished and that the present incarnation can reap the rewards from these efforts. The (c) indicates that such new patterns are being developed at the present time, while the (–) aspects point to the challenge and disintegration of such patterns. As with all aspects of Vulcan, this often carries over into the position of the Sun and its implications.

Vulcan/Uranus—is a very close and highly esoteric contact.[2] It involves the birthing of new forms for the expression of the Soul on the level of the human collective. Sometimes this occurs through violent or dangerous circumstances. Those men and women who can integrate the potency of this combination of energies within the context of their individual lives will be serving the collective purpose as a result of their work in the outer world. The (c) indicates some highly individualized way of accomplishing this focus of social development and reorientation. The (–) aspects can point to certain difficulties and social opposition to the accomplishment of their task. The (+) aspects make their work much simpler to accomplish, and give an ability to support or create the evolving social archetypes of the times.

Vulcan/Neptune—is not the easiest combination to understand or explain! My intuition focuses in on the relationship of Neptune as the Heart of the Sun, and thus the conveyor of the Love energy of the Creator. Perhaps Vulcan serves to eliminate any blocks to the externalization of this Loving Presence in one's life; that is, the inner Christ Principle. The combination of the First and the Sixth Rays can give rise to a "soldier of Christ" in no uncertain terms. The (–) aspects may lead one to becoming an "inquisitor"—one who is fanatical in breaking down other people's ways of spiritual devotion in order to replace them with his or her own. Certainly the (–) aspects will lead to a crisis in one's own focus of devotion and, depending on

---

[2]Please refer to the sections on the veiling of the Moon for greater details concerning the relationship of Uranus and Vulcan.

the nature of one's individual power, can externalize into creating the same crises for others. The (+) aspects between Vulcan and Neptune may well indicate that the individual's spiritual battles are involved with bringing about a greater inclusivity to humanity's collective spiritual destiny. The (c) would be quite variable in its effects, and would depend totally on the nature of one's spiritual evolution.

Vulcan/Pluto—gives an amazing focus of First Ray energy that is always present when Pluto is conjunct the Sun. On the Soul-centered level, the' combination of Pluto and Vulcan (and the Sun) is a very forceful expression of the Will/Power. Is the person then an agent for the Will-to-Destroy or for the Will-to-Love? Sometimes one has to be the former in order to serve the ultimate Purposes of the latter. Such is the quandary of a Pluto/Vulcan combination, especially when in (c) or (–) aspect. The (+) aspects between the two show success in the right use of will. All contacts of Vulcan and Pluto reveal a dynamic series of crises in the life that usually take one closer to fulfilling the goals of the Soul's Purpose.

Aspects of Mercury

Mercury/Venus—can never be more than 72 degrees apart; therefore, the only aspects they can form of any real importance are the conjunction, semi-square, sextile, and quintile. The placement of the sign Gemini should be carefully noted, as Mercury and Venus rule here from their respective levels. The potential harmony between these two bodies is evident when we note that Mercury relates pairs of opposites, bringing them into a focus of relationship which Venus can then harmonize, adding a definite spiritual quality to the expression of the energies concerned. The (+) aspects, and especially the (c), give a great potential for the infusion of the Soul's energy into the personality, especially in the areas of human relations, the arts, and the professions. The semi-square denotes the need to bring greater inner harmony into one's life, as this conflict between the Fourth and Fifth Rays can lead to a pedantic or otherwise unbalanced approach to relationships.

Mercury/Earth—can only be one of two aspects; either the opposition or, infrequently, when Mercury is farthest from the Sun (28 degrees), the inconjunction. The Third and Fourth Ray blend of these two bodies creates a relationship whereby mental energies are fusing into their proper forms for the working out of the individual's Earth-based dharma/task. The immediate tension of the opposition makes the focus of this relationship more clearly defined than when the two are in inconjunction.

Mercury/Mars—is usually a very harmonious combination from the Soul level. Its purpose is to clear a pathway so that personal desires do not interfere with the externalization of intuition. The (+) aspects facilitate the birthing of those Ideas which serve to support personal evolution and one's contribution to the collective. Mind works to reveal the Path, while Mars clears the way for its unfolding through the one-pointed energies of the Sixth Ray of the devoted planetary worker. The (c) intensifies one's efforts at creating a proper artistic or professional field through which one's Path may unfold. The (+) aspects give greater ease in the direction of the mental focus, and add drive and determination. The (–) aspects show some conflict between the desires of the lower self and the efforts of Mind to reveal the true direction of the Soul purpose.

Mercury/Jupiter—is a combination of the two planets which govern the Mutable Cross, ruling as they do Gemini and Virgo, Sagittarius and Pisces, from the personality level. The function of these two planets when in mutual aspect (and the work of the Second and Fourth Rays) is to blend dualities into harmonious syntheses which serve to expand the mind, so that it is capable of an increased loving and inclusive perception of reality. The (c) is a clear indication that the above is to be accomplished in the present incarnation. The (+) aspects reveal an inner understanding from the Soul level of the nature of synthesis, which we can rightly call "the Science of Soul Control." The (–) aspects reveal that lessons in duality are still a part of this individual's process of unfolding and that a focus of loving, nondualistic inclusivity has to be established.

Mercury/Saturn—is a most potent combination of mental energies. Mercury and the Fourth Ray create the proper relationships and forms for the expression of Mind. Saturn and the Third Ray work to create those patterns and structures whereby such ideas take on power and a dynamic focus of manifestation. When functioning through the (+) aspects, the mind is strengthened with the ability to give abstract ideas a practical expression. One is able to hold many ideas simultaneously, in consciously created structures of interrelationship. This is often accompanied by a clear and flexible vision of the potential realization of these concepts and ideas, and of their benefit to humanity. Yet flexibility easily becomes rigid patterning when these planets are in (–) aspect with each other. The mind may still be very strong, but its outer, practical expression is hampered by nonregenerative mental habit patterns. The (c) points to the continual need to birth new patterns and structures for the expression of Active Intelligence. It can give a practical but somewhat rigid outlook.

Mercury/Uranus—is a blending of two octaves of mental energy.[3] Intuition, organization, the ability to think in categories, and harmonious expression of ideas, are some of the many benefits that come from this combination. The blending of the Fourth and the Seventh Rays through these planets bestows an innate understanding of the ability to bring order out of chaos. When in (c) or in (+) aspect, the above, positive tendencies are emphasized. When in (−) aspect, there can be a great deal of confusion about the best way to express one's ideas. There are great urges to communicate and to synthesize, but methodology (order) is often lacking.

Mercury/Neptune—at its most spiritual, provides a joining of a Son of Mind (human being) with the Son of God (indwelling Christ principle). It is thus a potent focus for mystical insight into the Love which underlies all ideas and events. The urge to communicate this Soul-focused reality into the outer world is part of the task when the Fourth and Sixth Rays combine through these planets. Neptune rules spiritual desire, or the urge to manifest the Christ—"the destiny of all the nations." Mercury seeks to relate and communicate this Presence into the Minds of Men. When in (−) aspect—and often in the (c), as well—there is some confusion about the way to relate and clarify one's spiritual concepts and visions to oneself and to others. One becomes dissatisfied with the physical surroundings and one's relationship to them, as ungrounded, idealistic, spiritual aspirations tend to take over the life. The (+) aspects seem to bring about a greater balance and harmony between these two forces. If the individual is strongly anchored in the Soul, any combination of Neptune and Mercury will serve to increase spiritual insights and perceptions.

Mercury/Pluto—is a powerful combination which seeks to create transformations in people's minds so that they may be more receptive to the unfolding of the Path and the Soul's reality. When one is about to mount the Fixed Cross but is still strongly connected to the Mutable, this transformation and reorientation is a very personal one. It will indicate that the ideas and concepts of the personality have to be "killed off" so that they may be regenerated by the inclusivity of the Soul's mental expression. Once on the Fixed Cross, activities increasingly turn from the fulfillment of personality desires to service to the collective. The (c) and (−) aspects intensify the need for this redirection of mental energy. There is often a conflict about the right use of will,

---

[3]To me, the combination of Mercury, Saturn, and Uranus symbolizes the energies of astrology. Uranus gives archetypical awareness; that is, the ability to see the relationship between the macrocosm and the microcosm. Mercury bestows the Fourth Ray quality of relating the higher (abstract concepts regarding the nature of energy) through the lower (rational mind). Saturn adds structure and potency to Active Intelligence, as well as a sense of personal responsibility, which is so essential to one engaged in astrology professionally.

also, as the personality can use mind for self-serving purposes. The (+) aspects, when expressed on the Soul level, give a harmonious relationship between the Will/Power and the expression of Mind.

Aspects of Venus

Venus/Earth—is only possible through one minor (the sesqui-square) and two major (the inconjunction and the opposition) geometric angles. Of course, all three of these are (–) and challenging ones. In effect, the purpose of Venus in aspect to the Earth is to reveal to humanity (through right human relationships and the Laws which govern the Soul) that the "Light of Mind" is Love. As humanity is referred to in the Ancient Wisdom Teachings as the "Sons and Daughters of Mind," all connections between the Earth and Venus are lessons about the essential quality of love.[4]

Venus/Mars—bestows the clarity of the Fifth Ray energy of the Concrete Mind—reason—upon the passions of personal desires. Venus thus serves to modify Mars through this gift of the "Light of Mind" which is spiritual love. It is thus that the desire nature comes under the direction of the Soul. We should also keep in mind that it is through the relationship of Venus and Mars that the solar plexus center gains rapport with the Third Eye. The (c) points to an intensification of focus in this planetary relationship. Although this combination increases one's magnetism and personal attractiveness, the relationship between love and desire is not always so clear. The (–) aspects point to a direct conflict between the two, and thus between the energies of the Fifth and Sixth Rays. The (+) brings a fluid interchange between love and the nature of personal desires, allowing the entrance of the more spiritual qualities of the Sixth Ray into human relationships.

Venus/Jupiter—is the most benefic of all planetary interchanges (although Sun/Jupiter and Sun/Venus are very beautiful combinations, as well). Jupiter's task of blending the mind and the heart, and aiding in the fusion of the lower and Higher selves, is given a tremendous boost when in aspect with Venus. The (c) and the (+) aspects give spiritual insight into all human relationships, and bring out the highest quality of rapport in every situation in which the individual may find herself. Refinement, serenity, and the power to fuse any and all opposing forces are part of the many gifts which this combination

---

[4]Venus has a very special relationship with our planet—an esoteric and beautiful one. It would be worthwhile for the interested reader to explore this connection through further research in Blavatsky's *The Secret Doctrine* and in Bailey's *Esoteric Astrology*.

bestows. The (–) aspects still carry many of these benefits, but there is a tendency to desire personal popularity, and there is often a liking for theatrics—especially those with spiritual or philosophical over-tones. At times, the (–) aspects between Jupiter and Venus indicate a person who projects false idealism and inappropriate spiritual quali-ties into his or her relationships.

Venus/Saturn—can be a very difficult combination of energies from the personality level, as it often inhibits or denies the "love connec-tion." Yet it is one of the greatest gifts from the level of the Soul, as it teaches the individual about right responsibility in human relation-ships. Venus/Saturn is very much the embodiment of the Law of Karma, in most aspects of human life. The Third and Fifth Rays combine to allow the Light of Mind to dominate the personal life. This is not the best combination if one is very romantically inclined, as *it does not allow romanticism to proceed unless the love nature is following the Law*. The (c) requires that one create new patterns of human relations that exhibit a closer adherence to the Law of Right Human Relations. The (–) aspects continue to reveal that previously established patterns of interrelations are no longer suitable for the Soul's expression. The (+) aspects, however, show that one's patterns and attitudes toward relationships may indeed be quite suitable for Soul expression. As a result, there will be an increase and/or refine-ment in the nature of one's responsibilities toward others in this lifetime.

Venus/Uranus—reveals much about the process of the transference from the personal life to the impersonal life. The house that holds Libra on its cusp should be closely examined in order to see how its affairs relate on the Soul and personality levels. As group conscious-ness develops, the need for one-to-one relationships eventually syn-thesizes into the development of an individual-to-the-collective relationship. The (c) shows a gift for organizing people and for blending individual talents with those of the group. It is thus a very powerful (and harmonious) blending of the Fifth and Seventh Rays. The (+) aspects reveal that there is a great ease of communication and movement between people of all different types and interests, and makes the blending of the personal and the impersonal far easier than does the square or opposition between these two planets. The (–) aspects show that there may be some difficulty, both in the present and in past incarnations, in making the necessary transference from the attachment to personal needs to fulfilling the needs of others. In effect, Venus/Uranus aspects tend to embody the "Science of Relationship."

Venus/Neptune—from the level of the personality is a combination which, although artistically and aesthetically oriented, usually brings about a great deal of confusion in one's romantic life. One simply doesn't know how much to merge and to what degree self-sacrifice is necessary. Strong aspects between Neptune and Venus are often found in the horoscopes of those people aspiring to a Soul-centered life. *The Path of Discipleship is also a Science.* Venus and Neptune, the Fifth and the Sixth Rays, embody a very important aspect of this science— one that has to do with the awakening of the urge to sacrifice. On the Soul level, this aspect requires that the lower self be a conscious vehicle for the indwelling Christ Principle. Even with the (+) aspects, the path of reorientation of romantic idealism inherent in this combination can be quite difficult to achieve. The (–) aspects, and often the .(c), will definitely bring about conflicts in this area.

Venus/Pluto—is a combination which brings death and regeneration to all patterns of interrelationship that do not provide a proper channel for the expression of the Soul. Once the individual has learned the lessons of the right use of Will/Power, he or she may become a healer and help people to release themselves from such nonregenerative ways of dealing with others. The Concrete Mind can then be utilized as a means of communicating the Will-to-Love. The (c) and the (–) aspects indicate a certain compulsiveness in the urge to control others. There will most likely be at least one crisis of reorientation of the love nature during the course of the lifetime. This often comes about through the loss (not necessarily by physical death) of a cherished person. The result of this pain brings about the regeneration of one's life values in terms of human relationships. The (+) aspects ease the intensity of such circumstances, and also give one the opportunity to communicate the results of these lessons quite effectively with others.

Aspects of Earth

Earth/Mars—indicates the need to resolve any conflict that impedes the working out of our Soul purpose on this planet, through the interference of the personal desire nature. The (+) aspects reveal that there is a positive blending of the Third and the Sixth Rays. Thus there is a clear mental picture of what has to be done, and the drive and one-pointedness to do it. The (c) is also the opposition of Mars to the Sun, and thus, like the (–) aspects, between the Earth and Mars, can overstimulate the devotional urge to one's envisioned purpose, increasing the input from the solar plexus and creating an overzealous nature.

Earth/Jupiter—is a blending which allows, from the perspective of the (+) aspects, a harmonious fusion between heart, mind, and Earth-focused purpose in the present incarnation. The (c) and the (–)

aspects may overemphasize the scope of personal importance in the accomplishment of one's dharma, thus lessening some of the more inclusive qualities of Jupiter (and the Sun) and the Second Ray.

Earth/Saturn—is a very strong blending of Third Ray energies. The (+) aspects indicate the potential for the mind to be a highly useful tool in the structuring of one's purpose on Earth. Look to the aspects with Mercury, as the combination Saturn-Earth-Mercury is a very potent one for the practical expression of mental energy. The (c) and the (–) aspects, however, can inhibit the fluid externalization of one's use of Active Intelligence. The (c) is also the opposition of these two planets to the Sun. This indicates that more self-love has to be developed in order to engender a sense of self-actualization, and thus increase the creative potential of the present incarnation.

Earth/Uranus—gives the potential for organizational ability, intuition, and an ordered methodology. When these two planets are in (+) aspects, the Seventh and Third Rays combine to express the above qualities in the actualization of one's Earthly purpose. When in (c) or (–) aspects, a lack of cohesion and a disorderly approach to anchoring one's vision occurs. There is usually some problem that makes it very difficult to create new forms for the expression of one's creative potential in the present incarnation.

Earth/Neptune—indicates a potential conflict. When these planets are in (c) or (–) aspect, the struggle is between idealism and a practical approach to the use of Active Intelligence. The Third and Sixth Rays are very different, as the former is the strongest of the mental Rays, while the latter is a very potent force for the expression of the personal, emotional body. It takes a highly trained or developed Soul to be able to anchor and blend the focus of the personality (Sun) with the strong idealism inherent in Earth/Neptune (–) aspects. The (+) aspects, and even the (c) or the more difficult contacts, are always modified by the level of Soul growth. Neptune is the Heart of the Sun, and its contact with the Earth in the (+) aspects can reveal a very deep spiritual commitment to Love/Wisdom in the present incarnation. Some sacrifice of the personal desire nature will ordinarily have to be made in order to bring about the fullest realization of what this Soul-centered purpose may be.

Earth/Pluto—endows the individual with the ability to uncover the hidden resources in the physical realm, in order to complete or anchor his dharma on this planet. In the (+) aspects, the Will/Power can be focused in such a way that it eliminates and transforms any of the lower forces that seek to stand in the Way. The (c) or the (–) aspects can give to the personality an inordinate sense of personal power, thus creating a crisis in the right use of will.

Aspects of Mars

Mars/Jupiter—is one of the most potent combinations of planetary influences when combined and/or integrated positively into the life. It is very definitely the indicator of the "spiritual warrior" who does battle in the name of Love/Wisdom. When in the (+) aspects with Jupiter, the Sixth Ray influences of Mars serve the individual well by giving devotion to the Path. Courage blends with idealism in order to harmonize duality and to increase the presence of Love in the world. False or exaggerated altruism, exclusivity of belief, and devotion to personal spiritual concepts are some of the indications of the (–) aspects. The (c) tends to be more positive, and points to an orientation that refines and gives greater impetus to one's Path.

Mars/Saturn—is not the easiest of combinations from the level of the personality, especially in the (–) aspects, including the (c). The Third and Sixth Rays are in conflict, leading to the creation of mental patterns that seek to empower the personal desire nature. This leads to the blockages of such desires, frustration, and the eventual failure of goals based on those impulses coming from the solar plexus. But Mars is exalted in Capricorn, and the (+) aspects allow personal desires to come under the direction of Active Intelligence, thus clearing a pathway in the life for the right use of the Will/Power.

Mars/Uranus—can be extremely positive, when activated from the level of the Soul. Uranus is very closely connected to the sexual (sacral) center in the human organism. Mars is the dominating influence over the center of personal emotions (solar plexus). When these two bodies are in (+) aspect, and/or under the direct control of the Higher Self, they inspire the generation of those forms in the physical life that advance the devotion to the Plan for both the individual and for humanity. If the aspect is (–), or if these two planets are at work through the level of the personality, misuse of sexual energy may easily result. The Sixth Ray, one-pointed quality of Mars is then geared to the development of new and experimental sexual desires (through the Ceremonial Magic and Order of the Seventh Ray/Uranus). This can easily lead to the perversion of the personal will through misapplied sexual activity. The (c) indicates the potent and intense release of either the positive or negative influences of this combination, depending on the level of personal evolution.

Mars/Neptune—is a very powerful expression of the Sixth Ray. Whenever these two planets are joined by mutual aspect, the message is quite clear: a strong connection has to be made between the energies of the solar plexus and those of the indwelling Christ Principle. Thus, the desires of the lower self have to be given over to the needs of the Soul and its healing mechanism. This is a facet of the self-sacrifice inherent in Neptune. If the individual can create such a transformation in the present incarnation, he or she becomes a potent vehicle for the energies of Love/Wisdom, which stand so closely behind the Sixth Ray. The (+) aspects give courage and direction in the discovery (and sharing) of spiritual truth—the greatest of which is that Love/Wisdom rules in our solar system. The (c) and the (–) aspects indicate a certain degree of confusion relative to this Path of self-sacrifice, and the ultimate redemption of the lower self through devotion to the Life of the Second Ray.

Mars/Pluto—is a combination which, when active from the level of the personality, or when in (–) aspect, tends to stimulate the will to utilize the power of the lesser self for the goals of personal desires. One can be quite ruthless in carrying out the intense, compulsive expression of the lower nature. The opposition gives a great deal of tension between the will of the lower self and the impulsing urges of the Will-to-Good coming from the Soul. But such a conflict is more easily perceived with the opposition than with the other (–) aspects or the (c). The (+) aspects between Mars and Pluto allow for the Will/Power (expressing through the loving focus of the Soul) to align itself harmoniously with the lower self, thus stimulating the purpose of transformation and reorientation in one's individual and collective life experiences. The (c) is especially significant, in that it intensifies the urge to fuse the lower and Higher selves so that the energies of the solar plexus come directly under the influence of the crown center, and thus are a potent source for the Will-to-Good.

Aspects of Jupiter

Jupiter/Saturn—joins the energies of the Second and Third Rays. In effect, the interchange between Jupiter and Saturn creates parameters and structures for the expression of Love/Wisdom. When operating through the (+) aspects, this is a very potent and extremely creative fusion of forces, as Jupiter's task of blending influences takes on the proper channels of expression. Intelligence becomes activated through Love/Wisdom, while Love/Wisdom can formulate itself through the dynamics of Mind. The (c) serves to create new patterns through which Love and Intelligence may fuse and blend. Thus the (c) can give abundant creative opportunities, when operating from the Soul level. The (–) aspects, as well as the (c), when operating from the personality level, show that previous mental patterns and structures stop the flow of Love/Wisdom. The fusing qualities of Jupiter and the Second Ray are thereby inhibited by blockages in their channels of release or by crystallized thought-forms.

Jupiter/Uranus—combines the energies of the esoteric and exoteric rulers of Aquarius. This sign, and its placement by house cusp, should be noted in order to assess the effects of these two planets relative to their levels of expression. The functions of Uranus and the Seventh Ray are deeply involved with the fusion of Spirit and matter in order to produce the forms of life that properly express the Will and the Plan. When these energies are combined with those of Jupiter and the Second Ray, we have what the Tibetan calls a fusion of "planets of beneficent consummation." These bodies are especially important to the unfolding of the New Age, and when they combine in the individual's natal chart by (+) aspect, they indicate a person who can distribute and share those energies that condition the formulation of the coming Era. The deep thirst for new knowledge can be utilized by the Soul-centered individual for the service of humanity. When in (c), this urge is definitely intensified. The next conjunction of Jupiter and Uranus takes place at 5 degrees Aquarius in February 1997. What a wonderful and auspicious placement! The (–) aspects instill the same urge for shared understanding, but there is often an inconsistency of approach and a conflict of doctrines, making the fusing and synthesizing effects of these two planets difficult to align.

Jupiter/Neptune—is potentially one of the most beautiful and spiritual of combinations, as it joins Love/Wisdom to the devotion of the indwelling Christ Principle. When in operation from the level of the Soul, it bestows upon the individual a tremendous gift of healing and compassion. It allows for a very universal and inclusive approach to life, and definitely inclines one toward a mystical orientation. The (+) aspects keep the spiritual aspirations and urge to be of service in balance, while the (–) aspects make these energies difficult to integrate into the life. This is due to the fact that there is an overdeveloped sense of self-sacrifice, and a nature which is too altruistic and impractically idealistic. Disappointments based on the crashing down of self-created false idols (ideals) are often part of the life experiences. The result tears away spiritual glamour, revealing a greater (and often simpler) truth. As always, the (c) intensifies the experience inherent in the blending of these energies.

Jupiter/Pluto—is a powerful combination of the First and Second Rays that serves to destroy any barriers to the fusion of the lower and Higher selves. Strong Jupiter and Pluto aspects in the natal horoscope indicate a person who will serve to birth, transform, and expand spiritual concepts in people's minds and hearts. This can be done somewhat forcefully, through the conscious tearing down of previous ideals. The (c) is especially potent for, in addition to the above, it also indicates a deep pool of spiritual resources stored in the Higher Mind of the individual concerned. The (+) aspects embody the qualities mentioned above, but the experiences leading to the regeneration of one's spiritual awareness are more harmonious than those indicated by the (–) aspects. The latter constantly challenge one's beliefs, forcing one to dig ever deeper in the pursuit of Truth.

Aspects of Saturn

Saturn/Uranus—can be somewhat difficult to handle on the personality level, as the (–) aspects and the (c) serve to highlight a battle between that which is established and that which is new. When these angles of relationship are being expressed on the Soul level, the individual is often at the forefront of social development projects, fighting to unite the conservative and innovative sides to any issue. The (+) aspects give a fluid interchange between the Third and the Seventh Rays, allowing Active Intelligence an ease of expression into the forms and structures of society. As Capricorn is found on both the Third and Seventh Rays, there is a line of affinity between these two planets. The (+) aspects between Saturn and Uranus are therefore very harmonious in the creation of strong physical anchors for the externalization of the Mind of Creation and the individual Soul purpose.

Saturn/Neptune—is not the easiest combination of influences to integrate, as the Third and Sixth Rays are very different in their functions and effects. The (–) aspects and the (c) are particularly challenging, as the Mind finds itself in conflict with the emotional and devotional focus of Neptune and the Sixth Ray. This is especially true from the angle of the personality, where Neptune also strongly affects the solar plexus. The (+) aspects serve to fuse Active Intelligence with devotion to spiritual ideals and causes. The Mind can thus become a more highly spiritualized vehicle for the expression of the indwelling Christ Principle. The effects of Neptune's influence are also quite positive, as Saturn provides those effective channels for a more practical unfolding of devotion to one's spiritual ideals and field of service to humanity.

Saturn/Pluto—in any combination, is a very potent focus of the creative energies of the Will/Power. With the (c), the primary function of the fusion of these energies is to destroy any barriers to the construction of new forms of social institutions and societal enterprises that will be of benefit to the collective. The conjunction in Leo was in effect from September 1946 to July 1948 (while both planets were in this sign from August 1946 to May 1949), indicating a generation that would rebuild the world after the tremendous catastrophes of World War II. The (–) aspects have a great deal to do with uncertainty about the direction of the necessary destruction in one's (or society's) life in order for such rebuilding and regeneration to take place. There is a definite urge to wield power, but difficulty in executing this urge correctly. The (+) aspects take on the qualities of the (c) mentioned above, but with less intensity and greater harmony.

Aspects of Uranus

Uranus/Neptune—indicates a fusion of the Sixth and Seventh Ray rulers from the collective level of the Soul. These rulers are also the primary planets of the Piscean and Aquarian Ages. Those individuals with strong (+) aspects between the two are the harbingers of the New Age, and embody the energy of the cuspal forces that link one World Era to the other. The (+) indications lead to a harmonious fusion between devotion to spiritual ideals and the forms that such visions take in the practical world. The sense of the collective expression of the indwelling Christ Principle is very strong. The (–) aspects indicate individuals and a generation that can have some conflict between their spiritual ideals and their practical applications. The (c) aspects (which will occur within 1 degree of exactitude at 18 degrees Capricorn on April 19, 1992, and then exactly at 19 degrees Capricorn on February 2, 1993) indicate a strong fusion of these two Ray energies. The placement of the (c) in Capricorn emphasizes the Seventh Ray over the Sixth, and could indicate a generation that will be especially pragmatic (and perhaps quite formal) in the application of collective spiritual and social principles and ideals.

Uranus/Pluto—joins the First and Seventh Rays in a very close bond. This indicates that there is a Power to manifest the Will of the Plan into the outer world. Soul-centered individuals born during the last (c) of these two bodies (August 1962 to June 1969) will be very much involved in the dynamic creation of new forms for the expression of that Will-to-Good. As the (c) occurred in Virgo, the Second and Sixth Ray qualities of Love/Wisdom and Devotion will certainly modify the expression of the social transformations that this generation will seek to create. The (+) aspects are very much involved with the transformation of previous social structures and archetypes into the birthing of new collective patterns for society. The (–) aspects are also inclined to social change but, unlike the ease and fluidity of the (+) contacts, such reorientations are not particularly smooth, and may often occur during circumstances of great social upheaval.

Aspects of Neptune

Neptune/Pluto—combines the energies of the First Ray and the Sixth. The only major aspect that these two planets make is a sextile, which lasts from 1943 to 1998, and as a result, it has a great collective importance. These two bodies, when combined at such a 60-degree angle, produce a link between the Will/Power of the Creator and its expression through Devotion to the indwelling Christ Principle. The last fifty years of this century are blessed by this combination, and add to the healing and transformational circumstances experienced by humanity as we approach the New Age. Soul-centered people with this sextile serve to embody these energies through their positive individual and group-oriented activities. Those centered in the personality will only find that they are receptive to these efforts on the part of the New Group of World Servers and others who are oriented to Goodwill.

PART THREE

A GUIDE TO THE SOUL-CENTERED DELINEATION OF THE NATAL CHART

13

Points to

Ponder

I cannot too strongly reiterate the constant necessity for you to think in terms of energies and forces, of lines of force, and energy relationships. . . . The whole story of astrology is, in reality, one of magnetic and magical inter-play for the production or externalization of the inner reality. . . .

—Alice A. Bailey
Esoteric Astrology

In the previous two chapters, I have given a number of indications on the approach to the delineation of house, sign, Ray, and planetary implications. I would like to present a number of other helpful in-structions at this point that will aid the astrologer in his or her interpretation of the Soul-centered horoscope as it relates to the ordinary, personality-focused natal chart.

INTUITION

Intuition is a quality of the Soul and can be developed in anyone who is willing to make the necessary effort. The development of the astrologer's intuition is absolutely essential for the correct assessment of the relationship between the "two" horoscopes. Such an unfolding occurs through the astrologer's efforts at meditation and the deep contemplation of what has been gleaned from the Ancient Wisdom Teachings. It also comes from establishing a disciplined attitude of objective observation, both over one's own life and actions, as well as over the life around oneself. The "eye of the Observer" has to be opened through a sense of loving detachment, so that the mind and the heart consciously combine. All of this takes time, patience, and hard work, but, from the evolutionary perspective, it is an essential part of the training required to advance oneself. Intuition is also developed through service and sharing, as it requires an awareness of a whole outside of, and yet inclusive of, oneself.

Astrology seeks to measure and define Divine Creative Consciousness as it works to unfold Itself. I have always perceived astrology as an intuitive science, utilizing a system of logically interrelated points of reference for its expression. I felt this way years before coming in contact with the Work of the Tibetan and the more esoteric aspects of the Ancient Wisdom Teachings. The rational mind, concrete logistics, and physical measuring devices are quite limited, in this respect, and must be used as extensions of the higher human faculties of cognition. Intuition and its telepathic uses are fast becoming an ordinary instrument of communication among today's more advanced humanity.

Everyone has had the experience of thinking about someone, and having the telephone ring a few minutes later, only to find that that person has called. Sometimes the timing is even closer—one picks up the telephone to call a friend, and finds the friend on the line, even though the phone has not yet rung. Intuition and telepathic communication will evolve into a common tool for the vast majority of humankind as we progress into the New Age and beyond.

The accuracy of astrological interpretation, and the attunement to the unfoldment of celestial cycles as they relate to human activities, requires the astrologer to develop several faculties of awareness, all based on intuition:

1. An intimate contact with the thought-forms contained within the symbols of the twelve signs. We are told in the Teachings that such thought-forms were anchored in Atlantean times.

2. An attunement to the nature of the life forces in our solar system as they work through the planets. The basic definitions of these energies are simple enough to acquire—Jupiter equals expansion, Saturn equals consolidation, Mercury equals mental communication, etc. Yet, as we have been studying in this volume, the inner nature of the planetary Lives is far more profound. Intuition links our individual consciousness to the consciousness of these planetary life forces so that we come to know them as integrated aspects of ourselves.

3. A comprehension of the Ray energies, and then an attunement to their essential nature. We will thus come to understand the Rays as the primary sources of the planetary life energies.

4. An attunement to those mutations in the collective consciousness which affect us all. Thus, through intuition, the astrologer is able

to see the relationship between current world conditions and the nature of planetary transits, eclipses, and other astronomical and astrological factors. He or she can then relate these conditions in terms of their significance in the life and consciousness of the client.

INTERFACING

The great majority of us are working to align and integrate the energies of our personality with those of our Soul. It is therefore very important to be able to properly juxtapose these influences in the natal chart. It is through the one horoscope of birth that the "two" charts can be viewed simultaneously. This is accomplished by applying the following methodology:

1. Interpret the nature of the chart based around the Sun sign and the ordinary, exoteric planetary rulers of the signs and houses. This will give a very good assessment of the planets, aspects, and other astrological implications in the life of the lower self. The less evolved the consciousness, the more important will be the position of the planets by houses. The houses are those facets of life which indicate the areas of the attachment of the energies of the personality.

2. The Sun sign, with its exoteric planetary rulers, reveals the equipment of the personality for the present incarnation. It will serve as the background for the unfoldment of the Soul's purpose. The primary Ray of the Sun sign will reveal much about the nature of the personality. The Sun sign speaks to the astrologer about the immediate possibilities inherent in a given lifetime.

3. When we build our interpretation of the natal chart around the rising sign and the esoteric rulers of the signs and houses, the spiritual goals of the present incarnation reveal themselves. This is the Soul-centered chart, indicating Soul purpose. This Soul-centered horoscope opens our understanding of the spiritual future of the person whose chart is in front of us. It thus demonstrates those opportunities for true service and evolutionary advancement. The Soul-centered chart also shows the nature of a person's particular contribution to the collective unfoldment of humanity.

4. When we interface the horoscope of the Sun sign with that of the esoteric significance of the rising sign, we will then see the relationship of the Soul and the personality quite clearly. In this way we can judge how the present incarnation and current life situations either help or inhibit the linkage of the Soul and the personality. In effect, the path of this fusion indicates the crises and rites of passage which

permit the synthesis of the present life stream into the more eternal stream of the Soul's experience.

5. Your delineation of the esoteric horoscope should be superimposed over the exoteric chart. In this manner, you will obtain a clear picture of the relationship between the Higher and lower selves and their expression in natal astrology. In this respect, you must especially contrast the two dispositors (that is, the exoteric and the esoteric) of each of the planets and the houses. If the rising sign is Libra, for example, an understanding of Venus by sign, house, and aspect will tell you much about the basic temperament and personal comportment of an individual on the personality level. A similar examination of Uranus, however, will tell you a great deal about the direction of Soul purpose and growth. This kind of juxtaposition and contrast has to be done for each of the planets and houses. Should the dispositor be the same planet (as in the case of Leo and the Sun, Capricorn and Saturn, and Scorpio and Mars), you must interpret the planets from their two different levels of expression in order to properly assess this intermingling of forces in the person's life.

PLANETS AND RAYS

1. All of the chakras have Ray correspondences, as well as planetary ones. The relationship of the sacred and nonsacred planets to the chakras, and their implications about the Soul and the personality, should be carefully considered. Please refer to the diagrams, tabulations, and necessary chapters in this book for references.

2. It is very important to note the differences in the effects of the sacred and nonsacred planets in other areas, as well. The nonsacred planets tend to work more in the life of the personality, setting up certain conflicts that bring about a greater focus of Soul awareness. The sacred planets work to fuse and blend the Soul and the personality. Mars, for example, will definitely highlight the nature of the battle between the lower and the Higher selves (especially in the house in which it is found). Jupiter will serve to heal the wounds of such a conflict through its Second Ray fusing power and the inherent Love quality of its energy. By revealing its higher, spiritual significance, Jupiter, through its Wisdom aspect, would also help the individual use the information gleaned in such a battle to expand his or her consciousness.

3. Each of the planets is governed by one of the Rays. Note the influence of the Ray energies as they work out through the Soul and the personality in the natal chart. Blend your understanding of the Ray

forces with your knowledge of planetary implications. Saturn, for example, is closely connected to the Third Ray of Active Intelligence. It is also the planet of consolidation, structure, and limitation. Thus, the blended influence of this planet's Ray and archetypical energies would lead us to say that Saturn works to create those structures on the Earth and on the mental plane which aid in the expression of Active Intelligence. Thus, Saturn is most helpful in the unfolding of one's mental concepts and visions into more practical realities.

THE MOON AND THE VEILING OF PLANETS

1. The Moon indicates what is past. It is the vehicle for one's biological karma, and indicates a great deal about the physical body and the particular type of attachment that one may have to the form life. It acts as a container for previously alive thought-forms, experiences, and energies. Its traditionally interpreted effects are found to be significant only in relation to the lower self, which is very much moved into action through attachment and response to previous patterns of desires, emotions and instincts.

2. From the esoteric point of view, the Moon is a totally dead body. Its effect on the life of the Soul, and even on the life of a person who is struggling between the Mutable and the Fixed Crosses, is relatively nil. The Moon does serve, however, as a veil over other influences—specifically, those of Vulcan and Uranus. It is not necessary to repeat at this point what has already been written in earlier chapters about this veiling effect (as well as the relationship between the Sun and Neptune in this regard). But it is important to stress that the astrologer should experiment with substituting Vulcan or Uranus for the Moon, and Neptune for the Sun, in the Soul-centered chart. There is much to be learned from such interfacing and blending of influences. In most cases, the Moon will be veiling Vulcan in the earlier stages of Soul fusion, while she will be substituting for Uranus in the lives of men and women who have been walking the Path a bit longer.

3. To summarize, we can say that, from the perspective of the Soul-centered chart, the Sun is the present, the Moon is the past, and the rising sign points to the future.

14

The Delineation of the

Soul-Centered Horoscope

of Mahatma Gandhi

The human being in his eventual recognized group rela-
tionships is of more importance than appears in his indi-
vidual life, which the orthodox horoscope seeks to elucidate.
It only determines his little destiny and unimportant fate.
Esoteric astrology indicates his group usefulness and the
scope of his potential consciousness.

—Alice A. Bailey
Esoteric Astrology

Persons in power should be very careful how they deal
with a man who cares nothing for sensual pleasure, noth-
ing for riches, nothing for comfort or praise or promo-
tion, but is simply determined to do what he believes to be
right. He is a dangerous and uncomfortable enemy—be-
cause his body, which you can always conquer, gives you
so little purchase upon his soul.

—Gilbert Murray
Hibbert Journal

It is only fitting that we close this volume about the astrology of the
Soul by delineating the horoscope of one who was called "Mahatma"—
a title coming from two Sanskrit words, *maha* (great) and *atma* (soul).
The struggles of the Advanced Disciple of the Path in fusing and
balancing spiritual Ideas into forms for the advancement of humanity
are clearly seen through the intense Fourth Ray influence in this
horoscope.

Gandhi was born with Scorpio rising and Mercury, ruler of the
Fourth Ray, conjoined the Ascendant in that sign. The other Fourth

Ray body, the Moon, is at the Midheaven, in strong aspect to four planets which are all situated in signs of this Ray (Taurus and Scorpio). The importance of Scorpio and the Fourth Ray is further emphasized by the fact that all three rulers of Scorpio are in Fourth Ray signs. Mars, the Soul-centered ruler of the Ascendant, is in the first house in the sign of the Scorpion, while Pluto, co-ruler of Scorpio on the personality level, is in Taurus. Mercury, the Hierarchical ruler of Scorpio, is conjoined the Ascendant, which points immediately to the fact that he was destined to become an instrument of the Planetary Hierarchy of Masters and Teachers for the accomplishment of some major task.

Harmony through Conflict is very definitely the theme of the entire

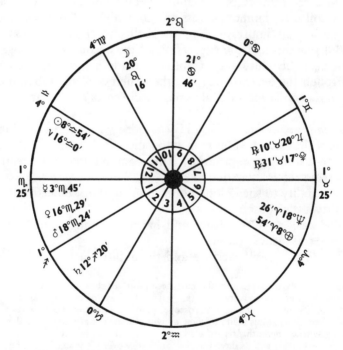

Horoscope 2: Mahatma Gandhi, born in Porbandar, India October 2, 1869 at 7:33 A.M. LMT

life of this Great Soul.[1] Not only is this revealed to us by the predominance of Fourth Ray signs and planets in the natal chart, but this
influence is markedly fixed through the conjunction of Venus (harmony) and Mars (conflict) in Scorpio (sign of the Fourth Ray and the
Path of the Disciple) in the first house (the Way of Soul unfoldment).

Gandhi would strive to build a new form of nationhood for his
people. He would repeatedly risk (and ultimately lose) his life, trying
to unite the forces of Islam and Hinduism into a single India of all
people living as brothers and sisters. He would develop the principle
of nonviolent protest that would form the basis for another Great
Soul's efforts at winning freedom for humanity—Martin Luther King,
Jr. Nonviolent protesting would become the foundation point for the
antiwar and antinuclear demonstrations up to the present time. This
will continue to be a principal method of transformation for mankind
in the future. In this respect, Gandhi created and anchored an archetype for collective human expression. Only a Great Soul is capable of
making such an impression on the collective consciousness. Lord
Jesus did this through the expression of the Second Ray. Moses was
an avatar of the Third Ray. Confucius made his principal contribution through the Seventh Ray. Mother Theresa is an embodiment of
the Sixth Ray of Devotion. Mahatma Gandhi's work manifested through
the Fourth Ray.

Personality equipment: Gandhi was born with the Sun in Libra in
the twelfth house. The Sun is in opposition to Neptune in Aries and
sextile to Saturn in Sagittarius. This combination is indicative of
several major characteristics:

1. The ability to spend long hours alone in deep, reflective contemplation (twelfth house).

2. The basic urge for peace and harmony, and a natural attunement to social justice (Libra).

3. The urge for self-sacrifice and the ability for the personality to

---

[1]Although several systems and formulas have been proposed regarding the determination of
one's actual Soul and personality Rays (as well as the Rays of the physical, mental, and
emotional bodies) through the natal horoscope, I am not fully convinced by any of them.
Nor have I been able, at this point, to come up with a system of astrological analysis myself
which fully satisfies me in this regard. Although I feel that the Soul Ray is permanent, the
Rays of the personality and its three vehicles can change over the span of a lifetime, relative
to the nature of personal evolution. Therefore, I have purposely avoided such a highly
speculative discussion in favor of stressing the Ray *influences* in a chart. The latter do not
change; that is, Scorpio on the Ascendant will always indicate a strong Fourth Ray expression for the Soul, no matter what the Ray of the Soul itself.

Michael Robbins, Ph.D., a clinical psychologist and highly respected esoteric astrologer,
has developed a psychological testing series based on the principles of the Seven Rays and
the information contained in Alice Bailey's books on esoteric psychology. This material is
very helpful in determining one's Ray makeup. Inquiries about this test (called the P.I.P.)
can be made through the Seven Ray Institute, 128 Manhattan Ave., Jersey City Heights, NJ
07307.

be a vehicle for some transcendental and transpersonal purpose (Neptune in Aries in opposition to the Sun).

4. The incorporation of a philosophical belief system that could be used to structure the energies of the personality in order to fulfill such a transpersonal purpose (Saturn in Sagittarius in aspect to Neptune and the Sun).

5. From a more esoteric perspective, when we substitute Neptune for the Sun, we see the direct expression of the Heart of the Sun. This brings forth a strong Sixth Ray influence, and Gandhi was deeply committed to his Hindu religion. He came from a family that worshipped Vishnu, the Second Ray (Soul aspect) of the Hindu trinity. In addition, his background was steeped in the philosophy of *ahimsa,* which means "nonviolence to all living things."

6. Saturn, planet of the Laws of Manifestation, and exalted in Libra, is sextile his Libra Sun. Gandhi became a lawyer, and through his efforts at achieving equality for his people in South Africa, he established those techniques that he would eventually use to overthrow British rule in India. This foreign influence can be seen from the following placements:

   a. Saturn is in Sagittarius, sign of jurisprudence and significator of all things foreign or at a long distance from one's birth.

   b. The esoteric ruler of the personality (Sun sign) is Uranus, which is located in the ninth house of foreign travel. The house position of the esoteric ruler of the Sun's sign indicates the place where those experiences unfold that serve to develop the personality into the vehicle for the Soul's purpose. From the Soul-centered approach, we know that the ninth house is the place where the knowledge of Cosmic Law is anchored. The ninth is the "home" of the Higher Mind, and is thus the vehicle of vision which endows one with an attunement to the unification of all belief systems. The placement of Uranus in this house, and its trine to the Soul-centered ruler of the horoscope (Mars in the first house), is a very clear indication of the alignment of the Soul's purpose with the equipment of the personality in the present incarnation.

Biological karma (the past): The Moon is in Leo in the tenth house. This is a very strong placement, with major aspects to Saturn, Neptune, Venus, Mars, Pluto, Jupiter, and Vulcan. The Moon is the focal point of both a Grand Trine in fire and a potent T-Square in fixed signs. Of the multitude of important factors contained in these aspects, let us examine several of the more dominant.

1. Gandhi came from a very religious family (Moon ruling the ninth house exoterically), in which the central figure promoting this adherence to religious tradition was his mother, Putlibai. The Moon's position in Leo, disposited by the Sun, shows the conditioning link

between the traditional past of Gandhi's ancient racial heritage and the present personality equipment.

2. His family were administrators in the government of the local princes of the Indian state of Gujarat. His father was the chief minister in this capacity, and had to keep the harmony between the rajas and the British authorities (strong Fourth Ray influence).

3. The Pluto-Jupiter-Moon contact is very much involved with the reorientation of philosophical concepts, and the creation of social systems based on these new ideas (Moon trine Saturn). The Moon-Mars-Venus aspects show that Gandhi would be continually involved in the creation of balance between opposing social forces.

4. The Moon, ruler of the ninth house exoterically, is trine to Neptune in Aries, which rules this house esoterically. This is an exceedingly important contact—one which brings out his devotion to spiritual unity among all people in his multiethnic nation.

5. Substituting Uranus for the Moon, we find that the urge for social reform was always a main thrust of Gandhi's life—from his early days in South Africa, where he campaigned for many years for equality for the Indian minority in that apartheid state, to his efforts at an independent India.

6. The Fifth Ray expression of the Moon sign adds a strong quality of precision and logic to Gandhi's efforts at creating social equality. The Moon in the tenth house serves to bring the entire Indian nation (that is, the past—Gandhi's collective, biological karma) into a struggle to birth itself into the twentieth century as an independent people. Not only is this the embodiment of the traditional meaning of the tenth house—social responsibility—it also represents the significance of the Soul-centered chart: the enforcement of the Plan of the Masters.

7. The Moon is linked by square aspect to Mars in Scorpio, the Soul-centered ruler of the Ascendant. She is also in square to the co-ruler of the Ascendant on the personality level, Pluto in Taurus. Gandhi had to struggle, with enormous efforts of will (Pluto and the First Ray), to break free from the past (British rule over India), to establish a new order for the future of his people, and to ensure India's place in the world (the square between Mars and the Moon). The tremendous difficulties, violence, and loss of life that would accompany these efforts (the culminating moments of which took place during World War II) are also indicated by the aspects of the Moon to Mars and Pluto.

8. The Sixth Ray is very strongly involved through Gandhi's unswerving devotion to his vision of a new India and a new humanity. The Moon is strongly in aspect to Mars and Neptune. The self-sacrifice of this position is shown from a purely physical perspec-

tive in Gandhi's use of fasting as a way to gain his spiritual objectives. The Moon signifies nourishment at its most basic level: food. This denial of sustenance and the willingness to make a martyr out of himself for the sake of his spiritual vision is very much an example of the combination of these three planets, as well as the combined influences of the Fourth and Sixth Rays. Mars is exactly inconjunct Neptune, thus strengthening the urge to do battle unto death. The contact of Venus to the Moon, Mars, and Neptune shows that this battle would tend to be a "passive aggressive" one. All India and the world would know that the Mahatma was in his bed, slowly starving, and that in order to save his life, great political compromises would have to be made. This behind-the-scenes control over vast energies, accomplished through apparently peaceful means, is also seen through Gandhi's numerous imprisonments, in which he would center the attention of hundreds of millions of people on himself and his objectives while he sat spinning in his prison cell (Sun in Libra in the twelfth house in aspect to—and substituted by—Neptune).

Soul Purpose (the future): From the Soul-centered perspective, Neptune in Aries is disposited by Mercury, which is also the Hierarchical dispositor of Mars in Scorpio. Mercury sits conjoined the Ascendant and is *totally unaspected to the rest of the planets by any of the six major angles of relationship.* Unaspected Mercury is not only a very potent vehicle for the expression of the predominant Fourth-Ray energies at work in this life, but allows the Mind to be a very free agent for Hierarchical impressions and purposes. Thus, none of the urges for self-sacrifice are accomplished through emotional centering in the solar plexus (Mars dominating). It was not passion, exclusivistic religious zeal, or fanaticism which motivated Gandhi. The Mahatma was attuned to the Plan from the Mind of Divinity, and was able to utilize his body—plus society's fear of and feelings of guilt associated with death—to bring about those great social upheavals that were part of the collective goal for humanity during his time.

Let's continue our examination of this Great Soul's horoscope through a house-by-house analysis:

FIRST HOUSE

Personality level: Gandhi's body was small and wiry, and he displayed a need for constant movement and the use of his hands (Mercury rising in Scorpio). He had tremendous personal magnetism, which drew people to him and made of him a very charismatic, although self-effacing, individual (Mars and Venus conjoined in

Scorpio). He would use this charisma and ability to synthesize various opposing social elements in the effort to materialize spiritual goals (Mars and Venus in aspect to Jupiter and Pluto, as well as to the Moon and Neptune). He wrote copiously; his collected works filled some eighty volumes (Mercury conjunct the Ascendant).

Soul level: The quality of his primary Ray type is the Fourth—Harmony through Conflict. It is this Ray that the Soul chooses as the focus for its expression in the outer world. Yet who could not say that standing behind this Fourth Ray energy is a deeper quality of the Second Ray that only seeks of Its children (humanity) peace, love, and a more evolved expression of consciousness? Is this not the eventual goal of all Souls? The expression of the manifested Will of Divinity in the life of the Mahatma was very much involved in service to humanity through healing differences and nurturing unity. This is seen through Mercury's esoteric rulership over his sixth house, and its placement directly on the Ascendant. This would be accomplished through the ability to relate differing segments of humanity into greater harmonious wholes. Mercury on the Ascendant with Venus conjoined Mars, the ruler of Scorpio, is indicative of this process.

Yet it should be noted that India was eventually separated, and the nations of Pakistan and Bangladesh came into being. This was not part of Gandhi's vision of unity, and his disappointment at India's division may be viewed astrologically through the square of Mars to the Moon in the natal chart. This indicates that the goal of the unity of his homeland (symbolized by the Moon) would not be achieved. Another indication of this failure is that the Sun, Soul-centered ruler of the tenth house (the culmination of the Soul's purpose) is in opposition to Neptune, which conjoins the Earth. Thus, Gandhi's vision had to give way to perhaps a higher Source for the destiny of the Indian subcontinent. Jupiter, the esoteric ruler of the fourth house (karmic results coming from the culmination of Soul purposes), is also in opposition to the ruler of the first house, Mars.

It might thus be speculated that Gandhi's mission was to free India from Britain, and to give his people a sense of national identity. The greater spiritual ideal that people of all races and religions could live together harmoniously in India was not to be realized in his lifetime. The Aquarian Age paradigm in this respect is for each of the nations of humanity to anchor its own identity in its own lands and cultures, just as it is vital that each of us anchor our individualized identities on the Path. The creation of Pakistan for the Moslem minority of India was thus very necessary. Gandhi's vision of a peace-filled and united India (and world) may become a reality when each race and nation is individualized through the unfolding of Love/

Wisdom. Then, the healing process of synthesis may take place and unify the world.

Finally, the fact that Mars is in Scorpio in the first house, conjunct Venus and trine Uranus, shows that his Soul purpose is very closely linked to the present incarnation, as the latter two planets disposit the Sun in Libra. Venus adds the strong Fifth Ray quality of the Concrete Mind. Gandhi was a lawyer who possessed a highly gifted intellect. His understanding of social movements (Venus trine Uranus) blends with his devotion to change and transformation (Pluto opposing Mars and Venus) in order to birth a new society for his nation (Moon veiling Uranus in the tenth house, square to Mars-Venus-Pluto-Jupiter).

SECOND HOUSE

Personality level: Jupiter in aspect with Pluto, Mars, and Venus in Taurus-Scorpio, and the Moon in Leo, would make huge resources available to Gandhi. Yet the nature of the geometric angles between these planets shows that on the personality level, the urge for the sensual pleasures money can bring was not at all Gandhi's way. There was a distinct and almost compulsive negation of material goods, except when they could be used as symbols for his Soul purpose; that is, his use of the spinning wheel to represent India's ability to create and administer its own textile industry. This archetypical use of material resources even extended to basic nutrition, as Gandhi often used fasting as a way to achieve his political/spiritual ends. Saturn in Sagittarius in this house (and its fine aspects to the Sun, Moon, and Neptune) indicates that a great deal of his personal resources were centered in the mental plane. It was his knowledge of law, on both social and spiritual levels, that should be seen as his real riches.

Soul level: The Earth, ruler of Sagittarius and the second house, is in Aries in the sixth house, trine to Saturn and widely conjunct Neptune. (It is, of course, in opposition to the Sun and Vulcan.) Thus, Gandhi's storehouse of life force (prana), as well as his spiritual strengths and resources, are expressed on the Soul level through the house of service to humanity. The Earth's position, especially in relationship to Saturn, reveals his inherent knowledge regarding the building of his individual Antahkarana, as well as the collective Antahkarana which would lead the Indian people to establish a closer contact with the Soul of their nation! It is in this collective capacity that the work of a Great Soul unfolds.

The connection between the Earth and Neptune (both of which are in Aries) reveals the importance of self-sacrifice as a tool for the accomplishment of his spiritual goals. The anchoring of spiritual resources and values would be accomplished through Gandhi's highly individualized efforts, as the dispositor of both Neptune and the Earth is Mercury, conjunct the Ascendant.

THIRD HOUSE

Personality level: With Capricorn on the cusp of this house, and the strong placement of Saturn in the natal chart, we can say that Gandhi's mental processes were highly structured and well planned. The idealistic and spiritual quality of his mind is seen through the trine between Saturn and Neptune. The other trine, between Saturn and the Moon, gives the ability to communicate with a wide number of people and to structure such communication so that many people (Moon in the tenth house) would be affected by his mental concepts. There is a strong sense of social responsibility attached to his need to communicate. Saturn's rulership over this house in the sign of Sagittarius is also indicative of the wide range of his published works and the vast amount of traveling he did in order to complete his tasks.

Soul level: Saturn is in trine with its Soul-centered dispositor, the Earth, which adds a very strong Third Ray quality to the expression of his mental energies, as both these planets and the angle itself are of this Ray. The combination of Saturn-Earth-Sun shows that Active Intelligence will be a most potent tool in the accomplishment of his life's work. It also endows Gandhi with a strong connection to *manas* (mind substance) out of which he could create the necessary concepts and links to the inner resources of the Soul (Saturn in the second house). Gandhi's steps along the Path would be accomplished while practicing and fulfilling both social and Cosmic Law abroad (Saturn in Sagittarius, ruler of the third house, in aspect to both the Soul-centered and personality-centered rulers of the ninth house).

FOURTH HOUSE

Personality level: Gandhi's entire home life and background was steeped in two interests: religion and the administration of social and political concerns. The ruler of the fourth house, Uranus, is in Cancer in the ninth house, revealing these two directions most clearly. Uranus trines Mars and Venus, showing that he would work as a crusader and pioneer regarding those social issues connected to his racial roots.

His early work in South Africa on behalf of Indians (both Moslem and Hindu) living and working in that country at the turn of the twentieth century bears witness to this. As his political and spiritual consciousness evolved, his concept of roots would expand and lead him to view the Family of Man as his own.

The square between Neptune and ninth house Uranus points to the intense social conflicts that he would encounter abroad. One of the most important philosophical principles fostered by Gandhi, and which actualized into a political movement, is called *Satyagraha,* which means "firmness in truth," and points to the transformation of injustice without inflicting suffering upon one's oppressors. Many times, however, suffering is seen to be inflicted upon those who passively resist their oppression, but who ultimately achieve victory by standing firm in their beliefs. This philosophy shows a very strong Sixth Ray influence, and is indicated astrologically by the powerful aspects Uranus creates with Neptune and Mars. If we also observe that there are six planets in fixed signs in this horoscope (including five in a very potent, angular T-Square), we can readily understand the "firmness" that underscored all of Gandhi's methodologies.

Soul level: Jupiter, esoteric ruler of the fourth house, is in a very close sextile to Uranus, ruler from the personality level. Whenever such a mutual, transcendental aspect occurs, it indicates that the Soul can easily express itself in the life of the personality, relative to the affairs of the house involved. To put it another way, it shows that the fusion of the Higher and lower selves is easy to achieve in terms of the energies of that house.

Jupiter conjunct Pluto in opposition to Mars (ruler of the Ascendant) shows that Gandhi would be an instrument of great upheaval in his own country. His ability to assess the reasons and find the ways for creating such total transformations is seen through the positions of all the aforementioned planets in relation to Jupiter. The fourth house influence brings about a karmic conclusion to his life efforts through the expression of the Second Ray (Jupiter), as the energies of this planet work to effectuate a new social order in the outer world (Uranus as exoteric ruler of Aquarius).

On the Soul level, Neptune's square to Uranus reveals a conflict between the Sixth and Seventh Rays. This square is especially potent, as Neptune is the esoteric dispositor of Uranus in the chart. It can thus be seen that Gandhi's devotion to certain spiritual ideals of unity and wholeness (Sixth Ray) would not be realized in the objective world of manifestation (Seventh Ray). Gandhi would often experience frustration in the ultimate realization of his spiritual and social visions. His own karmic lessons, requiring loving detachment from the results of his actions, would be very intimately involved with this set of circumstances. This is yet another facet of the work of the Dweller on the Threshold (of Initiation).

```
FIFTH HOUSE
```

Personality level: Neptune's inconjunction to Mars in Scorpio shows that Gandhi had to have experienced a tremendous struggle between the desire for the pleasures of the lower self and the Soul's urge to serve humanity. The keynote meaning of any aspect between Mars and Neptune is "sacrifice of the ego's need for self-assertion." In the life of a person on the spiritual path, this sacrifice usually results in the reorientation of desires in order to accomplish some transcendental purpose. Gandhi's need is to make the personality a vehicle for a profound and far-reaching focus of transformation (Neptune in opposition to the Sun). Thus he would no longer be the object of personal, one-to-one relationships (Libra), but the object of those relationships wherein he would be the counterpoint to an entire nation—or even, at times, to the world.

This means that he would find that his abundant sexual energies would be used for the transformation of much larger social issues. Mars is the ruler of the solar plexus (center of personal desires) in the personality chart, while Neptune (the Heart of the Sun) becomes the dominant force once the Soul and personality fuse. This battle must have been exceedingly difficult, as Mars is the dispositor of Neptune and conjunct Venus in Scorpio, indicating a very profound sexual and sensual nature. Gandhi was helped in the reorientation of his personal desires through the trine of Saturn in Sagittarius to Neptune, which gave discipline based on an understanding of Higher Law, as well as through his inherited, biological karma (Neptune and Saturn trine the Moon).

As we mentioned above, Gandhi came from a very religious family. His mother was an especially pious person, who greatly influenced the molding of his early character. In fact, when Gandhi went off to England to study law, he made a vow to his mother that while he was there, he would not touch wine, women, or meat. This is another indication of the Grand Trine of the Moon, Neptune, and Saturn. I find it very "coincidental" that the law college he attended in England was called the Inner Temple!

Soul level: Pluto is the ruler of the fifth house, and is in opposition to Mars. This shows the struggle between the Will and the head center, and the emotional nature of the personal desires centered in the solar plexus. Indeed, it would appear that this aspect represents a vital turning point in the direction of Gandhi's spiritual path, as Mars is the exoteric ruler of the Ascendant. This position points out a very essential meaning associated with this house from the Soul level: the fifth house is the area where Love manifests as the Will to merge with the Plan in the expression of one's particular focus of creativity. Pluto's conjunction to Jupiter in Taurus shows that a major facet of Gandhi's creative contribution would involve the practical expression of wide-reaching and inclusive philosophical concepts. This process involved a number of intense struggles for social transformation (the opposition to Mars and Venus), but resulted in the birthing of new forms of social and political structures into the collective conscious-ness of humanity (the square to the Moon, veiling Uranus, and the Moon's trine to Saturn) both in India and elsewhere.

From the perspective of the Rays, the Pluto/Jupiter conjunction in Taurus reveals that Gandhi's creative purpose would involve the joining of the energies of the First and Second Rays through a field of expression signified by a sign of the Fourth Ray. Thus Harmony through Conflict would be the means through which this great synthesis would come about. This is further emphasized by the fact that Venus (harmony) and Mars (conflict) are also conjoined in a Fourth Ray sign, in opposition to the Jupiter-Pluto conjunction. This set of aspects is worth the reader's contemplation.

SIXTH HOUSE

Personality level: The call to be of personal service is very evident in this horoscope, as the exoteric ruler of this house, Mars, is located in the first house. Neptune in the sixth, opposing the Sun, adds strength to this orientation, although it can be seen that, as Neptune is inconjunct Mars in Scorpio, Gandhi would act as a martyr in the performance of his work. This is evident by the fact that on several occasions, he almost starved himself to death in the pursuit of his aims. Mars, Sixth Ray personality ruler, is opposed to Pluto and Jupiter, which can lead to the fanatical pursuit of one's aims—especially if these are centered in one's spiritual beliefs.

Gandhi's health was very fragile as a result of these excesses (Nep-tune in the sixth opposed to the Sun and inconjunct Mars). His real strength was in his willpower, seen through Aries, First Ray sign, on the cusp of the sixth house, and the position of both Mercury and Mars. The techniques and skills that he used within the realm of his work and service were primarily centered on nonviolence. This can be seen by the fact that Mars (assertion), ruler of this house, is conjunct Venus (cooperation). Gandhi's immensely strong Fourth Ray influence helped him keep many opposing forces in a series of checks and balances. He was helped in this respect by the fact that his personality was operating through Libra (ruled by Venus) in the twelfth house. He thus was able to hold and balance considerable power from places of obscurity and imprisonment.

Soul level: The sixth house is ruled by Mercury in Scorpio on the Ascendant. This also shows that his service and work was to be carried out in a very direct and individualistic way. World Service was Gandhi's Soul Purpose—one that would be expressed through a tremendous focus on the Ray of Harmony through Conflict. Devotion to the Will/Power of Divinity (Neptune in Aries on the Soul level) would be one of his most important tools. In this respect, he would sacrifice his physical body (Mars inconjunct Neptune), and utilize all the powers of his personality (the Sun in opposition). Vulcan's influence would serve to shape the lower self so that it could be used as a tool for the Heart of the Sun. There is no doubt that Gandhi was a great Initiate. The Hierarchical ruler of Scorpio is conjunct the Ascendant, indicating that this Son of Mind would be utilized as a direct tool of the Planetary Hierarchy for the carrying out of the Plan for Humanity. His horoscope leaves no doubt as to his status as a Mahatma.

SEVENTH HOUSE

Personality level: Venus (seventh house ruler) is conjunct Mars in Scorpio in the first house and indicates an early marriage. In fact, Gandhi was married at the age of thirteen. Yet he was often separated from his wife and home (the square to the Moon) and eventually separated from his wife as an active husband when he renounced the expression of his sexuality (Venus conjunct Mars in Scorpio opposing Pluto) for his religious principles (opposition to Jupiter). His marriage was a very devout and loving one (Venus conjunct Mars, Sixth Ray ruler in a fixed sign), but also indicative of the duality of the Fourth Ray expression of Scorpio. His wife was his best friend (Venus trine Uranus). She provided him with a strong sense of psychological support and a loving foundation for his self-expression (Uranus ruling the fourth house and trine to Venus and Mars). Gandhi would have made some very important relationships with powerful people (Jupiter and Pluto in the seventh house), some of whom were opponents of his spiritual and social views (Jupiter/Pluto in opposition to Venus, ruler of the seventh). The mutual reception of Pluto and Venus (along with the contact to Mars) is a strong indication that he would be killed by an assassin (a secret enemy, as indicated by Venus's rulership over the twelfth house).

Soul level: Vulcan shapes the tools of the personality (conjunct the Sun) so that it may be a proper vehicle for the kind of self-sacrifice and service that will be needed to accomplish the Soul's purpose (opposition to Neptune and the Earth in the sixth house). It would be in combating the divisive and negative forces seeking to hold India in bondage that the Will/Power of the twelfth house Vulcan would express at its greatest strength. It would be through the harmonizing of opposites (Vulcan in Libra) that Gandhi would rise to the service of the world Savior, for his was definitely the externalized Path of the Martyr. Vulcan's connection to Saturn and the Moon is a clear indication that he had the ability to shape those new thought-forms (Vulcan in Libra, sign of the Third Ray, as well as sextile Saturn) which could be used in the establishment of a new society (Moon veiling Uranus in the tenth house).

I believe that his particular Dweller (seventh house) had a great deal to do with his adherence to the vision that absolute harmony could be created in a land of such intense diversities of belief and social custom as was the India of his time. His devotion to this ideal and its consistent frustration (Vulcan in opposition to Neptune) must have been the source of great suffering for him. In the end, his vision of a unified, peaceful, and independent India did not reach fulfillment. This can be understood astrologically if we see that Uranus, the exoteric ruler of the fourth house of endings, is in an extremely difficult T-Square with Vulcan and Neptune. Uranus disposits Vulcan esoterically, and is square to it. At the same time, Uranus is squared by its own esoteric dispositor, Neptune, while the latter is opposed to Vulcan.

EIGHTH HOUSE

Personality level: The fact that the ruler of this house, Mercury, is in Scorpio conjunct the Ascendant, shows that Gandhi would be able to transform other people's energies to suit his own purposes. This would be done through writing and lecturing, as the energies we are speaking about are mental in nature. Thus, Gandhi was very successful at changing people's minds so that their thoughts would align with his own. Another facet of the strongly Fourth Ray Mercury-in-Scorpio influence was Gandhi's ability to create a tremendous force in conflict with his own. He did this by setting forth those ideas and concepts which would be heavily opposed by the political status quo of his times. This opposition of forces would lead to those open struggles that would bring the attention of the world to his efforts.

Mercury is thus an extremely potent force in this chart. It is unaspected, and therefore stands as a pure archetype for the energies it represents. Gandhi would have had a very difficult time distancing himself from his own ideas, or even being able to see the validity of anyone else's opinions or concepts. In this respect, we can see that he needed to evolve and regenerate (eighth house function) the effects of Mercury on the personality level. In my opinion, this is a facet of the Dweller, insofar as it represents the need for release of the ego's attachment to the mental plane.

Pluto stands behind Mercury, as does Mars on the personality level. Both of these planets are in fixed signs of the Fourth Ray. Mars is a Sixth Ray body, while the First Ray of Will/Power works through Pluto. This means that Gandhi was exceptionally devoted in the most determined way to his ideas, and had the willpower to follow through on what he believed to be the truth. This facet of his character reveals yet another aspect of the Dweller in the steadfast and often fanatical devotion which Mercury's dispositor (Mars in Scorpio) endows. This quality of absolute adherence to his personal ideas and opinions would have been one of his greatest challenges. It would lead to the fusion of his Higher Will and Ideals with his lower mental body so that the Soul Purpose could be fulfilled. The above exemplifies the primary function of the eighth house, which is to provide the necessary arena of conflict for personal transformation, and the regeneration of the lower self. This must be accomplished in order to fuse the personality with the Soul.

Soul level: Venus, the Soul-centered ruler of the eighth house, is also in Scorpio, once again focusing our attention on the incredible Fourth Ray emphasis of this most advanced Disciple. Venus conjuncts Mars, ruler of the Ascendant, revealing that another facet of Gandhi's Higher Purpose was his liberation into world service and the ultimate victory of his Soul (see p. 344). The blending of the ruler of the Fifth Ray, Venus, with the planet ruling the lower expression of the Sixth Ray, Mars, indicates the struggle that Gandhi would have had to undertake as he repolarized his personal emotions and sexual desires to the impersonal creative expression of the Mind. Thus, passion gives way to insight, divisiveness to unity, and conflict to harmony.

When a Great Soul is at work, he or she influences an enormous number of people. The Buddha, Lord Jesus, Confucius, Moses, and more recently, Einstein and Dr. King (to name but a few of the Great Ones) anchored great gifts into the consciousness of humanity. Gandhi, in addition to sharing the science of nonviolence in order to achieve the blending of opposites (the quintessential significance of Venus), also helped to birth the Soul of a Nation! This is a most advanced use of eighth house energies for the purposes of the Plan.

Venus is trine Uranus, the esoteric ruler of Libra, thus bringing Gandhi's personality (the Sun) into the focal point of the great social upheavals instigated by this slight old man at his spinning wheel. This trine is the embodiment of the Law of Right Human Relations—the Law which Gandhi strove to serve.

NINTH HOUSE

Personality level: Since the exoteric ruler of the fourth house (Uranus) is in the ninth house, and the co-ruler of the fourth house (Saturn) is in Sagittarius, we can conclude that Gandhi must have spent a great deal of time away from his home, especially in the pursuit of his higher education. History bears witness to the truth of these astrologically based conclusions. As the ninth is also the house of publishing and legal activities, and its ruler, the Moon, is in the tenth house of career, it comes as no surprise that Gandhi became a lawyer, as well as a much-published author. The Moon is in very difficult aspects with Pluto and Jupiter, as well as with Venus and Mars. This indicates the many religious and social conflicts that would beset Gandhi's life. The Grand Trine of the Moon to Saturn and Neptune reveals Gandhi's ability to construct wide-reaching and inclusive social philosophies (Saturn in Sagittarius, Uranus in Cancer in the ninth) that from an idealistic point of view (Neptune in Aries) would be able to accommodate all differing orthodoxies and peoples into a national unit (Moon in the tenth). Cancer on the cusp of the ninth, and the Moon in the tenth, would also reveal the importance of his family's (and especially his mother's) influence on his spiritual life.

Soul level: From the perspective of the Higher Self, Neptune in Aries opposing the Sun is the ruler of the ninth house. This position signifies that Gandhi's Path was one of total personality surrender and self-sacrifice. The trine from Neptune in Aries to Saturn in Sagittarius indicates his attunement with Cosmic Law and the Ancient Wisdom Teachings. The harmonious link between these Sixth and Third Ray planets tells us that there was an ease and fluidity of contact between Gandhi's devotional nature and the revelation of those Ideas in the Mind of God which he personified. These two Ray influences are synthesized by a third—the Fourth Ray quality of the Moon in the tenth—which shows that this Devotion to Mind would be expressed through the conflicts inherent in this Ray quality.

When we understand the Moon as veiling the influence of Uranus, we come to see that the blend of Devotion and Mind was to be used to create a new archetype of social expression; that is, an independent and unified India. As mentioned previously, the T-Square of Neptune to Uranus and Vulcan could be the indication that the unification of his country would not be achieved. The ninth house and all of its implications are tremendously strengthened by the placement of the exoteric ruler (the Moon) in trine to the Soul-level ruler (Neptune). Thus, the Higher Mind and Its Teachings could filter down from the Soul level into the realm of Gandhi's biological inheritance, and be given out to the people of the world.

TENTH HOUSE

Personality level: When Leo is on the Midheaven, we can expect that an individual will want to shine forth and radiate his personality through his chosen career. Yet the ruler of this house cusp, the Sun, is in the twelfth house. It is quite amazing just how much of Gandhi's career was expressed through places of restriction and seclusion, such as prisons and sickbeds. Gandhi's greatest power came from behind the scenes; his influence was felt as it permeated into the very fabric of the collective consciousness of his people. As the Sun is opposing Neptune, the suffusion of a more individualized statement of the personality into the collective is even more apparent. The sextile from Saturn in Sagittarius gives self-discipline and philosophical support to Gandhi's professional activities. His was a personality that embraced India in both its spiritual and cultural heritage.

The Moon's placement in the tenth is strongly indicative of Gandhi's ability to reach the masses of people. The Moon is always the significator of the masses—in effect, the Family of Man. This is just as true in the horoscope of the personality as it is in the Soul-centered one. A highly evolved personality—one that is capable of being a successful vehicle for Soul control—will have the magnetism to do the collective work which is always part of the dharma of the Higher Self. The Moon in the tenth stands for a set of transcendentally linked circumstances which, by the Law of Correspondences, are intimately related. These contacts are: the biological mother (here ruling the ninth house of religion and higher learning), the family and heritage, one's race and nation, and finally, the human collective.

Soul level: When we examine the Sun as the ruler of the tenth house from the perspective of the Higher Self, a very beautiful picture unfolds before us. We now have to see the Sun as veiling Neptune, and to realize that it is the Heart of the Sun that is at work through the twelfth house. Gandhi would use his ability to infuse his loving consciousness into the collective to enforce the Plan of the Masters. The square of Vulcan to Uranus would serve to break down previous patterns of social archetyping and allow him to build a new nation.

The externalization of his field of service would come not only through the political movements he initiated (Uranus, dispositor of the Sun in Libra, trine to Venus and sextile Jupiter/Pluto), but through his ability to gradually and subtly direct the fate of hundreds of millions of people from his prison cell or tiny bedroom. The combination of the Sun and Neptune joins the energies of the Second Ray to those of the Sixth, and brings Devotion to Love/Wisdom. This is the underlying motivational key of his life, and reveals the presence of the Mother, the Healer, the One Great Soul, as the culmination of his spiritual purpose. He would be helped in the creation of the new thought-forms necessary to focus the birth of an independent Indian nation, and thus forge a new collective identity, through the work of Active Intelligence. This is seen by Saturn's sextile to the Sun and its trine to the tenth house Moon, the latter veiling Uranus.

ELEVENTH HOUSE

Personality level: This is the house which, on the personality level, is associated with organizations, political activities, and one's associates in general. Virgo, sign of service, is on the cusp and its ruler, Mercury, sits on the Ascendant of Gandhi's chart in Scorpio. We can thus say that the affairs of this house were of paramount importance to him. The strong first house contact of the ruler reveals his personal leadership of the many organizations which he initiated, and to which he gave creative impulse. The placement of Mercury in Scorpio indicates the power wielded by Gandhi to summon up collective energies and then transform and direct them according to his personal ideas and concepts.

Soul level: The spiritual hopes and wishes associated with the activities of this house are strongly connected to the Moon's placement in the tenth. We have already spoken at length about the implications of this position, but one of the most important is the establishment of his racial family and country of birth as an independent nation, free from colonial oppression. The Fourth Ray energies of the Moon (esoteric ruler of Virgo), and its difficult aspects with four angular planets also in signs of this Ray, indicate the problems and crises Gandhi would face in manifesting such visions into a physical reality. The tenth house position of the ruler of the eleventh house clearly indicates that such aspirations were very much part of his need to culminate the purpose of his Soul in the present incarnation. Thus the hidden Christ, the *anima mundi* latent in the sign Virgo, would reveal itself through the tenth house manifestation of Divine Will (Moon in Leo, First Ray sign).

TWELFTH HOUSE

Personality level: To me, this is the strongest house in the horoscope. Not only is the Sun (ruler of the Midheaven) placed here, but the two rulers of Libra (twelfth house cusp) are trine to one another. This indicates that the energies of the twelfth can externalize and interface quite easily between Soul and personality levels. As a result, Gandhi's great reserve of inner spiritual strength, his connection to the collective consciousness of his nation, as well as all the hidden resources of his Soul, were available to him for use in the outer world. As the two ruling planets involved are Venus and Uranus, the focus of this externalization is the Law of Right Human Relations.

Venus conjunct Mars in Scorpio, in opposition to Pluto and Jupiter, reveals that Gandhi was a man with many enemies. It is also indicative of the religious fanatic who assassinated him in 1948. Gandhi was always at work trying to balance opposing forces. This is not only inherent in his Libran personality, but also speaks about the collective energies needing to be brought into a harmonious whole so that a free India could be born into the community of nations. The Venus/Mars conjunction, square to the tenth house Moon, points to this struggle. Gandhi's nonviolent political provocations brought about what would appear be his own self-undoing (that is, prison terms and self-inflicted fasting and suffering). This is also an example of the more inharmonious contacts the twelfth house ruler (Venus) makes with the other planets in the natal chart.

Soul level: I have already spoken at some length about the nature of these twelfth house energies, especially the Sun/Saturn/Neptune contact, Uranus's square to Neptune, and the T-Square of Uranus, Neptune, and Vulcan. The strength of the twelfth house, and all of its planetary associations, shows that Gandhi had to be a light in the midst of a multitude of dark, unredeemed forces of ignorance. He was worshipped by hundreds of millions, and hated and feared by millions more. He had to balance the incredible hatred and prejudices of the Hindu and Moslem communities of India, while struggling to embody and radiate the healing power of Love/Wisdom. He had to battle to free his technologically backward nation from the greatest empire of the times, while working to blend the individual interests of the hundreds of local Indian princes and rajas. His strength lay in his connection to the Ancient Wisdom Teachings of his ancient faith (Uranus, Soul-centered ruler of the Sun and the twelfth house, posited in the ninth), and his ability to call upon the healing resources of the Soul in order to exteriorize its Purpose (Venus, exoteric ruler of the twelfth, conjunct the ruler of the Ascendant, and trine the esoteric ruler of the twelfth, Uranus).

Gandhi took upon himself the task of transforming the divisive forces and energies which surrounded him, releasing India from bondage and creating a new nation in the process. His was the Path of the World Savior, and exemplified the paradigm of the sainted martyr of the Piscean Age. Yet in his visions of social equality, in his work to free the lowest members of traditional Indian society, the "Untouchables" (calling them *Harijan* or the "Children of God"), and in his devotion to the Law of Right Human Relations, he served to forge a major link in the building of the world Antahkarana, which is to be the bridge of consciousness for the New Age.

A CLOSING WORD

The most exciting and important journey one can make is the involutionary quest of the Soul and the evolutionary aspiration of the personality. When they meet, you come Home. In that Dwelling Place, the life Purpose is revealed; knowledge becomes Wisdom; and Love becomes a reality at last.

It is my sincere wish that this volume will serve as a companion guide along your Way. It was written to stimulate rather than resolve, to initiate inquiry into the astrology of the Soul rather than to culminate such yearnings of the Higher Mind.

And more than anything else, I hope that it is worthy of the Love and Wisdom of the Tibetan Master, and adds to the collective efforts of the New Group of World Servers everywhere.

THE MANTRAM OF THE DISCIPLE

I am a point of light
within a greater Light.
I am a strand of loving energy
within the stream of Love divine.
I am a point of sacrificial Fire, focused
within the fiery Will of God.
And thus I stand.

I am a way by which men may achieve.
I am a source of strength,
enabling them to stand.
I am a beam of light
shining upon their way.
And thus I stand.

And standing thus, revolve
And tread this way the ways of men,
and know the ways of God.
And thus I stand.

Bibliography

The following is a research and study guide that will serve to amplify the teachings shared in this volume. Those titles preceded by an asterisk (*) have been used as direct references in the compilation of the present work.

Works about the Ancient Wisdom Teachings by Alice A. Bailey

There are some two dozen books and compilations available from this great source of the Ancient Wisdom Teachings. (These books are all published by the Lucis Publishing Co., P.O. Box 722, Cooper Station, New York, NY 10276, unless otherwise noted.) I recommend them all, but in terms of the present work, the following may prove to be most helpful:

Discipleship in the New Age, vol. 1, 1944.
Discipleship in the New Age, vol. 2, 1955.
Esoteric Astrology, 1951.

*   *Esoteric Healing*, 1953.
*   *Esoteric Psychology*, vol. 1, 1936.
*   *Esoteric Psychology*, vol. 2, 1942.
    Ponder on This—A Compilation, 1971.
    Serving Humanity—A Compilation. Pretoria, South Africa: Humanitas Trust, 1972.
    The Labours of Hercules. London: Lucis Press Ltd., 1974.
    The Soul and Its Mechanism, 1930.
    The Soul—A Compilation, 1974.

I would recommend that the following books be read after reading the ones listed above, if the student has a desire for a deeper understanding of the Ancient Wisdom and its applications:

A Treatise on Cosmic Fire, 1962.
A Treatise on White Magic, 1951.
Destiny of the Nations, 1949.
Glamour, A World Problem, 1950.
The Rays and the Initiations, 1960.

Other Works about the Ancient Wisdom Teachings

*   Blavatsky, H. P. *The Secret Doctrine*, vols. 1–3. Los Angeles: Theosophy Co., 1928.
    Eastcott, M. J. and N. Magor. *Entering Aquarius*. Tunbridge Wells, England: Sundial House Publications, 1971.
    ———. *The Plan and the Path*. Tunbridge Wells, England: Sundial House Publications, 1964.
    Leadbeater, C. W. *The Chakras*. Wheaton, IL: Theosophical Publishing House, 1927.
    ———. *The Inner Life*. Chicago, IL: Theosophical Press, 1927.
    Mees, G. H. *The Revelation in the Wilderness*, vols. 1–3. Deventer (Europe): N. Kluwer, 1951, 1953, 1954.
    Powell, A. E. *The Astral Body*. London: Theosophical Publishing House, 1926.
    ———. *The Causal Body*. London: Theosophical Publishing House, 1928.
    ———. *The Etheric Double*. London: Theosophical Publishing House, 1925.
    ———. *The Mental Body*. London: Theosophical Publishing House, 1927.

————. *The Solar System.* London: Theosophical Publishing House, 1930.

Purucker, G. de. *Fountain Source of Occultism.* Pasadena, CA: Theosophical University Press, 1974. (Edited by Grace Knoche, published posthumously.)

————. *Fundamentals of Esoteric Philosophy.* Pasadena, CA: Theosophical University Press, 1979.

Saraydarian, T. *The Hidden Glory of the Inner Man.* Agoura, CA: Aquarian Educational Group, 1968. (All of this teacher's writings are helpful.)

————. *The Magnet of Life.* Agoura, CA: Aquarian Educational Group, 1968.

Two Disciples. *Rainbow Bridge II.* Escondido, CA: Triune Foundation, 1981.

Other Works about the Seven Rays

In addition to the primary work on this subject by Alice A. Bailey found in *Esoteric Astrology, Esoteric Healing,* and *Esoteric Psychology,* vols. 1 and 2, the following books are recommended:

* Abraham, K. *Introduction to the Seven Rays.* Cape May, NJ: Lampus Press, 1986.

————. *Psychological Types and the Seven Rays.* Cape May, NJ: Lampus Press, 1983.

* Burmester, H. *The Seven Rays Made Visual.* Marina Del Ray, CA: DeVorss & Co., 1986.

Wood, E. *The Seven Rays.* Wheaton, IL: Theosophical Publishing House, 1925.

Other Works about Astrology

Collin, R. *The Theory of Celestial Influence,* vol. 1. New York, NY: Samuel Weiser, Inc., 1971.

Green, J. *Pluto: The Evolutionary Journey of the Soul.* St. Paul, MN: Llewellyn Publications, 1986.

Greene, L. *Saturn: New Look at an Old Devil.* York Beach, ME: Samuel Weiser, Inc., 1976.

Heindel, M. *The Message of the Stars.* Oceanside, CA: Rosicrucian Fellowship, 1940.

Hickey, I. *Astrology, A Cosmic Science.* 1970. Available through the estate of I. M. Hickey, c/o Helen C. Hickey, 103 Goldencrest Avenue, Waltham, MA 02154.

Jones, M. E. *Essentials of Astrological Analysis.* New York: Fabian Publishing Society, 1960. (This author's works are highly recommended.)

Leo, A. *The Art of Synthesis.* Edinburgh, Scotland: International Publishing Co., 1962.

———. *Esoteric Astrology.* London: L. N. Fowler & Co. Ltd., 1967. (All of this author's works on astrology are most valuable.)

———. *Jupiter—The Preserver.* New York: Samuel Weiser, Inc., 1973.

* Oken, A. *Alan Oken's Complete Astrology.* New York: Bantam Books, 1988.

Rudhyar, D. *The Astrology of Personality.* New York: Lucis Publishing Co., 1936. (All of this author's works are highly recommended.)

———. *The Pulse of Life.* The Hague, Netherlands: Servire, 1963.

———. *The Sun Is Also A Star.* New York: E. P. Dutton and Co., 1975.

Ruperti, A. *Cycles of Becoming.* Vancouver, WA: CRCS Publications, 1978.

Stahl, C. W. *Vulcan, the Intra-Mercurial Planet.* 1968. Available through John Van Zant, Neoteric Pathwork, 24 Colorado, Highland Park, MI 48203.

Weston, L. H. *The Planet Vulcan: History, Nature, and Tables.* American Federation of Astrologers, P.O. Box 22040, Tempe, AZ 85285–2040, 1987.

There are two other sources which may turn out to be great gifts to the reader:

Meditation Mount, P.O. Box 566, Ojai, CA 93023. There is no charge to receive bi-monthly booklets in the series *Meditation Group for the New Age.*

The Seven Ray Institute, 128 Manhattan Ave., Jersey City Heights, NJ 07307. Write for subscription rates for the *Journal of Esoteric Psychology,* published two or three times per year.

201 798 -7777

INDEX

Rays (*cont.*)
  6th (Devotion & Idealism), 62, 95,
    98–100, 105, 107, 108,
    111, 117–119, 127, 129–134,
    157, 161, 163–165, 178,
    182–184, 192, 193, 195, 196,
    198, 207, 212, 213,
    215–217, 239–241, 244–246,
    248, 254, 262–266, 269–271,
    274, 275, 289, 291–293, 295,
    296, 300, 307, 313, 314,
    316, 317, 319–321, 323, 324,
    326, 329, 330, 337, 338,
    341, 353, 355–359, 361, 363,
    364, 368, 369, 371, 372,
    374–377, 379–381, 392, 393,
    395, 399–402, 404, 405,
    407
  7th (Ceremonial Ritual & Order),
    61, 75, 76, 95, 98–100,
    103, 107, 112, 113, 117–119,
    127, 128, 130, 132–138,
    147, 156, 157, 161, 162, 165,
    178, 180, 183, 199–206,
    210, 222, 225, 228–233, 235,
    237, 239, 241, 245, 253,
    255, 262–266, 268–270, 274,
    276, 281, 282, 285, 288,
    292, 294, 297, 298, 300, 301,
    307, 308, 310–317, 319,
    320, 324, 328, 331, 332, 337,
    338, 353, 354, 356, 357,
    359, 362, 365, 371, 373,
    375–377, 379–380, 392,
    399, 400
Rays and the Initiations, The (Bailey),
  29, 140
Reincarnation, 43, 87, 88, 143. *See
  also* Law of Reincarnation
Ring-Pass-Not, 40, 41, 44
Robbins, Michael, 392n
Romanticism, 76
Rudhyar, Dane, 141
Rulers
  Hierarchical, 188, 189, 203, 212,
    234, 238, 376, 312, 390,
    391, 395, 402
  personality/exoteric, 52, 60–62, 65,
    76, 82, 104, 124, 136, 168,
    173, 180, 181, 195, 196, 200,
    202, 203, 210–212, 226,
    269, 273, 275, 277, 280, 281,
    285, 287–290, 293, 294,
    297, 300, 301, 306–309, 312,
    313, 315–317, 320, 324,
  326, 329–331, 338, 340, 344,
    346, 350, 354, 356–358,
    377, 387, 391, 394, 398–403,
    405, 406, 408, 409
Soul/esoteric, 49, 52, 61, 62, 65,
    76, 82, 107, 120, 124, 162,
    168, 173, 180, 182–184, 187,
    201, 202, 212, 217, 218, 232,
    234, 244, 245, 253, 258–265,
    267, 268, 271–275, 277, 280,
    281, 284, 287, 288, 290, 294,
    296–298, 300, 301, 305,
    307–309, 312, 314, 317, 320,
    321, 326, 330, 333, 335,
    337–340, 344–347, 350, 351,
    354, 356–358, 377, 387, 390,
    391, 393, 394, 398, 399, 404,
    405–407, 409
Rupa manas, 117

Sacrifice, 24, 120, 145–147, 164, 210,
    212, 224, 225, 227, 228,
    241–249, 255, 256, 264, 279,
    281, 288, 290, 292, 313, 318,
    319, 321–323, 326, 359, 362,
    363, 365, 366, 374–378, 393,
    395, 397, 400, 402, 403, 405
Sagittarius. *See* Signs
Saraydarian, Torkom, 349
Saturn. *See* Planets
Scapegoat, 224. *See also* Signs—
    Capricorn
Science of Relationships, 96, 97, 373,
    374
Scorpio. *See* Signs
Scorpion. *See* Signs—Scorpio
Sea-Goat, 224n, 228, 229. *See also*
    Cross Fixed; Signs—Capricorn
Secret Doctrine, The (Blavatsky), 3, 26n,
    40, 252, 255, 272, 302, 372n
Service, 10, 52, 58, 59, 63, 73, 128,
    129, 145, 146, 157, 159,
    188–191, 197, 198, 200, 206,
    209, 217, 223, 230, 232,
    242, 247, 251, 262–263, 265,
    269, 271, 272, 276, 279,
    284, 287–289, 293, 295, 300,
    301, 303, 305, 309, 324, 330,
    343, 371, 385, 387, 406, 407
  to humanity, 60, 69, 89, 114, 144,
    187, 199, 212, 214, 221,
    230, 234, 237, 238, 240, 264,
    267, 272, 277, 283, 284,
    301, 329, 330, 331, 332, 378,
    379, 396, 397, 400